34843

Underlining
R.H

GN
668
C6
1969

Codrington, Robert Henry
    The Melanesians; studies in their
anthropology and folklore.   Oxford,
Clarendon Press [1969]
    xv, 419 p.   illus., fold. map.   23cm.

    Reprint of the 1891 ed.

    1. Melanesians.

34843

MELANESIAN

ANTHROPOLOGY AND FOLK-LORE

CODRINGTON

STONE BUILDING AT GAUA, SANTA MARIA, BANKS' ISLANDS

(*From a sketch by the Author*)

[*Frontispiece*

THE MELANESIANS

STUDIES IN THEIR

ANTHROPOLOGY AND FOLK-LORE

BY

R. H. CODRINGTON

Oxford
AT THE CLARENDON PRESS

Oxford University Press, Ely House, London W. 1

GLASGOW NEW YORK TORONTO MELBOURNE WELLINGTON
CAPE TOWN SALISBURY IBADAN NAIROBI LUSAKA ADDIS ABABA
BOMBAY CALCUTTA MADRAS KARACHI LAHORE DACCA
KUALA LUMPUR SINGAPORE HONG KONG TOKYO

FIRST PUBLISHED 1891

REPRINTED LITHOGRAPHICALLY IN GREAT BRITAIN
AT THE UNIVERSITY PRESS, OXFORD
BY VIVIAN RIDLER
PRINTER TO THE UNIVERSITY
1969

PREFACE.

IT has been my endeavour in the following pages to bring together the results of such observations as many years' acquaintance with Melanesian people has enabled me to make. I had once hoped to have been able to give something more like a full account of the beliefs and practices of the natives of those islands concerning which I have had the opportunity of collecting information; but my stay upon my last return to the Melanesian Mission was too short for this, and I have now to put forth what I know to be very incomplete.

My observations and enquiries were carried on, and my notes were made, in the years from 1863, when I first visited the islands, to 1887, when I left the Mission; partly in the Melanesian Islands, but mostly in Norfolk Island, where natives of many of these islands have for many years been brought together for instruction. Twice during this period I made with natives of the various islands a systematic enquiry into the religious beliefs and practices of the Melanesians, and the social regulations and conditions prevailing among them. On the first occasion I had, as regards the Banks' Islands, the very valuable assistance of a native who was a grown youth before his people had been at all affected by intercourse with Europeans or had heard any Christian teaching—the Rev. George Sarawia, the first, and now for many years the leader, of the native clergy of that group. The results of these first enquiries appeared briefly in the Journal of the Anthropological Institute of February, 1881 ; and these were carefully reviewed by me during my last stay in Norfolk Island in 1866 and 1867. I was so fortunate then as to meet there several old friends and pupils who had come down, for their health's sake and for other reasons, after a residence as teachers among their own people. They had been living in their various islands in a position and at an age which would make them acquainted with the views and habits of their countrymen, and they were able, and, I believe, entirely willing, to communicate freely what they knew. It happened thus that I was able to go through the subjects which are treated of in this book with native instructors from the Solomon Islands, the Banks' Islands, and the Northern New Hebrides ; with Marsden Manekalea from Ysabel, Benjamin Bele from Florida, Joseph Wate from Saa, Walter Woser from Motlav, Arthur Arudulewari from Aurora, Lewis Tariliu from Pentecost, Martin Tangabe from Lepers' Island ; every one of them, in my opinion, a competent and trustworthy witness, though all were not equally intelligent.

It has been my purpose to set forth as much as possible what natives say about themselves, not what Europeans say about them. For this reason, though the results of my own personal observations are given, I have refrained from asking or recording, except in a few instances where acknowledgment is made, the information which my colleagues in the Mission would have abundantly and willingly imparted. No one can be more sensible than myself of the incompleteness and insufficiency of what I venture to publish ; I know that I must have made many mistakes and missed much that I might have learnt. I have felt the truth of what Mr. Fison, late missionary in

Fiji, to whom I am indebted for much instruction, has written : 'When a European has been living for two or three years among savages he is sure to be fully convinced that he knows all about them ; when he has been ten years or so amongst them, if he be an observant man, he finds that he knows very little about them, and so begins to learn.' My own time of learning has been all too short. I have endeavoured as far as possible to give the natives' account of themselves by giving what I took down from their lips and translating what they wrote themselves. It is likely that under the circumstances of such enquiries much of the worst side of native life may be out of sight, and the view given seem generally more favourable than might be expected ; if it be so, I shall not regret it.

I should have been glad if space had allowed me to treat at greater length the subject of the native Arts of Life, and to have given more of the Tales, which throw so much light upon native life and thought. The comparison of the Melanesian languages, customs, beliefs, and arts, with those of the islands of the Pacific and Indian Oceans, will fix the ethnological place of the Melanesian people while it aids the general study of mankind.

In conclusion, this book, though written by a missionary, with his full share of the prejudices and predilections belonging to missionaries, is not meant to have what is generally understood to be a missionary character ; but the writer is persuaded that one of the first duties of a missionary is to try to understand the people among whom he works, and to this end he hopes that he may have contributed something that may help.

WADHURST :
March 12, 1891.

CONTENTS.

—•◆—

CHAPTER I.

INTRODUCTORY.

CHAPTER II.

SOCIAL REGULATIONS. DIVISIONS OF THE PEOPLE. KINSHIP AND MARRIAGE CONNEXION.

CHAPTER III.

SOCIAL REGULATIONS. CHIEFS.

CHAPTER IV.

PROPERTY AND INHERITANCE.

CHAPTER V.

SECRET SOCIETIES AND MYSTERIES.

CHAPTER VI.

SOCIETIES. CLUBS.

CHAPTER VII.

RELIGION.

CHAPTER VIII.

SACRIFICES.

CHAPTER IX.

PRAYERS.

CHAPTER X.

SPIRITS.

CHAPTER XI.

SACRED PLACES AND THINGS.

CHAPTER XII.

MAGIC.

CHAPTER XIII.

POSSESSION. INTERCOURSE WITH GHOSTS.

CHAPTER XIV.

BIRTH. CHILDHOOD. MARRIAGE.

CHAPTER XV.

DEATH. BURIAL. AFTER DEATH.

CHAPTER XVI.

ARTS OF LIFE.

CHAPTER XVII.

DANCES. MUSIC. GAMES.

CHAPTER XVIII.

MISCELLANEOUS.

CHAPTER XIX.

STORIES.

LIST OF ILLUSTRATIONS.

B

NOTE.

The orthography in use in the various native languages is not generally here employed in native words, but it occasionally appears. In such cases it is enough to observe that $b = mb$, $d = nd$, n is ng, g is ngg, and that g and q represent peculiar sounds. Excuse must be offered for the very ill-looking ngg, representing the ng in 'finger'; a sound so distinct from the ng in 'singer' that it is impossible to use, as in English, the same symbol for both. It is necessary to note that ng here always stands as ng in 'singer.'

CHAPTER I.

THERE are four groups of islands, within that region of the Western Pacific to which the name of Melanesia has been given, that form a curved belt following roughly the outline of the Australian coast, at a general distance of some fifteen hundred miles, and turning away from the important outlying Archipelago of Fiji; these are the Solomon Islands, the Santa Cruz group, the Banks' Islands and New Hebrides, and New Caledonia with the Loyalty Islands. There is an undoubted connexion of race, language and customs among the people who inhabit these groups; a connexion which further extends itself throughout what is called Melanesia to New Guinea westwards, and eastwards to Fiji. The distinction between the Melanesian people of these groups and the Polynesians eastwards of Fiji is clearly marked and recognised, for the line which separates Melanesian from Polynesian falls between Fiji and Tonga. No such line can be drawn to mark such a boundary to the west till the Asiatic continent itself is reached. From the Polynesian islands of the East Pacific on the one side, and from the Asiatic islands of the Malay Archipelago on the other, two currents of influence have poured and are pouring into Melanesia, the former much more modern and direct, the latter ancient and broken in its course. Upon these currents float respectively the kava root and the betel-nut. The use of the betel is common to India, China, and the Melanesian islands as far to the east as Tikopia; the Polynesian kava has established itself in the New Hebrides, and is a novelty in some of the Banks' Islands; it has not been carried across the boundary of the betel-nut by the Polynesian settlers in the Reef Islands of Santa Cruz. The present work is not concerned at all with one of the four groups above mentioned, that of New Caledonia and the Loyalty Islands, nor with the larger southern members of the New Hebrides group; its view is confined, except for occasional illustration, to the Solomon Islands, Ysabel, Florida, Savo, Guadalcanar, Malanta, San Cristoval, Ulawa, to the Santa Cruz group, the Banks' and Torres Islands, and three of the northern New Hebrides, Aurora, Pentecost and Lepers' Islands. Within this field are contained certain islands inhabited by Polynesian colonists from the East who still retain their Polynesian speech. Such are Nupani, Pileni, Nukapu, and other reef islands of the Swallow group, where the physical characteristics of the Polynesian people may possibly be traced, but certainly are not conspicuous, having been lost by mixture with neighbouring Melanesians. In Rennell Island and Bellona Island, southern members of the Solomon group, the people are physically Polynesian; a lad from Bellona, who was in New Zealand with Bishop Patteson, was in name (Te Kiu), colour, tattoo, and speech very much a Maori. Men from the Polynesian settlements on Mae and Fate in the New Hebrides have found the language of Ontong Java like their own.

The discovery of these islands was prolonged through three centuries, and carried on by Spanish, French and English voyagers. The Spaniards found the Solomon Islands, Santa Cruz, the Banks' Islands, and the northern New Hebrides; the French added much later to the discoveries in these groups; the English found, under Captain Cook, the principal islands of the New Hebrides and New Caledonia, and have filled in the charts. The Dutch discovered Fiji. The earliest, and certainly most interesting, discoveries were those of the Spaniards; of Mendana in his two voyages of 1567 and 1595, and of Quiros and Torres in 1606 [1].

---

[1] Dr. Guppy, in his Solomon Islands and their Natives, has discussed these discoveries at length with special reference to the Journal of Gallego. By the kindness of Mr. Woodford I have read the narrative of Cotoira. In both the

Mendana, despatched by the Viceroy of Peru, reached in 1567 the first Melanesian land seen by Europeans, the great island which he named Santa Ysabel de la Estrella, and from thence the voyagers under his command discovered further and named the large islands Malaita, Guadalcanal, San Cristoval, and the lesser islands, Sesarga, which is Savo, Florida with its islets, Ulawa, and the small islands near San Cristoval. To these he gave the name of the Solomon Islands, to mark his conjecture, or to suggest the belief, that he had discovered the source of the riches of Solomon. In his second voyage of 1595, undertaken for the purpose of colonizing the Solomon Islands, Mendana discovered Santa Cruz, and attempted to form a settlement there ; an attempt abandoned after two months, in consequence of his death and the sickness of the remnant of his crews. Quiros had been with Mendana, and was allowed in 1606 to carry out a project he had been continually urging of recovering and colonizing the Solomon group. Fortune however made him the discoverer of the New Hebrides, when he believed himself to have reached the great Austral Continent, in the island which still bears the name he gave it of Espiritu Santo. The first Melanesian islands however that he saw were those now known as the Banks' Islands, one of which, Santa Maria, retains the name he gave it : Torres, after parting from Quiros, saw and named the Torres Islands. After an interval of more than a century and a half, the French voyager Bougainville, in 1768, added Pentecost, Lepers' Island, and Malikolo to the discovery of Quiros, naming the group the Great Cyclades, and found the great islands of Choiseul and Bougainville beyond those discovered in the first voyage of Mendana.

Polynesian word Te Ariki, the Chief, in the form Taurique, is given as the designation of the chiefs in Ysabel, where it is now entirely out of place. This is the less easy of explanation, as the other native words given appear to be those now in use. I may add that I have discussed the accounts of Mendana's discoveries, as related in Burney's and Dalrymple's collections, with natives of the Solomon and Santa Cruz Islands ; but unfortunately my notes on this subject have been lost.

In the next year Surville passed through the same group ;
the disastrous voyage of La Perouse ended at Vanikoro in
1785. The southern islands of the group, which have since
preserved the name he gave of the New Hebrides, were
discovered by Cook in his second great voyage in 1774, and
after these New Caledonia and the Loyalty Islands. Bligh, in
his wonderful boat voyage after the mutiny of the Bounty,
passed through and named the islands of the Banks' group.

The names given by the Spaniards to the Solomon and Santa
Cruz groups, and to the islands of Ysabel, Florida, Guadalcanar, San Cristoval, Santa Anna and Santa Catalina, to
Espiritu Santo in the New Hebrides and Santa Maria in the
Banks' Islands, have maintained themselves; some of the
French names have disappeared ; some, Aurora, Pentecost or
Whitsuntide, Star Island, Gulf Island (for Ugi), have taken
an English form. To some islands no new names have been
given, native names, or what were supposed to be such, having
been supplied by the natives, such as Ambrym, Api, Mallicollo ;
in some cases the native name, or what was taken for it, as
Malaita, has prevailed over the name given by the discoverer.
To ascertain the native name, and the proper orthography of
the native name, of an island is a matter of difficulty to
a visitor. Large islands seldom have a name; an enquirer
pointing to the island as a whole, is given the name of the
district or village to which he points, or perhaps that of some
islet between him and the mainland ; or he may take the
name of a man for that of a place [1]. Of the islands discovered

---

[1] The island of San Cristoval has been called Bauro by Europeans,
not by natives, from the name of a part of it. A village on that island
is marked on the Admiralty chart with the name of its chief. The island
of Florida and its language has got the name of Anutha, and Anudha,
from an islet between Mboli and Ravu. Bishop Patteson, on his visit in
1862, was given by a native boy on board the name, in the form Anudha,
of the islet Anuha, and took it for the name of the whole island. Melanesians
who could not pronounce th called it Anuta ; Banks' Islanders, taking the
first syllable to be the preposition ' at,' commonly used with names of places,
call it Nuta, and Nut. The large island of Ysabel may be seen in some maps
marked Mahaga, from a single village in Bugotu, the language of which was
made known by Bishop Patteson.

by Mendana in his first voyage, Ysabel, Guadalcanar, and
San Cristoval have no native names, though names of parts
are often taken to designate the whole ; the second of these,
so far as is known to them, is called Gera by natives of south-
east Malanta and San Cristoval ; and the latter has become
known as Bauro, from its most conspicuous part. It is strange
that the large island which has somehow got the name of
Malanta has a native name, at any rate all along the west side,
Mala or Mara. The native name of Florida is Nggela, the
same word as Gera ; and the island is known in Mala Masiki
as ' beyond Gela.' Savo is no doubt the island called Sesarga
by the Spaniards, who heard the name Sabo, and misplaced
it. The native Ulawa, heard by the Spaniards as Uraba,
has lost the Spanish name of La Treguada, and retains
on the charts Surville's Contrariété. The native name of
Santa Cruz, the discovery of Mendana's second voyage, is
Ndeni, from which the Nitendi of the charts has probably
been derived [1].

The discovery of the Banks' Islands and New Hebrides by
Quiros was preceded by a visit to Taumako, where he obtained
information concerning some sixty islands known to the native
voyagers. Nearly all of these probably are the small islands
inhabited, like Taumako, by people of the Polynesian race,

---

[1] There can be little doubt that Gallego's Florida is a part of the Nggela of
the natives, and probably Buena Vista is Vatilau. San Dimas, San German,
Guadalupe, have been shewn by Mr. Woodford to be parts of Florida as they
shew from the sea, not as the island is divided by unseen channels. The native
names of the lesser islands near San Cristoval are, Ugi for Gulf Island, the
Spanish San Juan ; 'Olu Malau, the Three Malau, for Three Sisters, Las Tres
Marias ; Owa-raha, Great Owa, for Santa Ana, and Owa-rii, Little Owa, for Santa
Catalina. It is remarkable how much more accurate Gallego's Aguare is than
the Yoriki of the charts or the Orika given by Dr. Guppy. Gallego's Hapa
may represent Owa, though not so well as Oo-ah or Oa. Uraba is really.
nearer the native Ulawa than Ulaua, the native tongue, like the Spanish,
readily interchanging l and r, w and b. How Mr. Brenchley got Ulakua
cannot be explained, nor why a new form Ulava is introduced. A correct
native name, it may be said, is rarely to be obtained from a trader; the early
sea-going visitors make the form which is to stand for the native name, and
hand it on. The only security is the writing of a native who knows.

who are great voyagers at the present day, and are easily distinguished by their Polynesian tongue, though where they lie near larger islands of Melanesian population, the appearance of Polynesians has been lost [1]. Many of these islands are easily identified, and lie away from the New Hebrides [2], but Quiros was led by his information to look for the large country of which he was in search towards the south, and he thought he found it in what he named Tierra Austral del Espiritu Santo. This island, now commonly known as Santo, has the native name of Marina. This was not the first land of the New Hebrides seen by Quiros; after having apparently seen the light of a volcano in the night, he found himself in the morning in view of three islands, one the present Aurora of the New Hebrides, and two belonging to the Banks' Islands, the volcanic cone, Merlav, called by him Nuestra Señora de la

[1] I have myself witnessed the arrival of eleven canoes from Tikopia among the Banks' Islands. The men said they had come to see the islands, and were hospitably received. One was shot at Ureparapara, and they departed. Shortly before this a canoe from Tikopia had been driven by the wind to Mota, and the men in her most kindly treated, and the same thing had happened before and has happened since. The difference in size, manner, language and dress between the Tikopians and Banks' Islanders was conspicuous. The true name is pretty certainly Chikopia, since the Mota people learnt Sikopia from their visitors; two Fijian islands are Cikobia = Thikombia.

[2] Chicayana is Sikaiana, Stewart Island; Guaytopo is Waitupu, Tracy Island, of the Ellice group; Taukalo is Tokelau; Nupani and Pileni are Reef Islands of Santa Cruz; Manicolo no doubt stands for Vanikoro. Bishop Patteson in 1866 found that the Reef Islanders of Santa Cruz visited Taumako and Tikopia. It is excusable at sight to take the Pouro of Quiros for Bauro in San Cristoval, but in my opinion the attempted identification must completely fail. In the first place, Pouro and Bauro are far from being the same in sound when the confusion of English spelling is got rid of; Quiros would never write ou for au. Secondly, Bauro is not and never was the native name of San Cristoval; it is a name picked up by Europeans, I believe by Bishop Selwyn of New Zealand, and adopted for European convenience. Gallego calls, and properly, a part only of the island Paubro. Thirdly, arrows with points in form of a knife (a fair description of some Lepers' Island arrows) are wholly out of place in the Solomon Islands. Fourthly, the certain identifications of the islands named do not lead in that direction. In the same way, when it is understood that the name of the island in the Malay Archipelago is Buru, in Dutch spelling Boeroe, there can remain very little ground for identifying it with either Bauro or Bulotu, in French spelling Bourotou.

Luz, and Santa Maria. After having visited the latter, he made his way to a larger island seen to the southward, and remained a month in the great bay of SS. Philip and James in Espiritu Santo. Merlav was renamed Pic de l' Étoile by Bougainville, and is now Star Island. The eight islands of the Banks' group are: (1) Star Island, Merlav; (2) Sainte Claire, Merig; (3) Santa Maria, Gaua; (4) Sugarloaf Island, Mota; (5) Great Banks' Island, Vanua Lava; (6) Saddle Island; (7) Bligh Island, Ureparapara; and (8) Rowa [1]. One of these, named Saddle Island by Bligh, has no native name as a whole; another, the Reef Island of Rowa, has no geographical name. The Torres group consists of four islands, Hiw, Tegua, Lo, and Tog, and is now known as Vava; there is no native name to the group. The native names of the three islands which with Espiritu Santo make up the northern New Hebrides are, Maewo, Aurora Island; Araga, Pentecost Island; and Omba, Lepers' Island. The two latter names present a difficulty, and

---

[1] Quiros named seven islands before he reached Espiritu Santo: San Raymundo, Los Portales de Belen, La Vergel, Las Lagrimas de San Pedro, El Pilar de Zaragoza, Santa Maria, and Nuestra Señora de la Luz. The two latter alone are known. Bligh named Ureparapara after himself, Saddle Island and Sugarloaf Island (probably the Pillar of Quiros) after natural features, and Great Banks' Island, with the whole group, after Sir Joseph Banks. Besides the geographical names, these islands have mostly three sets of names. An island has its name in the local form and in the Mota form, which has come into use through the employment of the Mota tongue as a common language in the Melanesian Mission. Thus Vanua Lava, Gaua, Ureparapara, Meralava, are the Mota forms of Vono Lav, Gog, Norbarbar, Merlav. Another set of names was used by natives when sailing between the islands, with a view of concealing their course from unseen enemies; Mota was *Ure-kor*, the place full of dried bread-fruit; Ureparapara, full of slopes, was *Ure-us*, full of bows, Meralava, *Ure-kere*, full of clubs, the best bows and clubs being got there; others were named after the food and other natural productions thought to characterise them. Misspelt and then misread, the rock Vat Ganai has become in maps the island Vatu Rhandi; by a misreading of Gaua, Santa Maria, which is to its native inhabitants Gog, got with traders the name of Ganna. The Torres group has got the name of Vava, with the preposition 'at' Avava, Ababa, from a part of one of the islands which Ureparapara people used to visit. Traders have fixed on Tog the name of Pukapuka, originally unknown among the natives. The Mota name for Lepers' Island, Opa, for Omba, has become well known.

bring in a point of much interest. In the native name of
Pentecost *a* is really the preposition '.at'; Omba with the same
preposition appears in charts as Aoba; it would be reasonable
therefore to write Raga as well as Omba, but custom in these
matters must be allowed to prevail. The interest of the
point lies in the connexion shewn by the common use of
this preposition in place-names between Melanesia, the Malay
Archipelago and Madagascar. Ethnological and historical
questions are inseparable from the consideration of place-
names; for example, the questions whether the Bauro of
the Solomon Islands is the same with the Bouro, properly
Buru, near the Moluccas, or whether Futuna of the New
Hebrides is named after Futuna, Horne's Island. About one
thing however there ought to be no disagreement; however
difficult it may be to ascertain a native name and its orthography, European names should be written in the language
to which they belong; San Cristoval, or Cristobal, not
Christoval; Espiritu Santo, not Spirito Santo or St. Esprit;
and where French names are retained, Contrariété Island and
Cape Zélée.

Between the time of the discovery of the Solomon Islands
by Mendana and the time in which the visits of whalers,
traders and missionaries have become frequent, within the
last thirty or forty years, very little if anything at all was
done by Europeans to influence the character of native life.
It is very interesting therefore to enquire in what particulars
the Spaniards' account of what they discovered differs from
what would be recorded by recent visitors. The place-names
mentioned, with less error than is common now, are those still
in use, Malaita for Mala, Uraba for Ulawa, Paubro for Bauro,
Aguare for Owarii. The names of persons mentioned are such
as are now in use; one of the few words not names to
be found in Gallego's narrative, *benau, panale, panay,* is clearly
pana, a kind of yam with prickles on the vines. In three points
it may be observed that Gallego reports what would not
have been lately seen. The natives are represented as attacking the Spaniards with bows and arrows everywhere,

except at San Cristoval, where darts are mentioned ; in recent
times a voyager would not have found bows and arrows
the usual weapon, but spears, except at Malanta.   Gallego
reports open cannibalism at Ysabel and Florida, whereas
no modern visitor would have seen it except at San Cristoval.
Nakedness is said by Gallego to have been complete, a point
in which Figueroa differs from him, and complete nakedness
would not have been found of late years anywhere but in
Malanta.   The probable conclusion is that, making allowance
for lapses of memory on one side and exaggeration of fact on
the other, the people, language, customs and condition of the
people in the Solomon Islands have not changed since
Mendana's discovery of 1567 [1].

The account of the visit of Mendana to Santa Cruz in
1595 and of the Spanish attempt to form a settlement is
ample and detailed ; and it was remarked by Bishop Patteson,
who was probably the first European after Mendana's party to
go about the native villages, that what he observed corresponded closely with the Spanish record.   It is only within the
last ten years that, by the courage and enterprise of the present
Missionary Bishop John Selwyn, the island of Santa Cruz has
again become open to friendly, and unhappily also to mischievous, approach.   The present writer has gone through
the account of Mendana's visit with natives of Santa Cruz,
whose comments were certainly interesting.   One point may
be mentioned ; the Spaniards, failing to get the people of the
main island to learn their language, sent to kidnap, after
the fashion which from the beginning seems to have been
natural to European visitors, some boys from the neighbouring
Reef Islands, whom they had observed to be more intelligent

[1] Mr. Woodford, in Further Explorations in the Solomon Islands, has
brought forward information from the Journal of Catoira, chief purser of
Mendana's fleet.   From this it appears that the use of the betel-nut was
already established.   Another native word, *na mbolo,* a pig, also occurs.
Much may be learnt as to the present condition of the Solomon Islanders
from Mr. Woodford's Naturalist among the Headhunters, as well as from
Dr. Guppy's book ; but there is no picture of native life so good as that given
in ' Percy Pomo.'

than those of Santa Cruz. When this was related to a
mixed group of Santa Cruz and Reef Island boys at Norfolk
Island, it was at once declared that the Spaniards were quite
right, that the Santa Cruz people now think the Reef Island boys
sharper than their own ; because it is the custom of their
fathers to take them with them on their voyages, which
Santa Cruz men do not do. The very short stay of the
Spaniards, soon assuming hostile relations, cannot be thought
to have affected native life at all; the looms with which
they weave their mats, their fowls, common till lately to other
islands with them, and many other things in which a
difference has been observed, are mentioned in the Spanish
narrative. There is nothing in the account of the discoveries
of Quiros in the Banks' Islands and New Hebrides to shew
any difference between the condition of the native people
then and in the later times, when they have become well
known to Europeans; but it may be observed that the
Spaniards began to kidnap, doubtless with good intentions,
and to recognise the 'devil' of the natives.

In the interval between the discoveries of Mendana and
Quiros and the visits of whalers and missionaries in the
present century, there is every reason to believe that all
memory and tradition of white men had died away in the
Solomon Islands and Santa Cruz [1]; Europeans appeared again
as perfect strangers. We are able therefore to conjecture
how the first explorers appeared to the natives, when we know
how we have ourselves appeared. To the old voyagers, as

----

[1] Bishop Selwyn of New Zealand began his missionary voyages in 1849,
and visited the Solomon Islands in 1850 ; he landed on sixty islands in 1857,
in which year the Banks' Islands became well known to him. In 1861 Bishop
Patteson, in H. M. S. Cordelia, became acquainted with Florida and Ysabel,
the yearly visits of the Melanesian Mission having before stopped short at
Guadalcanar. From that year forward the work of the Mission has been
regularly carried on within the limits of Ysabel to the west, and Mae,
later Pentecost, to the south. When the present writer made his first voyage
in the Mission vessel, the Southern Cross, in 1863, Bishop Patteson was
generally conversant with the people and the languages of the islands from
New Zealand to Ysabel.

to later discoverers, it was a matter of course that hitherto
unknown countries should be found, and that they should be
inhabited by men unlike themselves; but to the natives
it was a strange thing that there should be any men unlike
themselves, or any unknown land for them to come from.
There are still natives in these islands who remember when a
white man was first seen, and what he was taken to be. In
the Banks' Islands, for example, the natives believed the world
to consist of their own group, with the Torres Islands, the three
or four northern New Hebrides, and perhaps Tikopia, round
which the ocean spread till it was shut in by the foundations
of the sky. The first vessels they remember to have seen
were whalers, which they did not believe to come from any
country in the world ; they were indeed quite sure that they
did not, but must have been made out at sea, because they
knew that no men in the world had such vessels. In the
same way they were sure that the voyagers were not men ; if
they were they would be black. What were they then?
They were ghosts, and being ghosts, of necessity those of men
who had lived in the world. When Mr. Patteson first landed
at Mota, the Mission party having been seen in the previous
year at Vanua Lava, there was a division of opinion among
the natives ; some said that the brothers of Qat had returned,
certain supernatural beings of whom stories are told ; others
maintained that they were ghosts. Mr. Patteson retired from
the heat and crowd into an empty house, the owner of which
had lately died ; this settled the question, he was the ghost
of the late householder, and knew his home. A very short
acquaintance with white visitors shews that they are not
ghosts, but certainly does not shew that they are men ;
the conjecture then is that they are beings of another order,
spirits or demons, powerful no doubt, but mischievous. A
ghost would be received in a peaceful and respectful manner,
as European visitors have always in the first instance been
received ; a being not a living man or ghost has wonderful
things with him to see and to procure, but he probably brings
disease and disaster. To the question why the Santa Cruz

people shot at Bishop Patteson's party in 1864, when, as far as can be known, they had not as yet any injuries from white men to avenge, the natives have replied that their elder men said that these strange beings would bring nothing but harm, and that it was well to drive them away; and as to shooting at them, they were not men, and the arrows could not do them much harm. It is sad to think how generally the elder men have, from their own point of view at least, been right; iron, tobacco, calico, a wider knowledge of the world, have not compensated native people for new diseases and the weakening of social bonds [1]. White visitors have not meant to do the natives wrong, but they have in fact harmed them, and have not earned moral respect at any rate generally from them. Europeans have from the beginning of inter-course with Melanesian natives kidnapped them, and have persuaded themselves that they were doing them a service by bringing them into what is called contact with civilization; the natives have from the first resented the kidnapping of their sons, and their sons, however much they may have wished to go away and have rejoiced in what they have learnt and acquired, will hardly be said by any impartial observer to have done any good when they have returned; although indeed to some people the power of speaking a little 'pigeon English,' for their convenience, seems to be a great improvement to a native.

To a voyager among these Melanesian islands who has no special geological learning the generally volcanic character

---

[1] I believe there is no doubt that dysentery was unknown in the islands till natives returned from residence with Europeans. When the Nukapu men, whose kidnapping was the immediate cause of the death of Bishop Patteson, escaped from Fiji and made their way to their native island, dysentery, before unknown, broke out there. The absence of a native name for this and other diseases, is to some extent at least a proof of recent in-troduction. Within my own recollection syphilis, or the venereal disease which was taken for it, was unknown in the islands visited by the Mela-nesian Mission, except at San Cristoval, where alone intercourse with whalers and traders had been considerable. It has lately become widely known, and it is certain that it has been brought back by returned 'labourers,' male and female.

of them cannot fail to be apparent. The lofty land of Guadalcanar, rising to a height of 8000 feet, and the high mountains
of Espiritu Santo and New Caledonia, may be thought by
him to have some other origin ; but he cannot miss the still
active volcanos, or fail to observe that many islands have the
shape of those that are active in a more or less perfect or
ruinous condition. The vast cone of Lopevi in the New
Hebrides rises to an apparent point at the height of 5000 feet,
and has been seen to cast out smoke and ashes. Tinakula, as
it is called, near Santa Cruz, the native name of which is
Tamami, is a well-formed cone 3000 feet high. When Mendana was attempting his settlement in 1595, the point of the
cone was blown away; the volcano is now very active, throwing
out glowing masses of lava, which roll down into the sea.
The enormous crater of Ambrym, at the height of 2500 feet,
is the centre of vast rugged fields of lava, hitherto unapproachable ; round this main mass of the volcano there rise lateral
cones no longer active, forest-covered to their peaks, and
affording perhaps the most beautiful of Melanesian landscapes.
When the Solomon Islands were discovered Savo was active.
Some years ago an eruption was expected by the natives,
because the old people remembered or had been told of
considerable activity some fifty years before ; rumblings were
then heard and smoke was seen at Florida : the steaming
pool and hot stream flowing from it are often visited. In the
Banks' Islands, Vanua Lava is always steaming from its
sulphur springs. Great lateral cones on the north and east of
this island are now extinct, but the streams which rise in the
central mass run warm and stinking to the sea, and powder
the rocks with sulphur. In Santa Maria above Lakona there
are steaming vents on the ridge of the ancient crater now
filled by a lake, and on the hill Garat, which has been thrown
up within it, there is a group of hot pools, sulphurous
jets, and basins of boiling mud within the encircling ridge, from
which hot streams pour down into the lake [1]. Bligh Island,

---

[1] Any volcanic vent, from an active crater to a dead solfatara, is in the
Banks' Islands a *vuro*. Three of those near Lakona have names, one, a deep

Ureparapara, is a remarkable example of the type of Amsterdam or St. Paul's Island in the Indian Ocean; the sea enters the ancient crater, on the ridge of which, rising to nearly 2000 feet, is a steaming vent. Star Island, Meralava, is a massive cone rising so steeply to a height of 3000 feet, that it surprises strangers that it should be inhabited. From below the cone appears to terminate in a cup with a broken lip, but Bishop Selwyn and Mr. Palmer, who reached the top in 1881, found a more recent crater, which no doubt was active when Quiros discovered the island: there is now no recollection of activity [1]. In the New Hebrides, volcanic action has not yet exhausted itself on Lepers' Island; it is probable that besides the very conspicuous volcanos of Ambrym, Lopevi, and Yazur on Tanna, there are many solfataras and fumaroles as yet unnoticed in this group.

All these volcanic islands, whether still in active operation, or still fuming with latent fires, or long ago extinct, have dead and living coral round their base. The greater number of the islands lie in a ruined mass, in contrast to the cones of Lopevi and Tinakula; in some the volcanic form is hidden or

pool sluggishly bubbling and steaming, is the Old Woman; another briskly active is the Stranger's Wonder; another, the New Vuro, though evidently not very recent, is very active and noisy. In the largest pool, some twenty feet across, two jets of steam raise the water to the height of a couple of feet, and after rain very much higher. When I was there in 1875 a new vent had been lately opened by an earthquake.

[1] Some years ago a native lad from Mota told me that he with a companion had mounted to this crater. They found at the top a bare stretch of stones, and within the crater a lake of black water, covered with a thick black cloud; a heavy darkness filled the place, a huge bird soared round their heads, awe and horror fell upon them, and they turned and fled. It is easy to talk lightly about native superstitions. Mr. Palmer thus describes the crater. 'We could see nothing at first, as a cloud was over, but presently it lifted, and we saw a large deep crater with splendid precipitous sides, in some places fully three hundred feet high. There is a small pool of water at the bottom, and rather on one side a second perfectly round crater, which we also determined to look into. We descended through trees and mosses; I was much interested in finding the *tutu* of New Zealand (coriaria sarmentosa), which I have never seen anywhere else in these islands; the second crater goes down to a point, where the trees and ferns are of better growth.'

confused, in others lateral cones and craters plainly shew themselves; a dense forest growth generally covers all from base to summit. All alike have coral forming a certain pro-

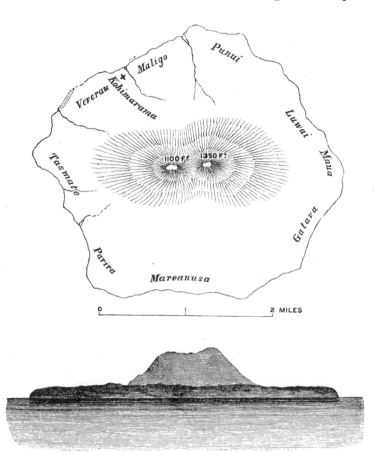

Mota.

portion of their mass, the rock of coral formation varying with its age. Elevated terraces of coral appear in Futuna and the Loyalty Islands. The figure of Mota, in the Banks' Islands, shews the primary cone with a shoulder of later discharges standing upon a broad coral base uplifted some 200 feet above the sea. On this raised surface lie blocks of volcanic stone, while the ravines cut deep through it by the torrents from above expose to view the madrepore and other corals of which it is composed; on the beach water-worn fragments of both coral and volcanic rock lie among the living coral. In the Torres Islands terraces formed by successive upheavals are conspicuous; nothing is seen but coral; in one of the islands, at least, the natives have to dig for volcanic stone that will bear heat for their ovens. In the Banks' Islands it may be said that the land is being elevated; a patch between Mota and Motalava has become much more shallow in the last few years.

Florida in the Solomon group is divided into three parts by two channels called *utuha*, and calls to mind the mainland of the Aru Islands, as described in Mr. Wallace's Malay Archipelago. Though the northernmost channel is pretty wide, the island in its native name, Nggela, and in native conception, is one, and neither of the three parts has a name of its own. A similar channel divides Mala masiki from Mala paina, little from great Malanta. In Florida, over the wider channel which is called from this *utuha ta na vula* the Moon Channel, there is a cliff white as chalk. In the Banks' Islands small barren patches, *rea*, of coarse grass here and there appear; in Florida large barren spaces of this kind are conspicuous, as they are on the opposite slopes of Guadalcanar, and change the aspect of the landscape to the eyes of one who comes from the forest-covered islands to the East [1].

[1] The islands may be roughly classified according to the use of stone or shell implements in them. In the Banks' Islands, Torres Islands, and Santa Cruz, they had only shell adzes, and used obsidian flakes for cutting and scraping. In the Solomon Islands, except in Rennell and Bellona, and the New Hebrides, the implements were of stone, and flakes of chert were used; but in the latter group on Lepers' Island, where the volcanic force is not yet exhausted, shell was the ancient use. Stone adzes in my possession from the Solomon Islands are of Andesite, a basaltic lava, from Florida compact andesite, from Ulawa altered andesite; from the New Hebrides, one from Ambrym is Gabbro, one from Pentecost is Bastite serpentine.

Whether there are in this part of Melanesia any atolls
properly so called may be a question. There are lagoon
islands of two kinds. The Reef Islands of the Santa Cruz
group show flat patches of sand and coral resting on the reefs;
such a one is Nukapu, where the lagoon is two miles across.
The Matema group, part of the same Swallow group, consists
of several sand islets resting on the edge of a very large
and irregular reef; two of the islets, which are only separated
at high tide, are very characteristically inhabited, Nufilole by
a score or two of Melanesians, and Fenua loa, as the name
imports, by Polynesian colonists from the East. On the other
hand, Rowa in the Banks' group consists of five tiny islets on
the bight of an irregular reef five miles long, the principal
islet being formed upon a jagged point of volcanic rock,
to all appearance a fragment of the edge of a sunken crater.

The *Tas* in the middle of Santa Maria in the Banks' Islands
is the only lake of considerable size known in Melanesia.
It is about five miles long, occupying the hollow of the
ancient crater, into which the steaming hill Garat has been
intruded; the waters pour out in a magnificent waterfall.
There is a much smaller lake in Vanua Lava which feeds
two fine cascades, and another on Lepers' Island with a
volcanic vent upon its edge. Bishop Selwyn in 1888 found
the lake at Tikopia covered with large water-lilies; the Tas
of Santa Maria will surely reward its first scientific visitor.

A few words may be ventured on the natural history of this
part of Melanesia. The cuscus common in the Solomon Islands
does not reach to Santa Cruz; it is believed to exist in
Espiritu Santo, where Quiros reported that there were goats.
The white cockatoo, abundant in the Solomon Islands generally,
does not pass the two straits that separate respectively Guadalcanar and San Cristoval, Malanta and Ulawa; but while
Ulawa does not strike the unlearned visitor as different in its
zoology from Malanta, the birds of San Cristoval seem few and
strange. Frogs stop short of Santa Cruz, abundant as they
are in the Solomons. A remarkable megapod is found in all
the groups, if not of more than one species at any rate with

different habits. At Savo, where without any attempt at domestication they have become private property, they lay in a carefully divided and appropriated patch of sand, and come out of the bush, as the natives say, twice a day to lay and look after their eggs. In the Banks' Islands and the New Hebrides they lay their eggs in the hollow of a decayed tree or in a heap of rubbish they have scratched together. In the Banks' Islands these birds are called *malau*, as they are *maleo* in Celebes[1]. The native breed of fowls still abounds in Santa Cruz ; the imported fowls seem to have destroyed and replaced them in all the more commonly visited places, though they were common thirty years ago[2]. Crocodiles are abundant in the Solomon Islands and Santa Cruz ; they are sometimes seen in the Banks' Islands, and one was lately killed in the Torres Islands ; they are known and named in the Northern New Hebrides. The name throughout is the same, *vua* or *via*, the Malay *buaya*, Malagasy *voay*. The natives of Ysabel maintain that they have four eyes, two for clear water, and two for mud. Snakes are not everywhere abundant ; at Mota in the Banks' Islands there are no land snakes, and the natives maintain that if imported they will not live ; in Vanua Lava and Saddle Island of the same group, those that live among the root-stems of the huge banyan-trees are said to attain an enormous size. The eels in the Tas of Santa Maria are sometimes more than thirty inches in girth. It is tantalizing to those who suffer so much from mosquitos in the islands now to know that Mendana, who was two months at Santa Cruz,

---

[1] Mr. Wallace remarks of the maleo of Celebes, that the difference between the sexes is so slight that it is not always possible to distinguish it without dissection. At Savo it is asserted that there is no distinction of sex, all are hens ; *ara mua pukua na tanotanodika*, they know no sexual impropriety.

[2] The rapidity with which imported fowls have replaced the indigenous breed is remarkable. I have no recollection myself of having seen native fowls, out of Santa Cruz, except in Lepers' Island and Florida. Mr. Woodford remarks, as a proof how little native tradition can be depended on, that natives assured him that there were no fowls in the Solomons until white men came. They meant, no doubt, fowls of the kind before them. I am not aware that any new name has come in anywhere in the Solomon Islands, as *kokok* has in the Banks' Islands, for the new fowls.

and Quiros, who lay a month in the great bay of Espiritu
Santo, both declare that in their time there were no
mosquitos, but it is probably the small house fly that is
meant. The variety of the mosquitos of the present time is
interesting with all the suffering they bring; in Mota there
is but one kind, which bites only in the daylight; in Vanua
Lava, in the rainy season, they drive the natives to bury themselves in the sea-sand for sleep. The same name for the
mosquito prevails from the Asiatic continent to Fiji; and the
odious blow-fly carries the same name and habits through all
the islands. Dr. Guppy commends the habits of the Birgus
latro to the attention of residents in the Pacific Ocean. The
account of it in Hazlewood's Fiji Dictionary describes how
the *ugavule* climbs cocoanut-trees, pierces and drinks the young
nuts, husks and breaks the old nuts and eats the meat; how it
is taken by tying grass round the tree it has ascended, so that
when descending backwards it reaches as it believes the
ground, and loosing its hold on the tree it falls and is stunned;
how it throws earth and stones into the face of its pursuers.
The same crab or lobster is called *ngair* in the Banks' Islands,
where the natives assert that when it seizes anything, such as
a man's hand, with the left and smaller claw, it holds till
sundown; on which account that claw has the name of
sundown, *loaroro*. They say also that when a *ngair* drops a
cocoanut from the tree upon a stone to break it, he will only
eat it if it is broken smooth; if the fracture is jagged he will
not touch it. The Wango people of San Cristoval go beyond
probable fact when they relate that on moonlight nights they
paddle over to the little island Biu, and quietly creeping up the
beach find these crabs occupied in a dance, two large and old
ones in the centre, beating time with one claw upon the other,
and the rest circling round and waving their claws as the
dancing natives wave their clubs; so surprised they are taken
in great numbers [1].

[1] The natives do not believe in the existence of anthropoid apes. They
believe in the existence of wild men, and Europeans for many years past have
interpreted this belief to imply the existence of apes. See Chapter xviii.

CHAPTER II.

THERE will be no attempt made here to deal with the Ethnology of Melanesia. The origin of the Melanesian people, in their various seats and in their various divisions, may be taken to be unknown; as they themselves apparently have no traditions and no opinions about the matter, and in the stories which pass among them represent themselves to have been created where they are. The variety of their languages, and to a much less extent of their arts and customs, shews that they have not come in one body into the islands they now inhabit; an examination of their languages discovers a very considerable underlying sameness; and the present book may be taken perhaps as an evidence of a large general resemblance in the religious beliefs and practices, the customs and ways of life, which prevail in the islands which are here embraced in a common view. As knowledge extends and detailed information is brought in from all sides, a connexion will no doubt be traced with regions beyond Melanesia; the loom, for example, peculiar to Santa Cruz alone among the islands here treated of, may connect the people of that group with those of the Caroline Islands; many things in common between Fiji and Madagascar besides language may bring those countries and much that lies between them into whatever ethnographic province the latter is held to belong to; but to endeavour to trace such connexion is beyond the present purpose, which is confined to the exhibition of the Melanesian people as they now appear. There are not wanting some myths of origin, over and above the stories of creation told of Koevasi, Qat, or Tagar. It is said at Saa for example, in Mara Masiki, that men sprung spontaneously from a sugar-cane of a particular sort, *tohu nunu* : two knots began to shoot, and the cane below each shoot burst asunder ; from one came out a man, and from the other a woman, the parents of mankind. It is of more consequence to observe the meaning of the words by which the people of the various islands describe themselves as men. It is said sometimes that people discovered in isolation from others call themselves merely ' men,' without a name for their race or nation, as if they thought themselves the only men in the world. In Melanesia, when natives were first asked who they were, they answered ' men,' meaning that they were not demons or ghosts, but living men ; and they did so because they did not believe their visitors to be men, but ghosts themselves, or demons, or spirits belonging to the sea.

In the native view of mankind, almost everywhere in the islands which are here under consideration, nothing seems more fundamental than the division of the people into two or more classes, which are exogamous, and in which descent is counted through the mother. This seems to stand foremost as the native looks out upon his fellow men ; the knowledge of it forms probably the first social conception which shapes itself in the mind of the young Melanesian of either sex, and it is not too much to say that this division is the foundation on which the fabric of native society is built up. There are no Tribes among the natives ; if the word tribe is to be applied as it is to the Maori people of New Zealand, or as it is used in Fiji. No portion of territory, however small, can be said to belong to any one of these divisions ; no single family of natives can fail to consist of members of more than one division ; both divisions where there are two, and all the divisions where there are more than two, are intermixed in habitation and in property ; whatever political organization can be found can never be described as that of a tribe grouped round its hereditary or elective chief. It is probably true

†

that in every account of Melanesian affairs given to the world tribes are spoken of; but a belief that every savage people is made up of tribes is part of the mental equipment of a civilized visitor; when one reads of the 'coast tribes' or the 'bush tribes,' nothing more is meant than the people who inhabit the coast or the inland part of some island.

There is, however, one very remarkable exception to this general rule of division in the Solomon Islands; it is not to be found in Ulawa, Ugi, and parts of San Cristoval, Malanta, and Guadalcanar, a district in which the languages also form a group by themselves, and in which a difference in the decorative art of the people, and in the appearance of the people themselves, thoroughly Melanesian as they are, can hardly escape notice. In this region, the boundaries of which are at present unknown, there is no division of the people into kindreds as elsewhere, and descent follows the father. This is so strange that to myself it seemed for a time incredible, and nothing but the repeated declarations of a native who is well acquainted with the division which prevails in other groups of islands, was sufficient to fix it with me as an ascertained fact. The particular or local causes which have brought about this exceptional state of things are unknown; the fact of the exception is a valuable one to note[1].

Speaking generally, it may be said that to a Melanesian man all women, of his own generation at least, are either sisters or wives, to the Melanesian woman all men are either brothers or husbands. An excellent illustration of this is given in the story of Taso from Aurora in the New Hebrides, in which Qatu discovers and brings to his wife twin boys, children of his dead sister: his wife asks, 'Are these my children or my husbands?' and Qatu answers, 'Your husbands to be sure, they are my sister's children.' In that island there are two divisions of the people; Qatu and his wife could not be of the same, Qatu and his sister and her children must be of the same; the boys therefore were possible husbands of

[1] 'Descent is still uterine in some parts of Fiji; most of the tribes, however, have advanced to agnatic descent.'—Rev. L. Fison.

Qatu's wife, but had they belonged to the other division their age would have made her count them her children rather than her brothers. It must not be understood that a Melanesian regards all women who are not of his own division as in fact his wives, or conceives himself to have rights which he may exercise in regard to those women of them who are unmarried ; but the women who may be his wives by marriage, and those who cannot possibly be so, stand in a widely different relation to him ; and it may be added that all women who may become wives in marriage and are not yet appropriated, are to a certain extent looked upon by those who may be their husbands as open to a more or less legitimate intercourse. In fact appropriation of particular women to their own husbands, though established by every sanction of native custom, has by no means so strong a hold in native society, nor in all probability anything like so deep a foundation in the history of the native people, as the severance of either sex by divisions which most strictly limit the intercourse of men and women to those of the section or sections to which they do not themselves belong. Two proofs or exemplifications of this are conspicuous. (1) There is probably no place in which the common opinion of Melanesians approves the intercourse of unmarried youths and girls as a thing good in itself, though it allows it as a thing to be expected and to be excused ; but intercourse within the limit which restrains from marriage, where two members of the same division are concerned, is a crime, is incest. In Florida in old times the man would have been killed, and the woman made a harlot; now that the severity of ancient manners is relaxed, money and pigs can condone the offence, but much more than is exacted if a man is found sinning with one who might possibly have become his wife. In the Banks' Islands, where the divisions of the people are two, if it became known that two members of one of them had been guilty of this disgraceful crime, as they considered it, the people of the other division would come and destroy the gardens of those who belonged to that in which the offence had been committed, and these would make no resistance nor complaint. It was

the same in Lepers' Island ; where the offending man had also
to make large payment to the near relatives of the woman
with whom he had offended, so as to appease their anger, and
'fence against' the fault.   Cases of incest of this kind were
always rare in all the islands, so strong was the feeling against
intercourse within the kin.   (2) The feeling on the other hand
that the intercourse of the sexes was natural where the man
and woman belonged to different divisions, was shewn by that
feature of native hospitality which provided a guest with a
temporary wife.   That this is done now or has lately been
done is readily denied in the Solomon and Banks' Islands, but
is not denied in the Northern New Hebrides ; there can be
little doubt that it was common everywhere.   But the woman
supplied to the guest was of necessity one who might have
been his wife ; the companionship of one of his own kin never
could be allowed.

It will be convenient in the more particular treatment of
this subject, to take examples first from the Banks' Islands and
Northern New Hebrides, where the people are divided into two
kins, and then from the Solomon Islands, where the divisions
are more than two.   The same two divisions run through the
Banks' Islands, with the Torres Islands and the Northern New
Hebrides.   A Banks' islander wherever he goes in his own
group knows his own kin, and if he passes to Aurora in the New
Hebrides he finds the same.   The Aurora men know well
who are their kin in Pentecost and Lepers' Island ; the Lepers'
islanders know theirs in Espiritu Santo.   Strange, therefore,
as the language is to a Mota man in Pentecost, or to a Lepers'
islander in Motalava, each is at home in a way which would be
impossible to him in the Solomon Islands[1].   In neither the
Banks' Islands nor the New Hebrides is there a name to distinguish the division or kindred ; nor is there any badge or
emblem belonging to either ; in their small communities
every neighbour is well known.   Each of the divisions is in

---

[1] A Lepers' Island youth staying at Mota was delivered from some little
difficulty with the remark, *O tanun we wia gai, gate tanun ta Qauro,* He is
a man of the right sort, not a Solomon islander.

Mota called a *veve*, in Motlav *rev*, a word which in itself signifies division. Those who are of one *veve* are said to be *tavala ima* to the others, that is 'of the other side of the house.' A woman who marries does not come over to her husband's side of the house ; she is said to be *ape mateima*, 'at the door,' the doors being at the ends of the native houses ; nor does the husband go over to the wife's side ; the children belong to the mother's side. All of the same 'side of the house' are *sogoi* to one another. Hence a man's children are not his *sogoi*, his kindred ; his nearest relations are his sister's children. There is no account seriously given of the origin of the two divisions in the Banks' Islands. Within the two *veve* there are certain families among the Banks' Island people, the members of which have a certain family pride, and endeavour to keep up by intermarriage the family connexion. The best known of these is the Lo Sepere family, from the place of that name in Vanua Lava, where Qat is believed to have lived [1]. Adoption is common, and has no particular significance. Childless parents naturally adopt a child of kin to the wife, so that the adopted child occupies the position of one born in the house ; but if, as sometimes happens, an orphan child from the husband's kin is adopted out of pity, it is brought up as of kin to the wife, and care is taken to conceal the fact of adoption. When the child grows up and by some chance finds out that he has been brought up on the wrong 'side of the house,' he will leave his foster parents, and go and live with his own *sogoi*. Much grief and bitterness is caused by such a discovery.

In Aurora, Maewo, the nearest of the New Hebrides to the Banks' Islands, with one of which, Merlav, there is a good deal of communication, the members of the two divisions

---

[1] The Lo Sepere family of Vanua Lava is the same with the Tupueviga of Gaua and the Anamele of Mota. On the other side of the house the Tapulia of Gaua and Merlav are counted the same with three groups at Mota, viz. Alo Gapmaras of Takelvarea, the Wotawota of Maligo, and the Liwotuqe of Gatava. These family groups lie within the *veve*, but do not take in all the *veve* ; neither side of the house is exhaustively divided into family groups.

speak of one another as 'of the other side,' *ta tavuluna* ; and
they have a story that the first woman, a cowry shell that
turned into a woman, called the men to her and divided them
into her husbands and her brothers, fathers and maternal
uncles, according to the present arrangements.　The presence
of families within the kin in this island is very remarkable.
There are several in the northern part of the island, mostly
named from the places where they are formed.　There is one,
however, named from the octopus, *wirita*, belonging originally
to Bugita, a place upon the shore.　The connexion between
this family and the octopus is obscure ; they have no notion
of descent from the *wirita*, and eat it as freely as other natives ;
but if a man of another family desired to get *wirita* for food,
he would take with him one of the *wirita* family to stand on
the beach at Bugita, and cry out, 'So-and-so wants *wirita*';
then plenty would be taken.　It seems rather as though the
residence of this family where *wirita* are abundant, and where
the beach would naturally be their preserve for fishing, had
given rise to a belief in a connexion and to a name.　Another
family named 'At the Wotaga,' from their home near a
certain fruit tree, would not bring up a light-coloured child ;
if such a one were among them they thought that they would
die [1].

In Araga, Pentecost Island, though irregular intercourse
between members of the same kin is punished by the destruction of the gardens of the offending side by the members
of the other, yet marriages within the kin are not unknown.
Those who contract them are despised, and even abhorred,
but money and pigs having been given and received, the
marriage stands.　In Lepers' Island, Omba, the two divisions
are called 'bunches of fruit,' *wai vung*, as if all the members
hang on the same stalk.　Their story is that when Tagar first
made men he made two, both male, and then one of these

---

[1] To these lesser divisions or family groups my informant (A. Arudulewari)
gives the name of *reve*, as to the two great kindreds.　For example, he and
Walter Gao are of t e Wirita family, Tarisuluana is of the Ta Wongi, a place
now deserted ; Vile is Ta Lau of the beach, Tilegi of Suwumea.

took a tuber of *qevu,* a kind of yam, and threw it at the other, who at once turned into a woman, and cried with a loud voice that many men should die because of women. This woman had two daughters, who fell out; and from one of these sprang one *waivung,* and from the second the other. In case of the adoption of a child by a foster-mother who is of the other 'bunch,' the secret of the kindred is carefully kept; the true state of the case is never mentioned by those who know it, until the time for marriage comes. This is done out of consideration for the feelings of the adopting parents; but the repugnance to marriage within the kin is too great to allow of permanent concealment.

The system of the division of the people into strictly exogamous kins is no doubt best seen and considered where the division is simple and separates the whole population on the one 'side of the house' and the other. Two questions may here therefore be suitably raised; the first, whether in this division there are traces of a communal system of marriage; the second, whether the system is sufficient to prevent that which it seems intended or maintained in order to prevent, namely, the marriage of persons too closely allied in blood. In regard to the first question it must be said, on the one hand, that the people have no memory of a time when all the women of one side were in fact common wives to the men of the other side, and that there is no occasion on which the women become common to the men who are not of their kin. The license of a gathering at a feast is confessed to be great, but it is disorderly and illegitimate, and is not defended on the ground of prescription. If a great man making a feast gives it to be understood that he will not allow the harmony of the gathering to be spoilt by jealous quarrelling about women, it is taken as a festive concession; if he gives out that people are to behave well, they know that any one who takes liberties will have to answer for it, not only, as on ordinary occasions, to the injured husband, but to the powerful master of the feast. The stories also of the creation of mankind, and particularly of woman, represent individual marriage.

When Qat wove Iro Lei with pliant rods and made her live, it
was to be his own wife ; his brothers tried to carry her off for
themselves, one woman among eleven of them, but they are
said to be stealing her, not claiming a right. When he
made men, male and female, he assigned to each man his
wife. On the other side is to be set the testimony, the strong
testimony, of words. This is given by the plural form in
which the terms for 'mother' and 'husband' or 'wife' are
expressed. In the Mota language the form is very clear ;
ra is the plural prefix; the division, side, or kin, is the *veve*,
and mother is *ra veve*; *soai* is a member, as of a body, or a
component part of a house or of a tree, and *ra soai* is either
husband or wife. To interpret *ra* as a prefix of dignity is
forbidden by the full consciousness of the natives themselves
that it expresses plurality. The kin is the *veve*, a child's
mother is 'they of the kin,' his kindred. A man's kindred
are not called his *veve* because they are his mother's people ;
she is called his *veve*, in the plural, his kindred, as if she were
the representative of the kin ; as if he were not the child of
the particular woman who bore him, but of the whole kindred
for whom she brought him into the world. By a parallel use
to this a plural form is given to the Mota word for child,
reremera, with a doubled plural sign ; a single boy is called not
'child' but 'children,' as if his individuality were not distinguished from the common offspring of his *veve*. The same
plural prefix is found in other Banks' Island words meaning
mother ; *rave* in Santa Maria, *retne* in Vanua Lava, *reme* in
Torres Islands. The mother is called *ratahi* in Whitsuntide,
and *ratahigi* in Lepers' Island, that is the sisters, the sisterhood,
because she represents the sister members of the *waivung* who
are the mothers generally of the children. Similarly the one
word used for husband or wife has the plural form. In Mota
a man does not call his wife a member of him, a component
part of him, but his members, his component parts ; and so a
wife speaks of her husband. It is not that the man and his
wife make up a composite body between them, but that the
men on the one side and the women on the other make up a

composite married body. The Mota people know that the
word they use means this; it was owned to myself with a
blush that it was so, with a Melanesian blush, and a protesta-
tion that the word did not represent a fact. The word used
in Motlav, part of Saddle Island, gives hardly the less con-
firmation to this interpretation of the Mota word because it
has not a plural form ; in Motlav *ignige* has the same meaning
with the Mota *soai* ; a man says of his leg or his arm *ignik*,
my member, one of my members, and he calls also his wife
ignik, while she calls him the same.

As concerns the second point in question, it is apparent that
the strict rule of exogamy as regards the kin leaves marriage
open to those who are very near in blood ; for a man is not of
kin to his own children, and a man is not of kin to his
brother's children. But although it is the intermarriage of
sogoi, members of the same *veve*, that is strictly forbidden,
and the descent is always counted by the mother, yet the
blood connexion with the father and the father's near relations
is never out of sight. Consequently the marriage of those
who are near in blood, though they are not *sogoi* and may
lawfully marry, is discountenanced. In Mota, for example,
the children of a brother and sister are thought too near to
marry. The brother and sister are both of one *veve*, A, as
children of one mother ; the children of the sister are of her
veve, A ; the brother's children are of the *veve* B, following
their mother, who must needs be of the other side of the
house. It appears then that the two cousins, children of a
brother and sister, are not *sogoi*, one being A and the other B,
and that they can marry. But they will not ; the match
will not be made ; if they married they would be said to 'go
wrong[1].' It will be seen that the succession to property
shews the same tendency, perhaps a recent tendency, to the
recognition of agnatic descent.

Florida, and the parts of the Solomon Islands adjacent to it,
afford an example of the division of the people into more than
two exogamous kindreds. In Florida these divisions are six,

---

[1] As in the case of Dudley and Agnes in the Mota pedigree further on.

called *kema,* and each has its distinguishing name. These are the Nggaombata, the Manukama or Honggokama, the Honggokiki, the Kakau, the Himbo, and the Lahi. But these six *kema* no doubt represent a much simpler original division ; for two of them have local names, of Nggaombata in Guadalcanar, and Himbo, the Simbo somewhat indefinitely placed among the islands to the west, from whence these two *kema* are known to have come. The Nggaombata and the Himbo, perhaps only as strangers, go together ; and the Lahi, a small division, are said to be so closely connected with Himbo that the members cannot intermarry. Whether Honggokama and Manukama are names of one *kema,* or of two divisions into which the one is separating, is a question. The Honggo-kama and the Honggo-kiki, the great and the little, are plainly parts of one original. It is not the case in Florida that an originally double division has simply split and split again ; but the settlement of foreigners has so complicated the arrangement that few natives profess to be able to follow it [1]. Yet the foreigners have undoubtedly brought with them a distinct sense of kinship with one or other of the local *kema.* The strict rule of exogamy is not a sufficient limit to the right of marriage ; here also, as in the eastern islands, it is supplemented by a strong public opinion as to what is right. A remarkable instance of this occurred a few years ago, when Takua, a considerable chief, took to himself the daughter of one of his wives. The girl was not, of course, of his own *kema,* and so far he was within his right, but the sense of decency and propriety of the people was outraged, and the man's influence as a chief was much diminished. In Bugotu of Ysabel there are three *vinahuhu*: Dhonggokama, Vihuvunagi, and Poso-

---

[1] This is illustrated by the case of Alfred Lombu, who, returning from Norfolk Island in search of a wife, proposed for a daughter of Takua, the chief of Mboli. The girl was not of the same *kema* in name with Lombu, and he maintained that he was not aware that his *kema* and hers were in fact the same ; but Takua imposed upon him a heavy fine, seeing an opportunity for possessing himself of the money accumulated for the marriage, and professing great indignation at the outrage on propriety.

mogo, not one of which now corresponds exactly with either of
the Florida *kema*. But the Dhonggokama, they say, is the same
as the ancient *kema* which has split into the Honggokama
and Honggokiki in Florida; and the other two may be well
believed to be themselves the divided other member of the
original pair. The meaning of the names of three of the
Florida *kema*, besides the two that are local, are known;
Honggo is cat's-cradle, Manukama is an eagle, Kakau is a
crab. It is evident that when the divisions of a people multiply names must be given them; where there are two 'sides of
the house' no name is needed for either, but when a man may
have wives and children of three or four kindreds not his own,
a name for each kin is necessary to maintain the matriarchal
system of descent through the mother.

It adds very much to the distinction between these *kema*,
that each has some one or more *buto* from which its members
must keep clear, abstain from eating, approaching, or beholding
it [1]. One of the very first lessons learnt by a Florida child is
what is its *buto*, its abomination, to eat or touch or see which
would be a dreadful thing. In one case, and in one case only,
this *buto* is the living creature from which the *kema* takes its
name; the Kakau kin may not eat the *Kakau* crab. The
Nggaombata may not eat the giant clam; the Lahi may not
eat of a white pig; the Manukama may not eat the pigeon;
the Kakau, besides their eponymous crab, may not eat the
parrot Trichoglossus Massena. The Manukama are at liberty
to eat the bird from which they take their name. If the
question be put to any member of these *kema* he will probably
answer that his *buto* is his ancestor; a Manukama will say
that the pigeon he does not eat is his ancestor; but an
intelligent native, describing this native custom, writes:—
'This is the explanation of the *buto*. We believe these *tindalo*
(the object of worship in each *kema*) to have been once living
men, and something that was with them, or with which they
had to do, has become a thing forbidden, *tambu*, and abominable,

---

[1] Thus in 'Percy Pomo' a man is horrified at seeing blue trousers, the
colour of some part of the inside of the shark, which was his *buto*.

D

buto, to those to whom the *tindalo* belongs.' He gives the
example of the clam of the Nggaombata. The ghost, *tindalo*,
of a famous ancient member of that *kema*, named Polika,
haunted a beach opposite Mage, and a large snake, *poli*, was
believed to represent him there. The Nggaombata could not
approach that beach, Polika was their *buto*[1]. On another
beach where they catch fish wherewith to sacrifice to Polika
is a *gima*, a clam, which they call Polika, and used to believe
to be in some way Polika; hence the *gima* in their *buto*.

There will occur at once the question whether in this we do
not find totems. But it must be asked where are the totems?
in the living creatures after which two of the divisions are
named, or in those creatures which the members of the several
divisions may not eat? It is true that the Kakau kindred
may not eat the crab *kakau*; but the Manukama may eat
the bird *manukama*. If there be a totem then it must be
found in the *buto*; in the pigeon of the Manukama and the
giant clam of the Nggaobata, which are said to be ancestors.
But it must be observed that the thing which it is abominable
to eat is never believed to be the ancestor, certainly never the
eponymous ancestor, of the clan; it is said to represent some
famous former member of the clan, one of a generation beyond
that of the fathers of the present member of it, a *kukua*. The
thing so far represents him that disrespect to it is disrespect
to him. The most probable explanation of these *buto* may
indeed throw light upon the origin of totems elsewhere, but
can hardly give totems a home in the Solomon Islands. The
buto of each *kema* is probably comparatively recent in Florida;
it has been introduced at Bugotu within the memory of living
men. It is in all probability a form of the custom which
prevails in Ulawa, another of the Solomon Islands. It was
observed with surprise when a Mission school was established

---

[1] *Na butodira Gaobata na tidalo eni*, That ghost is the *buto* of the
Nggaombata. The origin of the prohibition is respect for Polika; those of his
kema would not intrude upon the beach he haunted, nor would they eat the
clam, because the clam on the reef represented him. They have now looked
in vain for the snake.

in that island, that the people of the place would not eat
bananas, and had ceased to plant the tree. It was found
that the origin of this restraint was recent and well remembered; a man of much influence had at his death not
long ago prohibited the eating of bananas after his decease,
saying that he would be in the banana. The elder natives
would still give his name and say, 'We cannot eat So-and-
So.' When a few years had passed, if the restriction had
held its ground, they would have said, 'We must not eat
our ancestor.' This represents what is not uncommon also
in Malanta near Ulawa, where, as in Florida also, a man
will often declare that after death he will be seen as a
shark.

These divisions, *kema*, are not political divisions [1]. It is not,
as in the Banks' Islands where every house must needs contain
members of both divisions, that every *kema* will be represented
in every village, for one or two of the smaller may have no
member there; but every man's wife, or wives, and all his
children, must needs be of a *kema* different from his own, and
every village must have its population mixed. The property
of the members of each *kema* is intermixed with that of the
others. In a considerable village the principal chief is the
head of the *kema* which predominates there, and he exercises
his authority over all, while the principal men of the less
numerous *kema* are lesser chiefs. It is evident that the pre-
dominance of any *kema* cannot be permanent. A chief's sons
are none of them of his own kin; and, as will be shewn, he
passes on what he can of his property and authority to them.
If then in a certain district one kindred is now most numerous,
in the next generation it cannot be so, for the children of
those now most numerous will be naturally many more in

---

[1] When some outrage on white men has been committed the 'tribe' is
supposed responsible; but any party of natives concerned is sure to be
made up of members of both *veve* or several *kema*, and some of these probably do not belong to the place where the outrage is committed. Of the five
natives who cut off the boat at Mandoliana in 1880, only two were of the same
kema, and only one was at home at Gaeta.

number, and will none of them be of kin to their fathers.
Thus it was that twenty years ago the Nggaombata was the
dominant *kema* in Florida, and to be a great chief it was said
that a man must be Nggaombata ; but now the Manukama
are rising into the chief place, and supply the chiefs in many
districts of the island.

The system by which the Melanesian people are thus divided
into exogamous groups in which descent follows the mother,
receives of course the name of a Matriarchal system ; but it
must be understood that the mother is in no way the head of
the family. The house of the family is the father's, the
garden is his, the rule and government are his ; it is into the
father's house that the young bridegroom takes his wife, if
he has not one ready of his own. The closest relationship,
however, according to native notions, is that which exists
between the sister's son and the mother's brother, because the
mother who transmits the kinship is not able to render the
service which a man can give. A man's sons are not of his
own kin, though he acts a father's part to them ; but the tie
between his sister's children and himself has the strength of
the traditional bond of all native society, that of kinship
through the mother. The youth as he begins to feel social
wants, over and above the food and shelter that his father
gives him, looks to his mother's brother as the male representative of his kin. It is well known that in Fiji the
vasu, the sister's son, has extraordinary rights with his
maternal uncle. The corresponding right is much less conspicuous and important than this in the Melanesian Islands
west of Fiji ; but it is a matter of course that the nephew
should look to his mother's brother for help of every kind,
and that the uncle should look upon his sister's son as his
special care ; the closeness of this relation is fundamental.
The connexion of kinship through the mother with the great
exogamous group, and that of blood through the father with
his family, thus stand in clear recognition, and to a certain
extent necessarily conflict one with another. The connexion
caused by marriage between members of the groups and

families is a third relation equally felt and expressed in words. The terms therefore in which the various degrees of relationship are conveyed fall into three classes; the first of the kinship through the mother, the second of the family generally on father's and mother's side, the third those following on marriage.

A complete view of the system of relationship with the terms that express it, in any one native field in Melanesia, cannot indeed be taken to shew what everywhere prevails, but as giving a representative example is very valuable; the Mota system, which may well stand for that of the Banks' group, can perhaps be shewn completely and exactly.

(1) It has been said that all the members of each of the two exogamous divisions of the people are *sogoi*, that is of kin, to one another; the only other relation belonging to this kinship is that between the maternal uncle and his sister's children, male and female, expressed in the terms *maraui* and *vanangoi*. The uncle is *maraui* to his sister's child, the nephew or niece is *vanangoi* to the mother's brother; but the nephew is also called *maraui* to his uncle. The relation passes on to the second generation; the children of a man's sister's daughters are his *vanangoi*, they are still of his kin; but his sister's son's children are of the other *veve*, the special tie of kindred is broken; they are called his children, being brought up to stand in the same generation with their parents. A man's sister's child, his *vanangoi*, stands as if in the same generation with himself.

(2) Putting aside connexion by marriage, and the special relation of the *maraui* and *vanangoi*, which follows upon the passing of kindred through the mother, relationship generally can be arranged in four successive stages of generation; the grandparents, the parents, the children, the grandchildren. Take the present generation, *tarangiu*, of young married men and women; they are brothers and sisters; the generation above them are their fathers and mothers; the generation below them are their children; the generation below that will be their grandchildren, to whom again all who come before their

parents are grandparents and ancestors. The terms *tamai* and *veve* must be translated by father and mother, and are used generally to all of the same generation with the parents who are 'near' and belong to the family connexion. A child, son or daughter, is *natui*; grandparent and grandchild, ancestor and descendant, is *tupui*[1]. The terms equivalent to brother and sister are used on a different principle from that with which we are familiar, and according to which the sex of the person referred to determines the use of the word. In Melanesia, as elsewhere, one word describes the relationship of persons of the same sex, and the other word describes the relationship of persons of different sexes. Men are *tasiu* to men, and women *tasiu* to women; men are *tutuai* to women, and women *tutuai* to men. There is a further difference, the sex being the same, the elder man or woman is *tugui* to the younger, the younger man or woman is *tasiu* to the elder; but *tasiu* is the prevailing use. It may be observed in this system of terms of relationship that all of one generation, within the family connexion, are called fathers and mothers of all the children who form the generation below them; a man's brothers are called fathers of his children, a woman's sisters are called mothers of her children; a father's brothers call his children theirs, a mother's sisters call her children theirs. Upon this it has to be remarked that this wide use of the terms father and mother does not at all signify any looseness in the actual view of proper paternity and maternity; they are content with one word for father and uncle, for mother and aunt, when the special relation of the kinship of the mother's brother does not come in; but the one who speaks has no confusion as to paternity in his mind, and will correct a misconception with the explanation, 'my own child, *tur*

---

[1] It may be observed that the principal terms of relationship are generally the same, not only in the Melanesian islands here in view, but throughout the languages with which the Melanesian languages are connected; mother being an exception. Common words however are not always used in the same application, as the Florida *tubu* is no doubt the Mota *tupu*.

natuk ; his real father, *tur tamana* ; *tur tasina*, his brother not his cousin [1].'

(3) A general term *qaliga* embraces all of the other side of the house who have been brought near by marriage, fathers-in-law, mothers-in-law, sons- and daughters-in-law, and all their brothers and sisters. A man and his wife's brother call one another *wulus*, and a woman and her husband's sister call one another *walu* ; but the man is also called *walu* ; and both terms are extended to the cousins of the husband or wife. A woman does not call her husband's brother her brother-in-law ; she is nothing to him, though her children, being his brother's children, are called his. A man calls his daughter-in-law *tawarig*. There is, moreover, a term of marriage relation to which no equivalent exists in English ; parents whose children have intermarried call one another *gasala*, which may be translated fellow-wayfarers.

A genealogical table or pedigree of a Mota family (see p. 38) will supply examples of the various relationships subsisting, and make clear the application of the various terms. The two *veve*, the two sides of the house, are distinguished by the letters *A* and *B* for males, *a* and *b* for females. All *A* and *a*, *B* and *b*, are *sogoi* respectively, as belonging to the same side of the house ; and as besides they are ' near ' to one another by blood, they will call one another *tasiu* and *tutuai* when the relationship strictly conveyed by those words is absent. The prefix *Ro* marks a feminine name. The points in the pedigree marked with asterisks require some explanation, but are almost entirely covered by the principle that a man's sister's son, his *vanangoi*, takes his place in the family on the same

---

[1] Before the native use is well understood it is certainly perplexing and misleading. As an example, a boy named Tarioda came from Araga to Norfolk Island. Remembering a youth of the same name from the same island, I enquired if he had anything to do with him ; the boy answered that he was hi father, and that he had seen him and knew him, meaning that he was a cousin of his father's. Such an answer might well be the ground of a statement that paternity was very little thought of in the New Hebrides. English people probably had perfectly clear conceptions about family ties before they used the words uncle, aunt, cousin, nephew and niece.

A MOTA PEDIGREE.

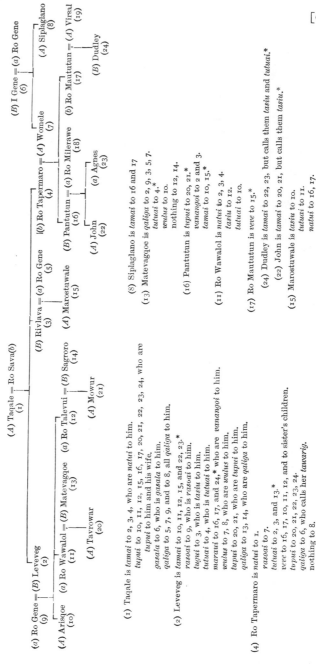

(A) Taqale = Ro Sava(b) (1)

(B) I Gene = (a) Ro Gene (6)

(a) Ro Gene = (B) Leveveg (9) — (2)

(B) Rivlava = (a) Ro Gene (3) — (5)

I(b) Ro Tapermaro = (A) Womele (4) — (7)

(A) Siplagiano (8)

(A) Arisqoe (10)

(a) Ro Wawalol = (B) Matevaqoe (11) — (13)

(a) Ro Talevui = (B) Sagroro (12) — (14)

(A) Marostuwale (15)

(B) Pantutun = (a) Ro Milerawe (16) — (18)

(b) Ro Maututun = (A) Virsal (17) — (19)

(A) Tavrowar (20)

(A) Mowur (21)

(A) John (22)

(a) Agnes (23)

(B) Dudley (24)

(1) Taqale is *tamai* to 1.
    tupui to 10, 11, 12, 15, 16, 17, 20, 21, 22, 23, 24, who are
        tupui to him and his wife.
    gasala to 6, who is *gasala* to him.
    qaliga to 5, 7, 9, and to 8, all *qaliga* to him.

(2) Leveveg is *tamai* to 10, 11, 12, 15, and 22, 23.*
    rasoai to 9, who is *rasoai* to him.
    tupui to 3, who is *tasiu* to him.
    tutuai to 4, who is *tutuai* to him.
    maravi to 16, 17, and 24,* who are *vanangoi* to him.
    wulus to 7, 8, who are *wulus* to him.
    tupui to 20, 21, who are *tupui* to him.
    qaliga to 13, 14, who are *qaliga* to him.

(4) Ro Tapermaro is *natui* to 1.
    rasoai to 7.
    tutuai to 2, 3, and 13.*
    veve to 16, 17, 10, 11, 12, and to sister's children.
    tupui to 20, 21, 22, 23, 24.
    qaliga to 6, who calls her *tawearig*.
    nothing to 8.
    wulu to 5, 9.

(8) Siplagiano is *tamai* to 16 and 17

(13) Matevaqoe is *qaliga* to 2, 9, 3, 5, 7.
    tutuai to 4.*
    vulus to 10.
    nothing to 12, 14.

(16) Pantutun is *tupui* to 20, 21.*
    vanangoi to 2 and 3.
    tamai to 10, 15.*

(11) Ro Wawalol is *natui* to 2, 3, 4.
    tasiu to 12.
    tutuai to 10.

(17) Ro Maututun is *veve* to 15.*

(24) Dudley is *tamai* to 22, 23, but calls them *tasiu* and *tutuai*.*

(22) John is *tamai* to 20, 21, but calls them *tasiu*.*

(15) Marostuwale is *tasiu* to 10.
    tutuai to 11.
    natui to 16, 17.

(20) Tavrowar is *tasiu* to 21.

level with his uncle, *maraui*, as if in the place of his mother.
Thus Leveveg is in fact great-uncle to John and Agnes, but
counts as uncle only because they are grandchildren of his
sister. The grandchildren of his brother are his grandchildren,
tupui, that is his great-nephews and nieces. For the same
reason Leveveg, who is in fact maternal great-uncle to Dudley,
counts as his maternal uncle, *maraui*, Dudley ascending into
his mother's place. So Pantutun is first cousin to the mothers
of Tavrowar and Mowur, and, being of the generation above
them, would be called father or uncle, *tamai*, and they his
children, if it were not that he is cousin to their mothers
through his mother, whose place therefore he takes on the
second ascending step, and becomes *tupui*, great-uncle. Thus
he is father, *tamai*, that is uncle, to his first cousins Arisqoe
and Marostuwale ; and his sister Maututun is their mother or
aunt ; because he ascends into his mother's place, who was
their father's sister. The same rule makes Dudley father or
uncle properly to his first cousins John and Agnes, though, as
they are of the same generation and older than himself, he
calls them improperly brother and sister : improperly, because
they are not his *sogoi*, and he could in strictness, though not
with public approval, marry Agnes. It is still more remarkable that John is properly father or uncle to his second cousins
Tavrowar and Mowur, who are much older than himself ; but
his father Pantutun is their great-uncle, *tupui*, and he is therefore their uncle, *tamai*, or as it naturally sounds to us their
father[1]. The case of Matevagqoe and Ro Tapermaro is distinct
from this : he married her brother's daughter, and to do that
must have been of her side of the house, her *sogoi*. If it had
been her sister's daughter, she and her niece's husband would
be *qaliga* ; but that cannot be between *sogoi*, so they call themselves cousins, brother and sister.

The pedigree here exhibited does not shew the polygamy

---

[1] It sometimes happens that a boy is in this way 'father' to one old enough
to be his natural father, or 'grandfather,' *tupui*, to one of his own age. When
it is so the formal relationship is practically merged in the general *tasiu*,
brotherhood.

which existed in its early stages, and it may be asked whether
the terms of relationship would not undergo some change in
such a case; whether, for example, the sons of the same father
by two mothers would not be distinguished from the sons of
the same father and mother.   The answer is that no difference
is made.   A man's wives, if he should have many, must all be
sogoi, of the same side of the house, calling one another sisters,
and calling each the other's children hers, whether they were
married to the same man or had different husbands.   This
does not however shut out altogether the relationship of
step-father and mother.   A man who has a son by one of his
wives who is dead, does not bring in a step-mother to the boy
if he adds another to his living wives; the woman would
come in as another mother, and the boy would take no notice.
But if a woman with children loses her husband, and becomes
the wife of a man who is not 'near' to her previous husband,
being of course *sogoi* but with no recent blood relation, the
man will come in as step-father, and the term *usur*, successor,
is applied to him, the connexion being called *usur-gae*, bond of
succession.   A looser connexion than this is enough to make
an *usur*; as when a boy's father has had a wife, not the
mother of the boy, who after becoming a widow marries
another man; the boy will take liberties with the man as
having come into his father's place; he will take yams from
his garden.   When a step-father sneezes the step-son will cry
out, *Matia revereve gam o sulate!* a sneeze to draw out a worm
for you! the notion being that the former husband has a
certain grudge against his successor, and sends a worm from a
point of land on which ghosts congregate.

Where, as in Florida and the neighbouring parts of the
Solomon Islands, the divisions of the people are three, four, or
six, and where a man may have a wife or wives from any one
of them but his own, it would seem likely to be more difficult
to keep accurate count of the various degrees of relationship
in which people stand to one another; and it is probable that,
though the native system is precise in following every step
and connexion, the people do in fact content themselves com-

monly with general terms. The special relation of the sister's
son to his mother's brother is of course conspicuous; each calls
the other *tumbu*; and this term is applied also to the father's
mother's brother by his grand-nephew, and by the great-uncle
to his sister's grandchild. In a generation of members of the
same *kema* all of them call one another *hogo* in the same sex,
and, with more or less attention to nearness of blood, brothers
and sisters; that is to say, an elder brother or sister is *tuga* to
one of the same sex, and a younger brother or sister is *tahi*,
while a brother or sister is *vavine* to one of the other sex.
With the exception of the mother's brother, the blood relations of the ascending generation are all father and mother,
tama and *tina*. In the generation above, with the exception
of the father's mother's brother aforesaid, who is *tumbu*, all
male and female are *kukua*. In descending a man's sons and
daughters, and his brother's and cousin's children, are *dale*,
distinguished as *dale mane* and *dale vaivine*, according to sex,
a man's sister's child being *tumbu*; and in the same way a
woman's children and her sister's and female cousin's children
and her husband's brother's and sister's children are all her
children, *dale mane* male, *dale vaivine* female. Descending to
the next generation, all are again *kukua* to their grandparents
and great uncles and aunts, and all above them; except that,
as aforesaid, the relation of *tumbu* subsists between a great-
nephew and his father's mother's brother. Husband and wife
are *tau*. A father- or mother-in-law, and son- or daughter-in-
law, is *vungo*, the term being applied widely to persons connected by marriage who are not of the same generation.
Brothers- and sisters-in-law, and generally persons of the same
generation connected by marriage, are *iva* to one another [1].

It would seem that the absence of exogamous divisions of
the population in that region of the Solomon Islands in which
descent follows the father (namely, in Malanta, about Cape
Zélée, in Ulawa, and in San Cristoval), must make the system

[1] The word *mavu*, which is used for 'namesake,' is also used as a term
of family relationship. Unfortunately the full list of Florida terms made by
me many years ago lacks a key.

of family relationship very different there from that which
has been described as prevailing in the Banks' Islands and in
Florida. To a very considerable extent no doubt this is so ;
but it is improbable that the peculiar closeness of relation
between a man and his sister's son should entirely fail to appear. Of this I have little evidence to offer [1] ; the families are
formed upon the father, and the only restriction upon marriage
is nearness in blood. To whatever extent, however, it may be
that descent through the father removes that characteristic
feature of the Melanesian family system which appears in the
relation between the maternal uncle and his sister's child, it is
certain that the main structure is the same as elsewhere ; that is
to say, that no terms corresponding to uncle and aunt, nephew
and niece, or cousin exist. All on the same level are brothers
and sisters, if children of brothers and sisters or of cousins ;
they look upon the children of brothers, sisters and cousins
as their children, and the children call them all fathers and
mothers ; the ancestors above father and mother, and the
descendants in the second and lower generations, are all united
under one general term, which covers ancestry and posterity
alike. At Wango in San Cristoval, where owing to immo-
rality and infanticide the population has been kept up by the
adoption of children from the bush, adopted children take the
position in the family which would have been theirs if they
had been born in it ; although no blood relationship exists, they
cannot marry those who are near through the adoptive father.
These children appear to be by traders called slaves because they
are bought ; the people themselves call them their children.

   The subject of marriage relations is incomplete without notice
of the reserve so remarkably exercised towards the persons
and names of those who have become connected by marriage.
This is conspicuous in the Banks' Islands, and makes but
little show in the Solomon Islands. In Lepers' Island, a

---

[1] From Rev. R. B. Comins I learn that at Wango and Fagani in San
Cristoval the term for the relation between the maternal uncle and his sister's
child is *mau*. The terms *iha, ifa, hungo, fungo*, are the Florida *iva* and
vungo ; *'ama, 'ina, 'asi*, are *tama, tina, tahi*.

singular reserve is strongly shewn, as it is in Fiji, by brothers
and sisters, and also by mothers and sons; but this reserve,
though its existence and its cause may well throw light upon
that exercised between those connected by marriage, has no
proper place here.   In Florida, in the Solomon Islands, there
is no difficulty about meeting, or mentioning the name of,
father- or mother-in-law, or any of a wife's kindred, and no
extraordinary marks of respect are shewn.   It is the same at
Saa.   The extraordinary separation of the sexes in Santa
Cruz and the neighbouring islands, however instructive to
observe in this connexion, does not follow on relation by
marriage.   In the Banks' Islands the rules of avoidance and
reserve are very strict and minute.   As regards the avoidance
of the person, a man will not come near his wife's mother;
the avoidance is mutual ; if the two chance to meet in a path,
the woman will step out of it and stand with her back turned
till he has gone by, or perhaps if it be more convenient he
will move out of the way.   At Vanua Lava, in Port Patteson,
a man would not follow his mother-in-law along the beach,
nor she him, until the tide had washed out the footsteps of the
first traveller from the sand.   At the same time a man and his
mother-in-law will talk at a distance.   A man does not avoid
his father-in-law, nor a woman hers.   A man does not avoid
his wife's brother, but will not sleep with him; he does not
avoid his son's wife, or his own wife's sister.   Boys and girls
who are engaged generally avoid one another, but through
shyness, not by rule.   Where the persons above mentioned do
not avoid one another, they are careful to shew respect in not
taking anything from above the head or stepping over the
legs of a father-in-law or wife's brother.   It is disrespectful
at all times for a young man to take anything from above an
elder man's head, for there is something naturally sacred,
rongo, about the head, and no one will take the liberty of
stepping over the legs of any but a brother or intimate friend.
To avoid the mention of a name shews a lower degree of
respect than to avoid a person.   A man who sits and talks
with his wife's father will not mention his name, much less his

wife's mother's name ; a man will not name his wife's brother,
but he will name his wife's sister, she is nothing to him. A
woman will not name, but does not avoid, her husband's
father ; she will on no account name her daughter's husband.
Two people whose children have intermarried, who are *gasala*,
will not name each other. The reserve with regard to the
name extends to the use of it, or of any part of it, in common
conversation. A man on one occasion spoke to me of his
house as a shed, and when that was not understood, went and
touched it with his hand to shew what he meant; a difficulty
being still made, he looked round to be sure that no one was
near and whispered, not the name of his son's wife, but the
respectful substitute for her name, *amen Mulegona*, she who
was with his son, and whose name was Tawurima, Hind-house [1].
Thus, referring to the Mota pedigree given on page 38, Leveveg could not use the common words *mate*, to die, or *qoe*,
pig, because of his son-in-law Matevagqoe; Virsal could not use
the common words *panei*, hand, or *tutun*, hot, because of his
wife's brother's name, or even the numeral *tuwale*, one, because
of his wife's cousin's name. To meet the difficulty caused by
this limitation of vocabulary, a word may be used improperly
like *paito*, shed, for *ima*, house ; or a knife may be called a
cutter and a bow a shooter ; but there is a stock of words kept
in use for this very purpose, to use which instead of the common
words is called to *un*. Thus the *un* words used in the cases
mentioned above would be *karwae* for *qoe*, *saproro* for *mate*,
lima for *panei*, *val* for *tuwale* [2]. This avoidance of the person
and of the name is ascribed by the natives themselves to a
feeling of shyness and respect, a certain inward trembling

---

[1] The word *amaia*, with him, is used not only for a wife's name but in place
of 'his wife'; *nan amaia wa*, then said his wife. In the case referred to,
Tawurima, the name of the daughter-in-law, contains the word *ima*, house.
The father of Tawurima, again, could not use the common word for to go, *mule*,
because it is part of her husband's name, Mulegona.

[2] These *un* words are particularly valuable, because they often shew a
connexion with other languages which does not appear in more common words.
Words are not invented for this purpose ; words are taken which lie
comparatively unused in the language.

which they say prevents their mentioning their own names also ; to blurt out a name is to take a liberty, to avoid the use of it shews delicate respect, and one will extend this respect to more distant connexions rather than apply it too narrowly. A native when asked the name of some other, will often turn to some bystander who answers for him, and the explanation is given in the one word *qaliga*. Respect is also shewn in Mota by using a dual pronoun in addressing or speaking of a single person; 'Where are you two going?' is asked of a *qaliga*, as if both husband and wife were present.

In the New Hebrides the practice is much the same. In Lepers' Island a man speaks to his mother-in-law, and she to him, but they will not come near ; when he speaks to her she turns away. A mother-in-law or father-in-law does not mind using the name of daughter's husband or son's wife in speaking of them to others, but cannot use it in addressing them. When a woman calls to her son-in-law she addresses him as *mim*, you in the plural; when she sends a message to him she says, using his name, 'They want Tanga to go to them,' that is, 'I want Tanga to come to me.' A daughter-in-law does not avoid her husband's father, a man sends his wife with messages to his father. A man will not speak at all the name of his wife's brother ; speaking of him he says, 'my brother-in-law,' speaking to him he says, 'you' in the plural; if he meets him in the path he turns aside, and asks 'Where are you (plural) going?' In this case only it appears that the name is never spoken ; the reserve among connexions by marriage is much less marked than that between brother and sister. No one will step across the legs of another, or take anything from over his head, especially a brother's ; that is thought a serious piece of disrespect. In the neighbouring island of Araga, Pentecost, the intercourse of fathers- and mothers-in-law with their daughter's husband or son's wife is very little restricted; the chief, if not the only, reserve in speaking is exercised by engaged couples before the giving of property for the girl is complete ; this is called *lalag*.

CHAPTER III.

SOCIAL REGULATIONS. CHIEFS.

IT has been shewn that the social structure in these Melanesian islands is not tribal, and it will have been observed
therefore that there can be no political structure held together
by the power of tribal chiefs; but chiefs exist, and still have
in most islands important place and power, though never
perhaps so much importance in the native view as they have
in the eyes of European visitors, who carry with them the
persuasion that savage people are always ruled by chiefs. A
trader or other visitor looks for a chief, and finds such a one
as he expects; a very insignificant person in this way comes
to be called, and to call himself, the king of his island, and
his consideration among his own people is of course enor-
mously enhanced by what white people make of him. The
practice moreover of the commanders of ships of war by which
local chiefs are held responsible for the conduct of their people,
and are treated as if they had considerable power, undoubtedly
increases their importance, nor can that result be regretted.
As a matter of fact the power of chiefs has hitherto rested
upon the belief in their supernatural power derived from the
spirits or ghosts with which they had intercourse. As this
belief has failed, in the Banks' Islands for example some time
ago, the position of a chief has tended to become obscure; and
as this belief is now being generally undermined a new kind
of chief must needs arise, unless a time of anarchy is to begin.
It will be well probably at the outset to give the account of a
chief's power and government in the Solomon Islands, the
Banks' Islands, and the New Hebrides, as supplied by natives

of those groups respectively, who well knew what they were
speaking about. A Florida *Vunagi* kept order in his place,
directed the common operations and industries, represented
his people with strangers, presided at sacrifices and led in war.
He inflicted fines, and would order any one to be put to death.
At Saa in Malanta the chief, *Maelaha*, is such by virtue of
descent, a remarkable difference existing in many points
between this people and Melanesians generally; the people
work in his gardens, plant for him, build a house or canoe for
him at his word. He inflicts fines, and can order a man to be
put to death. At Banks' Islands the *Tavusmele* or *Etvusmel*
in former days kept order, gave commands about the common
concerns of the place, arranged difficulties with neighbouring
villages, could order an offender (one for example who had bewitched or poisoned another) to be put to death, or to pay a
fine of pigs. In Lepers' Island the *Ratahigi* commands or
forbids in such matters as fishing, voyaging, and building;
he can order an offender to be shot or clubbed, or to give
a fine of pigs. In each of these cases it may be added that
the chief has with him young men who have attached themselves to him and carry out his commands, and that the
chief has no more property in or dominion over land than
another man. Further details as to the position and power of
chiefs in the various islands will be hereafter given.

A point of difference between the Polynesian and Melanesian sections of the Pacific peoples is the conspicuous
presence in the former, and the no less conspicuous absence
in the latter, of native history and tradition. In the
Melanesian islands, with one notable exception, the enquirer
seeks in vain for antiquity; the memory of the past perishes
quickly where all things soon pass away, where every building
soon decays, where life is short, and no marked change of
seasons makes people count by longer measures of time than
months. While any one lives who remembers some famous
man of the past his fame lingers, but it dies with the personal
remembrance; a man's ancestry goes back so far as living
memory extends; historical tradition can hardly be said to

exist. It is true that in Motlav, part of Saddle Island in the Banks' group, the people who now live in the islet of Ra and the coast opposite know where their families came from, from neighbouring islands, Mota, Vanua Lava, or from other parts of Saddle Island; but it was only lately they say that they came to live where they are. In Araga, Pentecost Island of the New Hebrides, they shew their original seat at Atabulu, a village still remaining and held in high respect. But the little history that remains, and is vouched for by a multitude of sepulchral stones, is lost in the legend attaching to a sacred stone, of winged shape, lying in the village place. It is called Vingaga, Flyer with webbed wings, and represents one Vingaga, who came floating in a canoe to shore and founded that town. People, *ata*, collected and abode with him, *bulu*; after a time he flew back to heaven. Ancient house sites, raised perhaps a yard above the ground, are to be seen at Atabulu, and at Anwalu near by, with stones over the graves of forgotten chiefs. In Maewo great heaps of stones mark the graves of great men of old times, such as none have been of late. In Motlav, near a famous and enormous *natu* tree, is a house-mound five feet high, where no habitations are now, and men say that it came down from his ancestors to the last man whose house stood on it; and this is but a single known representative of the *yavu* of a Fiji family of rank[1]. The remarkable exception to this absence of history or tradition is found at Saa in Malanta, and is so remarkable and characteristic of native life that the story must be told at length. The larger and principal part of the present inhabitants of Saa ani menu came from Saa haalu, inland not very far off, eleven generations ago. The migration took place under the following circumstances. There were four brothers at the ancient Saa, of whom the eldest was the chief; two were named Pau-ulo, the eldest Pauulo *paina*, the great, the second Pauulo *oou*, the champion;

[1] Mr. Fison writes, 'The higher the house-mound, the higher its occupant's rank: *sa cere na nodra yaru*, their house-mound is high, is still used to express that a family is of high rank.' The *yavu* is described as the ancestral town-lot on which the house is built.

the two younger had the same name, Ro Ute seu oo'u [1].
The chief was a quiet man; the two youngest, aided by the
second, were always fighting and damaging their neighbours'
property; all Pauulo Paina's money was spent in paying
compensation for their injuries and in making peace, and he
told them he must leave them and go away. The neighbouring
people, however, determined to make an end of their trouble ;
they collected, and began to surround the village of Saa as
night fell. Before their circle was complete the Saa people
learnt their danger, gathered their women and children, and
escaped unseen and unheard in the darkness, carrying with
them three drums, which remained at the present Saa within
the memory of old men yet alive. But when they were clear
of the enemy and safe outside their line, they remembered
that a bunch of areca-nuts from which Pauulo Paina had
already taken some to chew with his betel leaves, and which
would furnish means to the enemy of working his death
with charms, was left behind. The two Ute agreed that
one of them, if he died for it, must go for the nuts to save the
elder brother, and the younger of the two took on himself the
danger because he was the younger. The circle was now
closed round the village, but it was still dark, and the enemy
knowing nothing of the escape sat waiting for the dawn to
make their onset. The young Ute took his seat among them
as one of their party, and after a while said to them that he
would steal in and see whether the Saa people were safe in
their houses and could be surprised. Thus he passed through
to the empty village, climbed the palm with a rope round his
feet, gathered all the nuts remaining on the tree, and as he
came down so twisted the stem that when his feet touched
the ground it split into four, and fell with a crash upon the
house. The enemy hearing the sound thought that the Saa
people were not yet all asleep, and sat still; Ute managed to
pass through them unperceived with his nuts, and joined his
friends. Thus they escaped and descended towards the coast ;

[1] The two having the same name were the 'Bonito-gutter champions'; the
Saa *oo'u* being the Mota *wowut*, a fine fellow, a favourite, a hero.

and when they came to a fork where the path divided Pauulo Paina made a speech, saying that no fighters, bullies, thieves, or wizards were to follow him. One party then branched off with Pauulo Oou; and lower down a second separation was made, so that in the end three settlements were formed of people who counted themselves of kin. The inhabitants of what is now Saa ani menu received the fugitives with Pauulo Paina, and his descendants in the male line have ever since been the hereditary chiefs[1]. The descendants of the old inhabitants are now but few and of the lower orders, but they are still the owners of the land. It has never occurred to the Saa immigrants to dispossess them; the new-comers remain, even the chiefs, landless men, except so far as a little has been given to them and a little sold; they have always been allowed what they wanted for their gardens, and have been content. When the move was made there was no great difference in speech, and there is none now in words; but the older race speak very slowly, and may be distinguished now by that slow habit of speech.

There are then at Saa, and at the other two settlements founded by the refugees from the ancient Saa, a family of chiefs with a history, and with descent in the male line. All of that family are born in a certain sense chiefs, the eldest son succeeding to the position of his father as principal chief unless he be judged incompetent. If he turns out a bad, vicious man he loses respect and power, and his brother insensibly replaces him. Sometimes a man will retire because he knows his own unfitness[2]. The chief's power therefore

---

[1] The eleven generations from Pauulo to the present chiefs are kept in mind by the invocation of their successive names in sacrifices.

[2] At the time of writing the above there were three chiefs of high rank at Saa : the ostensible and acting chief was Dorawewe, but he is only the third son of his father, the late head chief. The son and heir of the eldest son was not yet grown up; respect was paid to him for his birth, but he had little power, and the less because his character was bad and he went after women, and so did not gain personal respect. Watehaaodo, uncle on the mother's side to the young man, and himself of the chief's family, was guardian to him, and thence was an important man. It should be observed that thus the particularly close relation

at Saa comes from his birth and personal qualities, not from his intimacy with supernatural beings and his magical knowledge ; he may have these, and is in fact pretty sure to have them, but if one, like Dorawewe now, sacrifices for the family, it is not as chief, but because he has had the knowledge how to do it passed on to him.   In the same way the chief curses in the name of a *lio'a*, powerful ghost, forbidding something to be done under the penalty of death, taboos, because of his ancestral connexion with that *lio'a*. He inherits wealth from his father, and adds to it by the fines he imposes and by the gifts of the people ; but no wealth or success in war could make a man a chief at Saa if not born of the chief's family [1].

The hereditary element is not absent in the succession of chiefs in other islands, though it is by no means so operative as it appears to be. A story hereafter to be narrated illustrates the manner in which a man becomes a chief in Santa Cruz. The most conspicuous chief in Florida at the time and in the place in which Europeans became acquainted with that island was Takua of Boli, whose position it may be safely said was never so exalted in the eyes of the natives as in the eyes of their visitors. He was not a native of Florida but of Mala, and his greatness rested in its origin on a victory in which as a young man he took a principal part, when a confederation of enemies attacked the people of Ta na ihu in Florida, where he was then staying. His reputation for *mana*, spiritual power, was then established ; and from that, as a member of a powerful family of the Nggaombata, with his brothers Sauvui and Dikea, his

of the mother's brother to his nephew maintains itself where the system has become patriarchal.

[1] The word used to designate a chief in Malanta, Ulawa, and San Cristoval, *ma'eraha, ma'elaha,* means literally great death or war, and shews that to the native mind a chief is a warrior. It is customary both at Saa and in Arosi, San Cristoval, to adopt by purchase into the chief's family a boy who promises to be a stout warrior, and to bring him up to be the fighting man and champion of the town. Such a one I remember to have seen at Ubuna in Arosi, a dwarf, whom his purchasers had taken to be a remarkably strong and sturdy child, when he was really a boy much older than they thought. He turned out to be a *maeraha* indeed who scorned to use a shorter spear than full-grown men.

influence increased. Thus according to a native account of the
matter 'the origin of the power of chiefs, *vunagi*, lies entirely
in the belief that they have communication with powerful
ghosts, *tindalo*, and have that *mana* whereby they are able to
bring the power of the *tindalo* to bear.' A chief would convey
his knowledge of the way to approach and to use the power
of the *tindalo* to his son, his nephew, his grandson, to whom
also he bequeathed as far as he could his possessions. Thus he
was able to pass on his power to a chosen successor among his
relations, and a semblance of hereditary succession appeared.
A man's position being in this way obtained, his own character
and success enhanced it, weakness and failure lost it. Public
opinion supported him in his claim for a general obedience,
besides the dread universally felt of the *tindalo* power behind
him. Thus if he imposed a fine, it was paid because his
authority to impose it was recognized, and because it was
firmly believed that he could bring calamity and sickness upon
those who resisted him; as soon as any considerable number
of his people began to disbelieve in his *tindalo* his power to fine
was shaken. But a chief had around him a band of retainers,
young men mostly, from different parts of the island some of
them, of various *kema*, who hung about him, living in his
canoe-house, where they were always ready to do his bidding.
These fought beside him and for him, executed his orders for
punishment or rapine, got a share of his wealth, and did all
they could to please him and grow great and wealthy with
him. They would marry and settle round him if strangers
in the place; and thus a chief and his retainers would be by
no means always the representatives of the people among
whom they ruled, and who sometimes have suffered for their
misdeeds [1]. The influence of a chief, if his band of retainers
is large, and the district in which he rules is populous, extends
widely in the island; his brother chiefs aid him, and, for a
consideration, carry out his wishes [2]. The power to impose a

---

[1] Julian Avenal, not Fergus McIvor, represents such a Melanesian chief.

[2] Some years ago the captain of one of Her Majesty's ships laid upon Takua
of Mboli the duty of apprehending a certain offender, and keeping him a

fine was an active one ; a chief forbids under penalty of a
fine, which is a form of taboo ; he orders one who has done
wrong or has offended him to pay a certain sum of money to
him.   Thus Takua imposed a heavy fine on the man who had
proposed to marry within the prohibited degrees, and the
offender had to hire an advocate to state his case discreetly,
apologize, and beg off a part of the fine.   The chief sends
women or boys to fetch the fine he has imposed ; these sit at
the man's door and *dae*, dun him by their presence and
demands, till he pays.   If he refuses, the chief sends his
retainers to destroy and carry away his property.   It is evident
that a chief of sense, energy and good feeling, will use his
power on the whole to the great advantage of the people ; but
a bad use of a chief's power is naturally common, in oppression,
seizing land and property, increasing his stock of heads, and
gaining a terrible reputation.   For example, a man who had
a private enemy would give money to a chief to have him
killed, as one did not long ago to Dikea ; Dikea would send
one of his young men to kill him.   But sometimes the man
would know his danger and send more money to the chief to
save his life.   Dikea would take both sums and do as he
pleased.

The power of a chief naturally diminished in old age, from
inactivity, parsimony, and loss of reputation ; and, to the credit
of the people, also if, like Takua when he took the daughter of
one who was already his wife, he did what was held by them
to be wrong.   In any case some one was ready, it might be by
degrees, to take the place of one whose force was waning.   A
chief expecting his death prepared his son, nephew, or chosen

prisoner till his return; so at least the captain's orders were interpreted to the
chief. Takua complained ; he could have him killed easily, he said, it would
cost him but a trifle to get that done, but to catch a man and keep him for ten
months would be very difficult and very expensive. Things are now changed
at Florida. Dikea of Ravu accused two men of taking fragments of his food
to charm him ; they fled to Olevuga ; Dikea sent money to Lipa, chief of that
place, to have them killed ; Lipa sent it back. Dikea then sent money to
Tambukoru of Honggo, asking him to attack Olevuga ; that chief refused, but
kept the money.

successor, by imparting to him his *tindalo* knowledge ; but this could not always be done, or the choice made might not be acceptable. The people then would choose for themselves, and make over the dead chief's property to their chosen head. Sometimes a man would assert himself and claim to be chief, on the ground that the late chief had designated him, or because he had already a considerable following (belonging perhaps to an increasing *kema*, as the dead chief to a decreasing one), or boldly standing forth and crying out to the people that he was chief. Without a chief a village would be broken up[1].

The very great part played in the native life of the Banks' Islands by the secret societies hereafter to be described, the *Suqe* and *Tamate*, has always obscured the appearance of such power as a chief would be expected to exercise. Any man whose influence was conspicuous was certainly high in these societies, and it would be wholly inconsistent with the social habits of the people that a man whose place in the Suqe was insignificant should have any considerable power. Hence chiefs as such have hardly been recognized by the missionaries engaged in this group, though traders have found chiefs and kings. When Mala many years ago forbade the use of bows, it was taken to be done by the power he had in all the societies

---

[1] Some years ago Lipa, the chief of Olevuga, was carried off as 'labour' to Queensland, and the chiefless place was in confusion ; but Dikea of Ravu in the neighbourhood, one of the same Nggaombata family, sent directions to Olevuga that the people should choose their chief, and then came over with his party, and took Kosapau, whom they had chosen, by the hand, putting him forward as their chief. The people then knew that he would.be supported, and obeyed him. But Lipa came back after a time, and Kosapau quietly took the second place. When Kalekona of Gaeta died there was no one to succeed him; the chiefs of the other districts, his cousins, came to get their share of the property, and were hospitably entertained ; but the chiefs of Honggo, Liukolilia and Tambukoru, of the Manukama *kema*, would have attacked the Gaeta people in their headless state, if Charles Sapimbuana, the Christian teacher, himself a Manukama, had not got pigs and money together and bought them off. Without a chief the Gaeta people would have dispersed ; no Christian could be a chief of the ancient sort, and the Christian teachers had all agreed among themselves that they would take no place of such authority.

in Vanua Lava and Mota. Still there was a name meaning
chief, *etvusmel, tavusmele,* and a native of Motlav who resided
some weeks in Florida, in the district where Takua was counted
a great chief, bears witness that he saw no great difference
between that *vunagi* and the *etvusmel* of his own home [1]. The
succession of the Etvusmel is declared by him to have been
from father to son, as far as can be remembered, an important
point to notice where descent in family goes by the mother; and
it is said that the chief was always of the great clan or kin,
the *veve liwoa,* an expression which also requires explanation.
The explanation is that in practice, as in the devolution of
property and in the handing on of religious and magic rites,
a man always put as far as he could his son into his own place,
and a rich and powerful man would secure a high place in the
Suqe for his son in very early years; thus the great man's
son would succeed to his place, and become to some extent an
hereditary chief. The father and the son would always be of
different sides of the house; and, as at Florida the chiefs were
generally of the *kema* which happened to be most numerous
at the time, so in the Banks' Islands, where the divisions are
but two, and each of them in alternate generations more
numerous than the other, the chief man was regularly found
on the most powerful side of the house. Thus it can be said
that the succession of Etvusmel at Motlav has been from
father to son as long as can be remembered, and will so continue, though with lessened consequence. Besides those who
were really chiefs many men were called 'great men,' and had
considerable influence in their villages, men who had been

---

[1] The name no doubt refers to the rank obtained in the Suqe club by
killing pigs; *Ta vus mele* is the man who kills for the *mele.* Even now when
the population of Motlav is Christian, they still among themselves call Stephen
Etvusmel at Losalav, and Abraham at Melwo, '*o sul we toga alalanrara, pa
gate nom mava tama we tuai,* the people remain under those two, but do not
regard them with the same respect as in old days.' At Losalav the former
Etvusmel, Molovlad, left a son who is now under Stephen; and when the latter
dies this John Semtambok will succeed. So they agree among themselves now,
on the ground that he is the son of the late chief, high in the Suqe club, and of
the side of the house that now predominates, i.e. of the *veve liwoa.*

valiant and successful in war, and were high in the Suqe ; that
is to say, men who were known to have *mana*, for a man's
charms and amulets made him the great warrior, and his
charms and stones made his pigs and yams to multiply, so that
he could buy his steps in the society. The cleanliness and order
of a Banks' Island village are not now what they were, since
the authority of the 'great men' has been diminished by the
increasing enlightenment of the young people.

In the Northern New Hebrides the position of a chief is
more conspicuous ; though perhaps only because those who
first made themselves acquainted with those islands have
always taken them to be very important people. A man high
in the Suqe, or a successful leader in war, had authority in
his village in the northern part of Aurora, but seems to have
had no designation as a chief. In Araga, Pentecost Island,
and in Omba, Lepers' Island, the remarkable designation of a
chief is Ratahigi, the word which stands for 'mother' in
those islands, and is no doubt identical with the Mota *ratasiu*,
brothers. The probable origin of the use of a word meaning
brotherhood or sisterhood as the name for the mother has
been already suggested (page 28) ; the use of it to designate
a chief seems certainly to point to the fact that the chief
is looked upon as the representative of the brotherhood, of the
kin. As has been pointed out, where there are two kindreds,
and the son is not of the father's kin, it is natural that each
kindred should preponderate in influence, because more in
number, alternately, and that as son succeeds father, one
of this kindred and the other of that, each in his turn should
belong to the kin which is in his time the great one. Hence
they say that chiefs are hereditary, father being succeeded by
son, or uncle by sister's son, in a general way as a matter of
fact, though not always nor by rule. The son does not inherit
chieftainship, but he inherits, if his father can manage it,
what gives him chieftainship, his father's *mana*, his charms,
magic songs, stones and apparatus, his knowledge of the way
to approach spiritual beings, as well as his property. The
present chief will teach his son his knowledge of supernatural

things, and hand over his means for using it; he will buy him up high in the *Suqe* society, and give him and leave him property; so the younger man is ready to take the place of chief when his father dies or fails through age. If a man has no son competent he may take his nephew; sometimes, the son perhaps being too young, a chief's brother will succeed him; sometimes a man will set himself up when no successor is acknowledged, or the people will choose some one to lead them. Some years ago Mairuru, the chief of Walurigi, was a very great man; he sent his son, a young boy, to be educated at Norfolk Island, and it was at once understood that a Christian education which shut out belief and practice of *mana*, shut him out from succession as a chief. If this son had settled in his father's village before the old man's death, he would no doubt have succeeded to some of his property and some of his consideration, but he was absent. When Mairuru died without an apparent successor, a certain man attempted to take his place; he went into the late chief's sacred haunt, his *tauteu*, in which he used to have his intercourse with the *wui*, spirits, and he declared that he heard some one whistle to him there. He told the people also that afterwards in the night he felt something come upon his breast, which he took in his hands, and found to be a stone in shape like the distinguishing part of a valued kind of pig [1] : then Mairuru, he said, himself appeared to him and gave him the *mana*, the magic chant, with which he was to work the stone for producing abundance of those pigs. When he showed the stone the people believed his story; but in the event nothing came of his *mana*, and Mairuru had no suc-cessor. It appears, therefore, that in Lepers' Island and in Araga, as elsewhere, the real ground on which the power of a chief rests is that of belief in the *mana* he possesses, with

---

[1] In certain breeds of pigs in the Banks' Islands and New Hebrides, which are much valued on this account, there occur individual females which simulate the male sex. These are in the Banks' Islands *rawe*; they furnish the finest tusks. Dr. Shortland has observed that the word *rawe* has in the Maori of New Zealand a sense which accounts for its application to these pigs.

which also the wealth he has inherited with it, and all his success in life, are connected. The power of such a man is exercised directly over the people of his own village, and if his reputation for *mana* spreads abroad, he will have a wide influence in his island and even beyond it ; young men from other parts, as well as the youths of his village, will come and live in his *gamali*, his *Suqe* club-house, and will carry out his orders even to the punishment of death in peace, and fight for him in war.

CHAPTER IV.

PROPERTY AND INHERITANCE.

In the character of property and in the laws of succession to property, there is hardly any difference to be found in the Melanesian islands with which we are concerned; in all it may be said that property is in land and in personal possessions; that there is a certain distinction between land which has been inherited and that which has been reclaimed from the waste; that there is no strictly communal property in land; and that with landed and personal property alike, the original right of succession is with the sister's children, except where, besides the very exceptional case of Saa, there comes in the succession of children to the property which their father has acquired for himself.

The land may be considered everywhere to be divided into three parts: (1) the Town lots; (2) the Garden ground; (3) the Bush. In Florida, (1) *Na Komu*, (2) *Na Matanga*, (3) *Na Leiao*; in Santa Cruz, (1) *Matalia*, (2) *Nabalo*, (3) *Nabanogabo*; in Mota, (1) *O Vanua*, (2) *O Utag*, (3) *O Mot*; in Lepers' Island, (1) *A Vanue*, (2) *A Labute*, (3) *A Labute virogi*, which in Araga are (1) *Vanua*, (2) *Lolgae*, (3) *Ute vono*; and these correspond to the *Yavu*, the *Qele*, the *Veikau* of Fiji[1]. Of

---

[1] Land tenure in Fiji has been described by the Rev. Lorimer Fison in a Paper printed in the Journal of the Anthropological Institute, February, 1881, and briefly as follows : ' The tenure of land is distinctly tribal, and the title is vested in all the full-born members of the tribe. The land is of three kinds : the *yavu* or town lot, the *qele* (*nggele*) or arable land, and the *veikau*

these three divisions of the land, the bush, the uncleared
forest, is not property; nor, as far as I am aware, do the
natives fix any limit up to which they consider the bush
to belong to the particular district or group of villages in
which they live, although probably they would resent the
felling of trees too near their own grounds. The gardens
and the sites of the villages are all held in property, and
pass by inheritance; so that every part has its owner for
the time, who possesses it as his share of the family property,
but who can by no means alienate it as if it were simply
his own. The chiefs, however powerful in some places they
may be, have no more property in the land or more right
over it in any of the islands than other men; they often
use their power tyrannically to drive away the owners of
gardens which they covet, and they are very willing to meet
the common European belief that a chief is the owner of
the soil, by taking a price for land which is not theirs to sell;
but the ownership of every piece is remembered and will be
asserted when occasion offers. The remarkable case of the
landless chiefs at Saa (page 50) shews how fixed is the right
of property in land. Before the coming of Europeans the
sale of land was, at least at Saa, not unknown, but was at
any rate uncommon; of late, especially in the New Hebrides,
much land has been sold to Europeans, some honestly and
effectively, some by transactions in which the title of the vendor
has been nothing but his willingness to receive some calico
and guns. In a true sale the consent of all who have an
interest in the property must be had, and the exact boundary
of each parcel of land defined; then the value of each piece
and of each fruit-tree has to be ascertained, and the claim of

or forest. The *veikau* is common to all members of a community, but the *yavu*
and the *qele* are divided and subdivided. Each owner, however, holds for the
household to which he belongs, the household holds for the clan, the clan for
the tribe, the tribe for the community, and the community for posterity. Each
generation has the usufruct only, and cannot alienate the land. The chiefs
have overridden this rule, but most unjustly.' This will stand for the
islands west of Fiji, with the important difference made by the absence of
tribes.

every single individual discussed and satisfied. A fruit-tree planted on another's land, with his consent, remains the property of the planter and of his heirs [1]. It is important also to observe that the property, whether in the villages or in the gardens, does not lie in large divisions corresponding to the divisions of the people for marriage purposes into two or more kins or clans, the *kema* of Florida, the *veve* of Mota, the *wai vung* of Lepers' Island; but all are intermixed. It is probable enough that in the original formation of each settlement the several divisions of the people worked together to make their gardens; as it is, families have formed themselves within the divisions, the land is held by families, sons work in their fathers' gardens who are not their kin; there cannot be a family, or married couple, in which two kindreds at least have not a share.

It is remarkable indeed how precisely alike in the Solomon Islands, the Banks' Islands, and the New Hebrides, the character of property in land reclaimed from the bush asserts itself to be; and how the same effect has been produced of introducing or strengthening the tendency towards the succession of the son to his father's property, in place of the right of succession through the mother. This will be shewn, together with the very general agreement in the whole character of landed property and succession to it, as the subject is treated in some detail with examples taken from the several groups, beginning with Florida in the Solomon Islands, and passing eastwards through Santa Cruz and the Banks' Islands to the New Hebrides.

In Florida the house sites in the *komu*, like the gardens of the *matanga*, are hereditary property; and, though there do

---

[1] In Fiji, ' Fruit-trees are often held by persons who do not own the land; but there is a curious distinction here. The property in this case is rather in the fruit than in the tree, and is therefore not considered to be in the land. You may take the fruit, but you must not cut down the tree without the landowner's permission. A remarkable distinction was made by one of my Fijian informants. He who has a tree on another man's land may cut it down and take it away; his axe does not touch the soil; but he may not dig the tree up by the roots, for his digging-stick would turn up the soil.'—Rev. L. Fison.

not appear to be any ancient village sites now occupied, the
old sites are well remembered and their proprietors known.
Members of the various *kema* dwelling intermixed on their
property in the village have their gardens intermixed in the
matanga. It happens naturally, as a village is not inhabited
by a local tribe, that some of the villagers have no property
of their own in the village or in the neighbouring garden
grounds, in which case their neighbours accommodate them
with what they want. The *matanga* property is never absolutely in the individual but in the *kema*, being looked upon
as having been cleared originally by the *kema*; portions are
occupied in hereditary succession by families within the *kema*,
by an original agreement which now has come to be a
right. These ancient family lands pass of right to members of
the same *kema*, ordinarily the sister's children. The whole
matanga near a town is seldom under cultivation at the same
time; some may pass, if the place is deserted, entirely into
bush again, but is never strictly *leiao*, for its character is
remembered.   In the neighbourhood of a prosperous village a
man, and his sons working with him, will often clear a piece
of bush land and make it *matanga*. This then passes to his
sons without question, being held to be his own, and so long
as it is clearly remembered how the land was acquired it
passes from father to son; but after a time the character of
the property may be forgotten, and the nephews of a deceased
proprietor will claim it from his sons and be supported by
their *kema*; serious quarrels arise in this way. A chief,
vunagi, differs in no way from another man in his right to
property in *komu* and *matanga*[1]. If a man plants a cocoa-
nut-tree, an areca palm-tree, or other useful tree on a friend's
ground, the tree goes to the planter's son, and if the landowner continues friendly will pass on without dispute. A

---

[1] Dikea the chief at Ravu drove away Logana and his family from that place
on the pretext that Logana's brother-in-law had set fire to his canoe-house, but
really to get possession of Logana's *matanga*, which was large and good. The
dispossessed family at Olevuga keep their eyes on the property, waiting for
Dikea's death to claim it.

man also can plant in his own *matanga* fruit-trees expressly
declared to be the property of his sons; at his death the
ground will pass to his nephews, his own kin, but his sons
will own the trees. Florida people are very reckless however
about destroying fruit-trees.

The succession to personal property in Florida is known to
be originally with the members of the *kema*, the kin of the
deceased. These will assemble after a death, and if the
deceased be not very rich, will eat up his pigs and his food.
A chief will sometimes take what he likes, but has no right
to do it. A man before his death will direct that his canoe is
to go to his son, and he will receive it; otherwise son and
nephew will each claim, and the stronger will get it. A rich
man's money is divided among brothers, nephews, and, if they
can get any, his sons, a fruitful source of quarrels; but a man's
wife, in prospect of his death, would hide a good deal of his
money, and when the crowd assembled for the division of the
inheritance had dispersed, would bring it out for herself and
her sons. Chiefs used to hide their money and valuable
property and *tambu*, taboo, the place; now, when the fear of
the *tambu* is gone, the young people search for these hoards
and take what they find. These Florida customs may be
taken as representing those of the surrounding islands of the
Solomon group. In Saa and its neighbourhood property of
course descends entirely in the patriarchal line. In Santa
Cruz a man's nephews regularly succeed to his property,
in land, pigs, money and other things; but the sons also in
some cases succeed. A man there also has property in trees
which are not on his own ground.

In the Banks' Islands also the town land, the *vanua*, and
the garden grounds, the *utag*, are so far private property that
the owner can be found for each piece; the owner being the
one who has for his life the possession of the portion of the
family land which he has inherited; the lands and houses of
the two *veve* are intermingled; the succession to the land is
rightly with the sister's children. Here also the *utag* is distinguished into the ancient hereditary cultivated ground, and

823142   F that which has been reclaimed from the *mot*, the uncleared forest, by the present owner or his recent predecessors. In the first case the nephews on their mother's side of the previous proprietor occupy the ground, each taking the piece he wishes for his own garden, and all having collectively a property in the whole. The land of the other character passes to the children of the man who has cleared the forest from it; his kin have no claim to it. The children divide it into separate lots, and do not in any way hold the property in common; the eldest son will take the oldest plantation, and the youngest will have the latest which has not yet borne its crop [1]. Here the patriarchal succession is fixed; in the other case it is coming in and has a recognized footing. It is common to make arrangements by which a man's children succeed him with the consent of the heirs at law. For example, when Woser's father died, who had held an *utag* at Motlav in common inheritance with his brother, Woser gave a pig to his uncle, and he thereupon relinquished his claim to half the property in the garden ground, which he did not use. The heir of the deceased, and the heir also in prospect of the deceased's brother, was the son of their sister; and to him Woser gave money to quiet his claim. Upon this Woser, with his two brothers and two sisters, entered upon the *utag* as if they had inherited it; that is, they occupied it by a common property in the whole and with a particular occupation of separate gardens. If a similar transaction were to follow upon the death of these present owners, who are not of their father's kin, the land would go to their children who will be not of their kin but of their mother's; the property will thus revert to the *veve* to which it belongs. Sometimes a man before his death begs his brother not to disturb his son in his garden; he agrees, and the son takes his father's place;

---

[1] There is no right of primogeniture. Daughters inherit of right equally with sons, but in fact they rather transmit the inheritance to their children. So in Fiji, 'Daughters can scarcely be said to inherit land. Land is given *with* them at their marriage, but it is not given *to* them. If they hold it at all it is only a means of transmitting the land to their children.'—Rev. L. Fison.

but the father was there of right, and the son has strictly no
right; he therefore gives money to the natural heirs, his
father's sister's children. In order to make a transaction of
this kind secure, the son will put the money for the redemption
of the garden upon his father's corpse when he is laid out for
burial; the nephews and heirs of the deceased take the money
from their dead *maraui* in the presence of the assembled people,
and never can deny that they have given up their right [1]. If
a man's children at his death are not rich enough to redeem
the whole *ulag* they redeem a part. It is a part of the
acknowledgment of the right of the sister's children, and a
part of the satisfaction for it, that fruits and other produce are
allowed them for a time out of the garden; for these are the
labour of the deceased, whose heirs his nephews and nieces of
his own kin are; the products of the new owner's work will
not be claimed. Property in trees is distinct from that in
land, and goes to the planter's children. In case therefore of
a sale of land there is much variety in the title to the parcels
of ground and in the ownership of the fruit-trees, the knowledge of which is most minute and accurate. The exact
limits of each bit of property are known, and the value of the
right to be extinguished is discussed and settled by common
consent [2].

The town lots in the *vanua*, the house sites, *tano ima*, are held
in the same way. When a young man makes his own home
he builds on the property of his kin, his mother's or his
maternal uncle's. It happens naturally that the elder sons

[1] A pig has been soon delivered from the hand of a dead man at his funeral,
probably with the same intention.

[2] Many years ago I completed the purchase of a piece of ground for a school
at Navqoe in Mota, and found the rights, and the limits and value of the rights,
of every man and woman concerned acknowledged and defined in a surprising
manner. Each parcel of the land was known by boundaries drawn from tree
to tree. The year before the purchase of another piece of ground for a similar
purpose had been supposed to be completed, but when payment was being made
at Navqoe the owner of a fruit-tree on the other ground put in his claim, which
he had before omitted to make. He was accompanied by the owner of the
ground on which the tree stood, who testified that the claim was good, for the
claimant's grandfather had planted it.

have left their father's house on marriage before his death, or
do so successively after his death; the youngest son then
remains with his mother and keeps the house. In a village
which is flourishing a new house is built on an old site,
which therefore rises in time into something of a mound; but
villages are seldom permanent. When a new village is begun
it may occupy an ancient site of late unused, in which case
the property in the town lots is well remembered, or it may
be a new occupation of ground for building. The *vanua* at
Losalav in Motlav has been formed round a house built by the
great-uncle of Woser, who gave two *rawe* pigs to the owner
of the *utag* for the ground, and thus became the landlord;
his daughter afterwards, though she received nothing in the
way of rent, was treated with respect by the householders
because they were not on property of their own.

Personal property—the pigs which are so much valued, the
money, canoes, ornaments, weapons, and the various implements used in native life—goes to the children generally; but
the right of the sister's children is still maintained. When a
man dies his brothers and kinsmen, *sogoi*, will come and carry
off his pigs unless the children buy them off; but if a man
before his death makes a sort of testament, *vatavata varvarnanau*,
declaring that he gives his property to his children and
distributing it, they will not be disturbed in their inheritance.
A great man often buried quantities of money, which was
never found. In Lakona, part of Santa Maria, 'a man will
hide some of his money; then if he have a good son who helps
him well in his garden or always gives him food, the father
will make his hoard known to him, that it may be his; if not
it is gone for ever.' In that place a man's money at his death
is carefully distributed in short lengths among his children
and his kinsmen, and his pigs are distributed in the same
way; the children give money and pigs to the kinsmen that
they may keep his personal belongings, and his land and fruit-
trees, which are then completely given up. In the case of the
death of a native in some place in which he has settled as
a stranger, or where he has been on a visit, his kinsmen, and

especially his sister's son, have a right to go and take what he may have left behind him ; but this is generally compounded for by a sum of money, *tulag*, after receiving which no further claim can be made. There is no doubt very often in such a case a suspicion or accusation of poisoning or witchcraft as the cause of death, for which compensation is demanded [1].

In the New Hebrides the ancient succession of the sister's son to his uncle's property appears to be strongly maintained in Araga, Pentecost Island, where the nephew succeeds to the house, the garden, and the pigs of his uncle, and the son takes nothing except what his father has given him in his lifetime ; and even if a man makes a garden for himself out of the bush it must go to his sister's son. It is very different, however in Lepers' Island, where the right of the sister's son seems to be barely recognized, and the property in the villages and in the gardens is held by individuals as their own, not as belonging to the *waivung*. The town lots are fenced round, so that the houses stand in enclosures. A man's son succeeds to his house property, but will not live in the house so long as his mother and sisters are there, on account of those restrictions upon intercourse which have been already mentioned. Houses are renewed in the same place, but not always on the same site, and villages are often shifted, the property in the ground being borne in mind. A man's garden-ground, *labute*, goes to his sons, who arrange the division of it among themselves, unless their father has expressed his will about it before his death. Women do not succeed to land, but have a right to a share in the produce of their father's gardens, which indeed their brothers are considered to hold partly for them. A man can make himself a new garden out of the unappropriated ground fit for gardens, the *labute virogi*,—loose, not tied up,—

---

[1] For example, Wete's son had gone over from Merlav to Merig, and there he died, having been charmed by means of a fragment of his food at the instigation of a man whose wife is Wete's sister. So on the return of the party, when the cause of death comes out, Wete shoots his sister with his gun, because her husband had been the cause of the death of his son. The whole transaction is looked upon as a matter of course (the woman not being much hurt); Wete is on the best of terms with his neighbours and relations.

and there cannot be any difference between this and his hereditary property. Gardens are all fenced. Fruit-trees planted on another man's land remain the property of the planter and his heirs. It is in the succession to a man's personal property that the rights of kinship assert themselves. On a man's death his sons distribute his pigs, money, and other possessions, among those of his *waivung*, a choice pig and a larger share of other things being given to the sister's son, because his special relationship is much regarded. A man, however, will make his will, expressing his wishes as to the disposition of his property before his death. The succession to property is a fruitful source of quarrels, and it is natural that opportunity should prevail over acknowledged right when the heirs are out of the way.

There appears upon the whole a remarkable tendency throughout these islands of Melanesia towards the substitution of a man's own children for his sister's children, and others of his kin, in succession to his property; and this appears to begin where the property is the produce of the man's own industry, with the assistance in most cases of his sons, as in gardens newly cleared from the forest, in his money, his pigs, and his canoes. The original right of a man's own kin, and especially his sister's sons, to be his heirs not only to the hereditary lands which have come down in the kin but to personal property, is yet strongly maintained, even at Lepers' Island, where the advance towards the patriarchal system has been so considerable. It is probable that even at Saa something still survives of what must have been the original custom of the ancestors of that people, as well as of the rest of the Melanesians. It is evident that the newer form of succession depends upon the assertion of paternity; and as it arises sometimes on the occupation of new ground, it may be thought to be strengthened by the formation of new settlements after the family has established itself within the kin.

CHAPTER V.

THERE is certainly nothing more characteristic of Melanesian life than the presence of Societies which celebrate
Mysteries strictly concealed from the uninitiated and from all
females. A dress, with a mask or hat, disguises the members
if they appear in open day; they have strange cries and
sounds by which they make their presence known when
they are unseen. In some cases, as in Florida and Aurora,
they make a public show of a piece of the handiwork of the
ghosts with whom it is pretended that they have been associating. Such societies are the Dukduk of New Britain
described by Mr. Brown and Mr. Romilly, the Matambala of
Florida, the Tamate of the Banks' Islands, the Qatu of the
Northern New Hebrides. A photograph from New Caledonia
shews a figure which can hardly be distinguished from that
of a *tamate* from the Banks' Islands, and Mr. Romilly mentions
an institution like the Dukduk in New Guinea. It is plain,
therefore, that this institution extends very widely through
Melanesia, and the Nanga of Fiji, though in some respects
different, cannot be thought to be entirely distinct from it;
yet it is remarkable that nothing of the sort has as yet been
found in Santa Cruz, or in the Solomon Islands east of
Florida [1].

---

[1] Of the two large islands of Guadalcanar and Malanta, only a very small
part has come under observation. The Santa Cruz people do not seem to be
closely connected with the Solomon islanders. When it is remembered that the

The Florida mysteries were believed to have been brought
from Ysabel, where nothing of the kind has as yet been
observed. This belief, how-
ever, serves to point to a
connexion with the Dukduk
of New Britain, in the name
of which a further connexion
may probably be found. In
all these societies the ghosts
of the dead were supposed
to be present; in the Banks'
Islands their name is 'The
Ghosts;' in Santa Cruz a
ghost is *duka*; in Florida
one method of consulting
the ghosts of the dead is
paluduka. It is very likely
therefore that in New
Britain the Dukduk are also
'The Ghosts.'

NEW CALEDONIA MASKER.

One very important point
of difference separates these
from the *bora* of Australia,
in which the grown youth

of the tribe are 'made young men,' and have imparted to
them some knowledge of the religious beliefs and practices
of the elders. Grown men and infants, married and unmarried, are equally admitted to the societies of Florida
and the New Hebrides; and if in the Banks' Islands it
is not customary to admit boys very young, there is certainly no limit of age as regards admission. It is no
doubt the case that where these societies flourish, a youth
who has not become a member of one of them does not
take a position of full social equality with the young men

Nanga appears to be limited to a part only of Viti Levu in Fiji, and for a long
time escaped notice there, it is reasonable to look for the discovery of many
secret societies in Melanesia which have not yet been observed.

who are members; and also that such a young man has
probably no wife. Such a young man has not been able to
meet the expense of initiation or of matrimony; his friends,
from carelessness or poverty, have let him grow up without
making proper provision for him; he remains uninitiated and
unmarried from the same cause ; but initiation is by no means
a preliminary step to matrimony. It is difficult, in view of
the strict secrecy and solemnity of the mysteries, to believe
that there is no knowledge imparted in initiation of a religious
character. The outer world of women and children, and the
uninitiated, *matawonowono*,—whose eyes were closed,—undoubtedly believed that the initiated entered into association with
the ghosts of the dead ; the strange cries and awful sounds
that proceeded from the sacred and unapproachable lodge of
the association, or from the forest when the members of it
were abroad, were more than human in their ears ; the figures
that appeared were not those of men. An accident would no
doubt sometimes make it plain that it was a man, some one
well known and recognized, who was figuring as a ghost ;
but then his disguise was not the work of mortal hands ; and
the shrewd conjecture that all the rest were as much men and
neighbours as the one whose fall revealed him might be
entertained, but would be dangerous to express. It was only
when the neophyte was admitted into the mysterious precincts that he found only his daily companions there, and
learnt that there was nothing to be imparted to him except
the knowledge how the sounds were produced, how the
dresses and decorations were made, and in some cases a song
and dance. There was no secret article of belief made known,
and no secret form of worship practised. The ordinary forms
of prayer and sacrifice were performed as elsewhere, though
here in connexion with these mysteries. There were no forms
of worship peculiar to the society, and no objects of worship
of a kind unknown to those without.

It is remarkable also that, as far as I have been able to
ascertain, there is nothing or very little that is obscene, or
more objectionable from a moral point of view than imposture

combined with a certain amount of tyranny and intimidation.
In some places the neophytes had to endure hardships or even
tortures, which were absent, however, in the Banks' Islands,
where these societies are very numerous. The property of
the uninitiated was plundered, and themselves beaten and
oppressed when the mysteries were at work ; all order and
industry were upset. At the same time hideous and obscene
orgies were absent ; a native convert to Christianity might go
into his lodge and find nothing there to offend him that he
did not find in the village ; an European visitor might go in
and find nothing more mysterious to be revealed to him than
the hats and dresses and the appliances for producing the
unearthly sounds.

The Fijian *nanga* as described by Mr. Fison and Mr. Joske,
to which the presence of women gives at once a different
character, must be taken as representing these secret societies
in that group, and it is reasonable to suppose direct connexion
in origin between this and those that flourish in the islands
further to the west. The institution in Fiji, however, is so
little conspicuous in the life of the people, probably because so
limited in distribution, that it escaped for many years the
observation of Mr. Fison himself. In the Banks' Islands
the *tamate* would very soon call for notice. If no special
celebration of the mysteries were being carried on, a visitor
would soon become aware that there were near every village
retreats frequented by most of his native companions, and
unapproachable by some. The members of the societies would
be proud to shew him these retreats and the wonderful works
of art they contained. Very few days would pass without the
appearance of some masked figures, or the sound of some
strange noise or cry. In that group the number of these
societies is surprising ; some very insignificant, local, or
recently started by individuals ; some select and respected ;
one found everywhere, the principal and apparently original
institution of the kind. In the Northern New Hebrides
this Great *Tamate* of the Banks' Islands is not found, but
others of the same character appear. I have seen a mask and

a secret lodge as far south as Ambrym. The figure in the photograph from New Caledonia is so nearly identical with that of a *tamate* of the Banks' Islands, that the identity of the institution may be conjectured, or at any rate a connexion

BANKS' ISLANDS TAMATE.

must be taken to exist. Between the Banks' Islands and Florida the interval is considerable; but scholars from Florida, on their way to Norfolk Island many years ago, recognized their own *matabala* in the *salagoro* of Mota, to which as strangers they were freely admitted. The result of their admission was fatal to the mystery in either institution. A Florida boy who had seen what the Mota *salagoro* was and contained, knew very well what sort of mysteries those were at home into which he had not yet been initiated, and he ceased to believe in their supernatural character. The uninitiated boys from the Banks' Islands heard in Norfolk Island from their Florida schoolfellows what they had seen, and the sacredness of the *salagoro* was lost for them. The secret was out many years ago, though in Florida the power of the mysteries was maintained till Christianity prevailed in the only part of the island in which the institution had a seat.

In the Banks' Islands the *tamate* has survived the introduction of Christianity. All belief in the supernatural character of the associations has long disappeared, all women and children know that the *tamate* are men dressed in disguises made by themselves, and that the sounds and cries are naturally produced. But these societies had so important a place in the social arrangements of the people that they have held their ground as clubs. It is not only in the Banks' Islands that secrecy and a costume have their attractions. The secrecy of the lodges is still maintained, the *salagoro* is unapproachable by women and the uninitiated, the neophyte has still to go through his time of probation and seclusion, and the authority of the society is maintained by too much of the high-handed tyranny of old times[1]. In truth, the social power of these societies was too great to be readily dissolved, and in the

---

[1] It was a matter of principle with Bishop Patteson not to interfere in an arbitrary manner with the institutions of the people, but to leave it to their own sense of right and wrong, and their own knowledge of the character of what they did, to condemn or to tolerate what their growing enlightenment would call into question. So there arose among his early pupils the doubt whether it would be right for them as Christians to continue members of the *tamate* societies, to seek for admission into them, and frequent their lodges. The bishop put it to them that they should enquire and consult among themselves about the real character of the societies ; did they offer worship and prayer to ghosts or spirits ; were they required to take part in anything indecent or atrocious ; did membership involve any profession of belief or practice of superstition peculiar to the members ? After consultation they reported to him that they could not discover anything wrong in itself, except the pretence of association with ghosts, which had already ceased to be serious, and the beating and robbing of the uninitiated, which it was quite possible for them to refuse to take part in and to oppose. The bishop therefore would not condemn the societies, and in the Banks' Islands they continue to exist, and indeed to flourish more than it is at all desirable that they should.

absence of any strong political organization the importance of
the position of a member of the largest and most exclusive of
the societies has been considerable. Many years ago I well
remember how in the early morning of one day in the island of
Mota a strange cry was heard repeated from every quarter,
shrill, prolonged and unmistakeable. It was the cry of the
tamate; the members of the Great *Tamate* were all out and in
possession of the island; *o vanua we gona,* the country was in
occupation, no one could go about, everything of the business
of ordinary life was at a standstill till the *tamate* should be
satisfied. Upon enquiry we were told that in the evening
before a man in anger had taken up his bow. In accordance
with the teaching of Bishop Patteson, and with the authority
of the great man of the island, the society of the Great *Tamate*
had forbidden the use of the bow and arrow in private quarrels
under penalty of a fine to them. On this occasion the man
who had been guilty of the offence hastened to atone for it
with a pig, and all was quiet again. It is not surprising that
membership in so powerful a society should be valued and not
readily resigned.

I. *The Banks' Islands.*—The Banks' Islands, with the
neighbouring Torres group, are undoubtedly the chief seat of
these societies, which are there universally called ' The Ghosts,'
o tamate, netmet. In the Torres Islands alone there are a
hundred of them, and every man belongs to four or five. The
chief society, the *tamate liwoa* of Mota, is present everywhere,
though in some places it is not so important as some more
exclusive one of local origin. Another association is distinguished by its peculiar dance, and differs from the others in
having no permanent lodge or club-house; this, the *Qat,*
is found in all the Banks' Islands, but not in the Torres
Islands. All these *tamate* associations have as their particular
badge a leaf or a flower. The very numerous and well-marked
varieties of the croton, which all have their native names,
furnish the leaves; the flowers are those of the many varieties
of hibiscus, all also named. To stick flowers in the hair, *rou,*
is very common; it is the particular part of the head which is

ornamented by the particular flower that marks the member
of the *tamate*.   To assume the badge without being a member
of a *tamate* is an offence against the society, to be punished
according to the power and position of the society offended.
In the Torres Islands, for example, one of the three great
tamate societies is *Nipir*, and its badge is a hibiscus flower worn
over the forehead.   If any one not a member should be seen
with this flower thus worn, a bunch of flowers and leaves
is set up in a public place by the society, and the offender
knows that he must forfeit a pig.   He brings his pig, ties it
in the open space in the middle of his village, and stands by
it ; one of the society then beats him for his presumption, and
after that he has to go through the regular initiation with the
payment of the entrance fees.

The origin of these societies in the Banks' Islands has no
light thrown upon it, as in Florida, by tradition, and must be
presumed therefore to belong to no recent times.   There is a
story that a woman received from a ghost, whom she saw in a
tree, an image with the hat and cloak of a *tamate*, and that
she kept this hidden behind a partition in her house.   It
became known that she had something wonderful concealed,
and she admitted men on payment to a private view.   When
those who had partaken of the secret became numerous enough
they took it out of the woman's hands, made a lodge for
themselves, were taught by the image, which was all the
while itself a ghost, how to make the dress, and thus set up
the first *tamate* association, with the strictest exclusion of
all women ever afterwards. ˙ From this story nothing can be
learnt concerning the origin of so widely spread an institution.
The multitude of minor associations, generally named after
birds, are however mostly local, and may be thought to be
modern.   Any one might start a new society, and gather round
him his co-founders, taking any object that might strike their
fancy as the ground and symbol of their association.   A
visitor to Norfolk Island having seen there a bird that was
strange to him, established on his return to Mota a society
called 'the Norfolk Island Bird.'   Some such new foundations

will succeed and flourish, some will fail; but the whole number
in the Banks' Islands and the Torres Islands must be very
great. Three or four may be common to all the group, some
few common to two or more islands, the rest more or less
closely localized. Some are exclusive with heavy entrance
payments, and are used by elder men of good position; some
are cheap and easy of entrance. I think it probable that
where the Great *Tamate* is powerful, all the members of the
other societies belong also to that and work together with it,
except the younger members of the least important, the
seclusion of which is comparatively little respected.

The lodge or secret resort of the Great *Tamate* is the *salagoro*,
established in some secluded place, generally amidst lofty trees,
in the neighbourhood of every considerable village or group of
villages. The path to it is marked where it diverges from the
public path by bright orange-coloured fruits stuck on reeds,
bunches of flowers, fronds of cycas, and the customary *soloi*,
taboo marks, forbidding entrance. These are repeated at
intervals till the winding path comes out into the open space
in which the building stands. Such marks are quite sufficient
to prevent intrusion, because they represent the whole force of
the association, not because they rest on any specially religious
sanction. The whole place is not sacred, *rongo*, it is set apart,
tapu, by a sufficient authority. No woman or uninitiated
person would think of approaching; foreigners are admitted
without difficulty; that is to say, those who do not belong to
those neighbouring islands in which the society is known to
have a place, Solomon islanders for example. If nothing in the
way of initiation or particular celebration should be going on,
the visitor will find only a few members in the place; some who
use it as a club for their meals, some whose business it is as
newly-admitted members to prepare the meals, keep the place
swept, and remain within for a fixed number of days. Very
likely a cocoa-nut will be pointed out as representing some one
whose personal attendance has been excused. The hats and
dresses worn at the last dance or public demonstration may be
inspected. The hats are really ingenious, and when new are

handsome. They are made of bark, painted with such
vegetable preparations as it is a secret of the fraternity to
compound, and adorned in bands and in rings round the eyes
on either side with the scarlet seeds of the *abrus precatorius.*
The hats receive the whole head, and come down upon the

TAMATE, VALUWA, BANKS' ISLANDS.

shoulders, where they meet the cloak with a fringe of cycas
leaves. The shape of the hats is very various; some have a
strange resemblance to the cocked hats of naval officers, and
it has been naturally supposed that the pattern has been taken
from them. But it is very unlikely that a naval officer has

ever been seen in a cocked hat in the Banks' Islands, and the
masks of that shape were certainly seen when masks were first
seen there by Europeans[1].   Besides these hats the house of

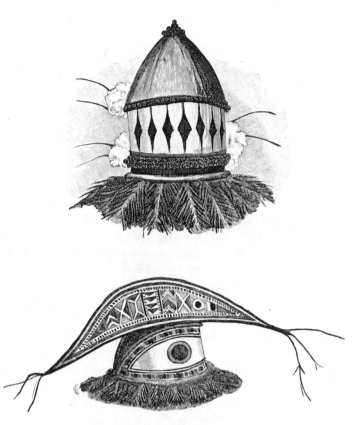

BANKS' ISLANDS TAMATE.

the *salagoro* will not be found to contain anything more than
the usual appliances for cooking : a certain disappointment is
probably experienced by every one who first penetrates into
the mysterious precincts.   There is one object, however, which

---

[1] It is true that when white men were seen with hats they were supposed by
the natives to wear what corresponded to their own masks.   The native name for

is not, or but lately was not, so readily made known. This is
the apparatus by which the peculiar, and certainly very
impressive, sound is made, which was believed by the outsiders
to be the cry or voice of the ghosts. This is a flat, smooth stone,
on which the butt-end of the stalk of a fan of palm is rubbed.
The vibration of the fan produces an extraordinary sound,
which can be modulated in strength and tone at the will of
the performer, and which proceeding in the stillness of day-
break from the mysterious recesses of the *salagoro*, may well
have carried with it the assurance of a supernatural presence
and power. The origin of this contrivance is thus narrated.
Two members of the Great *Tamate* in Vanua Lava going
together along the shore heard a strange and unearthly sound
as they approached a point of land, the usual haunt of ghosts.
They found this to be produced by an old woman sitting on
the beach and rubbing down shells for money upon a stone,
who was contriving to do her work and at the same time
shelter herself from the sun, by using the handle of her
palmleaf umbrella for the stick which holds the shell. The
men perceived the value of the discovery for the purpose
of their mysteries, ran in upon the woman and killed her,
and carried off the stone and her umbrella. This apparatus
does the work which the 'bull-roarer,' too well known in
the Banks' Islands to be used in mysteries, performs elsewhere.

    To obtain admission into any of these societies is to *tiro*.
Before admission can be obtained to the Great *Tamate*, the
candidate or his friends has to *usur* with a pig of the valued
kind called *rawe* ; and there is also a period of fasting to be
gone through. When he is admitted he is brought into the
salagoro, and deposits money at the successive stages of his
advance, marked by the *soloi* beside the path till he comes

---

a mask worn in one of these societies is the same as that given to the society
itself, *tamate*, a ghost ; and *tamate* has long been established as the name of
any European hat or cap. Hence it is natural rather to speak of these disguises
as hats than as masks, and useful perhaps to do so, to distinguish them from the
masks to cover the face which are in use elsewhere.

into the house. He has then to *goto*, remain secluded, so many
days before he can go back into his village, and after that
has to serve so many days more in the preparation of the
daily oven. The number of days of seclusion and of attendance, and the amount of the admission fees, vary with
the dignity of the society [1]. In Ureparapara, where the
Great *Tamate* is not of much importance, there are three chief
societies, *Ni Pir, No Vov, Ne Menmendol*, into which the admission is difficult; the new member has to *goto* for a hundred

---

[1] Mr. Palmer thus describes the initiation of children at Pek in Vanua
Lava. 'A number of children were about to enter the Salagoro, which was the
cause of the gathering. We passed through a tall screen of cocoa-nut leaves
some twenty feet high, made so as to hide the precincts of the Salagoro from
the uninitiated. In the courtyard of the village there was a group of children,
some babies carried in their fathers' arms, all boys; these were the candidates
for admission into the Salagoro. We waited for a short time, when some one
gave a signal, and one of the men gave a long, loud cry with all the strength of
his lungs, and then came rushing from a path inland a curious figure I had
seen dressing up for the occasion. This was the *tamate wasawasa* (the harmless
ghost) who was to conduct the children into the Salagoro. He came along with
a light, springy step, with two white rods in his hands, which he danced up
and down. All you saw of the man were his two legs. On his head was
a curious kind of hat or *tamate*; it is a mask with holes or slits in it,
through which he saw; long fringes made of cocoa-nut leaves blanched
covered his body entirely, and formed a kind of Inverness cape, through which
his hands protruded. A singular effect is given to the figure by the peculiar
high trotting action with which he rushes about, his leafy coat flying about him
with a rustling noise. He came leaping into the *tinesara* over a stone wall
with a springy bound, and danced round and round the group in the middle;
and then all at once with a shout rushed into the midst of them, and beat his
two white wands together till they were broken to shreds over the heads of
the group. One little fellow got frightened and rushed away, but he soon was
brought back again. Then the *tamate* retired into the enclosure, and the group
filed off in a procession round the *tinesara*, where a number of pigs were tied
to stakes. The pigs got a smack from each child; then they all went in single
file into the tall enclosure. As we watched them, the same little fellow who
was frightened before rushed back out of the screen, and after hiding himself
for a moment jumped up and rushed away into the bush, amidst a roar of
laughter. I heard afterwards that he ran away home, a distance of some five
or six miles. This was only the preliminary ceremony. These children will
have to remain in the enclosure forty or fifty days, till all the money and
pigs are paid for the privilege of belonging to this club.'—Island Voyage,
1879.

days, and after that to attend to the oven for another hundred
days. During his first hundred days he does not wash, and
gets so dirty that when he comes out he is not recognized;
so dirty is he, they say, that he cannot be seen. In this
island the Great *Tamate*, though it retains the name, has not
even a *salagoro*; a chamber for initiation is made in the
gamal, the house of the Suqe Club; the entrance payment
is small, and infants are admitted. In the Banks' Islands
also the lesser societies have no *salagoro*, whether they be
exclusive like the *Oviovi* or insignificant like the *Meretang*;
the lodge is the *sara*. From all the lodges equally women,
and the uninitiated, the *matawonowono* who have their eyes
closed, are strictly excluded. Women will venture to stand
near the entrance to the retreats of the lesser clubs, which
are often very little secluded from the public road; but
the *salagoro* of the Great *Tamate* and the *sara* of the important societies are very carefully respected. The croton
leaves which are the badge of each are well known; a
member of any one will mark with such a leaf the fruit-
trees or garden that he wishes to reserve for a particular
use, and the prohibition will be observed; he has behind
him the whole *tamate*[1], with whom an offender would have
to deal.

For the greater part of the year the *salagoro* or the *sara* is
used as a kind of club; the newly admitted members have the
duty of preparing a daily meal, which attracts some who have
no other engagement; it affords a convenient and somewhat
distinguished resort in the heat of the day. The European
visitor will be likely to find there any man he wishes to see;
he will find a meal there himself when he desires it; a yam
from the *salagoro* oven will be sent to him as a compliment,
of which no one will venture to partake whose eyes are still
unopened. From time to time the members rouse themselves

---

[1] Order is kept in the same way among themselves. If any one has made
a disturbance in the *salagoro*, a *makomako*, bunch of leaves, is set out, and
the culprit has to put money upon it, to *tape goro o makomako*, make his
atonement.

into activity, with a view to bring themselves into evidence,
to attract recruits, to impress the people with a sense of their
importance, and to enjoy a festival. Then they begin to make
new masks and dresses within their lodge, and the solemn
sound of the *linge tamate* warns all without that the mysteries
have begun. The country is said to be close, *o vanua we gona*,
no one can venture along the paths without the risk of being
beaten by the *tamate*. They assume the greatest license in
carrying off all they want, robbing gardens and stripping
fruit-trees for their feast, and then any one will suffer who
has spoken or acted without due respect to the society. The
ghosts in their disguise will rush into the villages, chasing the
terrified women and children, and beating any whom they can
catch ; the disadvantage of remaining outside as *matawonowono*
is made apparent [1]. Many of the lesser societies, composed of
those who are members also of the Great *Tamate*, whose power
is at their back, practise the same tyranny; but there are
some that do not terrify or beat, but come out to show their
finery and dance. A pretty and pleasant scene it is when two
or three figures dance forth into the sunshine of the village
place ; their heads concealed in masks in shape like the cowls
of Italian becchini, coming down in a point upon the breast,
and with round eyes painted on the sides, white, and glistening with scarlet seeds and the fresh green of the cycas fronds;
their bodies hidden in golden brown cloaks of sago leaves ;

---

[1] The smaller societies make their appearance with less pretence. ' On my
way home I met a wild and grotesque-looking party of men ; they belonged to
a *tamate* society, and they had been to pull a house to pieces in order to compel
the owner, or his son perhaps, to join them. They were adorned with hibiscus
flowers and croton leaves, their faces smudged with charcoal, and a leaf in the
mouth, each carrying a stick. Two or three of these had on a *tamate*, a hat and
mask, with a long fringe of leaves reaching down to the heels.' 'At this time
of the year, when they are baking bread-fruit, some of the young men dress up
in a mask and put on a dress of dried banana leaves, tied round the neck and
reaching to the ground, and they dance along with a rustling noise from the dry
leaves. They either talk gibberish or else in one of the neighbouring dialects.
The women and children are supposed to be frightened of them, but they often
give them their dried bread-fruit.' These are the Qasa.—Rev. J. Palmer's
Journals, Island Voyage, 1877, 1883.

each holding in either hand a cycas frond as a martyr in a picture holds his palm. The women and the little children crowd around full of admiration mixed with awe ; 'these are good *tamate*, they never beat or chase us.' In Ureparapara it is not the custom to beat the outsiders, but they are not slack in insisting on their rules. When an initiation into their *menmendol* is going on there must be no smoke of fire ; if smoke is seen anywhere, their *sagilo*, a bunch of their flowers and leaves, is set up, and a pig must be given for the offence.

In the part of the New Hebrides which closely adjoins the Banks' Islands these *tamate* societies are not so common as in those islands ; but there are in Aurora, Araga (Pentecost Island), and Ambrym, mysterious associations which have a retreat unapproachable by the uninitiated, and a mask and dress. In the southern parts of Araga there is said to be what is called a *tamate*, but information fails concerning it ; in Ambrym I have been taken into a secret place and shown a mask fashioned upon a skull and furnished with a wig of hair, and moreover decorated with the tusks of a boar. At any rate the Araga *tamate* is different from the *Qeta* to be hereafter described.

Different from these *tamate* societies in the Banks' Islands in having no permanent place of resort, and yet closely resembling them in all the most important characteristics, is the institution of the *Qat*, common to all the group. The great distinction of this, however, is the dance. The *tamate* will prepare and execute most elaborate performances of the dances of their islands, but the Qat itself is danced. For the initiation, whenever a sufficient number of candidates are forthcoming, an enclosure in a retired place is made by a fence of reeds, the two ends of which overlap to make an entrance, the shark's mouth as it is called, through which it is impossible to look. Here the neophytes remain, unwashed and blackened with ashes, for an appointed time, learning the dance and the song by which the steps of the dance are regulated. To obtain admission is, as with the *tamate*, to *tiro*, and money

has to be paid ; children too young to dance have the money
paid for them and enter ; when they are big enough they go
in again to learn the dance. Nothing can better represent to
a visitor the scene of an initiation into religious mysteries than
the jealously guarded enclosure from which in the dead of
night strange sounds and loud calls proceed, and the name of
which associates it with Qat, who may be taken for the god
whom they worship [1]. But the name *Qat* refers to the hats
and not to the *vui*; and enquiry does not discover any
religious meaning in the initiation. The neophytes learn a
dance difficult of execution and requiring much practice, not
because of a complicated figure, but from the rapidity and
accuracy with which the steps are stamped. The steps, as in
other dances, follow a song, and the tapping of a bamboo.
The Mota song is as follows: *Veve! la us mae, na ven toa, to
salsal, to salsal, Vevae, la us mae, na ven toa ;* ' Mother! bring
a bow hither, that I may shoot a fowl, a flying fowl ; Mother,
bring a bow hither, that I may shoot a fowl.' The same with
slight verbal change is what is used in Santa Maria, and no
doubt in the other islands also. As they dance this song is
silently followed, or sung in a low voice. There are other
songs learnt and sung in the *nin* which are not known to the
uninitiated : I have one from Gaua in Santa Maria, beginning
' Oh! make the fire and blow it into flame, we will finish
covering in our oven,' and having nothing in it which might
not be found in other songs. It may perhaps be thought that
the simple words of the song with which the *Qat* is danced veil
some mysterious meaning ; the initiated declare that it does
not. When the appointed time is come the newly instructed
dancers and the initiated come forth with lofty hats upon
their heads. These hats, in which the *Qat* was no doubt
originally danced, answer to the masks of the *tamate*, but are

---

[1] Thus Bishop Patteson described his first acquaintance with the Qatu at
Mota. On that occasion a small boy was detected looking into the enclosure
from a tree into which he had climbed ; he was seized and taken inside ; by
way of punishment he was covered with the leaves of the *kalato* nettle-tree
and he was compelled to join the neophytes.

high and pointed, resting on the shoulders ; they are now so
tall that they require guy ropes on either side to support
them, and it is impossible to wear them and dance. The Qat
dance is wonderful indeed. The open space in the middle of
a village on a moonlight night is lined with the spectators ;
the loud report of bursting bladders is heard from the wood
around ; one after another the performers, with a surprisingly
rapid stamping motion of the feet, enter upon the ground, and
come to an equally surprising sudden halt ; the leader carries
a length of bamboo made into a drum, with which he directs
and controls the dance ; the rest carry in their hands their
bows. When the dancers are numerous and expert the weight
and accuracy with which they beat the ground is wonderful ;
the island seems to shake beneath their feet. In Santa Maria,
whether at Gaua or at Lakona, the Qat is more elaborate
and difficult than in Mota or Motalava ; boys at Norfolk
Island will never undertake it. A practice of three or four
months is needed for this before newly-initiated performers
can venture to come out and dance. In former times, when
the newly-taught dancers made their first appearance, the old
members past their dancing days from far and near would
gather round with their bows in their hands and jealously
watch the steps ; if they saw an error they would shoot ;
and if any one were hit the blame was laid on the faulty
dancer ; there was no quarrel with the shooter and no compensation to be made.

II. *The New Hebrides.* In the Northern New Hebrides the
Qatu, with other institutions of the same kind, has its place
in Maewo, Omba, and Araga. In Omba, Lepers' Island, I know
no more than that there is a *Qatu*, the hats for which are made
in the shape of a shark ; from the other two islands information
is abundant. In Maewo, Aurora, there is more than one *Qatu*,
but one, the *Qatu lata*, is the chief. In all these there is
initiation with trial of endurance by torments and hardships,
but there is no secret imparted beyond the knowledge of the
song and dance and the making of the decorations. For the
initiation an enclosure is made with reeds near a group of

villages ; into these the neophytes are gathered, and here
they remain unwashed and with very little food and water
till the appointed time has expired, which may be thirty
days. During this time they learn a dance, and songs, but
they do not, as in the Banks' Islands, follow a song as they
dance. Little boys are not initiated, because they could not
endure the hardships and tortures to be gone through ; but
they can enter by proxy ; a man already initiated will go
through a formal initiation for them. There is no limit of
age, no period of life to which initiation is more appropriate
than another ; it is a matter of payment, of giving pigs, which
a wealthy man will give for his son or brother ; an infant and
a grown-up man are equally admitted. The mark of a member
of the *Qatu* is the flower of the *nalnal*, a scitamineous plant,
which no outsider is allowed to wear. Those who enter these
societies assume a new name, which however does not, as in
the neighbouring island, supersede the old one. They become
Tari, or *Vula* ; the young men, Tileg and Gao, though commonly so called, are Tari-koli and Vula-ngoda in the *Qatu*.
While the initiation is going on, if women assemble, as they
do, to hear the singing in the enclosure where the neophytes
are being taught, it is an allowed custom for men to carry
them off and ravish them. For a woman to see the newly
initiated until they have returned to ordinary life is a mortal
offence. They come out black with dirt and soot, and are not
to be seen till they have washed. Not long ago a girl from
the *Uta*, inland, saw by accident this washing. She fled to
Tänoriki, where the Mission school is, for refuge, but they
could not protect her. The Uta people sent for her and she
went, knowing that she could not fail to die, and they buried
her, unresisting, alive.

The great secret of the society is the making of the *Qatu*,
from which the name is taken, and which corresponds to the
qatu hats of the Banks' Islands, being in fact itself a hat or
mask. It is made of tree-fern trunks ; a pointed upright
part, large enough for a man to get within and carry it, and a
cross-piece pointed at the ends. This cross is daubed with the

white grated root of caladium, and painted with pigments only known within the society. The pointed top is adorned with a tuft of dracæna leaves ; the ends are connected and kept firm by sticks ornamented with sago-palm frondlets; two large eyes are painted on the front; the back is covered with the hairy plexus from the sago fronds. When completed, and the day appointed comes, a man within it carries this forth with three other men supporting it; in old days it was believed by outsiders to be the work of ghosts. The correspondence between this and the *tindalo* work of the Florida Matambala is as remarkable as it is complete.

An account of his initiation into the chief *Qatu*, that called *Qatu ta Gobio*, was written for me by a native youth while his memory was fresh on the subject. He was probably sixteen years old when with two others he passed through what he thus relates.

'Father, let me tell you how I went into the *Qatu*. I did not know what it was when my brother said to me, Now you are to go into the *Qatu*. Then I went, and there was a very great crowd in the place where they were celebrating the *Qatu*. Then my brother asked me, Are you strong? and I answered him and said, All right! If I should die, all right! After that I went where there was a building, a *gamal*, put up for the purpose not far from the village; my *malo* (dress) and ornaments were taken off, and I went inside. The *gamal* was narrow, low, and very long, and they had placed inside it two rows of *kalato* leaves (of the nettle-tree) sprinkled with salt-water, which met together about a yard from the ground. And I bent my knees and I ran into it. And that thing, the *kalato*, that they had put in the *gamal*, bites exceedingly, and they had heated the salt-water before they poured it on the leaves, not stalks, nothing but leaves, and they bite exceedingly. Then when I came out from that thing I cried as I never did before or since, and nearly fainted with pain ; and I neither ate nor drank water, but did nothing but cry for two days, and then I ate food. And the pig (one of his brother's which had been given as an entrance fee) they cooked in an oven; and they gave me some before it was done, and I ate it. After that I was thirsty, and they made a very small hole in the ground by stamping with the heel and poured cocoa-nut juice into it, and I drank. And they dashed water over me, which caused great pain. And the food that they gave me was extremely bad. When I was hungry they roasted a caladium root over the fire and gave it me underdone; and they trod my food into the ashes; and the water they poured on the ground, and then I drank the water. And if I had refused they would have beaten me to death; but I did not refuse, and I ate that food which they made so very bad for me. For my mashed food they mashed it on the ground; and they grated bananas that were not full grown to make *loko*, and stirred it together with dung; but we three did not quite eat up that *loko* that they made. Then we had to take up live embers in our hands; they stood round us with guns, and we laid hold on that burning fire; they commanded us to do it, and we laid hold of that fire. And we lay down on the ground and they trod upon us; they all ran over us, one of them taking the lead, and when he had stamped on us as he ran they all stamped on us. After that, when we rose from the ground, one man took a bow and pretended to shoot us. And we did not sit properly down, but lay down on the ground to eat our food, and our water also we lay down and drank. And with regard to that *Qatu* it is of tree-fern put together like planks, and we grated the *qeta* (caladium) and made the *Qatu* with it. And in the night after that we danced, and next morning we danced for the first time the *Qatu* dance; and after we had been thirty days in that *gamal* we killed a pig, and then went back into the village and stayed in the *gamal* and cooked that pig. And if one wishes to stay forty days in that *gamal* (i. e. of initiation) he then comes out; but that nettle will not soon leave him.'

Not satisfied with this experience, the same youth was afterwards admitted into another society in the way which he thus describes. 'Father, here again is another *Qatu* which

we call the *Taputae*, and exceedingly bad it is. It is well
that I should tell you the story of what they did to me.
It was thus. They dug a deep hole, but not very deep, and
brought a great quantity of dung and put it in the hole, till
it was full of that very nasty dung; and they also poured
water into the hole so that a man could sink in it. That
hole was not like the well here, but it was dug like the drain
by the *kumara* house beside the road; such it was, and I
got into it; and this body of mine was all dung, and my
hair also was all dung; and there was a man who poured a
great quantity of dung over me. Then I got out, and
washed myself in good water. But those others, grown up
men, did not get into that; they did nothing but cry.
Then some went away, and we danced in the night till morning, and then we danced the *Qatu* dance. After that we
killed a pig. And the women cannot eat that pig, nor can
some men, because they have not yet been initiated; and
that pig is all eaten up at once, none of it will be put by, it
will be eaten quite up.'

He adds that the bark' of the *varu*, an hibiscus, is beaten
out white for the decoration of this *Qatu*, and that the
initiated will take a bit of this bark, catch a fish for it, and
burn the bark as he cooks the fish, thinking that he will
thereby obtain *mana*, magical power, for catching that kind
of fish. If as he carries this bark he meets an outsider in
the path who sees it, he will either kill him on the spot, or else
he will take a pig from him, and the members of the Qat will
agree to eat the pig and let him live.

There is in the same island another institution of the same
character called the *Welu*. In this the neophyte lies down
on his face in a hole in the ground cut exactly to his shape,
and lighted cocoa-nut fronds are cast upon his back. He
cannot move, and he will not cry. The scars remain upon
his back—the mark of membership. While initiation into
this is going on there are certain trials or games. A bundle
of sticks is tied with a band of some creeper, and one of the
neophytes cuts at it with an axe. If he severs it with one

stroke his party score a gain; if he fails the initiated fall
upon the others and they fight. The two parties also play
the 'tug of war' with a large creeper; if the neophytes pull
the others over they go the sooner out of the enclosure; if
the others prevail they have to wait.

There are two things here which call for remark. The
expression 'dancing the Qat,' and the fact that each mystery
has its own dance, to learn which is the chief part of the

MASKED DANCERS AT AURORA.

initiation, recall the dances of the Greek mysteries, and the
African Bushman's use of 'dance' as equivalent to 'mystery.'
(Lang's Custom and Myth.) But it appears certain that in
these *Qatu* and *Welu* there is no secret knowledge conveyed,
no esoteric religious instruction given, no mystery but the
construction of the *Qatu* figure and the manner of the *Qatu*
dance. In the second place the question arises, why, if no
other advantage is to be gained than the position of an
initiated member, natives are willing to pay the entrance

fees and suffer as they do. But as it is certain that there is
no 'making of young men,' and that initiation is not a step
to matrimony, so it is equally certain that the social position
of a native depends very much upon his membership of the
most important of these clubs; an outsider could never be
a person of consequence; a man of good social position
would think it his duty to secure the same position for
his son by entering him early in the clubs to which he
himself belonged. To receive a new member with trials of
his endurance, to let him rise into equality only through
pain and contumely, has been, and may still be, the way of
Universities and Schools; and there is no reason why the
attraction of a mysterious secret which draws civilized men
should not work upon the savage. The native neophyte
also expected before his initiation that he really should
join in company with the ghosts of the departed; when
he was illuminated he enjoyed the deception of those who
followed him, and was well satisfied to eat their pigs and
take their money.

In the island of Araga, Pentecost or Whitsuntide, immediately south of Aurora, the institution is called the *Qeta*.
I have the description of it from one who was made a member
as an infant, but has seen all the proceedings of late years.
The rites are celebrated at uncertain intervals, whenever there
are a sufficient number of candidates forthcoming from a group
of villages; at intervals perhaps of six or ten years. Some
great man (or two or three of them together) presides and
manages the arrangements, and teaches the songs and dance;
the *Qeta* is said to be his or theirs. The scene of the meeting
is some *ute gogona*, a place on which *tapu* has been laid.
Many small houses are built there, in which the boys live
during the first part of their seclusion. Boys of all ages are
initiated, generally about the time of putting on the *malo*, the
dress worn by men; all are initiated sooner or later, none
grow up without it; to put on the *malo* and to enter the
Qeta are necessary steps in life. The entrance payment is
a mat given by the father, or guardian, one for each boy.

When the day appointed for the Qeta comes, all the initiated assemble at the place, and the women keep away. There is no enclosure, but when the ceremony begins a stick is laid upon the ground as a mark of entrance, and two companies of the initiated stand singing within the mark with a space between them. The boy who enters steps over the stick, and as he does so, if he has already a *malo*, they break unexpectedly his girdle string ; the *malo* falls and he enters naked. If the boy is too young to walk, he is carried over by his father or the friend who pays for him. The boys do not remain naked during the whole time of their seclusion, a fresh *malo* is given to each of them. My informant, himself initiated in his father's arms, began his story by saying that the *Qeta* was exceedingly bad. Being desired at the end of it to point out what there was exceedingly bad in the whole proceeding he referred to this, to expose a boy naked who had the *malo* was very bad indeed. When entered the neophytes stay in the houses, except when they come out to eat and sing and dance ; they have their bodies blackened with charcoal, and wear no ornaments. There are long rows of seats made on which the boys sit to eat ; the initiated feed them, giving each a bite, and the boys get nothing else to eat, though the initiated bring in food for themselves and eat it privately. The boys are taught a dance and song, singing aloud and dancing round the seats. The meaning of the song is trifling ; its use is to mark the steps of the dance. There is absolutely no secret, or any other knowledge communicated than that of the song and dance, and nothing else in the way of initiation. The time of seclusion is uncertain. After the first three days the greater number of the initiated go away; food runs short, though the boys have very small bites ; they begin to scatter a little, not going into the villages, but living in little houses near the gardens, the men looking after and feeding each household of boys. The whole time of seclusion lasts about five months, that is to say that yams are planted when it begins and the harvest is waited for. In the later time the restriction as to food is easier, but no fish or shell-fish is

allowed ; the beach is made *gogona*, unapproachable, on their
behalf; no one can go there to gather shell-fish.   During the
whole time of seclusion the boys are not allowed to wash, and
their bodies have become quite black.   The conclusion, therefore, of the whole thing is that when the first yams are dug
they assemble in one body and go down to the beach to wash
and eat.   The women then come and look at them.   After
this they return to their villages, and having become *tari*,
they assume a name with that prefix, Tariliu, Tarisuluana.
In all there appears to be no thought of intercourse with
ghosts or spirits ; but no doubt the master of the *qeta* makes
his prayers and offerings for success.

III. *Solomon Islands.*   From the New Hebrides to Florida
in the Solomon Islands is a long step, but in the Matambala
appears very plainly another form of the Qatu.   The seat of
it is a district of Florida called Belaga, where alone the rites
were celebrated, men from the other districts coming to be
initiated there.   The origin of the institution is ascribed to
one Siko, who came from Bugotu in Ysabel.   To him sacrifices
were made in their assemblies by a succession of men who had
received the office till the year 1883, when the last embraced
Christianity, and the Matambala came to an end.   The mysteries were celebrated at irregular intervals of six or ten years,
but the initiated formed a permanent body, and a certain part
of the beach at Belaga with the forest behind it was always
tambu, so that no uninitiated person might enter the precincts,
and no woman might pass along the beach.   Within this
sacred region there were twelve *vunutha* sanctuaries, and in
each one a sacred *vovoko* house was built ; but the two *vunutha*
at Materago and at Volotha were far more important than the
rest, and the houses built there so sacred that no man entered
them nor even approached them ; there were images in them
of birds and fish, crocodiles and sharks, the sun and moon, and
men.   The building of these two houses was the beginning
of the chief part of the proceedings.   In all that they did
they supposed themselves to be following the course of Siko's
actions.

I have a written account of the proceedings sent from Belaga by an old friend and pupil of mine, and explained to me in all particulars in Norfolk Island by a native of a neighbouring district, who remembered his own initiation perfectly well. I have also been furnished by Bishop Selwyn with the account given to him at Belaga, the seat of the Matambala, by initiated men. It is not easy in all points to connect the two accounts, and some of the particulars are described with unnecessary minuteness, but the general course and character of the proceedings are plain[1]. The month in which the whole begins is that in which the canarium almonds become ripe, and the *bigo*, the gathering of the first-fruits, hereafter to be described, is the first step in the ceremonial. The cracking of the nuts begins at Gole and goes through the twelve places to Buthinigai. The women and children set baskets in rows along the road when the new moon of *bigo* is seen, and the men gather the almonds from morning till nightfall, and fill the baskets with them. The next moon is the moon of sweeping, and they sweep the paths from Gole to Buthinigai, signifying that the paths are now reserved for the Matambala. Then follows the time of the close *tambu*, when the whole district becomes sacred, and the Teimbelaga, when they all assemble at Materago to see the *sasale* dance of Siko in the night.

On the following morning the Matambala, those already

---

[1] The native account begins, ' The Story of Siko who began it, a man from over sea. Siko was a man of former times, a countryman of Bugotu. And Doriki and he separated ; the reason of their separation was that Siko should not be chief, said Doriki, and Doriki should not be chief, said Siko ; and Doriki got the upper hand, so that Siko fled secretly, and made his way hither to Belaga ; he first came ashore down at Siota, and he liked the place there, but he looked back and still could see to Bugotu, so he put again into his canoe his men and property, and came along to Materago, where he could no longer see to Bugotu, and so there he dwelt. After that he divided them (the men with him) to twelve villages, to Gole, Vunavutu, Salesapa, Talabuga, Materago, Nagokama, Taiegu, Balotoga, Tangadala, Volotha, Mavealu, Buthinigai ; and he said to them, Let us do things as we did at Bugotu, said he to them. And he chose them to be chiefs in those villages,'—their names being given, one to each village.

initiated, go down to occupy houses that have been built upon the beach, and remain there till the proceedings are over. The initiated from each village take with them their friends who are to be admitted, but do not yet let them enter the *vunutha*, the sanctuary in the bush, where they themselves are occupied in making the structures of bamboo which are called the *tindalo*, the ghosts. These were of several forms. One called the *Voi* was described to the Bishop as a screen some ten feet long by nine high, made of bark painted and ornamented, and carried out by several men behind it into the open, where it could be seen by the women, children, and uninitiated, who firmly believed it to be not so much the handiwork of ghosts as an appearance of the ghosts themselves. Another, the *Koitaba-vunutha*, was so large that eighty or a hundred men inside it carried it down to the beach, where the outside population gazed at it. There was another instrument, the *Kuku*, a wooden club with a bird's head. One of the first proceedings of the Matambala men after the paths were swept, and the country was made close, was to cut down tall bamboos for these structures, tie them in bundles, and lay them in the sun to dry. 'After a while they brought these down to the *vunutha*, and added length to length till they were extremely long; and then they took vines and sago spathes and fastened them to the bamboos which they had prepared; and then they took coleus and turmeric; the coleus they chewed for the juice and squeezed wild oranges to mix with it and make it red; and the turmeric they pounded in a wooden pot. Then they painted with these things the sago spathes that they had fastened on to the bamboos, variegated and dazzling, very fearful for us to behold.' The *tindalo* figures, of which thirty or forty were made in one place, must have resembled the *Qatu* masks or hats of the Banks' Islands, though they were very much higher; for like them they were conical in shape, and were moved by men inside them. 'And when all was finished they appointed their day for the spectacle; and all the women and boys came out in the evening and viewed the *tindalo*, and all the men in the *vunutha* held up and brought

down the *tindalo* images to the beach ; and all the women and
the boys thought that they were nothing but ghosts, because
they did not know how they were made. After that they
appointed again the day after the morrow for the show, and
when that day came the women again came out into the open
for the spectacle. And when the show made in that way
was over, the men took the *tindalo* images back into the
vunutha, and burnt up with fire all those images. When that
was done, all the men came back to their villages from
the *vunutha*. And it was not possible to make known to
women and boys things of this kind ; but at length, when this
Gospel reached us, then it came out, so that all the women
and the boys and the uninitiated understood all about things
of this kind.'

The uninitiated were called *telegai*, the neophytes the new
Matambala. As in the Banks' Islands and the New Hebrides,
there was no knowledge communicated, except of the fact that
whatever was done was the work of men and not of ghosts,
which was no doubt a surprising revelation. Still, however, we
may be sure that the Matambala, new and old, firmly believed
that the art of making the images and the course of all their
proceedings had been taught by Siko, now a *tindalo*, and that
they were guided and enabled by the supernatural assistance of
Siko and his companions, now *tindalo*, and by the ghosts also of
their eminent predecessors in the Matambala, all of whom as
well as Siko were invoked with sacrifices. But there was no
esoteric doctrine taught, nor any secret imparted beyond that of
the making of the images. On this point the witness of the
initiated is as clear in Florida as in the Banks' Islands and the
New Hebrides. A certain rite, or mark, of initiation there
was ; the candidate clasped a tree, and was touched in six
places with a fire-stick on shoulders, loins, and buttocks.
When thus branded they were told that they were now Siko's
men, or Siko's messengers. In admission to these mysteries,
also, there was no limit of age, and no time of life more appropriate than another. Grown-up men were admitted, who
generally came from other parts of the island ; at Belaga

and the immediate neighbourhood the boys were initiated
whenever the ceremonies took place. Young children, even
sucklings, were made Matambala ; for the latter they would go
into the villages and beg milk from the women, since the
infants could not come out of the sacred precincts and the
women could not go in ; they were branded with the slender
midribs of the leaflets of the cocoa-nut.   Nothing was paid for
entrance to the Matambala. The initiation of the new members
was not performed till they had been some time living in the
houses on the beach, while the mysterious figures were being
constructed in the secret places in the wood ; it was part of
their preparation that they should be frightened by the bird-
headed clubs, the *kuku*, and they were threatened with death
if they revealed the secrets.   Altogether they remained away
from their homes three months.

During the whole of this time the Matambala, under cover of
the terror of their pretended association with ghosts, and
taking advantage of the closing of the paths, were playing
tricks and robbing in all the country round. They would
come as far as to Gaeta to steal pigs to sacrifice to Siko ; they
would cut down trees to fall across the roads, and no one
dared remove them ; they would pull down cocoa-nut palms
and big trees with ropes in the night as a proof that the
ghosts were abroad, for no mere man could be supposed so
strong as to overthrow them.   From time to time they
sacrificed to Siko.   More than once also they made their
appearance in the villages.   ' When the bamboos have been
cut down, they appoint a three days' space for the going up
inland of the ghosts (that is, of the Matambala), and when the
three days' space is past, then about the time of the clock
striking ten at night the ghosts go up.   And all the women
in the villages have been making *tutu* and *gola* (mashes of food)
since morning.   And when the night has come the men of the
Matambala down at the beach take *buro* (bull-roarers), and
seesee (bundles of cocoa-nut fronds to beat over a stick), and go
up inland with them and approach the village ; and they beat
the *seesee* and whirl the *buro*, and come into the village ; and

they whistle and cluck, and all the women in the village shut
fast their houses and are much afraid, because they think that
they are surely ghosts ; and they take the *tutu* and the *gola*,
and give it to the ghosts outside. Then all the men cry
mbuembue, and go down back again to the shore. After that,
again, they fix their day for the going up of the ghosts, and
they fix the fourth day; and when the fourth day has come,
and it is night, then they take again as before the *seesee* and
the *buro*, and go out again, and go and beat the *seesee* and
whirl the *buro*, and whistle and cluck ; and again they give
them the *tutu* and *soisombi* mixed with almonds ; and then all
the men cry *mbuembue*, and go down again to the beach.' The
women prepared small holes in the wall of the house, through
which to push out the food to the Matambala, a contrivance to
prevent them from feeling the hands of the men. When the
women hear the whistle they ask, ' Who are you, are you Siko ? '
and the man whistles in answer and takes the food. Great
care was taken lest the men should be seen when the ghosts
were believed to be about, and the Matambala were covered, as
elsewhere, with a cloak of leaves ; but in the daytime they
went among the women, gave notice of what the ghosts were
going to do, and called attention to what had been done by
them.

The downfall of this superstition and imposture has been
complete. It had long been undermined by the free admission
of Florida boys and young men into the *salagoro* of the Banks'
Islands, and the knowledge acquired there of what ghost
mysteries really were. No Matambala celebration had taken
place for some years ; all the young people knew how the
thing was done, though the elders did not give up their belief
in Siko, or the notion that there was something supernatural
about it. At length, as said before, the man who knew how
to sacrifice to Siko became a Christian, the sacred precincts
were explored, bull-roarers became the playthings of the boys,
and the old men sat and wept over the profanation and their
loss of power and privilege [1].

[1] 'I was sorry one day to hear that a lot of Gaeta young men had been

I know of no other Matambala or similar institution in the Solomon Islands; but in Malanta and Ulawa there is a period of seclusion for a boy as he grows up, which to a Banks' islander appears to be an entrance into the *salagoro.*

chaffing some old fellows who came from Materago to such an extent that they sat down and cried bitterly.' Journal of Rev. A. Penny, under whose teaching the downfall of the mysteries was brought about.

CHAPTER VI.

SOCIETIES. CLUBS.

In every village and group of houses in the Torres Islands, the Banks' Islands, and the Northern New Hebrides, is conspicuous a building which does not appear to be a dwelling-house. In a populous village of the Banks' Islands it is very long and low, with entrances at intervals along the sides below the wall-plate, with stone seats or a stone platform at the main entrances at either end, and low stone walls planted with dracænas and crotons near the same, with the jawbones of pigs and backbones of fish hanging under the eaves; and very often the clatter of pounding sticks in wooden vessels and white clouds of steam make known the preparation of a meal. This is a *gamal*. The same name, and a building of the same general character, with some difference of form, is to be found in the New Hebrides as far south as the Shepherd Islands at least. What are called 'Chiefs' houses' in New Caledonia probably represent the same. In some of the Banks' Islands, again, a visitor on entering a village would see one or more platforms squarely built up of stones, with high, pointed little edifices upon them, open in the front like shrines, the embers of a fire below, and above an image grotesquely shaped in human form. He would naturally take these for shrines of idols with the altars of sacrifices to them; but these also are *gamal*; the little edifice is the eating-place of a man of rank; the fire has cooked his food, which none but he in that place can eat, and the image is the emblem of his degree. In another island of the same group a *gamal* may be seen with

one end newly built and loftier than the rest, or else with one
end in ruin while the rest is in good repair and full occupation.
Here again there is a man, perhaps two or three, lately raised
to a new degree, for whom a special eating-place has been
prepared ; or the men of high degree have all died out from
the village, and no one of lower rank can enter into their
place.   Within, these long buildings are found to be divided
across by log fences, the *tingtingiav*, the fire-boundaries ; each
division contains its oven, with the appliances for cookery
around ; log pillows and mats complete the furniture.   The
gamal is a club-house, and the club is called the *Suqe*
in the islands where I have any considerable acquaintance
with it.

In all the Melanesian groups it is the rule that there is in
every village a building of public character, where the men
eat and spend their time, the young men sleep, strangers are
entertained ; where as in the Solomon Islands the canoes are
kept ; where images are seen, and from which women are
generally excluded ; the *kiala* of Florida, the *oha* of San
Cristoval, the *madai* of Santa Cruz, the *tambu* house of traders,
the *bure* of Fiji ; and all these no doubt correspond to the
balai and other public halls of the Malay Archipelago.
But these are not club-houses, as are the *gamal* houses of the
Suqe, which serve indeed to a considerable extent for public
purposes, because almost every man is a member of the club,
but are in fact the homes of a society in which every one has
his place according to his rank in the society.

The name *Suqe* is the same as that of the *Wui*, the supernatural personage, Supwe of the New Hebrides, but it is
doubtful whether any connexion between the two really
exists ; for in the Banks' Islands, where the society is in
great vigour, there is no *Vui* Suqe known, and in Whitsuntide of the New Hebrides, where the *Wui* Supwe is recognized,
the society has another name.   Nothing is known of the
origin of the club.   It is not connected with the secret
societies of the ghosts, and is not a secret society of the same
kind.   The club-house is in the open, and every one, except

when new members are admitted, can see what is going on,
though women are most strictly excluded.   It is a social, not
at all a religious, institution ; yet, inasmuch as religious
practices enter into the common life of the people, and all
success and advance in life is believed to be due to *mana*,
supernatural influence, the aid of unseen powers is sought for
by fasting, sacrifices, and prayers, in order to mount to the
successive degrees of the society.   To rise from step to step
money is wanted, and food and pigs ; no one can get these
unless he has *mana* for it ; therefore as *mana* gets a man on
in the *Suqe*, so every one high in the *Suqe* is certainly a man
with *mana*, and a man of authority, a great man, one who may
be called a chief, whom traders may call a king.   A man who
has got to the very top and emerged, *me wot*, is a very great
man indeed ; he has the title of *Wetuka*, as if he had reached
the sky ; he is of a rank which very few have attained, and
without his consent, to be obtained by substantial payment,
no one can be advanced at all.   In the Banks' Island stories
the poor lad or orphan who becomes the Fortunate Youth
rises to greatness by the *Suqe* ; he takes the highest grade in
this instead of marrying the king's daughter.   In the absence
of any more directly political arrangements among the people,
it is plain that a valuable bond of society is furnished by the
Suqe, in which the male population generally is united, and in
which a considerable power of control is vested in the elder
and richer men, who can admit or reject candidates for the
higher ranks as they think fit.   The great mass of the natives
never rise above the middle rank, many never arrive at that ;
but almost all, for the exceptions are very rare, are brought
while still boys into the society.   A man who has never
entered has the nickname of a *lusa*, a kind of flying fox which
does not gather with the flocks of the common sort.   At
entrance and at every successive step money has to be paid to
those who have already attained it, and a feast more or less
costly given according to the rank to be attained.   Hence,
while hardly any lad is so friendless as not to enter the
lowest division, hardly any live to rise to the highest place ;

unless indeed they have entered very young, have had their
early steps bought for them, and have been very prosperous
in their undertakings. The higher steps are occasion of large
popular gatherings and feasts, with songs and dances, and
come near to the *kolekole* hereafter to be described ; there are
hats also and images appropriated to these highest ranks.

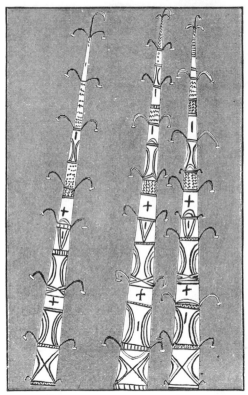

NATIVE DRAWING OF 'LANO' HATS.

The number of ovens and ranks varies in different islands;
the people of each think their own *Suqe* the correct one ; but
all acknowledge the value of the respective ranks, though they
may be attained under very various conditions.

In the Banks' Islands the *Suqe* of Mota has many steps
and ovens, all *av-tapug*. Beginning with the lowest : (1) *Rur-*

won, (2) *Avrig*, (3) *Qat tagiav*, (4) *Avtagataga*, (5) *Luwaiav*, (6) *Tamasuria*, (7) *Tavasuqe*, (8) *Tavasuqelava*, (9) *Kerepue*, (10) *Mele*, (11) *Tetug*, (12) *Lano*, (13) *Poroporolava*, (14) *Wometeloa*, (15) *Welgan*, (16) *Wesukut*, (17) *Wetaur-o-meligo*, (18) *Tiqangwono*. The lowest are commonly skipped over or taken together ; on the other hand, there are three degrees under the eleventh name, and two under the twelfth. Some of the names carry a meaning with them : *avrig*, the little fire ; *kerepue*, the bottom of the bamboo water-carrier ; *mele*, the cycas, which has a certain sanctity ; *poroporolava*, great joking ; *wometeloa*, the face of the sun ; *wetaur-o-meligo*, catches the clouds ; *tiqangwono*, shoots and completes. The *lano* wears a very tall conical hat, like that of the *Qat*, but sometimes forked ; the *poroporolava* has an image of a man ringed black and white ; the *wometeloa* an image of a man carrying on his head with outstretched arms a disk representing the firmament, with heavenly bodies painted on it. These images are carried about at the feast which celebrates the step in rank, and are afterwards set up in the little *gamal* in which the great man cooks his food ; the hat is worn by the new *lano* at the feast he makes, and is afterwards to be seen leaning against the *gamal*. At Gaua in Santa Maria the ovens are not so many ; boys begin high up, so that a Gaua boy often ranks with a gray-haired Mota man. Those who reach the higher ranks build a *gamal* on a lofty platform of stones for every oven or step, for which at Mota they are content to raise the *gamal* end. In the Torres Islands, or at least in one of them, there are only seven ovens and degrees of ranks in the *Huqa*, as the *Suqe* is there called, and in the *gamal*, the first being the *avlav*, big fire, which is rather on the threshold of the *gamal* than in it. Young boys do not enter into the club there. In all these islands the distinction between each successive stage is strictly marked ; any one stepping over the boundary to the oven above him would be trampled to death by those on whom he had intruded.

The way of entering the *Suqe* and making further advances in it is fixed and elaborate. The candidate must have in the first place his introducer, a boy's mother's brother by rights, whose good-will some months before must be secured by the present of a pig, which is made over formally to him with a slap upon its back. Having undertaken to make the *suqe* for his candidate, the patron makes a feast for him with a dance, decorating the village square with male pandanus flowers, and setting out money for him ; the partakers of the feast, including the candidate, make him a present of a little money, and he makes a return present to them ; they *vene*, shoot, and he *sar*, compensates. For the lowest grade in Mota the *vene* money is only half a fathom, returned with a full fathom ; for the higher grades very much money is required, and sometimes money fails and pigs are brought in. A boy who has no property of his own is supplied by his father or some friend with what is necessary for engaging the patronage of his uncle, upon whom the expense chiefly falls. In the higher grades the candidate for advance still has his patron, but the expenses fall upon himself, aided by his friends with gifts, *mategae*, of pigs and money; his wife's father is expected to be liberal in this. The candidate makes a return to the patron as liberally as he can for all that he has done in his behalf. The formal entrance into the society, or into a higher grade in it, has two parts. When the time comes, a day having been appointed and made known, the women leave the village before nightfall, and the members meet in the *gamal*. The candidate goes into the division in which is the fire and oven to which he is to belong. His patron breaks the string of some money and sheds it into a basket ; the others put on the money a garland of bamboo leaves in the lower degrees, of cycas leaves for the *mele*, cycas, rank and all above it. This is to *soso makomako*, to fill the garland. The new member then sits, and some one who is chosen for his fluency of speech discourses to him, tells him that it is his duty to work for his oven and not to complain if his duties are hard. They then give him a bit of an almond, and each member takes a bit in his hand ; they all hold the almond to their lips, and at a certain word they *negneg*, eat together. The

word is only this, ' I give you food from my fire.' Then the
money in the basket is distributed ; they *sese makomako*, pull
apart the garland. The *gana tapug*, the ceremonial eating, is
thus finished in the night; next morning, nowadays, comes
the *wol tapug*, the buying of the *suqe*; in former days an
interval of ten days came in. The new member now breaks
his money strings, touches the food of various kinds that he
has provided, which he could not do before for he had been
fasting for some days, and distributes his money and food to
every fire-place in the *gamal.* A general feast follows. He
himself has to *goto*, to remain in the *gamal* and eat only from
his *av tapug*, his *suqe* fire, for so many days according to his
rank ; for the middle ranks five days or ten, for the highest
ranks many more. The feast made at the entrance to a
higher rank is a public one, the distinction between the food
cooked in the ceremonial fire, the *av tapug*, and the rest
being carefully preserved. Where, as in the highest ranks,
there are but few present who can eat from the oven newly
reached, food from it is sent to a distance to men of the same
rank. The pigs also, the chief provision and mark of an
abundant hospitality, are not killed and consumed at the
feast ; they are sent off to different quarters, with a slap from
the newly-raised member of the club, by whom or in behalf
of whom they have been given, and sometimes with a
ceremonial representation of being killed. For the lower
ranks, or in a wealthy family where it is a matter of course
that a boy should have his steps bought for him, the feast is
a merry-making of the neighbours ; crowds flock to the great
feasts and dances which are made when the highest steps are
taken, and when the new man desires to make the most of his
social elevation. There was a dress, *malo-saru,* used only on such
an occasion, now no longer to be seen ; a kind of cape, in
four oblong parts, beautifully made in coloured matting, the
highest product of Banks' Island art. The candidate for such
steps would not be seen for many days before, being confined
in an inner chamber in the *gamal,* and fasting there. On such
an occasion, moreover, logs of a tree called *palako* are brought

out, which are supposed to be heavy with the ghostly power which they contain and symbolize, that *mana* without which nothing important can succeed.   The incidents of one of

'MALO-SARU' DANCING DRESS.

these feasts are thus described : 'Seven *palako* logs dressed in cycas leaves and flowers were brought in on the shoulders of men of rank, who walked as if the weight was heavy on

them. Then, preceded by a man carrying aloft in a dish the
money paid for the *palako* by the giver of the feast, the
bearers danced round with them as if with burdened steps.
A drum was beating all the time, and singing going on.
The newly-advanced giver of the feast danced out and round,
kicking up his heels behind him, and carrying a palm-leaf
umbrella before his face, because of his modesty, they said, in
his new position. Then a man of high position in the *Suqe*
pranced forth and made a speech. The correct thing seems to
be to pant a good deal, as other people cough, to disguise a
want of eloquence; it shews that the orator is a man of substance, well fed and short-winded. He trotted backwards and
forwards before the palakos, with his new messmate at his
heels modestly covering his face. His speech was interpreted
as to this effect: " This man has had difficulty in getting into
this position; he has been a long while about it, but we have
now let him in. He has spent a great deal of money on
these palakos and decorations, and he gives many pigs; he
does the thing very handsomely." Then the pigs were
brought out one by one and smacked by the giver of the
feast, as he handed them over to another great man who
decided where they were to go. There were four or five great
fat beasts, each with his own name, and several more of lesser
dignity. As each pig was smacked, three other great men
blew a loud blast on conch-shells. Then the new man laid
out his money on the ground, and the conchs were blown
again. The last act of the ceremony was the appearance of
another great man with a bow and arrows. He and the
modest host, with his palm-leaf over his face, capered about for
a while, and then he made his speech to this effect: " The
man who undertook to introduce this new member to his
present position is dead; but I have taken him up instead.
He has done handsomely—pigs, money, and everything that
is right." Then he rushed at the biggest pig, whose name
was Puss, and shot him with two arrows, much to his disgust.
This was only a form of killing the pig, for the arrows were
quite light ones. After this the host himself made a little

speech. I could not hear what he said; he had not been allowed to eat for five days, and was weak; but I was told that it was to the effect that some people had said the money was not enough, and now here was some more.'

Though women are completely excluded from the *Suqe* of the men, they have something of the sort among themselves, which is called improperly by the same name. They admit to grades of honour on payment of money and making of a feast, and so become *tavine motar*, women of distinction. By their *Suqe* they become rich in money, with which to help their husbands in their steps in rank, and they plant their own gardens for the feasts. Thus they advance to be tattooed, to wear shell bracelets, to put on an ornamented *pari*, the woman's scanty garment, to decorate their faces with red earth, in all which glories the *tavine worawora*, the common woman, can have no share. But this is in the way of *kolekole* rather than of *suqe*; two things which become so connected in the higher ranks of men that an account of one is incomplete without an explanation of the other.

A *kolekole* is a feast with dancing and singing made in connexion with a certain object, and giving a certain rank marked by its appropriate ornament. A man makes such a feast for himself, or for his son or nephew. When one has reached the highest place in the *Suqe*, he can still advance in the world by *kolekole*; and he often accompanies with these his regular progress in *Suqe* rank. The story of the Little Orphan exhibits in a succession of these festivals a picture of native grandeur and success. When a man builds a new house he will *kole* it, and a *nule*, a grotesque image, will remain as a memorial at the door. When a new *gamal* for the *Suqe* is built, or when a man adds a compartment for the oven to which he has lately risen or is to rise, there is a *kole-gamal*. A stone is brought up from the beach and placed near the *gamal*, or a *wona*, a platform of stones, is built up, and a feast is made to *kole* it. The maker of the feast, or the youth in whose honour it is made, dances on the stone, and can wear upon his ankle afterwards a *wetapup*, an orna-

ment of the fine feathers from near the eyes of fowls, dyed
crimson and woven into a string, and the stone remains
as a memorial. A *kolekole ngere qoe* gives the right to wear
a necklace of *wetapup*, and the hero of the occasion dances
in a hat. Another kind gives the right to wear a pig's tail
in the hair; I have seen a man at Maewo with five and
twenty. If a man had a wonderful or rare thing in his
possession, brought from foreign parts perhaps, as a white
cockatoo from the Solomon Islands, he might *kole* this; or
more probably he would take advantage of another man's
feast, and dance about exhibiting it. Orators mounted on the
gamal roof, or on the new-built house, would harangue the
crowd, setting forth the virtues of the giver of the feast;
others would go about with baskets of his money proclaim-
ing his liberality; the decorated *palako* logs heavy with
mana would be carried in; pigs would be dismissed to distant
villages with a smack from the giver; crowds from all parts
assembled; dancers and drummers exerted themselves in view
of the morrow's payment; women competed with new songs
for a prize and honour. It was a great thing for a man to
have a large assemblage at his feast, and a great satisfaction
to his enemy to prevent it; each would therefore use charms
to further his purpose. A man would rub the leaves of a
scented ginger-plant, or a strong-smelling erythrina, in his
hands overnight and hang them over the fire; he would chop
the twigs and leaves, singing over them a charm; he would
chew and puff all night to get *mana*; in the morning he
would blow his shell trumpet to spread abroad the influence
of his leaves, which would *avut*, draw a multitude to the feast.
A counteracting charm from the adversary would make men
feel disinclined to go. Another decoration to be obtained by
giving a dance and feast is the *urai non Qat* of Mota, *noran
Qat* of the Torres Islands, where perhaps it is now most
practised, the head anointing of Qat. The head is smeared
over with a mixture of a certain dust from a tree with the
juice of coleus leaves and native oranges and salt water, which
makes a brilliant red colour. There is another preparation of

823142   I

yellow colour. The *Vui* Ro Som in the Story of Ganviviris, when she made her appearance with all the ornaments that money could procure the right to wear, was thus adorned.

A feast of the same kind is held to commemorate a deliverance, a *Vovo* feast; when the famine and misery following on a disastrous hurricane had passed away at Mota, and food was once more abundant, then they celebrated a *Vovo* feast; such a feast was made by a native of the same island when he had quite recovered from a slight wound received at Santa Cruz; he danced about exhibiting his hat with the arrow through it.

In the northern part of Maewo, Aurora, in the New Hebrides, the *Suqe* is now nearly extinct; the old members use the *gamal* as a convenient resort, but no one cares for admission. The reason for this in a great measure is that a place in the *Suqe* was in old times valued for the advantages it carried with it after death. A native wrote that 'the reason for *Suqe* is this, that hereafter when a man comes to die, his soul may remain in happiness in that place Panoi; but if any one should die who has not killed a pig, his soul will just stay on a tree, hanging for ever on it like a flying fox. On this account no man likes his son to remain without anything being done; it is a matter of the first importance for him that he should get many pigs and seek money (i. e. mats), so that hereafter when all is prepared he may give that money to those who have already killed pigs, and that he may be all right.' Consequently, on the birth of a son a man s first care was to give a pig in his name to make a beginning of *Suqe* for him. But a place in the *Suqe* carried with it here also the same rank and consideration as in the Banks' Islands; among children even, one whose father had not given a pig for his admission would be despised; and when a man had killed his pigs properly afterwards on his own account his position in society was secured. ' He can adorn himself with pigs' tusks, and with that white shell-money that we have, and with the leaves of trees most thought of, croton and dracæna or cycas, and he thinks to himself, Now I am clear of trouble, there is nothing that weighs upon me now.' My friend adds that 'there are some now who have perceived that there is no truth in this; and these things they say are the deceits and vanities of the world.'

In Omba, Lepers' Island, the *Huqe* is in full vigour; a *gamali* is a necessity for a man to eat in, if there be but a single dwelling-house. There are not many ranks and ovens; a Lepers' Island *gamali* appears to a visitor from the Banks' Islands short and lofty. There are but four ranks in the society, and therefore but four divisions, *diringi*, in the *gamali*; the lowest the *toa*, the fowl; the second *moli*; the third *levusi*, meaning many; the highest *vire*, which means having fruited or flowered. But there are more ovens than one for each rank, and the member has to eat his way up through them before he can pass to the next division. So there are in one *gamali* five ovens for *moli*, and two for *levusi*. When a man has reached the highest rank of *vire* he can go on with it, making another feast and taking another name as often as he pleases, becoming every time a greater man. The lowest step does not confer a title, but a new name is assumed with the higher ranks, shewing the rank. These names, however, are not commonly used; no one, for example, calls Tangamben *Molimbembe*, Moli-butterfly, the name belonging to his Moli rank; but the number of names is great which belong to a man who has passed through all ranks and become many times a *Vire*. Age has nothing to do with entrance into the society, or with rising in the ranks; it is merely a matter of giving pigs and mats, which serve for money. There is nothing whatever of initiation; all males, except very little boys, are members and eat in the *gamali*. Their friends help the boys at first; but it is the great aim of all to rise and gain social position. A boy has a fowl, *toa*, given him to start in life, and a fowl buys him his first step, the *toa*; his fowls multiply, and he changes some of them for a young sow; so his property increases, and as he grows richer he desires to take each further step. The higher ranks of the *Huqe* give much power and authority, because those who have reached them can always keep back those who wish to rise, and the good-will of each one of them has to be secured. There is less strictness than in the Banks' Islands in the rule which keeps each man to his own oven ; one can descend from his own above and eat in a lower division, and if one should encroach on the place above him he would suffer only a fine of pigs.   There is the same system of entrance as in the Banks' Islands, by which a patron introduces the new member and makes his *huqe* for him, gifts which are to a considerable extent reciprocal.   The patron is properly one of the same family division, the uncle on the mother's side, or the brother. Thus, in the case of a boy whose rich father bought him up at once in early childhood to the rank of *moli*, the first step was to give a pig to the members of the boy's *waivung*, as an acknowledgment that he was intruding on their province, that the patriarchal was intruding on the matriarchal system. Afterwards his father gave him a pig, with which a feast was made in his name, and each person who took a piece of the pig gave a mat in return ; the man who took the head gave a mat a hundred fathoms long.   Of these mats the boy gave his father fifty in return for the pig.   Then he gave mats, or they were given in his name, to the *moli* whom he was to join ; and when he first went to eat at their oven they made a little feast for him.   His friends on his mother's side gave in his name a pig to his father, and made him a feast.

At Whitsuntide Island, Araga, the word *Loli* takes the place of *Suqe*, but the thing is the same.   All the male population are in fact members of the society ; wherever there is a dwelling-house, there is also a *gamal*.   The divisions with the ovens, *matan gabi*, are twelve; (1) *ma langgelu*, the stage of youth; (2) *gabi liv hangvulu*, the oven of ten tusks; (3) *ma votu*; (4) *gabi rara*, the oven of the ery-thrina leaf, which is the badge of the rank ; (5) *woda*, the stone-wall seat by the front of the *gamal*, on which no one below this rank may sit.   These five are the inferior steps which fathers see that their boys take as soon as possible, and as quickly as they can afford to buy them up. Though the lowest is nominally that of grown youths, no

child is too young to be admitted for whom the father, or
more properly the mother's brother, provides the entrance
payments and presents of pigs and mats. Here, too, though
in principle the mother's kin should take charge of the boy's
advancement, the father in practice generally makes it his
own business. The sixth step, *moli*, is the first that is
important ; the youth takes the great *loli, ma loli gaivua*, and
assumes a name with the prefix *Moli*. There are three steps
of *moli*. The ninth rank is *udu*, the tenth *nggarae*, the eleventh
livusi, the last *vira*. The patron, or father, of the new *moli*
gives him when he attains that rank some of that white and
beautiful shell-money, which, however, is not used as money,
but is much valued for ornament. This is worth many pigs,
and is worn on the arm or wrist in the string, or woven
into an armlet. These family jewels remain as heirlooms, and
are made up afresh for the successive wearers. Internal
discipline is severe ; one who should intrude into the division
of the *gamal* above his own would be clubbed or shot. To rise
to the higher *moli* and the steps beyond is the ambition of
every young man, and his friends are bound to help him ; for
this sacrifices are made, and *mana* sought from Tagar. For
gaining new steps in rank many pigs are wanted, many mats,
abundant supplies of food ; such things come to the man
supernaturally, he must have *mana*. The *Vira* is seldom
reached ; the man of that rank, like Viradoro now, is in fact
the chief ; he has great *mana* and the favour of Tagar, or he
could not have risen to be what he is ; his authority is paramount in the *Loli*, for none can rise without his consent, and
every one is a member of the society and hopes to rise ; he
has been fortunate in war, or he would not have survived ;
he comes of a family of rich and leading men who bought his
first steps when he was a child, and by whose wealth he has
bought the higher ; he is the great man, the Ratahigi.

CHAPTER VII.

RELIGION.

The religion of the Melanesians is the expression of their conception of the supernatural, and embraces a very wide range of beliefs and practices, the limits of which it would be very difficult to define. It is equally difficult to ascertain with precision what these beliefs are. The ideas of the natives are not clear upon many points, they are not accustomed to present them in any systematic form among themselves. An observer who should set himself the task of making systematic enquiries, must find himself baffled at the outset by the multiplicity of the languages with which he has to deal. Suppose him to have as a medium of communication a language which he and those from whom he seeks information can use freely for the ordinary purposes of life, he finds that to fail when he seeks to know what is the real meaning of those expressions which his informant must needs use in his own tongue, because he knows no equivalent for them in the common language which is employed. Or if he gives what he supposes to be an equivalent, it will often happen that he and the enquirer do not understand that word in the same sense. A missionary has his own difficulty in the fact that very much of his communication is with the young, who do not themselves know and understand very much of what their elders believe and practice. Converts are disposed to blacken generally and indiscriminately their own former state, and with greater zeal the present practices of others. There are some things they are really ashamed to speak of; and there are others which they think they ought to consider wrong, because they are associated in their memory with what they know to be really bad. Many a native Christian will roundly condemn native songs and dances, who, when questions begin to clear his mind, acknowledges that some dances are quite innocent, explains that none that he knows have any religious significance whatever, says that many songs also have nothing whatever bad in them, and writes out one or two as examples. Natives who are still heathen will speak with reserve of what still retains with them a sacred character, and a considerate missionary will respect such reserve ; if he should not respect it the native may very likely fail in his respect for him, and amuse himself at his expense. Few missionaries have time to make systematic enquiries ; if they do, they are likely to make them too soon, and for the whole of their after-career make whatever they observe fit into their early scheme of the native religion. Often missionaries, it is to be feared, so manage it that neither they nor the first generation of their converts really know what the old religion of the native people was. There is always with missionaries the difficulty of language ; a man may speak a native language every day for years and have reason to believe he speaks it well, but it will argue ill for his real acquaintance with it if he does not find out that he makes mistakes. Resident traders, if observant, are free from some of a missionary's difficulties ; but they have their own. The 'pigeon English,' which is sure to come in, carries its own deceits ; 'plenty devil' serves to convey much information ; a chief's grave is 'devil stones,' the dancing ground of a village is a 'devil ground,' the drums are idols, a dancing club is a 'devil stick [1].' The most intelligent travellers and naval

[1] It may be asserted with confidence that a belief in a devil, that is of an evil spirit, has no place whatever in the native Melanesian mind. The word has certainly not been introduced in the Solomon or Banks' Islands by missionaries, who in those groups have never used the word devil. Yet most unfortunately it has come to pass that the religious beliefs of European traders have been conveyed to the natives in the word 'devil,' which they use without knowing what it means. It is much to be wished that educated Europeans would not use the word so loosely as they do.

officers pass their short period of observation in this atmosphere of confusion. Besides, every one, missionary and visitor, carries with him some preconceived ideas; he expects to see idols, and he sees them; images are labelled idols in museums whose makers carved them for amusement; a Solomon islander fashions the head of his lime-box stick into a grotesque figure, and it becomes the subject of a woodcut as 'a Solomon Island god.' It is extremely difficult for any one to begin enquiries without some prepossessions, which, even if he can communicate with the natives in their own language, affect his conception of the meaning of the answers he receives. The questions he puts guide the native to the answer he thinks he ought to give. The native, with very vague beliefs and notions floating in cloudy solution in his mind, finds in the questions of the European a thread on which these will precipitate themselves, and, without any intention to deceive, avails himself of the opportunity to clear his own mind while he satisfies the questioner.

Some such statement as this of the difficulties in the way of a certain knowledge of the subject is a necessary introduction to the account which is given here of the religion of the Melanesians; and it is desirable that the writer should disclaim pretension to accuracy or completeness. The general view which is presented must be taken with the particular examples of Melanesian belief and customs in matters of religion which follow.

(1) The Melanesian mind is entirely possessed by the belief in a supernatural power or influence, called almost universally *mana*[1]. This is what works to effect everything which is

---

[1] Professor Max Müller, in his Hibbert Lectures of 1878, did me the honour of quoting the following words from a letter. ' The religion of the Melanesians consists, as far as belief goes, in the persuasion that there is a supernatural power about belonging to the region of the unseen; and, as far as practice goes, in the use of means of getting this power turned to their own benefit. The notion of a Supreme Being is altogether foreign to them, or indeed of any being occupying a very elevated place in their world. . . There is a belief in a force altogether distinct from physical power, which acts in all kinds of ways for good and evil, and which it is of the greatest advantage to possess or control.

beyond the ordinary power of men, outside the common processes of nature; it is present in the atmosphere of life, attaches itself to persons and to things, and is manifested by results which can only be ascribed to its operation. When one has got it he can use it and direct it, but its force may break forth at some new point; the presence of it is ascertained by proof. A man comes by chance upon a stone which takes his fancy; its shape is singular, it is like something, it is certainly not a common stone, there must be *mana* in it. So he argues with himself, and he puts it to the proof; he lays it at the root of a tree to the fruit of which it has a certain resemblance, or he buries it in the ground when he plants his garden; an abundant crop on the tree or in the garden shews that he is right, the stone is *mana* [1], has that power in it. Having that power it is a vehicle to convey *mana* to other stones. In the same way certain forms of words, generally in the form of a song, have power for certain purposes; a charm of words is called a *mana*. But this power, though itself impersonal, is always connected with some person who directs it; all spirits have it, ghosts generally, some men. If a stone is found to have a supernatural power, it is because a spirit has associated itself with it; a dead man's bone has

This is Mana. The word is common I believe to the whole Pacific, and people have tried very hard to describe what it is in different regions. I think I know what our people mean by it, and that meaning seems to me to cover all that I hear about it elsewhere. It is a power or influence, not physical, and in a way supernatural; but it shews itself in physical force, or in any kind of power or excellence which a man possesses. This Mana is not fixed in anything, and can be conveyed in almost anything; but spirits, whether disembodied souls or supernatural beings, have it and can impart it; and it essentially belongs to personal beings to originate it, though it may act through the medium of water, or a stone, or a bone. All Melanesian religion consists, in fact, in getting this Mana for one's self, or getting it used for one's benefit—all religion, that is, as far as religious practices go, prayers and sacrifices.'

[1] The word *mana* is both a noun substantive and a verb; a transitive form of the verb, *manag, manahi, manangi,* means to impart *mana,* or to influence with it. An object in which *mana* resides, and a spirit which naturally has *mana,* is said to be *mana,* with the use of the verb; a man has *mana,* but cannot properly be said to be *mana.*

with it *mana*, because the ghost is with the bone ; a man may
have so close a connexion with a spirit or ghost that he has
mana in himself also, and can so direct it as to effect what he
desires ; a charm is powerful because the name of a spirit or
ghost expressed in the form of words brings into it the power
which the ghost or spirit exercises through it.   Thus all
conspicuous success is a proof that a man has *mana* ; his
influence depends on the impression made on the people's
mind that he has it ; he becomes a chief by virtue of it.
Hence a man's power, though political or social in its character, is his *mana* ; the word is naturally used in accordance
with the native conception of the character of all power and
influence as supernatural.   If a man has been successful in
fighting, it has not been his natural strength of arm, quickness
of eye, or readiness of resource that has won success ; he has
certainly got the *mana* of a spirit or of some deceased warrior
to empower him, conveyed in an amulet of a stone round his
neck, or a tuft of leaves in his belt, in a tooth hung upon a
finger of his bow hand, or in the form of words with which he
brings supernatural assistance to his side.   If a man's pigs
multiply, and his gardens are productive, it is not because he
is industrious and looks after his property, but because of the
stones full of *mana* for pigs and yams that he possesses.   Of
course a yam naturally grows when planted, that is well
known, but it will not be very large unless *mana* comes into
play ; a canoe will not be swift unless *mana* be brought to
bear upon it, a net will not catch many fish, nor an arrow
inflict a mortal wound.

(2) The Melanesians believe in the existence of beings
personal, intelligent, full of *mana*, with a certain bodily form
which is visible but not fleshly like the bodies of men.   These
they think to be more or less actively concerned in the
affairs of men, and they invoke and otherwise approach them.
These may be called spirits ; but it is most important to
distinguish between spirits who are beings of an order
higher than mankind, and the disembodied spirits of men,
which have become in the vulgar sense of the word ghosts.

From the neglect of this distinction great confusion and misunderstanding arises; and it is much to be desired that missionaries at any rate would carefully observe the distinction. Any personal object of worship among natives in all parts of the world is taken by the European observer to be a spirit or a god, or a devil; but among Melanesians at any rate it is very common to invoke departed relatives and friends, and to use religious rites addressed to them. A man therefore who is approaching with some rite his dead father, whose spirit he believes to be existing and pleased with his pious action, is thought to be worshipping a false god or deceiving spirit, and very probably is told that the being he worships does not exist. The perplexed native hears with one ear that there is no such thing as that departed spirit of a man which he venerates as a ghost but his instructor takes to be a god, and with the other that the soul never dies, and that his own spiritual interests are paramount and eternal. They themselves make a clear distinction between the existing, conscious, powerful, disembodied spirits of the dead, and other spiritual beings that never have been men at all. It is true that the two orders of beings get confused in native language and thought, but their confusion begins at one end and the confusion of their visitors at another; they think so much and constantly of ghosts that they speak of beings who were never men as ghosts; Europeans take the spirits of the lately dead for gods; less educated Europeans call them roundly devils. All Melanesians, as far as my acquaintance with them extends, believe in the existence both of spirits that never were men, and of ghosts which are the disembodied souls of men deceased: to preserve as far as possible this distinction, the supernatural beings that were never in a human body are here called *spirits*, men's spirits that have left the body are called *ghosts*[1].

---

[1] The Melanesian Mission, under the guidance of Bishop Patteson, has used in all the islands the English word God. He considered the enormous difficulty, if not impossibility, of finding an adequate native expression in any one language, and further the very narrow limits within which such a word if it

There is, however, a very remarkable difference between the natives of the New Hebrides and Banks' Islands to the east, and the natives of the Solomon Islands to the west; the direction of the religious ideas and practices of the former is towards spirits rather than ghosts, the latter pay very little attention to spirits and address themselves almost wholly to ghosts. This goes with a much greater development of a sacrificial system in the west than in the east; and goes along also with a certain advance in the arts of life. Enough is hardly known of the Santa Cruz people, who lie between, to speak with certainty, but they appear to range themselves, as they rather do geographically, on the side of the Solomon Islands. In Fiji it is the established custom to call the objects of the old worship gods; but Mr. Fison was 'inclined to think all the spiritual beings of Fiji, including the gods, simply the Mota *tamate*,' i.e. ghosts; and the words of Mr. Hazelwood, quoted by Mr. Brenchley (Cruise of the Curaçoa, p. 181), confirm this view. Tuikilakila told one of the first missionaries how he proposed to treat him. 'If you die first,' said he, 'I shall make you my god.' And the same Tuikilakila would sometimes say of himself, 'I am a god.' It is added that he believed it too; and his belief was surely correct. For it should be observed that the chief never said he was or should be a god, in English, but that he was or should be a *kalou*, in Fijian, and a *kalou* he no doubt became; that is to say, on his decease his departed spirit was invoked and worshipped as he knew it would be. He used no verb ' am' or ' shall be '; said only 'I a *kalou*.' In Fiji also this worship of the dead, rather than of beings that never were in the flesh, accompanies a more considerable advance in the arts of life than is found in, for example, the Banks' Islands. It is plain that the natives of the southern islands of the New Hebrides, though they are said to worship ' gods,' believe in the existence and power of spirits other than the disembodied

could be found must be used, since the languages are at least as many as the islands. It is difficult to convey by description the ideas which ought to attach to the new word, but at least nothing erroneous is connoted by it.

spirits of the dead, as well as of the ghosts of men. When a missionary visitor to Anaiteum reported that the people 'lived under the most abject bondage to their *Natmases*,' and called these 'gods.' he was evidently speaking of the ghosts, the *Natmat* of the Banks' Islands, for the word is no doubt the same. The belief in other spirits not ghosts of the dead, appears equally clear in the account given of the sacred stones and places, which correspond to those of the northern islands of the same group, and in the 'minor deities' said to be the progeny of Nugerain, and called 'gods of the sea, of the land, of mountains and valleys,' who represent the *wui* of Lepers' Island and Araga. There does not appear to be anywhere in Melanesia a belief in a spirit which animates any natural object, a tree, waterfall, storm or rock, so as to be to it what the soul is believed to be to the body of a man. Europeans it is true speak of the spirits of the sea or of the storm or of the forest ; but the native idea which they represent is that ghosts haunt the sea and the forest, having power to raise storms and to strike a traveller with disease, or that supernatural beings never men do the same. It may be said, then, that Melanesian religion divides the people into two groups ; one, where, with an accompanying belief in spirits never men, worship is directed to the ghosts of the dead, as in the Solomon Islands ; the other, where both ghosts and spirits have an important place, but the spirits have more worship than the ghosts, as is the case in the New Hebrides and in the Banks' Islands.

(3) In the Banks' Islands a spirit is called a *vui*, and is thus described by a native who was exhorted to give as far as possible the original notion conveyed among the old people by the word, and gave his definition after considerable reflection :—' What is a *vui* ? It lives, thinks, has more intelligence than a man ; knows things which are secret without seeing ; is supernaturally powerful with *mana* ; has no form to be seen ; has no soul, because itself is like a soul.' But though the true conception of a *vui* represents it as incorporeal, the stories about the *vui* who have names treat

them as if they were men possessed of supernatural power. The *wui* of the Northern New Hebrides are the same. In the Solomon Islands it is difficult to get any definition of a spirit except that there are beings which were never men, and have not the bodily nature of a man. In San Cristoval such a being is called *Figona* or *Hi'ona*. Such was Kahausibware, a female, and a snake. The name *hi'ona* is known in Malanta also, but used with no very clear application; they believe there also in *urehi*, not living men, nor the ghosts of dead men, that haunt big trees in the forest and snatch away the souls of men. These are seen like ghosts, but are not sacrificed to or invoked. The name *vigona* is known also at Florida, and is applied to beings whose power exercises itself in storms, rain, drought, calms, and in the growth of food; but these the natives decline to admit to be simple spirits, thinking they must once have been men; and doubtless some so called were men not long ago. One being only is asserted there to be superhuman, never alive with a mere human life, and therefore not now a ghost; one that now receives no worship, but is the subject of stories only, without any religious consideration. This is Koevasi, a female. How she came into existence no one knows; she made things of all kinds; she became herself the mother of a woman from whom the people of the island descend. She was the author of death by resuming her cast-off skin; she was the originator of the varying dialects of the islands round; for having started on a voyage she was seized with ague, and shook so much that her utterance was confused. Wherever she landed the people caught from her an almost unintelligible speech. The chill of this ague remains in the river Kakambona in Laudari, Guadalcanar; Koevasi washed in it, and the water is now so cold that to wade into it makes one ill.

These spirits, such as they are, have no position in the religion of the Solomon Islands; the ghosts, the disembodied spirits of the dead, are objects of worship; the *tindalo* of Florida, *tidadho* of Ysabel, *tinda'o* of Guadalcanar, *lio'a* of Saa, *'ataro* of San Cristoval. But it must not be supposed that every

ghost becomes an object of worship. A man in danger may
call upon his father, his grandfather, or his uncle ; his nearness of kin is sufficient ground for it. The ghost who is to
be worshipped is the spirit of a man who in his lifetime had
mana in him ; the souls of common men are the common herd
of ghosts, nobodies alike before and after death. The supernatural power abiding in the powerful living man abides in
his ghost after death, with increased vigour and more ease of
movement. After his death, therefore, it is expected that he
should begin to work, and some one will come forward and claim
particular acquaintance with the ghost ; if his power should
shew itself, his position is assured as one worthy to be invoked, and to receive offerings, till his cultus gives way
before the rising importance of one newly dead, and the
sacred place where his shrine once stood and his relics were
preserved is the only memorial of him that remains; if no
proof of his activity appears, he sinks into oblivion at once.
An admirable example of the establishment of the worship
of a *tindalo* in Florida is given in the story of Ganindo,
for which I am indebted to Bishop Selwyn. There was a
gathering of men at Honggo to go on a head-hunting
expedition under the leading of Kulanikama the chief
(himself afterwards a ghost of worship), and Ganindo was
their great fighting man. They went to attack Gaeta, and
Lumba of Gaeta shot Ganindo near the collar-bone with an
arrow. Having failed in their purpose they returned to
Honggo, and said they, 'our friend is dead.' But as he still
lived they took him over to Nggaombata in Guadalcanar,
brought him back again, and put him on the hill Bonipari,
where he died and was buried. Then they took his head,
wove a basket for it, and built a house for it, and they said he
was a *tindalo*. ' Let us go and take heads,' said they ; so they
made an expedition. As they went they ceased paddling in a
quiet place and waited till they felt their canoe rock under
them ; then said they, ' Here is a *tindalo*.' To find out who
he was they called the names of *tindalos*, and when they
called the name of Ganindo the canoe shook again. In the

same way they learnt what village they were to attack.
Returning successful, they threw a spear into the roof of
Ganindo's house, blew conchs, and danced around it crying,
'Our *tindalo* is strong to kill.' Then they sacrificed to him,
fish and food. Then they built him a new house, and made
four images for the four corners, one of Ganindo himself, two
of his sisters, and another. Then, when eight men had
carried up the ridge covering for the house, eight men
translated the relics to the shrine. One carried the bones
of Ganindo, another his betel-nuts, another his lime-box,
another his shell trumpet. They all went in crouching, as if
under a heavy weight [1], and singing slowly, ' *Ma-i-i, ma-i-i, ka
saka tua*, hither, hither, let us lift the leg ;' the eight legs
were lifted together, and again they chanted ' *ma-i-i, ma-i-i,*'
and at the last *mai* the eight legs went down together. With
this solemn procession the relics were set upon a bamboo
platform, and sacrifices to the new *keramo* were begun ; by
Nisi first, then by Satani, then by Begoni, the last, at whose
death some four years ago the sacrifices ceased, and the shrine
fell to ruin before the advance of Christian teaching. To the
natives of Florida this Ganindo was a *tindalo*, a ghost of
worship, a *keramo*, a ghost powerful for war; he would be
spoken of now by some Europeans as a god, by others as a
devil, and the pigeon-English speaking natives now, who
think that 'devil' is the English for *tindalo*, would use the
same word. The belief in Florida and the neighbouring parts
is fixed that every *tindalo* was once a man ; yet some whose
names are known to every one, Daula and Hauri, associated
respectively with the frigate-bird and the shark, have passed
far away from any historical remembrance; Daula, indeed,
under the name of Kaula [2], is venerated at Ulawa. Some
also of the *keramo*, the *tindalo* of fighting, are known in
Florida not to have been men of the island, but famous
warriors of the western islands, where *mana* they think is

---

[1] The weight of *mana*, as in the *palako* logs, page 108.

[2] As the Florida *dale*, child, is in Ulawa *kale*, and Wango *'ataro* is Saa
'akalo.

stronger; who have only been known, and that of late years, in Florida in their spiritual state and power, but never in human form. At any rate the objects of religious worship are all *tindalo*; and every *tindalo* was once a man.

(4) Taking the islands of Melanesia, as many of them as come here into view, as a whole, it is found that Prayers and Offerings are made everywhere to spirits, to ghosts, or to both. The prayers are perhaps in some cases constraining charms, are certainly often forms of words believed to be acceptable to the being addressed, and known only to those who have special access to him. But there are also natural calls for help in danger and distress. The offerings or sacrifices, whether made to spirits or to ghosts, and differing a good deal in eastern and western islands, have various motives. Some are propitiatory, substituting an animal for the person who has offended; some deprecatory; some are offered to conciliate and gratify with a view to gain; some only to shew proper attention and respect or even affection; but the notion of propitiation is not at all commonly present. There is no priestly order, and no persons who can properly be called priests. Any man can have access to some object of worship, and most men in fact do have it, either by discovery of their own or by knowledge imparted to them by those who have before employed it. If the object of worship, as in some sacrifices, is one common to the members of a community, the man who knows how to approach that object is in a way their priest and sacrifices for them all; but it is in respect of that particular function only that he has a sacred character; and it is very much by virtue of that function that a man is a chief, and not at all because he is chief that he performs the sacrifice. Women and children generally are excluded from religious rites. In close connexion with religious observances come the various practices of magic and witchcraft, of doctoring and weather-doctoring; for all is done by the aid of ghosts and spirits.

CHAPTER VIII.

SACRIFICES.

THE simplest and most common sacrificial act is that of throwing a small portion of food to the dead ; this is probably a universal practice in Melanesia. A fragment of food ready to be eaten, of yam, a leaf of mallow, a bit of betel-nut, is thrown aside, and, where they drink kava, a libation is made of a few drops, as the share of departed friends, or as a memorial of them with which they will be gratified. This is done perhaps with the calling of the name of some one recently deceased or particularly in remembrance at the time, or else with a general regard to the ghosts of former members of the community. It is hardly thought that this becomes in fact the food of the departed, but somehow it is to their advantage, at any rate it pleases them. At the same time the living friends like to feel and shew remembrance of the dead who have sat with them around the oven ; and it is an opportunity of getting help from ghostly power, for which prayer is made. In the New Hebrides and Banks' Islands this domestic rite has not, so far as my knowledge goes, developed into any formal sacrifice, as it has in the Solomon Islands ; for it may be surely thought that the sacrifices of the latter islands have had their origin in such offerings to the dead. To place food on a burial-place or before some memorial image is common ; and to do this is to offer a kind of sacrifice, even if as in Santa Cruz the offering is soon taken away and eaten. But the natives do not call either of these offerings a sacrifice, do not use for either the words for which in English no other translation can be found. The sacrifices, in the more restricted sense, of the Solomon Islands are widely different from those of the New Hebrides and Banks' Islands; in the western islands the offerings are made to ghosts, and consumed by fire as well as eaten; in the eastern islands they are made to spirits, and there is no sacrificial fire or meal. In the former nothing is offered but food, in the latter money has a conspicuous place.

(1) A Solomon Island sacrifice has been excellently described by a native of San Cristoval. 'In my country,' he wrote, 'they think that ghosts are many, very many indeed, some very powerful, and some not. There is one who is principal in war; this one is truly mighty and strong, When our people wish to fight with any other place, the chief men of the village and the sacrificers and the old men, and the elder and younger men, assemble in the place sacred to this ghost; and his name is Harumae. When they are thus assembled to sacrifice, the chief sacrificer goes and takes a pig; and if it be not a barrow pig they would not sacrifice it to that ghost, he would reject it and not eat of it. The pig is killed (it is strangled), not by the chief sacrificer, but by those whom he chooses to assist, near the sacred place. Then they cut it up; they take great care of the blood lest it should fall upon the ground; they bring a bowl and set the pig in it, and when they cut it up the blood runs down into it. When the cutting up is finished, the chief sacrificer takes a bit of flesh from the pig, and he takes a cocoa-nut shell and dips up some of the blood. Then he takes the blood and the bit of flesh and enters into the house (the shrine), and calls that ghost and says, " Harumae! Chief in war! we sacrifice to you with this pig, that you may help us to smite that place ; and whatsoever we shall carry away shall be your property, and we also will be yours." Then he burns the bit of flesh in a fire upon a stone, and pours down the blood upon the fire. Then the fire blazes greatly upwards to the roof, and the house is full of the smell of pig, a sign that the ghost has heard. But when the sacrificer went in he did not

go boldly, but with awe ; and this is the sign of it ; as he
goes into the holy house he puts away his bag, and washes
his hands thoroughly, to shew that the ghost shall not
reject him with disgust ; just as when you go into the really
Holy House you take off your hat from your head, a sign that
you reverence the true Spirit.' The pig was afterwards eaten
by the worshippers. To sacrifice in this way is called *hoasi*,
the ghost to whom the sacrifice is made *'ataro*. It should
be observed that Harumae had not been dead many years
when this account was written, the elder men remembered
him alive ; nor was he a great fighting man, but a kind and
generous man, thought to have much *mana*. His shrine was
a small house in the village, in which relics of him were kept.
No one since his time had died whom the people thought
worthy of such worship; had it been so Harumae would have
been neglected.

In Florida, as has been said, the objects of worship are
tindalo, to whom the food consumed in the fire is offered as
their portion. Some are commonly known by name, others
are known only to one man and another who has found out
or been taught how to approach them, and calls each *tindalo*
his own, *nagana*. We are concerned here with sacrifices ; public,
as offered to a well-known *tindalo*, powerful in such things as
concern the general well-being ; and private, offered by individuals to the *tindalo* of whom they have particular knowledge[1].
In every village there was the *tindalo* accepted at the time,
and the chief was the sacrificer. He had received from his
predecessor the knowledge how to ' throw ' the sacrifice to this
tindalo, and he imparted this knowledge to his son or nephew,
whom he designed to leave as his successor. The place of
sacrifice was near the village, an ancient one or newly made,
according to the time in which this *tindalo* had been in vogue,
an enclosure with a little house or shrine in which relics were

---

[1] The word for which ' sacrifice ' is used as equivalent is in Florida *sukagi*,
in Bugotu of Ysabel *havugagi*. The sacrificer sacrifices with the offering to the
tindalo in or at the place of sacrifice, *na mane sukagi te nia sukagi na hanu
vania na tindalo ta na malei ni sukagi.*

preserved. When a public sacrifice was performed the people of the place assembled, boys but not women being present, near but not in the sacred place. Food is prepared, but not eaten till the sacrifice has been offered. The sacrificer alone enters the sacred place or shrine, and takes to it his son, or the person he has instructed. He makes a fire of small sticks, muttering words of *mana*, but he must not blow it. He takes some of the prepared food in a basket lined with dracæna leaves and others peculiar to this *tindalo*, some mash of yam or something of that kind; part of this he throws upon the fire, calling the name of the *tindalo*, and the names of others with it; he tells him to take his food, and makes petition for whatever is desired. The fire blazes up, a favourable sign that the *tindalo* are present and blow the fire; the bit of food is consumed[1]. What remains the sacrificer takes back to the assembly and eats, giving some of it to his assistant. Then the people receive from him their portions of the food prepared, and eat it or take it away. While the sacrificing is going on there is a solemn silence. If a pig is killed on the occasion, the heart in Florida, at Bugotu the gullet, is burnt upon the sacrificial fire. One *tindalo* commonly known, whose worship is not local, is Manoga. At sacrifices offered to him little boys are present, and sometimes even women partake of the sacrificial food. ' He who throws the sacrifice when he invokes this *tindalo* heaves the offering round about, and calls him; first to the east, where rises the sun, saying, If thou dwellest in the east, where rises the sun, Manoga! come hither and eat thy *tutu* mash! Then turning he lifts it towards where sets the sun, and says, If thou dwellest in the west, where sets the sun, Manoga! come hither and eat thy *tutu*! There is not a quarter towards which he does not lift it up. And when he has finished lifting it he says, If thou dwellest in heaven above, Manoga! come hither and eat thy *tutu*! If thou dwellest in Buru or Hagetolu, the Pleiades or Orion's belt; if below in

---

[1] It is denied that the food has a spirit, *tarunga*, corresponding to the *tarunga* which is the soul of a man; but the food offered is *tarungaga* (with the adjectival termination), 'has a spiritual character.'

Turivatu; if in the distant sea; if on high in the sun, or in
the moon; if thou dwellest inland or by the shore, Manoga!
come hither and eat thy *tutu*!' This Manoga belongs particularly to the Manukama or Lahi division of the Florida people,
each division, *kema*, having a *tindalo* whom they worship as
peculiarly their own, and whom they vaguely call their
ancestor; Polika of the Nggaombata, Barego of the Kakau,
Kuma of the Honggokama, Sisiro of the Himbo, *Tindalo tambu*,
whose personal name is not known, of the Honggokiki. As
these divisions are intermixed in the villages, though one is
generally more largely represented in any one of them than
the others, sacrifices are offered in each village or group of
villages to each of these *tindalo* of the divisions; and the
sacrificer is the man who knows the particular leaves and
creepers and species of dracæna, and ginger and shavings of a
tree, and words of *mana* with which the *tindalo* is approached,
knowledge which he has received from his predecessors. The
sacrificer then of the dominant family division of the place is
in fact the ostensible chief, the sacrificers of the less numerous
divisions are minor chiefs. With the worship of these *tindalo*
of larger and wider cultus is combined by the sacrificer that of
lesser and more private *keramo* of fighting whom he knows.
The local *tindalo* at the time in vogue, such as Ganindo,
occupies a middle place between the general and particular
objects of sacrificial worship. There are also the *tindalo* known
to every one, who are particularly powerful in certain spheres,
as Daula in the sea, and Pelu, one of the *vigona*, in gardens,
and Hauri in fighting; but only those who know the proper
way to approach them can sacrifice to them before a voyage or
planting or a fight.

There were two general sacrifices in the year, in which the
people of a village took part. The first, the *bigo*, was when
the canarium nut, *ngali*, so much used in native cookery,
was ripe[1]. None could be eaten till the sacrifice of the first-
fruits was offered. The knowledge of the way to do this, and

---

[1] This sacrifice is described by Mr. Woodford (p. 26). In that part of
Guadalcanar, where *l* is dropped in many words, *tindalo* becomes *tindao*.

the consequent authority to open the season, was handed down with the knowledge of the *tindalo* concerned. The man who has the knowledge observes the time, and some day in the early morning he is heard to shout. He climbs a tree, gets some nuts, cracks them, eats, and puts some on the stones in his sacred place for the *tindalo*. Then the people generally can gather for themselves; the chief sacrifices with food in which the new nuts are mixed on the stones of the village sanctuary; each man who has a *tindalo* does the same in his own sacred place. About two months after this there is another general sacrifice called the *sukagi karango*, when the food generally has been dug; a man who digs up his yams, or gets in whatever harvest he has, makes his private sacrifice besides. At the general sacrifice pig or fish is offered.

The private sacrifices of individuals are offered in the same way. A man has gained for himself, or had imparted to him, the knowledge of the leaves and bark and vines that some *tindalo* delights in, and with these he approaches him in the sacred place, *vunutha*, which is his own, and offers to him to keep himself in favour or to obtain something from him. There he invokes his familiar *tindalo*, joining with him some others, and offers in the fire his bit of food. A man will commonly have his *keramo*, a *tindalo* of killing, who will help him in fighting or in slaying his private enemy. He will pull up his ginger-plant, and judge from the ease with which it comes out of the earth whether he shall succeed or not; he will make his sacrifice, and with the ginger and leaves on his shield and in his belt and right armlet will go to fight. He curses his enemy by his *keramo*, 'Siria eats thee, and I shall slay thee;' and if he kills him, he cries, 'Thine is this man, Siria! and do thou give me *mana*.' Manslaughter without the help of a *tindalo* would be dangerous to the manslayer; the slain man's ghost would have power over him unless the *mana* of the *keramo*, a stronger ghost, were on his side. In case of failure the ghostly power on the enemy's side has been shewn to have the greater strength. A man must needs have his *keramo*, even if he had to buy one; if what his father or uncle taught and gave him did not succeed he tried another. A relic of the *keramo* (himself but lately a fighting man), a tooth or some hair in a little bag, was hung round the neck; or the contents of the bag might be only a stone. These amulets, *bomboso*, were kept in the house, and were called a man's *keramo*, just as relics were called *tindalo*. The *vigona*, as has been said, have influence over weather and in gardens. If a man himself knows one he can operate for himself, otherwise he pays a *mane nggehe vigona* to do it for him. Such a one goes into the middle of the garden with mashed food in the palm of his left hand, and he strikes it with his right hand as he calls on his *vigona* to come and eat. He says, 'This produce thou shalt eat; give *mana* to this garden, that food may be good and plentiful.' He digs holes at the four corners, and buries the leaves proper to his *vigona*, to give ghostly power to the garden, that it may be fruitful and to guard it; stones are used for the same purpose. As the yams, or *pana*, grow they are twined with the special creeper and fastened with the wood which the *vigona* loves. These *tindalo* of the gardens must not be offended by the entrance of men who have eaten pig's flesh or fish, or the flesh of the *kandora* cuscus, or shell-fish; three or four days after they have eaten such things they may approach, the food offensive to the *vigona* having left their stomachs the crop will not be hurt. When the yam vines are being trained the men sleep near the gardens, and never approach their wives; should they do so and tread the garden it would be spoilt. The man who has his own *vigona* can bring his power to bear in doing damage to another man's garden, being either moved by his own grudge or paid to do it; backed by his own *vigona* he offends the *vigona* of the garden he designs to spoil by laying putrid things there. If after this the crop is good, the first *vigona* has been shewn to be stronger than the other. The names of sixteen of these *vigona* are generally known. When the crop is dug a portion of the fruits is burnt in sacrifice to the one concerned.

Human sacrifices were occasionally made; but there was no

sacrificial feast upon the flesh as when a pig was offered ; only
little bits were eaten by those who desired to get fighting
mana, by young men, and by elders for a special purpose.
Such sacrifices were thought more effectual than others, and
advantage was taken of a crime, or imputed crime, to take a
life and offer the man to some *tindalo*. So within the memory
of men still young, Dikea, the chief of Ravu, condemned one
Gisukokovilo to death for stealing tobacco, and the grown lads
of Handika ate bits of him cooked in the sacrificial fire. The
same Dikea offered a human sacrifice in the year 1886. Two
calamities had fallen upon Dikea. One of his wives proved
false, and he sent her away, vowing that she should not return
till he had sacrificed to Hauri. Also his son had died, and he
made a vow that he would kill a man for him. Some thought
that he would kill a man to bury with the boy, but he did not.
He dug up his buried son that he might see him once more ;
and again, according to the common practice, he took up his
skull and set it in his sacred place. It was widely known
that Dikea had made his vow, and that he would pay well for
some one to kill. The Savo people had bought a captive boy
in Guadalcanar, lame and nearly blind, and him they brought
and sold to Dikea for twenty coils of money. The boy, ignorant of the language, did not know his fate. Dikea, laying his
hand on the victim's breast, cried ' Hauri ! here is a man for
you,' and his followers killed him with clubs and axes. His
head was taken to set up with Dikea's collection of skulls, his
legs were sent away to make known what had been done, but
none of him was eaten : ' So Dikea sacrificed to Hauri with
that boy.' In Bugotu of Ysabel the sacrifices, *havuyagi*, are
the same with those of Florida ; only the dwellers along the
coast sacrificed human victims, and this practice they said, as
in Florida, had come to them from further west. When the
head of an enemy killed in a fight was brought in triumph,
bits were cut off and burnt in sacrifice. A captive would be
taken to the sacred place, the burial-place of the *tindatho* to
whom the sacrifice was to be made, and there bound hand and
foot. Then the men of the place, following the chief who led the

sacrifice, each beat him on the breast with their hands, calling on the *tindatho*, and giving him the victim. This was enough sometimes to cause death, otherwise they cut his throat. Then the sacrificer burnt a bit in the fire for the *tindatho*. Did the men assembled eat of the sacrifice? Bera, the principal chief, at any rate used to do so till Wadrokal went there as a teacher; he would cook an arm in the oven and eat it, having first sacrificed with a portion. Only six years ago Soga at Mang-gotu sacrificed a man. He accused some Bugotu visitors of charming one of his own friends to death; eight of them he killed, but one he bound and took to the place where his friend was buried; there he offered him to the ghost, now a *tindatho*, of the man supposed to have been bewitched; but he did not eat of the sacrifice. In these, however, and in the lesser sacrifices, there is not commonly present the notion of propitiation, nor perhaps of substitution. When, as in the case of Dikea, misfortune is supposed to have followed on some offence, the offended *tindalo* is propitiated by the sacrifice, and this is done in case of sickness. But generally the object is rather to gain the favour and to retain the good will of the disembodied spirit.

In Saa, near Cape Zélée in Malanta, there is found in some sacrifices a distinct substitution of the victim for the person on whose behalf the offering is made. The ghost of some departed warrior or otherwise powerful man becomes a *lio'a*; that of a warrior, if on experiment he is found to act, is like the *keramo* of Florida, a ghost of battle or of killing, *lio'a ni ma'e*. The names of many, as of recent chiefs, are generally known, but some are known only to those who have learnt the means of access to them. There is no one word used for sacrificing; there are seven rites which an educated native of the place classes with the sacrifices of other islands. (1) The simplest is called *Tau taha*, as when one returning from a voyage puts food to the case containing the relics of his father, as did Ara'ana. In the course of a voyage also, when landing on an uninhabited islet, they will throw food and call on father, grandfather, and other deceased friends, and in any danger will do the same. Three other sacrifices have much in common, and it depends on the person called in and consulted to determine which shall be used. (2) One is called *'unu qo*, this is, burning a pig. This is offered in case of sickness, or when the failure of a garden crop shews that some *lio'a* has been offended. A man known to be able to sacrifice is called in, and is ready to say that he knows what *lio'a* has caused the mischief. To him is sent a small pig, which is to take the place of the person whom the ghost *lio'a* is plaguing ; and he takes it to the sacred place of that *lio'a* somewhere under a tree, strangles it, and burns it whole in a fire kindled on the sacred stones or on the ground. He burns with it also grated yam and cocoa-nut mixed with fish ; and then he stands and calls with a loud voice on the *lio'a* of the place, and with him he calls the names of all the ghosts of his family, his ancestors, and all who are deceased, down even to children and to women, and he names the giver of the pig for the food of these *lio'a*. A bit of the mixed food he leaves unburnt, wraps it in a dracæna leaf, and puts it by the relic case of the man to whose ghost he has been sacrificing. He is rewarded for his services by a present of food. (3) Another is called *toto 'akalo*, clearing the soul. It is performed in the house of the sacrificer, who cooks a little pig or a dog, and cites the names of the *lio'a* who are causing the trouble, calling upon them to *toto*, clear away the mischief, whether sickness, charm, or curse, and to make the afflicted party clean. Then he takes the pig out and throws it into the sea, or sets it on a stone in the sacred place of the *lio'a* he has addressed ; 'he will not put it in a common place; it is holy, it has taken away the mischief, it has made clean.' (4) The third of these is called *toto epa hanua*, clearing well the place, and is performed in the house of the sick person for whose benefit it is offered. They cook a pig or dog in the oven, cut it up, and lay all the parts in order. Then the sacrificer comes and sits at the head, and calls all the names of the dead members of the family of the *lio'a* in order downwards, saying, 'Help, deliver this man, cut short the line that has bound him.' Then the pig is eaten by all present, except the women; nothing is burnt. The remaining sacrifices are those of first-fruits. (5) When the yams are ripe they fetch some from each garden to offer to the *lio'a*. All the family who consider a certain line of ancestors to be the *lio'a* with whom they are concerned in this matter assemble, without the women, at the sacred place belonging to them. One goes into the sacred place with a yam, and cries with a loud voice to the *lio'a*, 'This is yours to eat,' and puts the yam by the skull which is in the place. The others call quietly upon the names of all the ancestors and give their yams, very many in number, because one from each garden is given to each *lio'a*. They add also *awalosi*, the edible flower of a reed. This offering of first-fruits is made in the early morning. If any one has in his house a relic, head, bones, or hair, he takes back a yam to set beside it. (6) First-fruits of flying fish. These fish, like the bonito, require a certain supernatural power to catch them; it is not every canoe that goes after flying fish. When the season comes the men get their floats ready, and the women go into the gardens to dig new yams and make grated food. The men then get a few flying fish, and sacrifice with them. Some *lio'a* are sharks, and to them the first-fruits are offered. Some have sacred places ashore with figures of sharks set up, before which cooked flying fish are laid; some ghost-sharks have no place on shore, and to them the fish are taken out to sea, their names are called, and the fish shred to them for their food. (7) The new canarium almonds cannot be eaten till the first-fruits have been offered to the *lio'a*, and a similar offering is made of the dried almonds before they are eaten, with added flying-fish.

A sacrifice in San Cristoval has been already described. In case of sickness, where a certain malignant ghost named Tapia is believed to have seized on a man's soul and bound it to a banyan-tree, a sacrifice of substitution is offered. The man who has access to Tapia is employed to intercede; he takes a pig or fish to the sacred place and offers it, saying, 'This is for you to eat in place of that man; eat this, don't kill him'; and he is then able to loose and take back the sick man's soul so that he may recover.

At Santa Cruz, when a man of consideration dies, his ghost becomes a *duka*. A stock of wood is set up in his house to represent him. This remains, and is from time to time renewed, until after a time the man is forgotten, or the stock is neglected by the transference of attention to some newer and more successful *duka*. When the stock is first put up, a pig is killed, and the two strips of flesh from along the back-bone inside are put before the stock as food for the *duka* represented. These do not stay long, but are taken away and eaten. When the stocks are renewed the same is done again; and from time to time offerings of food are made to the *duka* before the stock, laid there for a time, and then taken up and eaten. In case of danger at sea, a *duka* is called by name, a man's father or a deceased chief, or a certain Lata who is not remembered as a man, and a bit of food is thrown out; 'This is for you to eat.' Betel-nuts are placed on sacred stones for the *duka*. When a garden is planted they spread feather-money and red native cloth round it for the *duka*, and take it away again. A patient who has recovered from sickness under the treatment of a native doctor gives a pig for the *duka* concerned in the cure; and when a pig is killed a bit of meat is placed before the stock that represents him. Offerings of first-fruits of yams are made in the same way, in the form of mash or pudding. The economical offerings of Santa Cruz may be explained by the belief that the *duka*, themselves immaterial, have taken the immaterial substance of their gifts; the gross material therefore may be taken by fleshly men.

(2) The character of what may be called sacrifices in the Banks' Islands and Northern New Hebrides differs very much from that of the sacrifices of the Solomon Islands in two respects; the offerings are as a rule made to spirits and not to ghosts, and there is no use of fire to consume what is offered. It is true that fragments of food are thrown for the ghosts of the lately deceased; by an action no doubt closely connected with the sacrifices of the western islands, but not with the

notion of a sacrifice as these more eastern people understand it. In the use of the word in the Banks' Islands which has been taken as equivalent to ' sacrifice,' viz. *oloolo*, it is important to observe that the word is not employed in reference to the spirit to whom the offering is made, but to the man himself who presents the offering to the spirit [1], which is the same thing as to say that the word *oloolo* does not exactly mean to sacrifice. Still there is a sacrificial offering, and it is a means of propitiating a spirit after an offence, as well as a means of obtaining what is desired. Food also is by no means commonly the thing offered ; in the Banks' Islands perhaps nothing but native money is the offering.

The spirits who are approached with these offerings are almost always connected with stones on which the offerings are made. Such stones have some of them been sacred to some spirit from ancient times, and the knowledge of the way to approach the spirit who is connected with them has been handed down to the man who now possesses it. But any man may find a stone for himself, the shape of which strikes his fancy, or some other object, an octopus in his hole, a shark, a snake, an eel, which seems to him something unusual, and therefore connected with a spirit. He gets money and scatters it about the stone, or on the place where he has seen the object of his fancy; then he goes home to sleep. He dreams that some one takes him to a place and shews him the pigs or money he is to have because of his connexion with the thing that he has found. This thing in the Banks' Islands becomes his *tano-oloolo*, the place of his offering, the object in regard to which offering is made to obtain pigs or money. His neighbours begin to know that he has it, and that his increasing wealth has its origin there ; they come to him therefore and obtain through him the good offices of the spirit he has come to know. He hands down the knowledge of this to his son or nephew. If a man is sick he gives another who

---

[1] A man is said to *oloolo* with the money to the man who knows the stone ; the latter is said to *oloolo* on the stone on behalf of the former, the former to *oloolo* to the latter in regard to the stone ; neither is said to *oloolo* to the *vui* spirit.

is known to have a stone of power,—the spirit connected with which it is suggested that he has offended,—a short string of money, and a bit of the pepper root, *gea*, that is used for kava; the sick man is said to *oloolo* to the possessor of the stone. The latter takes the things offered to his sacred place and throws them down, saying, 'Let So-and-So recover.' When the sick man recovers he pays a fee. If a man desires to get the benefit of the stone, or whatever it is, known to another, with a view to increase of money, pigs or food, or success in fighting, the possessor of the stone will take him to his sacred place, where probably there are many stones, each good for its own purpose. The applicant will supply money, perhaps a hundred strings a few inches long. The introducer will shew him one stone and say, 'This is a big yam,' and the worshipper puts money down. Of another he says it is a boar, of another that it is a pig with tusks, and money is put down. The notion is that the spirit, *vui*, attached to the stone likes the money, which is allowed to remain upon or by the stone. In case the *oloolo*, the sacrifice, succeeds, the man benefited pays the man to whom the stones and spirits belong. If a man goes to sacrifice for success in fighting, he takes great care lest nothing sharp should prick or scratch him, or a stone bruise him; in the one case he would be shot, in the other he would be clubbed.

Some of these objects of sacrificial worship are well known, but can only be approached by the person to whom the right of access to them has been handed down; there must be between the worshipper who desires advantage and the spirit who bestows it not only the medium of the stone, or whatever other material object the spirit is connected with, but also the man who through the stone has got a personal acquaintance with the spirit. In Vanua Lava, at Sarewoana near Alo Sepere, the legendary home of Qat, there is still the stump of a tree which Qat cut down for his canoe, an aged stump with young shoots springing from it; men who are cutting a canoe make sacrifices at this stump, throwing down money there that their canoe may be swift and strong and never

wrecked. It does not appear that any one comes between the
offerer and Qat in this, perhaps because Qat is known to every
one.   There is no doubt often a sacrifice, *oloolo*, made in the
way of propitiation ; but a *vui* is not a malignant spirit that
will do harm unless propitiated.   If a man has heedlessly gone
into a sacred place and is afraid that he has offended the spirit
belonging to it, he will make his offering to the man whose
sacred place it is, that he may appease the spirit ; and in the
case of sickness there is always the presumption that some
spirit has been offended.   A man whose familiar spirit is
associated with a snake, an eel, owl, crab or some such
creature, visits it and makes his offerings to keep in favour
with it, or to obtain its favour for some one from whom he
receives money for an offering.   They say that a man who has
a *mae*, an amphibious snake to which a certain awful character
belongs, as his familiar, goes to the sacred place it haunts and
calls it till it comes.   He sits down and the snake crawls over
him, putting its tongue into his mouth, which he sucks.
He scatters money for the spirit, for he does not offer to the
snake but to the spirit, *vui*, that is with the snake and manifested in it.   He does not invoke or pray to the spirit, but he
may pray to the ghosts of his predecessors in this particular
mystery.   When a man visits his familiar in this way no one
else is present, and the doubt has occurred to the native people
whether there be a snake at all.   It is certain that when
a man has died who has been in the habit of receiving money
to offer to the snake, and another who has received instructions
from him as his successor has gone to reopen so profitable a
connexion, the creature has not been found ; but then it is
also concluded that the man and the snake die together.
Money in this same way of sacrifice, if so it can be called,
is scattered in a deep hole in a stream, or in a pool among
the rocks upon the beach ; wherever some impressive touch of
natural awe comes upon the native mind it apprehends the
presence of some haunting *vui*, and is moved to an act of
worship ; but it is not to the stone or stream or tree, or to the
spirit of it, that the offering is made ; the *vui* is a person as a

man is, and its presence makes the place sacred. The number of
men who in old times had a sacred place with a familiar spirit
of their own was large, probably most of the grown-up men
had one; there was no priestly order, no sacred buildings,
nothing to make a public show.

In the Northern New Hebrides, spirits are approached very
commonly at stones, and offerings are made to them upon the
stones, to secure their favour or to reconcile them if offended.
This is all the sacrifice there appears to be at Maewo,
Aurora Island; they use no word that can be translated
'sacrifice,' unless it be *turegi*, which means to lay an offering
upon a stone. A certain offering, however, is made to a ghost;
if a man's pig is lost he will go to the grave of a kinsman,
put on the stones above it, *qaru*, a tuft of dracæna or croton
leaves, and say, 'Get me back my pig.' The ghost will drive
the pig back into the village. To offer thus is *malai o qaru*.
At Whitsuntide, Araga, there are stones connected with spirits
in sacred places which are known only to those who have
discovered them, or have been introduced into acquaintance
with the spirits by their predecessors. At these stones sacrifices
are made. A young man wishes to get on in the Loli Society,
to become rich, to live to be old, the main object being to be
a great man in the Loli. Such a person makes his offering of
a pig or mats to the man who is acquainted with the spirit,
ma dugu boe lalainia; for they say, as in the Banks' Islands,
that the offering is not made to the spirit, but to the man who
knows him. This go-between keeps the pig for himself. He
goes to the sacred place taking the suppliant with him; then
he mutters to Tagaro the spirit, 'This man has given us two
a pig, let him be great, let him be a full-grown man.' After
this the suppliant can go and make his requests in the sacred
place by himself. Sometimes a very young cocoa-nut is broken
and the juice poured over his head as a sign that he is admitted. They also put such a young cocoa-nut on the stone as
an offering. Such sacrifices are made for sunshine, rain, and
abundant crops. Offerings also are made to the ghosts of
powerful men recently deceased, either at their graves or

where they are supposed to haunt. Men who know these
and have access to them, take mats, food, pigs, living or
cooked, into the sacred place and leave them there. At
Lepers' Island they *drugu* to the men who have access to
spirits, *wui*, in connexion with stones, giving money and pigs
to them for their intercession ; but offerings are not commonly made directly to *wui*, or to ghosts either. Offerings
are made at sea near certain dangerous rocks ; a tuft of pig's
hair or a fowl's feather from the cargo, or a bit of food, is
thrown into the sea for Tagaro, that he may give a safe passage to the canoe. Bishop Patteson noted in the course of his
last voyage, that at Ambrym it was the practice for great
men to burn a pig entirely, without any accompanying prayer,
in their *Suqe*, with the view of obtaining *mana*. This must be
looked upon as a sacrificial act.

NOTE.—The sacrifices of the Solomon Islands may well be traced to the
desire of making the deceased still sharers of the common meal ; what is offered
and burnt is common food. The further step of begging the offended ghost to
take all and spare the sick is taken at Saa and San Cristoval. It should be
remarked that there is nothing whatever to connect these sacrifices with the
buto (page 32), which, if anything, may be taken for a totem. To connect the
offering of money, in the Banks' Islands, to a spirit who is never the ghost of
a man, nor at all the animating spirit of a natural object, with the sharing of
the common meal with the deceased, is much more difficult. If there be a
Melanesian sacrifice to a god it is to a *vui*. To offer money is apparently to
give what man most values, and what the spirit also loves.

CHAPTER IX.

A MELANESIAN native in danger, difficulty and distress, will naturally call upon the beings in whose power to help him he believes. He will upon occasion do this with exclamations which express his feelings. This from his point of view would not be prayer, because it has no formal character. There are also songs, incantations, charms, which have power in them by virtue of the names or words contained in them. These are not addressed directly to the beings whose power they bring to bear, and would not be called prayers. There are besides invocations which may be called prayers, that is formal addresses to beg for succour or for aid. But it is certainly very difficult, if not impossible, to find in any Melanesian language a word which directly translates the word prayer, so closely does the notion of efficacy cling to the form employed. Addresses which may be called prayers in the Solomon Islands are of course made to the beings to whom they look there for other than human aid, to the *tindalo*, ghosts now powerful of men deceased. The invocations used at sacrifices are prayers; and those may properly be so called which are used at sea. Thus at Florida to Daula, a *tindalo* generally known and connected with the frigate-bird: 'Do thou draw the canoe, that it may reach the land; speed my canoe, grandfather, that I may quickly reach the shore whither I am bound. Do thou, Daula, lighten the canoe, that it may quickly gain the land, and rise upon the shore.' They invoke also Bagea as their grandfather; the word *bagea* meaning shark, and any *tindalo* that has taken up its abode in a shark, or is represented by one, being called Bagea. They call also upon their immediate forefathers when in danger on the sea ; one on his grandfather, another on his father, another on some dead friend ; calling them with reverence, and saying, ' Save us on the deep, save us from the tempest, bring us to the shore.' Daula is invoked to aid in fishing : 'If thou art powerful, *mana*, O Daula, put a fish or two into this net and let them die there.' After a good catch he is praised : ' Powerful, *mana*, is the *tindalo* of the net.' They rub fishing-lines with the leaves appropriated to such a *tindalo*. In San Cristoval the *'ataro* ghosts are applied to for help in battle, in sickness, and for good crops; but *lihungai*, the word they use, conveys rather the notion of charm than of prayer; the formula is handed down from father to son, or is taught for a consideration. So at Saa a man who has no special connexion with a *lio'a* ghost will, in danger at sea, call on his father or grandfather ; but one who knows some particular *lio'a* uses some particular form of words he has learnt in which power over the elements resides, and when he has done that, calls on the man now dead who introduced him to the *lio'a* and taught him the incantation, and after that again upon his father and his grandfather.

The *tataro* of the Banks' Islands, which may be called a prayer, is strictly an invocation of the dead, and is no doubt so called because the form begins with the word *tataro*, which certainly is the *'ataro* of San Cristoval, that is a ghost of power. The Banks' islanders are clear that *tataro* is properly made only to the dead ; yet the spirits, *vui*, Qat and Marawa are addressed in the same way. A man in danger on the sea will call on deceased friends, particularly on one who has been in life a good sailor ; but if he only cries out as he might in common life that is no *tataro*, which must be a form of words. The use of *tataro* in Motlav is thus described. A man is sick, and the cause of his sickness is suggested to be an offence against some sacred place near which he remembers himself to have intruded. Then the man to whom the sacred place

belongs will, for payment, go and *tataro* for him there
morning and evening. He calls aloud the name of the sick man,
and listens for an answering sound, the cry of a kingfisher or
of some other bird ; if he hears a sound he calls 'Come back'
to the life or soul of the sick man, runs back to the house
where he lies, and cries 'He will live,' meaning that he brings
back the life. If it happens that on his way to the sacred
place a lizard runs up upon him, it is enough, he has the life
and goes back with it. If a man who has a stone is going to
it to offer, *oloolo*, upon it, and he sees a rat, crab, iguana, or
lizard on the way, he scatters a little loose money for it, and
says a *tataro* that he knows. When the oven is opened for a
meal, one of the men will break off a bit of food and throw it
against the side wall of the house with a *tataro*. In the same
way when water is poured into the oven to make the steam,
there is a *tataro* used against an enemy, or to get rain or
sunshine. Some Mota forms are as follows. On opening an
oven, when a leaf of cooked mallow is thrown for some dead
person : '*Tataro*—this is a lucky bit for your eating ; they
who have charmed your food, have clubbed you (as the case may
be), take hold of their hands, drag them away to hell, let them
be dead.' If after this the man at whom it was directed is
heard to have met with an accident, 'Oh ho !' says the other,
'my curse in eating has worked upon him, he is dead.' When
water is poured into the oven : '*Tataro*—pour it on the head
of him down there who has laid plots against me, has clubbed
me, has shot me, has stolen this thing of mine (as the case
may be), he shall die[1].' On making a libation of kava before
drinking : '*Tataro*—Grandfather! this is your lucky drop of
kava ; let boars come in to me ; let *rawe* come in to me; the
money I have spent let it come back to me, the food that is
gone let it come back hither to the house of you and me.'

---

[1] 'Prayer in Fiji generally concluded with malignant requests as to the
enemy. "Let us live, and let those that speak evil of us perish. Let the
enemy be clubbed, swept away, uttery destroyed, piled in heaps. Let their
teeth be broken. May they fall headlong into a pit. Let us live, and let our
enemies perish."'—Rev. L. Fison.

On starting on a voyage: '*Tataro*—Uncle! Father! plenty of boars for you, plenty of *rawe*, plenty of money; kava for your drinking, lucky food for your eating in the canoe; I pray you with this, look down upon me, let me go on a safe sea.' Or when the canoe labours with a heavy freight: 'Take off your burden from us, that we may speed on a safe sea.' Another was used over the oven in the *gamal* of the Suqe club, the hole in which the fire is made: 'Grandfather! may it be—Father! my Uncle! my Greatuncle! we two will go on with a hundred fathom of money of yours; look down upon us two, do not look unfavourably upon us two; let money abound to us two, boars, *rawe*, food; let our *suqe* go on to the end; let not our outrigger be broken; you sit and look after us two; let us two go on well, with no unfavourable looks upon us; let us two come straight on in the hole of us three, in the hot *suqe* hole of us three, let the *suqe* come forth and advance.' There is no difference between these and the invocations of the spirits, *vui*, Qat and Marawa, except that these latter which follow, not being addressed to the dead, are not properly *tataro*. These three were used at sea: 'Qate! you and Marawa, cover over with your hand the blow-hole from me, that I may come into a quiet landing-place; let it calm well down away from me. Let the canoe of you and me go up in a quiet landing-place.' 'Qate! Marawo! look down upon me, prepare the sea of you and me, that I may go on a safe sea. Beat down the head of the waves from me, let the tide rip sink down away from me, beat it down level that it may go down and roll away, and I may come into a quiet landing-place.' 'Qate! Marawo! may it be— let the canoe of you and me turn into a whale, a flying-fish, an eagle; let it leap on and on over the waves, let it go, let it pass out to my land.' In answer to such prayers as these it was supposed that Qat and Marawa would come and hold fast the mast and rigging of the canoe, preserve it from danger, and speed it on its course.

In the Northern New Hebrides, in Aurora, they use the same word *tataro* for a form of words used for example in a storm at sea, a spell that works by the supernatural power residing in the words and in the names of the spirits mentioned.   When in distress and danger they call to a dead father or friend, ' Take care of your canoe and mine,' it is a cry, not a *tataro*.   The word is also used in Whitsuntide and Lepers' Island, and with probably the same limited application in strict native usage.

CHAPTER X.

BEINGS of a more or less distinctly spiritual nature, who
at any rate never were men, have their place in the beliefs and
in the stories of the Banks' Islands and the New Hebrides
very much more than in the Solomon Islands. Koevasi,
already mentioned, in Florida and Kahausibware in San Cristoval belong to the latter group, and may well be supposed
to be the same personage under different names. Both were
never human, yet in some way originators of the human
race; both were female, both subjects of stories, not objects of
worship. Kahausibware was a Hi'ona, a being of superhuman character, dwelling on the mountain of Bauro, the
central mass of San Cristoval, in the time of the infancy
of the human race. She was a snake in outward form.
There was in the same place a woman, a human being, the
offspring in some way of Kahausibware. In those days all
the fruits of the earth grew without labour, and all was of the
best; it was Kahausibware who made men, pigs, and other
animals, cocoa-nuts, fruit-trees, and all the food with which the
island is now furnished, and death had not yet appeared. The
woman one day went to her work, and left her infant in the
house in charge of the spirit snake, who was so much annoyed
by the screaming of the child that she coiled herself round it
and strangled it. The mother came in while the folds of the
serpent's body were still wound round her child, and seizing
an axe she began to chop the snake to pieces. As she
chopped it asunder the parts came together again; but the

snake at last could bear it no longer, and cried out weeping,
'I go, and who will help you now?' She made her way
down to the sea accordingly, and her track became a water-
course. Leaving the island, she swam across first to Ugi, but
from thence she could see the Bauro mountain; she went on
further to Ulawa, and thence again to the south-east end of
Malanta, but even there in clear weather she could see her
former home. She crossed therefore to Marau, the south-east
part of Guadalcanar nearest to San Cristoval, where the view
of the mountain of Bauro is shut off by the nearer hills; there
she rests till the present day. Since her departure all things
in San Cristoval have deteriorated. Snakes upon the Bauro
mountain are venerated as the progeny or representatives of
Kahausibware; but they are simple snakes, and she was a
Hi'ona, or Figona.

In the Banks' Islands and in the Northern New Hebrides
the purely spiritual beings who are incorporeal are innumer-
able and unnamed. These are they whose representative form
is generally a stone, who haunt the places that are sacred
because of their presence, and who connect themselves with
certain snakes, owls, sharks, and other creatures. There is in
these things a medium of communication with them, and
they are powerful to assist those who can approach them, and
also to injure men, though they are not of a malignant nature.
They are certainly believed to have no body; yet it is
impossible for the natives to conceive of them as entirely
without form. Men, therefore, have declared that they have
seen something, indistinct, with no definite outline, grey like
dust, vanishing as soon as it was looked at, near a stone, and
this must have been a spirit, *vui, wui*. But the same word is
used to describe beings who are corporeal, and individually
known and named. The natives will deny that these have
bodies as men have, and assert that they are of the same
nature as those which are incorporeal; but yet in the stories
that are told about them they figure as men, though possessed
of powers which men can never have. Consistency can
hardly be expected; the native mind indeed aims high when

it conceives a being which lives and thinks and knows and
has power in nature, without a gross body or even form; but
it fails when it comes to deal with an individual being of such
a nature. Hence the stories represent a *vui* like a man with
larger powers; a native seeing some new and wonderful
foreign work will cry 'A vui made it!', and receiving home
a boy grown up in absence cries '*Me vui gai!* He's a vui to
be sure!'

It is remarkable again that of these superhuman beings
who are called *vui* or *wui* in the Banks' Islands and New
Hebrides, and whose actions are like those of men, there seem
to be two kinds or orders. Qat in the Banks' Islands stories
and Tagaro in the New Hebrides stories move like heroes or
demigods amidst a lesser folk of dwarfs and trolls as full of
mysterious magic power as they are, but comparatively rude
and easily deceived. These lingered in the islands when Qat
and his brothers and Tagaro and his brothers left them; they
have been seen of late in human form, smaller than the native
people, darker, and with long straight hair. Marawa, the
friend of Qat, was one of these. A man living in Vanua
Lava but a few years ago, named Manlepei, going to the
river side in early morning, saw a little man with long
hanging hair, and followed him up the valley in which the
river runs, till they came to a narrow gorge closed by a rock.
The *vui* rapped upon this with his hand and it opened to him;
and as Manlepei followed close behind, it shut again upon
them both. They were in a cave which was the vui's house.
He said that he was Marawa, and that he would appear again
to the man if he would go back to the village and bring him
money. Manlepei prospered ever after through Marawa's
aid, and he made no secret of the source of his prosperity; he
was always ready to receive money from his neighbours on
Marawa's behalf, and to procure for them a share in his good
will. It is not long either since a female *vui* with a child
was seen in Saddle Island, close to the house of a man who
had often found a fine yam laid for him on the seat beside
his door, and had observed that his money-bag was still full

after he had paid a debt. There was a woman living a few years ago in Mota whose father was a *vui*. Popular stories shewed how these beings were believed to be at hand in the affairs of men. A woman working in her garden heard a voice from the fruit of a gourd asking her for food ; when she pulled up a caladium or dug a yam another immediately came into its place ; but when she listened to another *vui* playing on his panpipe, the first in his jealousy conveyed away the garden and all. In these stories, and no doubt in common belief, there was a certain confusion between these spirits and ghosts of the departed.

Some *vui*, spiritual beings, yet in some way corporeal, figure strangely in the stories of Mota as *Nopitu*, and of Motlav, in another form of the same word, as *Dembit*. There is often a difficulty in understanding what is told about them, because the name Nopitu is given both to the spirit and to the person possessed by the spirit, who performs wonders by the power and in the name of the Nopitu who possesses him. Such a one would call himself Nopitu ; rather, speaking of himself, will say not ' I,' but ' we two,' meaning the Nopitu in him and himself, or ' we ' when he is possessed by many. He would dance at a festival, such as a *kolekole*, as no man not possessed by a Nopitu could dance. He would scratch himself, his arm or his head, and new money not yet strung would fall from his fingers ; Vetpepewu told me that he had seen money fall from a Nopitu at a *kolekole*—bags full. One would shake himself on a mat and unstrung money would pour down into it. He would take a cocoa-nut to drink, and the by-standers would hear money pouring out instead of the liquor, and rattling against his teeth, and he would spit it up upon the ground. Tursal has seen at Mota a woman vomit native money—a Nopitu possessed by such a spirit. To obtain the favour of the Nopitu men would offer, *oloolo*, as at a sacrifice, to the man possessed ; would give him a red yam and almonds ; he would eat the yam raw, and be heard crunching money with his teeth. If a young cocoa-nut was offered he would open the eye and drink, and then give it back full of money.

But a Nopitu would also manifest itself in a different manner. A party would be sitting round an evening fire, and one of them would hear a voice as if proceeding from his thigh, saying, 'Here am I, give me some food, I am hungry.' He would roast a little red yam, and when it was done fold it in the corner of the mat on which he was sitting. In a little while it would be gone, and then the Nopitu would begin to talk and sing in a voice so small and clear and sweet, that once heard it never could be forgotten; but it sang the ordinary Mota songs, while the men drummed an accompaniment for it. Then it would say, 'I am going;' they would call it, and it was gone. Then a woman would feel it come to her, and sit upon her knee; she would hear it cry 'Mother! Mother!' She would know it, and carry it in a mat upon her back like an infant. Sometimes a woman would hear a Nopitu say 'Mother, I am coming to you,' and she would feel the spirit entering into her, and it would be born afterwards as an ordinary child. Such a one, named Rongoloa, was not long ago still living at Motlav. The Nopitu, like other spirits, were the familiars only of those who knew them, and these were often women. If a man wished to know and become known to a Nopitu, he gave money to some woman who knew those spirits, and then one would come to him.

The place of Qat in the popular beliefs of the Banks' Islands was so high and so conspicuous that when the people first became known to Europeans it was supposed that he was their god, the supreme creator of men and pigs and food. It is certain that he was believed to have made things in another sense from that in which men could be said to make them. To the present day a mother chides a sleepy, fractious child, or one crying with hunger, with the words, 'Do you think you are going to die? Don't you know that Qat made you so?' If a pig comes indoors to sleep in bad weather, the man who drives it out says to it, 'Qat made you to stay outside.' These are not serious sayings; but it was believed that Qat had made some creatures and fixed the natural condition of

things in the world. The regular courses of the seasons are
ascribed to him, the calm months from September to December,
when the *un*, Palolo sea-worm, comes, the yearly blow, and the
high tide in the month *wotgoro*; but irregular rains, winds
and calms are put to the account of the men who could influence other *vui* spirits so as to produce them. The name of Qat
is given also to remarkable objects and effects in nature ; when
fish die in the sea from excessive heat of the sun, Qat is said
to have poisoned them ; a kind of fungus is his basket, a fungia
coral is his dish, the sulphur at the volcanic vents in Vanua
Lava is his sauce, a beam of light shining through the roof in
the dusty air is his spear; and the flying shadow of a solitary
cloud over the sea is the shadow of Qat. With all this it is
impossible to take Qat very seriously or to allow him divine
rank. He is certainly not the lord of spirits. He is the hero
of story-tellers, the ideal character of a good-natured people
who profoundly believe in magic and greatly admire adroitness
and success in the use of it ; Qat himself is good-natured,
only playfully mischievous, and thoroughly enjoys the exercise
of his wonderful powers[1]. When he is said to create he is
adding only to the furniture of the world in which he was
born, where there were already houses and canoes, weapons,
ornaments, products of cultivated gardens and of such arts of
life as the natives possessed when they were first visited
by Europeans. It is difficult for the story-tellers to keep him
distinct from ordinary men, though they always insist that
he was a *vui*; and though he certainly never was a man, the
people of the place where he was born in Vanua Lava, Alo
Sepere, claim him as their ancestor.

It would be in vain to look for a connected history of Qat
from his birth to his disappearance ; he is the central figure of
a cycle of stories which vary in different parts of the islands
of the Banks' group. All agree that he was born in Vanua

---

[1] One can hardly help observing the absence of obscenity and ferocity from
these stories. Obscene tales, or parts of tales, no doubt are told where they
are acceptable, but they do not make any considerable part of the commonly
repeated legend.

Lava, and that finally he departed from the world. There are no doubt many of his feats and adventures which the natives have kept to themselves. The story which follows is translated, with additions from other sources, from the Mota of the late native Deacon Edward Wogale, himself of the Sepere stock.

The Story of Qat. Qat was not without a beginning, but he had a mother whose name was Qatgoro (otherwise Iro Ul), and this mother was a stone that burst asunder and brought him forth. He had no father, and he was born on the road. He grew up and talked at once. He asked his mother what his name was, saying that if he had a father or an uncle on his mother's side, one of them would name him ; then he gave himself the name of Qat. He had brothers also. The first was Tangaro Gilagilala, Tangaro the Wise, who understood all things, and could instruct the rest ; the second was Tangaro Loloqong, Tangaro the Fool, who was ignorant of everything, and behaved like a fool ; the others were Tangaro Siria, Tangaro Nolas, Tangaro Nokalato, Tangaro Noav, Tangaro Nopatau, Tangaro Noau, Tangaro Nomatig, Tangaro Novunue, Tangaro Novlog ; eleven of them, all Tangaro, twelve in all with Qat. The names of the last nine are made up of the names of the leaves of trees and plants, Nettle-leaf, Bread-fruit-leaf, Bamboo-leaf, Cocoa-nut-leaf, Umbrella-palm-leaf, added to Tangaro, which is no doubt the same with the Tagaro of the New Hebrides and the Tangaroa of the Polynesians. These all grew up as soon as they were born, and they took up their abode in the village Alo Sepere, where their mother, turned into a stone, may yet be seen. There Qat began to make things, men, pigs, trees, rocks, as the fancy took him. But when he had made all sorts of things he still knew not how to make night, and the daytime was always light. Then said his brothers to him, ' Hallo! Qat, this is not at all pleasant, here is nothing but day; can't you do something for us?' Then, seeking what he could do with the daylight, he heard that there was night at Vava, in the Torres Islands ; so he took a pig and tied it, and

put it into his canoe, and sailed over to Vava, where he
bought night, *qong*, from I Qong, Night, who lived there.
Others say that he paddled to the foot of the sky, to buy
night from Night, and that Night blackened his eyebrows,
and showed him sleep that evening, and taught him in the
morning how to make the dawn.   Qat returned to his brothers
with the knowledge of night, and with a fowl and other
birds, to give notice of the time for the return of light.   So
he bade them prepare themselves bed-places ; and they platted
cocoa-nut fronds and spread them in the house.   Then for the
first time they saw the sun moving and sinking to the west,
and called out to Qat that it was crawling away.   'It will
soon be gone,' said he ; 'and if you see a change on the face of
the earth, that is night.'   Then he let go the night.   'What
is this coming out of the sea,' they cried, 'and covering the
sky?'   'That is night,' said he ; 'sit down on both sides of
the house, and when you feel something in your eyes, lie down
and be quiet.'   Presently it was dark, and their eyes began to
blink.   'Qat! Qat! what is this? shall we die?'   'Shut
your eyes,' said he ; 'this is it, go to sleep.'   When night had
lasted long enough the cock began to crow and the birds to
twitter ; Qat took a piece of red obsidian and cut the night
with it[1] ; the light over which the night had spread itself
shone forth again, and Qat's brothers awoke.   After this he
occupied himself again in making things.

According to the story told at Lakona, in Santa Maria, Qat
and Marawa (another *vui* who here corresponds to the Supwe
of Maewo and Araga) dwelt in their place at Matan, near to
the mountain Garat, where the volcanic fires still smoulder.
They two made men in this way.   Qat cut wood of dracæna-
trees into shape; he formed legs, arms, trunks, heads, and
added ears and eyes ; then he fitted part to part, and six days
he worked about it.   After this he fixed the time of six days
for them to come to life.   Three days he hid them away, and

---

[1] Hence the expressions, *o maran me teve*, the morning has cut, and *o mera
ti lamasag*, the dawn strikes upon the sky, *mera* being a common word
for red.

three days he worked to give them life. He brought them forth and set them up before his face; then he danced to them and saw that they moved a little; he beat the drum for them, and saw that they moved more than before. Thus he beguiled them into life, so that they could stand of themselves. Then he divided them, setting each male by himself and giving him a female, and he called the two husband and wife. Three women he made, and three men. But Marawa made his of another tree, the *tavisoviso*; he worked at them six days also, and set them up, and beat the drum for them, and gave them life as Qat had done for his. But when he saw them move he dug a pit, covered the bottom of it with cocoa-nut fronds, and buried his men and women in it for six days. Then when he scraped off the earth with his hands to view them, he found them all rotten and stinking; and this was the origin of death among men.

According to the story as told in Mota, Qat made men and pigs at first in the same form, but on his brothers remonstrating with him on the sameness of his creatures, he beat down the pigs to go on all fours and made men walk upright. Man was made of clay, the red clay from the marshy riverside at Vanua Lava. The first woman was Iro Vilgale. Qat took rods and rings of supple twigs and fashioned her as they make the tall hats for the *qatu*, binding on the rings to the rods, and covering all over with the spathes of sago-palms: hence her name from *vil* to bind, and *gale* to deceive. When all was finished he saw a smile, and then he knew that she was a living woman.

Qat had, however, a wife, a female *vui*, Iro Lei by name, but he had no children. His brothers, who had no wives of their own, envied him the possession of the beautiful Ro Lei, as well as of his excellent canoe, and were always conspiring to get both into their own hands. When his work of creation was completed, Qat proposed to his brothers that they should cut canoes for themselves, and they began to work, each choosing a different kind of tree. Qat cut down a large tree well suited for a canoe, and worked secretly every day, but made no

progress in his work; every day when he returned to work he
found the wood that he had chopped away replaced, and the
tree made solid again. At length one evening when he had
finished his day's work he lay down to watch, making himself
small, and covering himself with a large chip which he drew
away from the rest and hid. Presently he saw a little old
man with long white hair creep out of the ground and begin
to replace the chips, each in the place from which it had
been cut, till the tree trunk was almost whole again. But
there was one defective place to which the chip belonged
which Qat had hidden, and the old man began to search for it,
and Qat watched. After a while he saw it and advanced to
take it; but Qat leapt up from under it, lifting up his shell
axe to cut him down. But Marawa, the spider, another very
powerful *vui*, for this was he, entreated Qat, 'Ah, friend, don't
kill me, and I will make your canoe all right again;' and he
worked at it, and soon finished it with his nails [1]. When
all the canoes were finished, Qat bade his brothers launch
their own, and as each was launched he lifted his hand, and
one by one they sank. Then Qat and Marawa appeared in
the one that they had made, paddling swiftly about, to the
astonishment of the brothers, who had not known that Qat had
even begun to work. Having amused himself with their
mortification, he recovered their canoes for them in the night.
After this his brothers tried with many deceits to destroy Qat,
so that they might possess themselves of his wife and his
canoe. One day they took him to the hole of a land crab
under a stone, which they had already so prepared by digging
under it that it was ready to topple over upon him. Qat
crawled into the hole and began to dig for the crab; his
brothers tipped over the stone upon him, and, thinking him
crushed to death, ran off to seize Ro Lei and the canoe. But
Qat called on Marawa by name, 'Marawa! take me round about
to Ro Lei,' and by the time that his brothers reached the

[1] Hence, when iron was seen in the form of nails, it was called at Mota
Marawa's finger-nails, *pis Marawa*, and *pismarawa* is now a widely accepted
name for nails.

village, there was Qat to their astonishment sitting by the side
of his wife. On another occasion they cut half through the
bough of a fruit-tree, and persuaded Qat to go out for the nuts.
When he fell as the branch broke, and as they thought was
killed, Marawa again saved him ; and when they ran to seize
his wife, they found him lying with his head upon her lap.
Qat was himself always ready to play tricks on his brothers,
but not in malice. One moonlight night he induced them to
go and shoot flying foxes, and as they were going covered
himself with boards, and flew up into a pandanus-tree and hung
there like a bat. His brothers saw him, shot at him, and hit
him. He spat out blood upon the ground, and they, making
sure that he was wounded, mounted one after another into the
tree to take the bat. As each one shot and climbed after him
he flew off, and returned to hang again. When all had shot
and climbed up he flew home, took out the arrows which had
stuck into his covering of boards, and hung them up in the
gamal. When his brothers returned he asked them what sport
they had ; and when they told how they had shot and hit a
wonderful bat, he made them look at the arrows and judge
whose they were. Iro Lei took her part in these tricks. One
day when Qat and his brothers were sailing in their canoes
they saw a woman on a point of rock, who called each of them
as he came near to come and have some of her food. Each as
he drew near and saw that she was an old woman rejected her
offer ; but Qat came up and took her into his canoe. They
had rejected his much-coveted wife, for this was Ro Lei
in disguise.

Again they consulted how they might destroy him, and
determined to entrap him while snaring birds. They prepared
each one for himself his place in a nutmeg-tree, each in succession further and further from the village, and the tree for
Qat much further away than all. Then they took Qat out
and shewed him his place. Qat mounted into his tree, and as
soon as he was busy with his snares his brother nearest to
him descended from his own place, ran beneath the tree
where Qat was sitting, and said, ' My nutmeg, swell! ' The

nutmeg-tree instantly grew so large in the trunk that Qat's arms could never clasp it, and all its boughs and branches equally swelled out. But Qat did not at first discover this, because he was busy setting his snares ; his brother who had laid the spell upon the nutmeg-tree ran back, collecting the others as he went into the village ; they seized and carried off Ro Lei, dragged down the canoe into the sea, and paddled off at once. The island had already sunk out of their sight when they blew their shell trumpet to let Qat know that they were gone. When he heard it he knew what had happened, and would have followed them, but the size of the swelled branches of the nutmeg-tree made it impossible for him to descend ; he tried and tried in vain, and then lifted up his voice and wept. His friend Marawa, the Spider, heard his cries, and came to ask him what was the matter. ' I can't get down,' said he ; ' my brothers have played me this trick.' ' Down with you,' said Marawa, whose hair was exceedingly long and loose ; and he sent up his hair to Qat, who descended by it and ran into the village. There he found the rollers of his canoe alone remaining, and sought his wife in vain, for his brothers had taken off his wife and his canoe to be their own. Then Qat went inside his house, and took his cock's-tail plume, and his string of the smallest shell-money, his red earth, and his shell hatchet, and asked his mother for his banana fruit. ' They have plucked them all,' she answered, ' except these little ones at the end of the bunch.' ' Pluck them all off,' said Qat. Then he took a cocoa-nut-shell bottle and stowed all his things and his food within it, made himself small and took his seat within it, and bade his mother count three waves, and at the fourth small wave to throw it into the sea. So Qat floated on and on in the bottle till he came up to the canoe in which his brothers were, for they had not yet reached land. Then he floated along before the bow of the canoe, and where he drifted they were forced to follow. By-and-by he took one of his bananas and ate it, and threw the skin into the sea where the canoe would come along. His brothers saw it, and remarked that it was like those

bananas of Qat's that they had taken ; they enquired among
themselves who had been eating a banana, and when all denied,
Tangaro the Wise spoke out : ' You fellows,' said he, ' it is
Qat who has eaten this banana, and has thrown the skin of
it here for us, to give us notice that he is not dead, but that he
has escaped and is following us.' But the rest of them would
not listen to him, declaring that Qat was dead. The same
happened again when he threw out for them another banana
skin. After this they saw the bottle itself in which Qat was
floating, close up to the canoe, and one of them took it up,
thinking that it was a good cocoa-nut, but when he smelt it
and found the smell bad, he threw it away again. This they
did one after another, except Tangaro the Wise, who did not
happen to observe it. Then Qat floated quickly to the shore
of Maewo, and emerged from his bottle ; he colours his hair
with the red earth, binds his small shell-money round his
head, sticks his cock's-tail plume in his hair, takes his seat on
the top of a male pandanus-tree on the beach, and there he
sits and waits for his brothers to come to land who were still
in the canoe. Presently they came through the reef and up
to the shore, and then they looked up and saw him sitting
in the pandanus, and enquired one of another who it was
sitting up there. ' It is Qat,' said Tangaro the Wise ; but
his brothers argued that he could not have made his way
thither, seeing that he was already dead. ' That is Qat, and
no mistake,' said Tangaro the Wise ; for he knew better than
his brothers about this and all other things. So they brought
their canoe to land, but had no need to haul it up, for Qat
made the rocks to rise and bear it high and dry. Qat leaped
down upon them with his axe, and hewed the canoe to pieces
for them with this song,—' Chop, chop the canoe ; whose
canoe is it ? Marawa's canoe. My brothers tricked me about
twisting a string—swell nutmeg-tree—and draw the snare.
I had one canoe, my canoe slipped off from me.' So he
chopped the canoe to pieces before their face. After this he
made friends with them, and bade them live in harmony
together.

Another remarkable series of adventures were Qat's encounters with Qasavara. This was a *vui*, very strong, a great fighter, tyrant and cannibal, who dwelt in the island which was the home of Qat and his brothers. One day the brothers went to bathe, and found floating down the stream a fruit of the Tahitian chestnut, a *make*. The others took it up one after another and rejected it, thinking it was not good, but Qat took it and found it good, and gave it to his mother to cook. Each of the brothers as he returned from bathing went to their mother for food. She had nothing but Qat's *make*, and they each took a bit of it; Tangaro the Fool finished it. Qat sent them to get some more, and following up the stream down which this fruit had floated they came upon the tree. They climbed upon it to gather the chestnuts, and Tangaro the Fool dropped one upon the house of Qasavara, over which the branches hung. Out came the ogre in a rage, seized and killed the brothers, and put them in his food-chest. Qat waited five days, then took his bow and arrows and shell hatchet and went in search. Following the stream he found the tree, and divining what had happened, brought out Qasavara by dropping a *make* on his house. They fought, and Qat killed Qasavara; then, searching for his brothers, he found their bones in the food-chest. He revived them by blowing through a reed into their mouths, and bidding them, if they were his brothers, laugh. Another adventure not very consistent with this is thus narrated. Qasavara falling in with Qat and his brothers invited them to his village, and made a fire in his oven for them. When it was evening he told them that they were to sleep by themselves in his *gamal*; but they, knowing that they would be killed, were exceedingly afraid. Night fell and they were very sleepy, and Qat called them to come to bed. He rapped asunder with his knuckles one of the rafters of the *gamal*, and they all got inside and slept. In the middle of the night Qasavara and his men took clubs and bows and came to kill Qat's party, but not finding them in the sleeping places went back disappointed. At the approach of day the cock crew, and Qat awoke his brothers,

bidding them crawl out at once, lest they should be seen
leaving the rafter by daylight. So they came out; and
when it was clear day Qasavara and his men running to the
gamal found Qat and his brothers chatting together. 'Where
did you sleep?' asked they. All of them answered that they
had slept in the place appointed for them; but Tangaro the
Fool cried out, 'We slept in this rafter here,' to the great
indignation of his brothers. Qasavara's party again as the
night drew on took counsel how they might kill them in the
rafter; but that night Qat rapped a side post with his
knuckles, it opened and they slept within it. Qasavara's
party came in the night and smashed the rafter, found no
one there, and again retired. Next morning again they
came into the *gamal* and found Qat and his brothers sitting
unconcerned; and again Tangaro the Fool confessed they
had been sleeping in the side post. Next night again Qat
opened the great main post and they slept in it, and again
Qasavara came and smashed the side post, and found no one
there. Tangaro the Fool again made known their retreat,
though he had been warned and scolded by his brothers.
Qasavara now determined to try another course, and to kill
them as they were sitting at a feast; that night Qat opened
the ridge pole with a rap and they all slept in it. Knowing
what was intended, Qat made his preparations to save his
brothers by planting a casuarina-tree; and he gave them his
instructions what they were to do. 'When they are getting
the food ready,' he said, 'wash your hands with the salt-water
in the bamboo water-vessels till they are empty; and then
when they are looking for salt-water, and wanting some one
to go and fill the vessels, two of you are to offer to go; and
two are to go at once; and when you get some way off smash
the bamboo vessels on the ground, and climb up into the
casuarina-tree. All of you are to do this.' They all agreed,
and did as they were bid. Then, when the oven was all
covered in, Qasavara's men cried out 'Hallo! there is no salt-
water! who will fetch some?' 'We two,' said two of Qat's
brothers; and they went, and smashed the water-vessels and

climbed into the casuarina-tree. Qasavara's men waited for them till they were tired, and then asked some others to go; two more of Qat's brothers went, and smashed the vessels and climbed into the tree. So it went on till all his brothers were in the tree, and Qat alone was left beside the oven with Qasavara and his men. Then as they opened the oven Qat sat with a large handful of food-bags beside the oven, and as they were taking out the food Qasavara struck at Qat with his club and missed him. Qat leapt away from him to the other side of the oven, and taking up food from within it cried, 'This for my brother, this for my mate,' and stowed it in the bags. Qasavara leapt across after him, struck at him and missed him again; and Qat again jumped across, took up food with the same cry, and stowed it in his bags. So it went on till all the food in the oven was taken, and all the bags were full. Then Qat rose and ran to his brothers, and Qasavara after him, hitting at him with his club and missing him as he ran, chasing him till he reached his brothers. Then Qat jumped away from him into the tree, and Qasavara climbed after him. Qat's brothers were gathered together on the tree top, and Qat climbed to them, and there they sat still, for they could climb no higher. Then Qasavara climbed close to them, and stretched out his club at arm's length to strike them; but Qat cried out 'My casuarina, lengthen!' So the casuarina elongated itself between Qat's party and Qasavara, and left him far below. But Qasavara climbed after them again, and again came close to them; and again Qat cried, 'Lengthen, my casuarina!' and again the tree lengthening itself carried Qat and his brothers away from Qasavara. So it went on till the tree top reached the sky. Then said Qat, 'Bend down, my casuarina!' and the tree bent its top down to Tatgan, and they all one after another got down to the ground there, and Qat the last of them. And as he reached the ground he held fast on to the top of the casuarina and waited before letting it go; and Qasavara followed down after them and reached the end. Then cried Qat, 'Now I revenge myself.' 'Ah, Qat!' cried

Qasavara, 'do me no harm; take me kindly for one of your household, and I will work for you.' 'No, indeed,' said Qat, ' but I will revenge myself for the mischief you have done me.' So he let go the tip of the casuarina-tree, and the tree sprang back and flipped off Qasavara, and his head knocked against the sky, and he fell back upon the earth; and there he lay at length upon his face, and turned into a stone. And now they offer sacrifices at that stone for valour; if any one desires to be valiant and strong in fighting, he offers at that stone, which they say is Qasavara [1].

The stone apparently is not at Tatgan in Vanua Lava, where it should be; so they say it is in Gaua; but it is agreed that Qat and his brothers took up their abode at Tatgan. It was, however, from Gaua that the story makes Qat to have taken his departure from the world. Where now in the centre of that island is the great lake, the Tas, there was formerly a great plain covered with forest. Qat cut himself a large canoe there out of one of the largest trees. While making it he was often ridiculed by his brothers, and asked how he would ever get so large a canoe to the sea. He answered always that they would see by-and-by. When the canoe was finished he took inside it his wife and brothers, collected the living creatures of the island, even those so small as ants, and shut himself with them inside the canoe, to which he had made a covering. Then came a deluge of rain; the great hollow of the island became full of water, which burst through the surrounding hills where now descends the great waterfall of Gaua. The canoe tore a channel for itself out into the sea and disappeared. The people believed that the best of everything was taken from the islands when Qat so left them, and they looked forward to his return. When for the first time Bishop Patteson and his companions went ashore at Mota, some of the natives now living remember that it was said that Qat and his brothers were returned. Some years after that a small trading vessel ran

---

[1] As Qasavara fell from heaven the women in their fright held their hands above their heads, but the men held theirs before their breasts; consequently from that time forth men grow bald and the breasts of women protrude.

on the reef at Gaua, and was lost. The old people, seeing her
apparently standing in to the channel of the waterfall stream,
cried out that Qat was come again, and that his canoe knew
her own way home. It is likely now that the story will be
told of eight persons in the canoe ; but it is certain that the
story is older than any knowledge of Noah's ark among the
people.

It is very probable that Lata, who is said by the people of
Santa Cruz to have made men and animals, is regarded by
them as Qat was regarded by the people of the Banks'
Islands ; and Tinota is a *duka* of the same kind with Lata.
A story which is told of Natei, now the chief man at Nelua in
Santa Cruz, shews a belief also in such beings as the Banks'
islanders believed to dwell with them in their islands, and
called *vui*. The story is doubtless much older than Natei, as
the similar story of Manlepei in Vanua Lava was doubtless
told of some other man, and by some other man of himself,
long before his time. The present younger generation at
Santa Cruz seeing Natei a great man, and taking it of course
that his greatness came by supernatural assistance, tell this
story of him. When he was a young man, they say, he was
following the upward course of a narrow valley looking for
birds to make feather-money, and advanced far inland into the
forest. A person met him and asked him who he was, and he
answered that he was a man. To Natei's like enquiry the
same answer was made. This person then took him by a very
good path up the valley, which narrowed into a ravine. This
opened again into a space in which were good gardens and a
village. The people there enquired of Natei where he lived,
and promised him that they would visit him at Nelua in five
days ; then he returned. Five days after the people of Nelua
saw some people coming to their village, whom they took to
be men from some inland place, and enquiring for Natei. His
house was shewn to them and they entered it, and were never
seen again. When he arrived and went into his house he
found it hung round with feather-money brought to him by
his visitors. It was known then that these were not mere

men, and it was remembered that they had long, straight hair. After this people would give Natei money and other things to obtain the favour of his friends, with whom he still kept up communication, and from that time he has thriven and risen in the world.

The nearest of the Banks' Islands to the New Hebrides is Merlav, Star Island, and there Qat and his brothers are the subjects of the stories common in the rest of the group. The northernmost of the New Hebrides and nearest to Merlav is Maewo, Aurora, and there Qat, though not unknown, is not recognised as a spirit, but Tagaro takes his place. Qatu they said was a great man of old times, very high in the *suqe*, as men used to be and are no longer now. But Tagaro was a *wui*. Of any *wui* the belief in Maewo was that he had no bodily form; any old man there would so describe one. Yet the stories of Tagaro, who was a *wui*, deal with him as the stories of the Banks' Islands deal with Qat. Of the brothers of Tagaro nothing is to be told, but his companion was Suqe-matua, who in all things was contrary to him. Tagaro wanted everything to be good, and would have no pain or suffering; Suqe-matua would have all things bad. When Tagaro made things, he or Suqe-matua tossed them up into the air; what Tagaro caught is good for food, what he missed is worthless. Tagaro lived at Mambarambara, and particularly at Hombio, not far from Tanoriki. He was not born there, but there he lived, made his canoe, built his house and his *gamal*, and created and raised his food. His life was full of wonders; his cocoa-nuts increased as he ate them; dry nuts out of which he scooped the meat filled up again. Finally Tagaro became angry because some one stole his pig, and went off to Mamalu, no one knows where; he turned the island upside down, and went off eastwards in his canoe from the east coast of the island, taking with him the best of everything, and never to return. He put out the fire, but threw back a fire-stick; his shell trumpet lies on the beach in the form of a rock; Lepers' Island is his canoe. His place at Hombio is very sacred; his yams still remain there, and trail over a *gamal* called the *gamal*

dam, the yam *gamal*. There is also one *wui*, Gaviga, and some
say another, who rules over the dead ; but the multitude of the
purely spiritual, incorporeal beings that are called *wui* belong
to the sacred stones.   In Araga, Whitsuntide Island, immediately south of Maewo, Tagaro has ten brothers, besides Suqe,
who accompanies and thwarts him.   Tagaro came down from
heaven, made men and other things, and went back again to
heaven.   Suqe belonged to the earth ; his head was forked,
therefore he had two thoughts in it.   Whatever Tagaro did or
made was right, Suqe was always wrong ; he would have men
die only for five days ; he wanted to have six nights to one day ;
he planted the scooped meat of the yam, not the rind.   Tagaro
sent him to a place where is a bottomless chasm, somewhere
inland in Araga, where he rules over the ghosts of the dead.
Tagaro when on earth, though a *wui*, had a human form, with
superhuman power.   He made the plain country by treading
the ground with his feet; where he did not tread are the hills.
He had no wife or children of his own kind, but he became
the father of a boy on earth.   The boy kept asking his mother
who his father was, and was told that he was in heaven.   Then
he must needs go to heaven to see his father, and his mother
made him a bow and an arrow of an *ere*, a flowering reed.   He
shot up and hit the sky ; his *ere* turned into something like the
aerial root of a banyan, up which the two climbed to heaven.
There they found Tagaro sitting in a *salite*-tree, and fashioning
images of himself out of the fruit.   One of these he threw to
the boy, who took it to his mother.   She recognised the
features, and told the boy it was his father.   Tagaro consented
to go back with them ; but as he descended he cut the line
above them and below himself, and went back to heaven,
while they came down to Atambulu, the original seat of men
in that island.

There are also many *wui*, all connected with stones and
sacred places, whose names are only known to those who have
access to them.   These also may be seen, in rain or towards
nightfall, and they give men food.   When they appear they
have long hair, sometimes long nails, and wear an old *malo*

waist-cloth. But these appear to be confused with the wild mountain creatures in human form, of whom tales are told in all the islands; for one that Tapera saw not long ago was a Sarivanua of the hills, standing in the rain by a banyan-tree, with bananas in his hand. He was like a man with small legs; when spoken to he did not answer, and when struck he did not feel. The multitude of *wui*, whose stones and haunts are sacred, are unknown by name, and have no form of body.

In Omba, Lepers' Island, a spirit, *vui*, is thus defined: spirits are immortal; have bodies, but invisible; are like men, but do not eat and drink, and can be seen only by the dead. But there are' others 'also that appear in bodily shape. Some are known by name, of whom the most remarkable are Nggelevu, who presides over the dead, and Tagaro and his brothers or companions. Suqe is not known in all parts of the island; his place is perhaps supplied by Tagaro-lawua, who answers also to Tangaro-loloqong in the Banks' Island stories. It was Tagaro who made fruit-trees, food, pigs, and lastly men, and he is still invisibly active in human affairs, and therefore invoked in sickness and all difficulties. Tagaro-lawua, the Big, was a boaster and incapable; Tagaro-mbiti, the Little, was exceedingly knowing and powerful; if Tagaro is spoken of it is Tagaro-mbiti who is meant. As Qat is represented by Tagaro-mbiti, so Merambuto, also a *vui*, answers to Qasavara. He, like the other, tried to catch Tagaro's party by night and kill them, but Tagaro made them all sleep in a shell. Next morning Tagaro-lawua let out the secret, and Tagaro-mbiti made them sleep elsewhere. All the stones that are sacred are connected with Tagaro, though other spirits also are concerned; all charms have their power from the name of Tagaro in them. There are besides, as in the neighbouring islands, spiritual beings, *vui*, not of the same order as Tagaro. They are super-human in nature and in power, and they can be seen. There is a man still living who one day followed his two wives down to the beach, and noticed there that some cocoa-nuts had been stolen from a heap he had made. Following footsteps he

found two female *vui*, who said they were hungry. He
promised them food and brought it to them—four baskets-full.
One of the women was beautiful, the other full of sores.
They asked him which he would have, and he answered that
he would take them both. Thereupon each gave him a stone
full of *mana*, one to get him ten barrow-pigs, the other for ten
sows; and they promised always to help him to get pigs, that
he might mount to greatness in the Suqe. These women
were *vui*, whose power lay in pigs; nevertheless, to this day,
when the man's wives go down to the beach for their fishing,
they find fish caught and lying ready for them. It is well
worthy of notice that Merambuto and his fellows are represented
not only as to a certain extent mischievous and unfriendly, but
also easily deceived and ignorant. This appears clearly in the
story of Merambuto and Tagaro-mbiti in the tree, where
Merambuto did not know and dreaded as something unknown
the conch-shell trumpet, as a Motlav story also represents a
vui as afraid of the sound of a drum. On the side of Lepers'
Island which is nearest to Araga the story of Suqe is told, and
he is represented as always in the wrong, though he shares
the work of creation with Tagaro. They two made the land,
and the things upon it; when they made the trees the fruit
of Tagaro's was good for food, but Suqe's bitter; when they
made men, Tagaro said they should walk upright on two legs,
Suqe that they should go like pigs; Suqe wanted to have men
sleep in the trunks of sago-palms, Tagaro said that they
should work and dwell in houses; so they always disagreed,
and the word of Tagaro stood. It was Tagaro also who went
to Maewo and brought back night in a shell. When he let
it out and darkness crept over the sky, men wept and beat
their houses. Tagaro is represented also as the father of ten
sons, of whom Tagaro-mbiti, the Little, was the last, and
exceedingly small. His brothers went out to work, but he
stayed at home with a sore on his leg. They planted the
leaves of the edible caladium, the top shoot of the banana, the
vine of the yam; but when they were gone he took the crown
of the caladium, the suckers of the banana, the rind of the yam,

and planted them.   His brothers scolded him for idleness, not
knowing what he had done ; but when the season came round
and they had nothing to eat, he shewed them his garden full
of abundant food.   It was Tagaro also (but Qatu in the
Maewo story) who married the winged woman—a Banewono-
wono or Vinmara, Web-wing or Dove-skin—from heaven.   This
was not exactly a spirit, *vui,* but one of a party of women with
webbed wings like those of bats.   These women flew down
from heaven to bathe, and Tagaro watched them.   He saw
them take off their wings, stole one pair, and hid them at the
foot of the main pillar of his house.   He then returned and
found all fled but the wingless one, and he took her to his
house and presented her to his mother as his wife.   After
a time Tagaro took her to weed his garden, when the yams
were not yet ripe, and as she weeded and touched the yam
vines, ripe tubers came into her hand.   Tagaro's brothers
thought she was digging the yams before their time and
scolded her ; she went into the house and sat weeping at the
foot of the pillar, and as she wept her tears fell, and wearing
away the earth pattered down upon her wings.   She heard
the sound, took up her wings, and flew back to heaven.

Beings called Tavogivogi must be classed as spirits : they
are certainly not human beings, and correspond to the
mysterious snakes called *mae,* which in neighbouring islands
are believed to assume the form of men.   A Tavogivogi is
not thought ever to have the appearance of a snake ; one of
them appears in the form of a youth or woman, in order to
entice one of the opposite sex, and the young man or woman
who yields to the seduction dies.   There is no outward sign
of the real character of the Tavogivogi, but the test is to
ask the name of a tree, and a wrong answer will shew that
there is deceit.   Successful or not the Tavogivogi suddenly
disappears, 'like a bird,' but in the form of a bird or other
creature.   The young man goes home and sickens; he remembers the sudden disappearance, knows what has befallen
him, and never recovers.   The name means 'changeling,' from
the word, in the Banks' Islands *wog,* to change the form.

CHAPTER XI.

It is almost certain that idols find no place in the account which I now proceed to give of sacred places and objects as I am acquainted with them in Melanesia. It is true that the word is commonly enough used to describe any kind of image of native workmanship, whether there be really something of a sacred character attached to it, or none whatever. The people of San Cristoval, Ugi, and Ulawa were conspicuous for their fondness for carving and the skill with which they worked ; a man among them would amuse himself by shaping a soft stone or bit of wood into a figure of a man or bird, or fish, as well as in carving by way of decoration what he made for use. I have seen at Fagani (Ha'ani) in San Cristoval a remarkably clever group over the apex of a gable, which represented a man climbing up to shoot an opossum, and the animal looking down upon him from the top of the pole in the most natural attitude. This would hardly be taken for an idol, but is as much an idol as many figures which have found their way into museums as such. The canoe-houses, common halls, public-houses, called in those parts *oha*, were full of carvings in the constructive as well as decorative parts. Some of these, the posts for example which support the ridge-pole and purlins, are often figures of men, who would be loosely called ancestors by the principal people of the village, and these would be treated with respect ; sometimes food and betel-nuts would be seen laid before them. But these had no sacred character, further than that they were memorials of deceased great men, whose ghosts visiting their accustomed abodes would be pleased at marks of memory and affection, and irritated by disrespect. There was no notion of the ghost of the dead taking up his abode in the image, nor was the image supposed to have any supernatural efficacy in itself. In any *oha* in Malanta may be seen an image of a shark, a sword-fish, or a bonito, before which portions of food are placed; and these figures will be said to be fathers, grand-fathers, ancestors of those who thus respect them. These are indeed receptacles of the dead, not of their spirits, but of their mortal remains or relics; such cannot be called idols. Although too they sometimes make other images and give the names of the dead to them by way of remembrance, they do not pray or sacrifice at such images, nor are they thought holy. In Florida a rudely-shaped image of a man might often have been seen in a sacred place near a village or by the sea-shore, with cocoa-nuts tied to it or food laid at its feet; this would be a *tindalo*, an image representing some powerful man deceased; the food would be for him to eat; the image was sacred. That is to say, the image was a memorial of some *tindalo*, and was not thought to have power in itself, or to be inhabited by the ghost of the departed. Images representing a *tindalo* were also cut on the posts of the canoe-houses, mere memorials not much regarded, and approached without respect.

The stocks set up in Santa Cruz to represent the dead are the simplest of memorials. In the Banks' Islands tree-fern trunks cut into very rude figures of men were often seen— memorials made at funeral feasts, having really no sacred character at all. In the same islands the images carried about at the Suqe feasts, and afterwards set up in the eating-places proper to the rank they represent, may well be taken for idols by those who are not acquainted with their meaning; and so indeed may the figure, the *nule*, into which the post of a house is cut, the building of which is celebrated by a *kolekole*. In the New Hebrides, at Ambrym, images of the dead whose death-feasts are to be celebrated are very elabo-rately prepared, not with any attempt at representing the figure of the particular deceased, but in conventional form ; sometimes carved out of tree-fern trunks, sometimes fashioned with wickerwork and sago spathes, and painted and adorned. Some shut up from common view by bamboo screens may probably belong to secret societies. In the same island drums are set up for funeral feasts with fantastic faces cut upon them, and these remain as in a manner images of the deceased, taken by visitors for idols or devil-drums. In the neighbouring islands similar images are made.

Sacred places have almost always stones in them ; it is impossible to treat separately sacred places and sacred stones. But whereas some places are sacred because stones are there, the stones seen in other places have been taken there as part of the furniture of a sacred place. Some places also and stones may be said to have the origin of their sacredness in graves or relics of the dead, and so have had their character given them by men ; while others are sacred because the stones are there, the stones being sacred because associated with a spirit. It is well here to recall the distinction which seems so important between ghosts, the disembodied spirits of men deceased, and spirits, of another order from the souls of men, which have never been connected with a human body ; and to remember that, speaking generally, the religion of the Solomon Islands is concerned with ghosts, that of the Banks' Islands and New Hebrides with spirits.

The sacred places and objects of the Solomon Islands shall be first described ; and first of all those which belong to sepulture. In Florida a sacred place is called *vunuha*. These places are sometimes in the village, in which case they are fenced round lest they should be rashly trodden upon, sometimes in the garden-ground, sometimes in the bush. A *vunuha* is sacred to a *tindalo*, ghost of power, and sacrifices are offered to the *tindalo* in it. In some cases the *vunuha* is the burial-place of the man who has become *tindalo*, in others his relics have been translated there ; in some cases there is a shrine, and in some an image. There are generally if not always stones in such a sacred place ; some stone lying naturally there has struck the fancy of the man who began the cultus of the *tindalo*; he thinks it a likely place for the ghost to haunt, and other smaller stones, and shells called *peopeo*, are added.   When a *vunuha* has been established everything within it is sacred, *tambu*, and belongs to the *tindalo*.   If a tree growing in one were to fall across a path no one would step over it.   In entering a *vunuha* a man who knows the *tindalo* and sacrifices goes first, those who go with him treading in his footsteps; in going out no one will look back, lest his soul should stay behind.   No one would pass a *vunuha* when the sun was so low as to cast his shadow into it; the ghost would draw it from him.   If there were a shrine in a *vunuha*, only the sacrificer would enter it.   Within it were the weapons and other properties used by the object of worship when alive, some said to be of great antiquity[1].   The school-boys now have broken down the shrines and pelted the images, and the teachers have carried off the weapons.   Dikea, a chief at Ravu, had ten *vunuha* of his own, one close to a garden that he wanted to enlarge.   He was afraid to desecrate the sacred place himself lest the *tindalo* should do him mischief; he therefore sent for Gura and Kerekere, two young Christian teachers, to do it for him, because they would not be afraid. They took their scholars and went, the other boys not venturing near.   They found in the *vunuha* one large stone in its natural bed, with smaller stones, *peopeo* shells, and leaves of ginger round it, all of which they threw about.   The two *tindalo* to whom the place was sacred, Koli and Kukui, appeared afterwards in dreams to the heathen men, and threatened the desecrators; Dikea waited till it was clear that they were none the worse, and then enlarged his garden.

At Saa in Malanta all burying-places where common people are interred are so far sacred that no one will go there

---

[1] The *vunuha* of Pelosule at Olevuga contained an image thought to be of great antiquity; a club sent to me from it is of a form never now seen in use.   I have an adze taken from the *vunuha* of Murini at Belaga, on which the soot from sacrificial fires remains.   The Rev. A. Penny has some *tindalo* relics believed by the natives to be very ancient.

without due cause ; but those places where the remains of
people of rank are deposited, where sacrifices are offered, and
which may be called family sanctuaries, are regarded with
very great respect.   Some of these are very ancient, the *lio'a*,
or powerful ghost, who is worshipped there, being a remote
ancestor.   It sometimes happens that the man who has
offered the sacrifice in such a place dies without having fully
instructed his son in the proper chant of invocation with
which the *lio'a* ought to be approached.   The young man who
succeeds him is then afraid to go there often, and begins a
new place, taking some ashes from the old sacrificial fire-place
to start the new sanctuary.   It is not common in that part of
Malanta to build shrines for relics, but it is sometimes done
when the *oha*, canoe-house, is full.   Such shrines are common
in San Cristoval in the villages, and in the sacred places
where great men have been buried.   To trespass on these
sacred places would be always likely to rouse the anger of the
ghosts, some of whom besides are known to be of a malignant
disposition.   Such a one is Tapia, whose haunt is at the
mouth of a river near Ha'ani, and sacrifice to whom has
been already described.

   There are sacred places, however, in the Solomon Islands
which are not places of sepulture, though none probably the
sacredness of which does not depend on the presence of a
ghost.   In Florida the appearance of something wonderful
will cause any place to become a *vunuha*, the wonder being
an evidence of the ghostly presence.   For example, a man
planted in the bush near Olevuga some cocoa-nut and almond-
trees, and not long after died.   There then appeared among
the trees a white *kandora*, cuscus, a great rarity.   This was
assumed to be the appearance of the dead man, now a *tindalo*,
and was called by his name.   The place became a *vunuha* ; no
one would gather the cocoa-nuts and almonds till two young
Christian men of late have taken the sacred place and trees
for a garden.   Through this same part of the forest ran a
stream full of eels (which Olevuga people will not eat), among
them one so large that it was thought to be a *tindalo*, the

abode or representative of some one dead; no one would
bathe in that stream or drink from it, except one pool in its
course which for convenience was not considered sacred.   In
Boli also there was a sacred pool with a *tindalo* eel.   In
Bugotu, in Ysabel, is a pool which is the abode of a ghost of
ancient times, and into which scraps of any person's food are
thrown whom his enemies wish to charm.   If the food is
quickly devoured by the fish, which are abundant in the pool,
the man will die ; if otherwise, the man who knows the place
and the ghost reports that the *tindalo* is unwilling to do
harm, his own friendly intervention having been probably
paid for by the one who knows that his life is aimed at.   To
obtain good crops food is laid on stones in these sacred places,
and for success in fishing fragments of cooked fish ; money
also is laid upon them in small quantities, the proprietor, so
to speak, of the *vunuha*, who is acquainted with the ghost, in
each case offering on behalf of those who desire the good
offices of the *tindalo*.   Stones have thus a considerable place
among the sacred objects of the Solomon Islands, though not
a very conspicuous place, wherever their situation or something
in their appearance has associated them with some powerful
ghost.   Those that are in open places are so far treated with
reverence that no one will go too near them, much less sit or
tread upon them, while those in secret sacred places become
in a way altars for sacrifice.   But as in time the ghosts
become superseded by later successors, there remains but a
vague respectful feeling towards these stones.   Small sacred
stones acquire a redoubled efficacy as they take their place
among the relics and implements of the deceased man of
power, now himself become a ghost of power; his sacrifices
had been wont to reach the *tindalo* whose presence was
secured to him by that stone, and now the presumed attachment of his ghost to the same gives credit and efficacy to the
sacrifices offered near it or upon it to himself.

Living sacred objects in the Solomon Islands are chiefly
sharks, alligators, snakes, bonitos, and frigate-birds.   Snakes
which haunt a sacred place are themselves sacred, as belonging

to or serving as an embodiment of the ghost; there was one in Savo, to look upon which caused death.   In San Cristoval there is a special reverence for snakes as representatives of the spirit-snake Kahausibware.   Sharks are in all these islands very often thought to be the abode of ghosts, as men will before their death announce that they will appear as sharks, and afterwards any shark remarkable for size or colour which is observed to haunt a certain shore or rock is taken to be some one's ghost, and the name of the deceased is given to it. Such a one was Sautahimatawa at Ulawa, a dreaded man-eater to which offerings of porpoise teeth were made.   At Saa certain food, such as cocoa-nuts from certain trees, is reserved to feed such a ghost-shark, and there are certain men of whom it is known that after death they will be in sharks, and who therefore are allowed to eat such food in the sacred place.   Other men will join themselves to their company; a man will speak as with the voice of a shark -*lio'a* in him, and say, 'give me to eat of that food.'   Such a man, if it appears that he is really *saka*, possessed of supernatural power, will after his death be counted himself as a shark*lio'a*; but it is possible that he may fail.   In Saa and in Ulawa if a sacred shark had attempted to seize a man and he had escaped, the people would be so much afraid of the shark's anger that they would throw the man back into the sea to be drowned. These sharks also were thought to aid in catching the bonito, for taking which supernatural power was necessary.   There was not long ago near Makira in San Cristoval a shark very much respected, and fed with pig's flesh ; it was believed to have grown so large within a circle of rocks in which it lived that it was no longer able to pass through the narrow entrance.   Sharks are very commonly believed to be the abode of ghosts in Florida and Ysabel, and in Savo, where they are particularly numerous ; hence, though all sharks are not venerated, there is no living creature so commonly held sacred as a shark, and the *tindalo* of the shark, *bagea*, seem even to form a class of powerful supernatural beings.   In Savo not long ago Lodo had a shark that he used to feed, and to which he used

to sacrifice. He swam out to it with food, called it by its
name, and it came to him. He had received his association
with this shark from his ancestors, in the same way in which
the connexion with other ghosts on shore and the knowledge
of them was handed down from generation to generation; for
this shark was a *tindalo*. There was the same association
with alligators; a chief of Bugotu within my memory had
such a connexion with one, in which his son at Norfolk
Island thoroughly believed. There was a story current also
of an alligator which would come out of the sea and make
itself at home in the Florida village in which the man whose
ghost was in it had lived; it was called by his name, and
though there was one man who had a special connexion with
it and was said to own it, it was friendly with all, and would
let children ride upon its back; but it must be confessed that
though its existence was everywhere asserted, the village
where it could be seen was never ascertained. A lizard seen
to frequent a house after a death was taken to be the ghost
returning to his old home. The sacred character of the
frigate-bird is certain; the figure of it, however conventional,
is the most common ornament employed in the Solomon
Islands, and is even cut upon the hands of the Bugotu people;
the oath by its name of *daula* is solemn and binding in
Florida, where Daula is a *tindalo*; as the *kaula* it is sacred at
Ulawa; just as many ghosts take up their abode in sharks,
many also and powerful to aid at sea are those which abide in
these birds. The ginger-plant has a certain sacred character
in Florida and the neighbouring islands; and so have besides
the various objects, living and inanimate, from which the
respective divisions of the people refrain as a matter of
religious obligation.

In Santa Cruz there are stones about which stories are told
connecting them with the *duka*, whether ghosts or other
spirits, which are the objects of worship; and on these betel-
nuts are placed as offerings. Passing eastwards to the Banks'
Islands and the New Hebrides, a region is reached in which
religion concerns itself chiefly with spirits that never were

embodied in men, and in which therefore sacred places and objects are generally such because of their connexion with spirits. Burial-places are certainly held in respect, especially the graves of men of importance in their time; a certain sacredness attaches to all belonging to the dead; but it is to the presence of a spirit, *vui*, that the special quality of most sacred places and objects belongs. In the Banks' Islands the difference between a naturally sacred character and that which follows upon an authoritative separation from common uses is marked by the use of two words, *rongo* and *tapu* or *tambu*, (recognised in English as taboo,) corresponding with which in the New Hebrides are *sapuga* and *gogona*. A naturally sacred, *rongo, sapuga,* character is given by the presence of a spirit, or association with one; and in by far the greater number of instances it is found that a spirit is associated with a stone. In the Banks' Islands a man would happen upon a boulder of volcanic or coral rock, and would be struck with a belief that a spirit was connected with it. The stone then was *rongo*, and the place in which it lay was *rongo*; the man constituted himself the master of the sanctuary; it was his *marana* within which none but himself, or those brought in by him, could come. Some stones are known to all, and are of more common access. At Losalav in Saddle Island there is near the beach a natural ring of stones which has been from time immemorial a sacred place. The people call the ring a fence, the space within it a garden, and the stones that lie within yam, banana, kava pepper, and other roots and fruits commonly planted by them. These stones were used for offerings of money and sweet-smelling leaves, in the belief that the plants corresponding to the stones would flourish and abound. The character and influence of the spirit connected with any sacred stone was judged by the shape of the stone. If a man came upon a large stone with a number of small ones beneath it, lying like a sow among her litter, he was sure that to offer money upon it would bring him pigs. Such a stone is Ro Tortoros at Mota; another Merina found and named from its shape the Pig; his wealth in pigs resulted from his discovery.

A stone with little disks upon it, a block of ancient coral, was good to bring in money; any fanciful interpretation of a mark on a stone or of its shape was enough to give a character to the stone and to the spirit associated with it ; the stone would not have that mark or shape without a reason.   Many of these stones had names of their own, as above, as Puglava, ' much money out at interest,' at Luwai, and as more than one named simply Money.   The spirits belonging to these stones are nameless ; their connexion each with its own stone is not clearly defined ; the stone, they say, is not the body of the spirit, nor is the spirit like the soul of the stone, for a stone certainly has no soul ; they say that the spirit is at the stone, *o vui ape vatu,* or near the stone, and it is the spirit not the stone that acts.[1] Some of these stones have an ancient established sanctity; only the few who know how to approach the spirit will visit them for sacrifice, all others pass by with awe, and will not tread the sacred ground about them.   If by some mishap one finds that he has intruded on a sacred place, he hastens to engage the services of the man who knows the stone, to make an offering to the spirit, lest he should suffer from accident or sickness.   There are some stones that have a sinister reputation, as those near which an accident has happened; and there are some upon which it is dangerous for a man's shadow to fall ; it is well to make offerings upon these, to keep the spirit in good humour.   A stone which is good for success in fighting is also likely to do harm if not treated with due observance ; some stones have the name of *galaqar,* as though they would spring up like a trap upon the trespasser.   Large stones as they naturally lie have a high place among the sacred objects of the New Hebrides.   In Aurora some of these are believed to have been produced in the ancient time of universal darkness, *qong tali,* when, if two men were sitting at all apart, a stone would grow up out of the ground between them ; such are to be seen in the forest now, tall as a house and of strange shapes.   These have no names, as some others have had from ancient times ; the common name for all sacred stones is *matiu.* Some are *vui* who have turned into stones ; some in the sea are

men of old time turned into stones ; some never were anything
but stones, but have a *vui* connected with them ; some stones
above the waterfall are called the 'dwellers in the land,' the
native people of the stream, and these have all their names.
They have much spiritual power, for they are in a way the
bodily presentment of the spirits to whom the stream belongs.
When men go eel-fishing, they secure success by offering a bit
of the first they catch upon the appropriate stone.   Sacred
stones of all kinds have spiritual power, *mana*, as belonging to
spirits, in various degrees and to be obtained for various
purposes.   Some cause sickness of the soul, some have great
power in a charm, when a bit taken with a prayer is pounded
up with a fragment of the person's food to whom mischief is
to be wrought.   Sometimes in Aurora a stone is smeared with
red earth ; in Pentecost and Lepers' Island one is anointed
with the juice of a young cocoa-nut.   In the last-named
island no other offerings are made on stones ; men go to them
in the sacred places in the forest and call upon Tagaro.   There
are also stones in the sea near Lepers' Island which belong to
spirits, and which people in canoes will not approach lest
sharks should eat them.

   The stones hitherto referred to are stones as they naturally
lie, the presence of which, because of their association with a
spirit, makes the ground about them a holy place, a *tano rongo*,
or *ute sapuga*.   But small stones that could be carried about
had an active part in the native life of the Banks' Islands and
the New Hebrides.   The following are examples from the
Banks' group.   No garden was planted without stones buried
in the ground to ensure a crop.   A piece of Astræa coral-stone
water-worn on the beach often bears a surprising likeness to a
bread-fruit.   A man who should find one of these would try
its powers by laying it at the root of a tree of his own, and a
good crop would prove its connexion with a spirit good for
bread-fruit.   The happy owner would then for a consideration
take stones of less marked character from other men, and let
them lie near his, till the *mana* in his stone should be imparted
to theirs.   Likeness to other fruits or tubers would be the

ground of a belief in similar powers.   Stones were much used
by weather-doctors.   To make sunshine it might be enough
only to smear a standing stone with red earth ; but it was
very effectual to wind about a very round stone, a *vat loa*,
sunstone, with red braid, and stick it with owls' feathers to
represent rays, singing in a low voice the proper spell, and
then to hang it on some high tree, a banyan or a casuarina in
a sacred place.   The stone to represent the sun might also be
laid upon the ground with a circle of white rods radiating
from it for its beams.   There are stones of a remarkably long
shape called in the Banks' Islands *tamate gangan*, that is,
' eating ghost ' ; these are so powerful from the presence with
them of a ghost, not of a spirit, that if a man's shadow fall on
one it will draw out his soul from him, so that he will die.
Such stones therefore are set in a house to guard it ; any one
sent to his house by the owner in his absence will call out
his sender's name, lest the ghost should think he has bad
intentions and do him a mischief.   Other stones, also connected with ghosts, have such power that when the owner of
one puts it under his pillow and dreams of another man, that
man will die.   One who has such a stone is paid by an enemy
to destroy a man in this way, and ' dreams him to an end,' *ti
qore mot*.   These stones are exceptional as deriving their power
from the dead.   Some again are called *tangaroa*, a name no
doubt the same with that of the brothers of Qat.   These a
man would carry with him in a bag, or hang up in his house.
If one went into a house where these stones were hanging and
meddled with the property of the owner, and after a while an
accident were to befall him, it would be said that the *tangaroa*
had done it.   Others, called *tarunglea* and *varasurlea*, were
swung about in an invaded place to take away the courage of
the invaders.   Others were hung as amulets, *soasoa*, about a
man's neck to keep him safe in danger; others, again, would
straighten the aim and strengthen the arm to shoot.   There
were others that women would take with them to bed in
hopes of children.   The stones on which, or with reference to
which, sacrifices are made are by no means always such as

naturally lie *in situ,* but are small, and may be lost.   In such
a case the owner of the stone, knowing that ghosts have
hidden it, cries to them and they restore it; although such a
tano-oloolo is such by virtue of its association not with ghosts
but spirits.

Lepers' Island may supply examples of the use of portable
stones in the Northern New Hebrides.   Besides those which
lie naturally in the bush, in the *tauteu,* the sacred spot in
which Tagaro is invoked, there are sacred stones which have
more or less *mana,* and are effective for various purposes.   Some
are hung up in bags in the house.   Some of these are inherited from ancient times, and some are new; some are good
in fighting, some will produce food, some will cause a failure
of crop; none will cause a large general crop for the year
(that must be done by forms of words), and none are good for
fishing.   None are used in planting a garden; in that the
juice of a young cocoa-nut is sprinkled with charms upon the
ground, and the shells are set up at the sides.   Each stone has
its appropriate charm with Tagaro's name, sung over it when
it is put to use.

Though the superstitious regard for stones is so commonly
shewn, and the superstitious uses of them are so multifarious,
there are yet practices with regard to them in which the natives deny that there is any superstitious or religious meaning
and intent, natural as it is that an observer should suppose it.
Such is the practice of throwing stones upon a heap by the
way-side.   Such a heap is to be seen at Valuwa in Saddle
Island; each travelling stranger as he arrives casts his stone
upon it.   The natives declare that their notion is that days
accumulate like stones; a man as he adds his stone to the
heap 'puts his day upon it.'   At Pun in the same island is a
heap of fruits of various trees; a stranger as he comes gathers
any fruit by the wayside and adds it to the heap.   In each
case it is a custom of the place; the people there like it to be
kept up, because the heaps shew how many visitors they have.
Between Valuwa and Motlav the path runs between two large
stones: travellers going from Motlav to Valuwa kick the

stone to the right as they pass, and say, 'Let Valuwa be near
and Motlav far;' travellers to Motlav kick the other stone
and say, 'Let Motlav be near and Valuwa afar.' This again
is an old custom, not seriously thought of. Another custom
common to the Banks' and Solomon Islands is that of throwing
sticks, leaves, or stones upon a heap at a place of steep descent,
or where a difficult path begins. They 'throw away their
fatigue;' they certainly do not acknowledge that they make
a prayer or offering [1].

Streams, or rather pools in streams, are sacred in the Banks'
Islands by reason of the presence of a spirit. There is at
Valuwa a deep hole into which no one dares to look; if the
reflection of a man's face should fall upon the surface of the
water he would die; the spirit would lay hold upon his life by
means of it. Trees are sacred in a sacred place; a banyan
often harbours in the labyrinth of its stems and roots a sacred
snake, that is, a spirit, and is therefore itself sacred. There
are, however, two trees which have a certain inherent sacredness
of their own, the casuarina, *aru*, and the cycas, *mele*. Nothing
can be more weird and ghostly than an aged casuarina standing
alone on a wind-beaten beach or rising on a lofty cliff, with
bare grey stem and shadowless foliage, never without a voice
whispering in a calm or shrieking in a breeze. The presence
of one of these trees gives a certain sanctity and awfulness to
a place; hence to translate the word 'sanctuary' the best

---

[1] Many years ago I observed beside a path in a wood in Norfolk Island a
little heap of sticks evidently thrown there by Melanesian boys passing on their
way to fish at the foot of steep cliffs of difficult descent. I enquired of my
companions, who smiled and did not answer. Long after, having read Mr.
Forbes' Naturalist's Wanderings in the Eastern Archipelago, I put the question
again to boys from the Banks' Islands and from Florida. Both gave the same
account, that it was done to ensure a safe descent in that place, and that it was
common in their islands; both declared that there was no thought of sacrifice
or offering, and no prayer, only, if anything was said, the words 'There goes
my fatigue.' Mr. Forbes mentions a similar practice twice, once in Sumatra
(p. 166), where the porters placed handfuls of leaves on a stone and prayed for
a dry day and good luck; and again in Timor (p. 481), where at the commence-
ment of a steep and precipitous descent the natives laid leaves and twigs on a
mound 'to ensure a safe descent.'

Mota word is *tano-aruaru*, place of casuarinas. The cycas is also sacred, *rongo*, but it is cut down without hesitation by the natives if it be in the way. Crotons and dracænas have a certain sacredness in connexion with the dead. In Araga, Pentecost Island, there is a strange belief that the cycas-tree turns into a young man or woman, like the snake to be here-after mentioned; only the ear remains unchanged, it shews a leaflet of the tree.

The living creatures which are most commonly held sacred in the Banks' Islands and New Hebrides are sharks and snakes; all kingfishers have at least something of a sacred character, and some owls, crabs, lizards, eels, and such things as haunt a place sacred because of the presence of a spirit. In the Banks' Islands a shark may be a *tangaroa*, a sort of familiar spirit, or the abode of one. Some years ago Manurwar, son of Mala, the chief man in Vanua Lava, had such a shark, for which he had given money to a Maewo man to send it to him. It was very tame, and would come up to him when he went down to the beach at Nawono, and follow along in the surf as he walked along the shore. Tursal, my informant, had himself seen it do this. This corresponds with what has been above related of Lodo and his shark at Savo; and the difference is instructive that in the Banks' Islands the shark was a spirit and in the Solomon Islands it was a ghost. In the New Hebrides some men have the power, as the natives believe, of changing themselves into sharks, as may be seen in the story of Tarkeke. A great deal of superstition is con-nected with snakes, not only because one is sure to be seen about a sacred place, but because the reptile is often thought to be otherwise connected with a *vui*, spirit, to have a spirit near it. In Mota there are no land-snakes; in the other islands of the Banks' group some of enormous size are said to live in banyan-trees, and are held sacred. At Valuwa there are snakes which strangers are not allowed to see, lest some misfortune should follow. Ordinary snakes are killed. Those that are held sacred are not fed or worshipped, but such as are the familiars of individuals who know them receive sacrifices.

In the New Hebrides snakes are perhaps more regarded than in the Banks' Islands. A native of Pentecost Island, if he sees one in a sacred place or in a house, will think that there is some reason for its appearing to him; he will pour over himself the juice of a young cocoa-nut, and ever afterwards expect to find the world go well with him through the influence of the spirit, or it may be of the ghost, associated with the reptile. In Lepers' Island if a snake haunts a man's house, more particularly if it be a great man's house, they are persuaded that it is a spirit; it is *gogona*, not to be lightly approached; it brings good luck to the house, and makes the owner rise in the *huqe* society. The house itself is treated with respect; no one will throw a stone at it, or mount upon it; the snake would resent such disrespect and make the offender ill.

There is an amphibious sea-snake marked with bands of dark and light colour, which in the Banks' Islands and New Hebrides is always more or less dreaded whenever it is seen. In these islands it is generally called *mae*, and it is this kind of snake which becomes the familiar spirit of those who have, or profess to have, intercourse with it. In Araga, Pentecost, every *mae* is believed to have the supernatural power of *mana*; one will do harm to men by taking away bits of their food into a sacred place, upon which their lips will swell and their bodies break out with ulcers. Some men turn into these snakes, and these snakes again turn into men. A *mae* does not behave like an ordinary snake; it shews that it is something different, for example, by washing its young. In a certain *gamal*, clubhouse, in Araga, is a hollow piece of the wood of a certain tree they call *bugo*, in which is water. In the night a mother *mae* used to come and wash her young one in this water; the people sleeping there used to hear it cry and knew what it was. They made a pipe to imitate the cry exactly, and use it now. The belief is most strong in all these islands that this snake turns itself into a young man or woman, generally into a young woman, to tempt one of the opposite sex; to yield to the temptation causes death.

It is possible to discover the deceit, but the discovery is
often made too late. In Araga the changed *mae* may be
known by the skin under the neck, which remains unchanged.
It was only lately that a youth died at Vathuqe in that
island who had been enticed by a changeling girl ; he saw
her neck and came back and told his people ; they tried the
proper remedy of smoke in vain. There is another test used
in that island ; the suspected temptress is induced to sit upon
a nettle-tree, and is convicted by her ignorance of its character.
In the Banks' Islands a young man, as one has related his
experience to myself, coming back from his fishing on the
rocks towards sunset, will see a girl with her head bedecked
with flowers beckoning to him from the slope of the cliff up
which his path is leading him ; he recognizes the countenance
of some girl of his own or a neighbouring village ; he stands
and hesitates, and thinks she must be a *mae*; he looks more
closely, and observes that her elbows and knees bend the
wrong way; this reveals her true character, and he flies. If
a young man can strike the temptress with a dracæna leaf she
turns into her own shape and glides away a snake. At Gaua,
Santa Maria, a man met one of these standing or variegated
snakes, as they call them, *mae tiratira, valeleas,* on the beach
at night in the form of a woman of the place. Seeing by her
reversed joints what she was, he offered to go to the village
and bring her money. When he returned he found her waiting for him in her proper form as a *mae;* he scattered money
upon her back, and she went off with it into the sea. More
lately in the same place a young man just returned from
'labour' in Queensland, saw one of these in the form of a
young married woman of his village. She turned into the
stalk of a creeper, as in that island it is believed that these
creatures do. It is believed also that if the man can cut the
creeper short he will live ; this young man accordingly broke
this vine off short and got safe home. But since that time
there has been something in the night disturbing those who
sleep in the same club-house with him, and he has confessed
that it is this snake-woman who comes to him in the night ;

and all believe him. Sometimes a young man will run home at
night and lose his senses ; they are sure that he has been with
a *mae*. Sometimes one will come in and lie down and sicken ;
they press him, and he confesses what he has done and seen,
and then he dies. Nothing seems to be more fixed in the
minds of natives, even those who have some education, than
the persuasion that all this is true.

The sacred character of the kingfisher is remarkable, and
the reason of it hard to find. In San Cristoval a kingfisher
pecks the head of the lately separated soul which has not yet
realized its condition, and it sinks into a ghost ; the natives
therefore kill it, but young ones spring up from the blood of
every one they kill. In the Banks' Islands every kingfisher,
sigo, is sacred, *rongo* ; a spirit is connected with it; not one is
ever killed or eaten. It is a singular thing that they make
halcyon days ; it is the name of the kingfisher that carries the
magic power in the charm for sunshine, for the *sigo* is thought
to control storms and rain, and the charm calls on it to eat
the rising waves and make a calm. They declare that there
are kingfishers at sea as well as on land, some of a species only
seen at sea away from land. If a man going out on a journey
hears a kingfisher cry, he thinks it is angry and forbids his
going ; he therefore sings a charm : ' *Tagar we me-e, nelehet
ni van barbar, ne lee we ni ver gor nangek me-e !* Good luck to
me, let mischief pass beside me, let good hap come round
before my face [1] !'

---

[1] In prose Mota ' *Togara wia ma, o lea we tatas ni van parapara, o lea we
wia ni viro goro nanagok ma.*'

CHAPTER XII.

MAGIC.

THAT invisible power which is believed by the natives to cause all such effects as transcend their conception of the regular course of nature, and to reside in spiritual beings, whether in the spiritual part of living men or in the ghosts of the dead, being imparted by them to their names and to various things that belong to them, such as stones, snakes, and indeed objects of all sorts, is that generally known as *mana*. Without some understanding of this it is impossible to understand the religious beliefs and practices of the Melanesians; and this again is the active force in all they do and believe to be done in magic, white or black. By means of this men are able to control or direct the forces of nature, to make rain or sunshine, wind or calm, to cause sickness or remove it, to know what is far off in time and space, to bring good luck and prosperity, or to blast and curse. No man, however, has this power of his own ; all that he does is done by the aid of personal beings, ghosts or spirits; he cannot be said, as a spirit can, to be *mana* himself, using the word to express a quality; he can be said to have *mana*, it may be said to be with him, the word being used as a substantive. In the New Hebrides, the Banks' Islands, the Solomon Islands about Florida, as in New Zealand and many of the Pacific Islands, the word in use is *mana*. In Santa Cruz a different word, *malete*, is used, which bears however the same meaning. At Saa in Malanta all persons and things in which this supernatural power resides are said to be *saka*, that is, hot. Ghosts that are powerful are *saka* ; a man who has knowledge of the things which have spiritual power is himself *saka* ; one who knows a charm which is *saka* mutters it over water, *saru'e*, and makes the water 'hot,' *ha'asaka*. The people of Mala Masiki, the lesser part of the island, which is cut in two not far from its south-eastern end by a narrow channel, think that the men of the larger part, Mala Paina, are very *saka*. If one of these visiting the Saa people points with his finger, *suisui*, there is danger of death or calamity; if one of them spits on a man he dies at once. By whatever name it is called, it is the belief in this super-natural power, and in the efficacy of the various means by which spirits and ghosts can be induced to exercise it for the benefit of men, that is the foundation of the rites and practices which can be called religious ; and it is from the same belief that everything which may be called Magic and Witchcraft draws its origin. Wizards, doctors, weather-mongers, prophets, diviners, dreamers, all alike, everywhere in the islands, work by this power. There are many of these who may be said to exercise their art as a profession ; they get their property and influence in this way. Every considerable village or settle-ment is sure to have some one who can control the weather and the waves, some one who knows how to treat sickness, some one who can work mischief with various charms. There may be one whose skill extends to all these branches ; but generally one man knows how to do one thing and one another. This various knowledge is handed down from father to son, from uncle to sister's son, in the same way as is the knowledge of the rites and methods of sacrifice and prayer ; and very often the same man who knows the sacrifice knows also the making of the weather, and of charms for many purposes besides. But as there is no order of priests, there is also no order of magicians or medicine-men. Almost every man of considera-tion knows how to approach some ghost or spirit, and has some secret of occult practices. Knowledge of either kind can be bought, if the possessor chooses to impart it to any other than the heirs of whatever he has besides.

There is no doubt that those who exercise these arts really

believe in the power of them as much as the people on whose
behalf they exercise them.   In some cases there is conscious
deceit, such as has been many times confessed by those who
have become Christians.   A young woman of my acquaintance
in the Banks' Islands had a reputation for power of healing
toothache by a charm which had been taught her by an
aged relative deceased.   She would lay a certain leaf rolled
up with certain muttered words upon the part inflamed ; and
when in course of time the pain subsided, she would take out
and unfold the leaf, and shew within it the little white maggot
that was the cause of the trouble.   When Christian teaching
began in the island she made no difficulty about disclosing
the secret, and all laughed over it together.   It is likely
enough also that a weather-doctor observed for himself, and
was taught by his predecessor to observe, the signs of change
and steadiness in weather, and brought his charms to work or
kept them back according to his observations.   But the means
he used seemed to him to be so naturally effective, and had
been so often followed by the results at which they were
aimed, that he seriously believed in them ; and if sometimes
they failed conspicuously, as when at Ysabel the weather-
doctor's own house was blown down by a storm on the very
day on which he had warranted a calm, there was also the explanation that another counter-charm had been at work and
had been stronger.   Such a supposition tended to confirm
much more than to weaken the belief in the power of weather-
doctors.   It is not only in Melanesian islands that whatever
confirms a belief is accepted and whatever makes against it is
not weighed.   Those who practised the various kinds of magic
did believe very much in their own art.

Though those who practise these various arts cannot be
separated into various classes or orders, or even regarded as
an order by themselves, inasmuch as they are mixed among
the population, and practise as they know some more some
fewer arts, it will be almost necessary to classify their
practices.   These may be arranged under the heads of Sickness, Weather, Witchcraft, Dreams, Prophecy and Divination,

Ordeals, Poison, Curses. In all these whatever is done is believed to be effected by the *mana* of spirits and ghosts, acting through various media, and brought to bear by secret forms of words to which the power to work is given by the names of the spirits or ghosts, or of the living or lifeless things to which this mysterious influence is attached.

(1) *Sickness.* Any sickness that is serious is believed to be brought about by ghosts or spirits; common complaints such as fever and ague are taken as coming in the course of nature. To say that savages are never ill without supposing a super-natural cause is not true of Melanesians; they make up their minds as the sickness comes whether it is natural or not, and the more important the individual who is sick, the more likely his sickness is to be ascribed to the anger of a ghost whom he has offended, or to witchcraft. No great man would like to be told that he was ill by natural weakness or decay. The sickness is almost always believed to be caused by a ghost, not by a spirit. It happens, indeed, as in the New Hebrides, where spirits are the chief objects of religious regard, that a man knows that he has trespassed on a sacred place belonging to some spirit, or has an ill-wisher who has a spirit for a helper, and supposes therefore when he is ill that a spirit has brought his sickness on him. But generally it is to the ghosts of the dead that sickness is ascribed in the eastern islands as well as in the western; recourse is had to them for aid in causing and removing sickness; and ghosts are believed to inflict sickness not only because some offence, such as a trespass, has been committed against them, or because one familiar with them has sought their aid with sacrifice and spells, but because there is a certain malignity in the feeling of all ghosts towards the living, who offend them by being alive. All human powers which are not merely bodily are believed to be enhanced by death; the ghost therefore of an ill-conditioned powerful man is naturally thought ready to use his increased powers of mischief.

Thus in Florida it is a *tindalo*, that is, a ghost of power, that causes illness; it is a matter of conjecture which of the

known *tindalos* it may be. Sometimes a person has reason to
think, or fancies, that he has offended his dead father, uncle,
or brother. In that case no special intercessor is required;
the patient himself or one of the family will sacrifice, and beg
the *tindalo* to take the sickness away; it is a family affair.
Sometimes a sick man thinks it is his own familiar *tindalo*,
and leaves his house to avoid him. If the cause of sickness is
a matter of conjecture, a *mane kisu*, one who understands these
things, a doctor, is called in. He will say that he knows the
offended ghost ; if it be a child he will say that it has trod in
the sacred place, *vunuha*, of some *tindalo* whom he calls his own ;
or else the parents will guess or enquire where the child has
been, and will send for the *mane kisu* who has influence with
the *tindalo* of that place. The doctor called in will bind upon
the patient the leaves belonging to his *tindalo*, will chew
ginger and blow into the patient's ears and on that part of the
skull which is soft in infants, will call on the name of the
tindalo, and beg him to remove the sickness. When he makes
his request, speaking in a low voice, he is said to *kokoe
liulivuti*, to speak, as the word is now used, in prayer. If the
sickness continues, another *tindalo* or another *mane kisu* is tried.
If no conjecture can be made as to the ghost probably offended,
any *mane kisu*, for a fee in money, will undertake to get his
own *tindalo*, who must know, to intercede with the one who is
doing the mischief. In some cases it may be a likely guess
that some one who has ill-will towards the sufferer has set his
tindalo to afflict, as they say to eat, the patient ; he then may
take money to call off the eating ghost. If he will not do this,
another more powerful *tindalo* may be engaged through
another *mane kisu*, who will prevail over the original assailant
and drive him off. While these remedies are being tried the
patient either recovers or dies ; if he recovers, the doctor under
whose treatment he began to mend has the credit and good
payment ; if he dies, the power of the *tindalo* that has prevailed
throughout is established. There is also mixed with this
treatment something like the use of medicine, the effect of
which, however, is always supposed to depend upon the *tindalo*

engaged.   The *mane kisu* knows certain herbs, and warms them
in a cocoa-nut shell over the fire; the steam applied to the
patient drives away the pain or the disease.   For cough
an infusion is drunk, the leaves being thrown away.   The
doctors also practise massage, kneading, squeezing, and rubbing
the body and limbs of the patient.   In Ysabel (and no doubt
also in Florida) the doctor called in will discover the *tindatho*
who causes the complaint he has to treat, by suspending a
stone or heavy ornament at the end of a string which he holds
in his hand, and calling over the names of the lately deceased;
when the name of him who causes the disease is called the
stone swings in answer.   Then it remains to ask what shall be
given to appease the anger of the ghost—a mash of yams,
a fish, a pig, a man.   The answer is given in the same way;
whatever is desired is offered on the dead man's grave, and the
sickness goes.

In Wango in San Cristoval the natives not long ago believed
that the ghosts, there called *'adaro*, actually fought with one
another over the sick with spears.   A man would have a
grudge against another, and pay a wizard to bring an *'adaro* to
'eat' him, to do him mischief.   It would become known that
he had given a pig, as it might be, to that wizard, and the
man whose life was aimed at, or his friends, would go to
another wizard, and by a larger fee secure as they hoped a
stronger *'adaro* for their side.   The two ghosts would fight it
out, or probably more than one would be engaged on either
side; the man would sicken, die, or keep his health, according
to the issue of the unseen battle.   Ghosts that haunt the sea
are believed to shoot men on the reefs or in canoes with fish
darted at them invisibly; or if, as often happens, a flying-fish
or gar-fish springs from the waves and strikes a man, they say
that an *'adaro* shoots it; it is no common fish, the man will die.
Sick persons are commonly treated with ginger and other
roots and leaves, and with water over which a charm has been
muttered to give it healing power from an *'adaro*.

In Santa Cruz the cause of sickness is an offended *duka*,
ghost or spirit, and the doctor called in is a *mendeka*, a man

with whom is the *malete*, which corresponds to the more
common *mana*, and who has a *duka* belonging to himself; for
example, at Neula, where Neobla is the *duka* in vogue, they
always send for Neobla's *mendeka*.   The doctor comes and sits
by the sick person, expecting the coming of the *duka* to him.
Presently he cries with a loud voice that he is come, and then
he gives the reason, supplied him by the *duka*, why the man
is sick, and directs what satisfaction is to be made.   The
doctor always receives a fee.   If the patient dies, the reason

MAN FISHING SHOT BY A SEA-GHOST.   NATIVE DRAWING.

given is that some other *duka* with whom the doctor is not on
good terms has been at work; if he recovers he gives a pig
for the *duka*, and a bit of it is put before the stock which
represents him.   Sometimes an offended *duka* will shoot a
man, and the *mendeka* will extract the arrow-head, working it
down from above into the sick man's foot with sweet herbs
and cocoa-nut juice, singing in a low voice and muttering his
charms, and finally bringing out a splinter of tree-fern wood
from the sole.   Sometimes very bitter juice squeezed out of
certain leaves is given to the patient to drink, sometimes the

treatment of a local pain is to squeeze leaves and herbs upon the part; but it is the *malete*, and not the natural property of these medicines, that works the cure.

In the Banks' Islands the *gismana* practised the same arts with his brethren of the west [1]. He worked the cause of pain and disease downwards, and extracted it; he stroked the seat of pain and spat; he sucked out or bit out from the seat of pain a fragment of wood, bone, or leaf; for swellings he chewed certain herbs and leaves and blew, *pupsag*, upon the place; he used fomentations and poultices of mallow leaves, for example, with some knowledge of the healing and soothing properties in them; he gave the patient to drink water from a hollow in a sacred stone, or water in which stones full of *mana* for this purpose had been laid, from which probably European medicine came to be called *pei mana*; and all was done by virtue of the *mana* conveyed in the charms sung over the remedy employed, songs which were themselves called *mana*, or in the muttered words, *wosag*, which took the disease away. Women had a share in the practice of this art; some of them knew the charms by which the soul of a sick child which a ghost was drawing away could be recalled, and the ghost driven off; the woman blowing on the child's eyes and calling the name of the attacking ghost. The *gismana* by no means confined himself to the care of the sick, all ways of working by means of *mana* were in his line of practice; women, however, did not

---

[1] 'One of our native mission agents in Fiji assured me very earnestly that he had the power of expelling disease-causing spirits, and he gave me a minute description of his treatment. He passed his hands over the patient's body till he detected the spirit by a peculiar fluttering sensation in his finger ends. He then endeavoured to bring it down to one of the extremities, a foot or hand. Much patience and care were required, because these spirits are very cunning, and will double back and hide themselves in the trunk of the body if you give them a chance. "And even," he said, "when you have got the demon into a leg or an arm which you can grasp with your fingers, you must take care or he will escape you. He will lodge in the joints, and hide himself among the bones. Hard indeed it is to get him out of a joint! But when you have drawn him down to a finger or a toe, you must pull him out with a sudden jerk, and throw him far away, and blow after him lest he should return." '—Rev. L. Fison.

practise harmful arts [1]. In the New Hebrides the healing of the sick belongs in Aurora to the *gismana*, in Lepers' Island to the *tangaloe ngovo*, in Pentecost to the *mata tawaga*, to those, that is to say, who have the knowledge of the songs and charms, believed to have come down from Tagaro himself, by which *mana* is conveyed and applied. In Aurora those who dream have the larger practice. In Pentecost and Lepers' Island the juice of a very young cocoa-nut, on which the doctor has blown, with a charm muttered or sung, is drunk by the patient or rubbed upon him, and water, with *mana* imparted to it in the same way, is also used. Sickness is generally supposed to be caused by ghosts, but as the sacred places and objects which may be profaned or lightly used belong to spirits, these are believed often to be angry, and to inflict pain and disease. The power of a spirit is also brought by a charm or curse to harm a man; it is natural, therefore, that in the treatment of the sick recourse should be had to spirits, and above all to Tagaro, rather than to ghosts. The name of Tagaro controls both ghosts and spirits. In Pentecost the doctor will forbid some kind of food to the patient, and when he recovers bring him some of it to eat as a proof that he is well. In both islands women know how to relieve pain. In Pentecost the women use leaves as poultices, and when they take them off profess to take away with them the cause of pain—a snake, a lizard, something from the beach; 'but,' says a native who has undergone the treatment, 'no one sees the thing but the women, and the pain remains.' In Lepers' Island the female practitioner rubs the patient downwards with a bunch of leaves, such as she knows to have the proper qualities, singing and muttering her charms. She will work one day upon the head, and go on working downwards day by day, squeezing and

---

[1] 'They have a nice woman or two on the island (Mota) who are credited with a knowledge of bone-setting. One is a sensible woman, an old friend of mine, so I went for her and set her to work. She pokes and pulls about, and manages to get the bone into its place.'—Rev. J. Palmer. The extreme dislike of natives, of the Banks' Islands at least, to washing when they are sick does not seem to have any superstitious origin; they dread a chill.

rubbing and drawing down the cause of pain, till she produces
at last in her bunch of leaves a stone or a bone, or the bit of
food perhaps by which the patient has been bewitched.   In
Pentecost if a man is delirious they say a *mae*, that snake of
mysterious nature, is in his stomach.   A doctor will then
breathe his charm into a dry cocoa-nut husk which he has set
on fire ; the patient sits over the smoke, and the snake, which
is a ghost or spirit, is driven out.

(2) *Weather*.   In all these islands it is believed that spirits
and ghosts have power over the weather ; it follows, therefore,
that the men who have familiar intercourse with spirits and
ghosts are believed to be able to move them to interfere for
wind or calm, sunshine or rain, as may be desired.   The
spirits and ghosts also have imparted power to forms of words,
stones, leaves, and other things, which therefore of themselves
affect the weather ; and there is also a certain natural congruity between some of these things and the effect they
produce, which seems to make them suitable vehicles of power.
The men, therefore, who have and know these things have
with them *mana* which they can use to benefit or to afflict
friends and enemies, and to turn either way as it is made
worth their while to turn it.   There are everywhere, therefore,
in these islands weather-doctors or weather-mongers who can
control the aërial powers, and are willing to supply wind,
calm, rain, sunshine, famine, and abundance at a price.   These
were generally also masters of other charms than those which
affect the weather, some knew one weather charm and some
another ; but there were generally in a community enough
for all requirements.   Their arts once secret are now pretty
well known.   In Florida the *mane nggehe vigona*, when a calm
was wanted, tied together the leaves appropriate to his *vigona*
and hid them in the hollow of a tree where water was, calling
upon the *vigona* spirit with the proper charm.   This process
would bring down rain to make the calm.   If sunshine was
required he tied the appropriate leaves and creeper-vines to
the end of a bamboo, and held them over a fire.   He fanned
the fire with a song to give *mana* to the fire, and the fire gave

mana to the leaves. Then he climbed a tree and fastened the bamboo to the topmost branch ; as the wind blew about the flexible bamboo the *mana* was cast abroad, and the sun shone out. To stop sunshine ginger-leaves were bound tight together with others and kept in the wizard's bag.

In the seafaring life of the Solomon Islands the maker of calms is a valuable citizen. The Santa Cruz people also are great voyagers, and their *mendeka* wizards control the weather on their expeditions, taking with them the stock which represents their *duka*, and setting it up in the cabin on the stage of the canoe. The presence of his familiar *duka* being thus secured, the weather-doctor will undertake to provide fair wind or calm. In the same island to get sunshine the wizard puts up some burnt wood into a tree ; to get rain he throws down water at the foot of the stock of Tinota, an ancient *duka* ; to make wind he waves the branch of the tree which has this power ; in each case he chants the appropriate charm.

The same things were done and similar methods followed in the Banks' Islands with the *mana* songs and *mana* stones [1]. The art is the same in the New Hebrides. To get rain the Aurora *gismana* puts a tuft of leaves which are *mana* for the purpose into the hollow of a stone, and upon this some branches of the piper methysticum, used for kava, pounded and crushed ; to these he adds the one of his collection of stones which has *mana* for rain ; all is done with the singing of charms with Tagaro's name, and the whole is covered over. The mass ferments, and steam charged with *mana* goes up and makes clouds and rain. It will not do to pound the pepper too hard, lest the wind should blow too strong. This pepper is very powerful also for weather-making in Lepers' Island. To make a hot sun, the wizards hold branches of the plant, which they have

---

[1] As above, page 184. 'There was a large shell filled with earth, and a rounded oblong stone standing up in it, covered with red ochre, the whole thing surrounded by sticks, a sort of fence with a creeper twined in and out. I innocently asked my friend what this was ; "*Me vil goro o lan nan wa vus*" he answered, "the wind is fenced or bound round, lest it blow hard." I asked whether the wind would not blow hard, and he answered "No, not while that lasts. When it rots then it can blow again."'—Rev. J. Palmer.

already filled with *mana* by charms sung over them, over the
fire in a house; as they wilt, dry up and burn, so will the land.
To make a famine they hang cocoa-nut fronds, yams, and other
food over the fire with the pepper branches. For rain they take
plants which have much juice in them, and leaves and stalks
of the *via*, the gigantic caladium, and crush them all together
with songs to give them *mana*; then all is put into a basket,
and hidden in the hollow of a tree where water lies. To make
a calm, leaves of a reed which is very light indeed, or pepper
stalks, are cut in lengths and hung up in a tree. All the
charms have their power because of Tagaro's name in them.

Together with weather-charms may be classed those used
in the Banks' Islands to assist a sow in her first litter of
pigs: such as beating her back with branches of a pepper
closely resembling that used for kava, strewing the blossoms of
the *wotaga*, Barringtonia, upon her back, laying cocoa-nut
fronds on her, breaking a bamboo water-vessel over her back so
that the salt-water may run over her, hanging a bag full of
native almonds above her head; all being done with the appropriate form of words. Nets also used for the first time are
charmed with leaves and the song *mana* for the purpose. In
Lepers' Island when a large new canoe is finished, and is for the
first time to be used, a very young cocoa-nut is made *mana* with
a song which bids the canoe be swift, successful in trading, and
victorious in fighting, and it is then put on the outrigger.
Then they make a short trial of the new canoe, and afterwards
start with the conch trumpet and store of mats to trade for
pigs. It would be hard indeed to draw a limit to the use of
charms which, substantially the same in character with these,
assist those who know them or pay for them, or else injure or
obstruct their enemies. In prospect of a fight, for example,
besides his amulets and stones, a man in the Banks' Islands
would strengthen his hand to shoot and kill by drinking an
infusion of very bitter herbs and bark; and by chewing other
leaves and puffing forth their magic influence would dis-
hearten an approaching enemy.

(3) *Witchcraft.* The wizards who cure diseases are very

often the same men who cause them, the *mana* derived from spirits and ghosts being in both cases the agent employed ; but it often happens that the darker secrets of the magic art are possessed and practised only by those whose power lies in doing harm, and who are resorted to when it is desired to bring evil upon an enemy. Their secrets, like others connected with *mana*, are passed down from one generation to another, and may be bought. The most common working of this malignant witchcraft is that, so common among savages, in which a fragment of food, bit of hair or nail, or anything closely connected with the person to be injured, is the medium through which the power of the ghost or spirit is brought to bear. Some relic such as a bone of the dead person whose ghost is set to work is, if not necessary, very desirable for bringing his power into the charm ; and a stone may have its *mana* for doing mischief. What is needed is the bringing together of the man who is to be injured and the spirit or ghost who is to injure him ; this can be done when something which pertains to the man's person can be used, such as a hair, a nail, a leaf with which he has wiped the perspiration from his face, and with equal effect when a fragment of the food which has passed into the man forms the link of union. Hence in Florida when a scrap from a man's meal could be secreted and thrown into the *vunuha* haunted by the *tindalo* ghost, the man would certainly be ill ; and in the New Hebrides when the *mae* snake carried away a fragment of food into the place sacred to a spirit, the man who had eaten of the food would sicken as the fragment decayed. It was for this reason a constant care to prevent anything that might be used in witchcraft from falling into the hands of ill-wishers ; it was the regular practice to hide hair and nail-parings, and to give the remains of food most carefully to the pigs[1]. In the Banks' Islands the fragment of food, or what-

---

[1] There is little doubt that the common practice of retiring into the sea or a river has its origin in the belief that water is a bar to the use of excrement in charms. It is remarkable that at Mota, where clefts in rocks are used, no doubt also for security, the word used is *tas*, which means sea.

ever it may be, by which a man is charmed is called *garata*; this was made up by the wizard with a bit of human bone, and smeared with a magic decoction in which it would rot away. Or the *garata* would be burnt, and while it was burning the wizard sang his charm; as the *garata* was consumed, the wizard burning it by degrees day after day, the man from whom it came sickened, and would die, the ghost of the man whose bone was burning would take away his life. If then any man who knows he has an enemy has reason himself to think that something has been taken from him, or his friends hear that a *garata* from him is in some wizard's hands, he or they will give money to get the fragment back; and the enemy again and his friends will give more to secure the continuance of the charm. In Aurora the fragment of food is made up with certain leaves; as these rot and stink the man dies. In Lepers' Island the *garata* is boiled, together with certain magical substances, in a clam shell with charms which call on Tagaro. It is evident that no one who intends to bring mischief to a man by a fragment of his food will partake of that food himself, because by doing so he would bring the mischief also on himself. Hence a native offering even a single banana to a visitor will bite the end of it before he gives it, and a European giving medicine to a sick native gives confidence by taking a little first himself [1].

Another charm is common to both eastern and western islands, which is called in the Banks' Islands *talamatai*. A bit of human bone, a fragment of coral, a splinter of wood, or of an arrow by which a man has died, is bound up with the leaves which have *mana* for the purpose, with the *mana* song; by this means the power of the ghost is bound into the charm, and the *talamatai* is secretly planted in the path along

---

[1] ' He (Soga in Bugotu) was quite willing to try (quinine and brandy), so I proceeded to mix it solemnly before them all. Then ensued a curious scene. "Taste it," said Hugo. This I did, and he followed suit, and then all Soga's people had a little sip served out in a shell. This was to show there was no harm in the medicine.'—Bishop Selwyn.

which the person at whom the charm is aimed must pass, so that the virtue of it may spring out and strike him with disease. The tying and binding tight of the *talamatai* while the charm is chanted is what gives the magic power, and if the fibre to make the string is rolled in making it upon the skull of a former practiser of the art, its efficacy will be the greater [1]. The *talamatai* was made but lately in Valuwa in Saddle Island; but the wizard who tied the last brought out all his magic apparatus before the people of his village and smashed it with an axe. In Lepers' Island the same thing is called *rango*.

Another remarkable engine of mischief is called in the Banks' Islands *tamatetiqa*, ghost-shooter. Since this is used also in Florida it may be supposed to be common to all these islands. A bit of bamboo is stuffed with leaves, a dead man's bone, and other magical ingredients, the proper *mana* song being chanted over it. Fasting in the Banks' Islands, but not apparently in the Solomon Islands, adds power to this and other charms. The man who has made or bought one of these holds it in his hand, with the open end of the bamboo covered with his thumb, till he sees his enemy; then he lets out the magic influence and shoots his man. Some years ago in Mota a man named Isvitag waiting with his ghost-shooter in his hand for the man he meant to shoot, let fly too soon, just as a woman with a child upon her hip stepped across the path. It was his sister's child, his nearest of kin, and he was sure he had hit it full. To save it he put the contents of the bamboo into water, to prevent inflammation of the invisible wound, and the child took no hurt. A striking story was told me by Edwin Sakalraw of Ara of what he saw himself. A man in that islet was known to have prepared a *tamatetiqa*, and had declared his intention of shooting his enemy with it at an approaching feast; but he would not tell who it was that he meant to kill, lest some friend of his should buy back the power of the charm from the wizard who had prepared it.

[1] According to the Mota expression they bind, *we vil*, a *talamatai*, and pour, *we wuro*, over a *garata*.

To add force to the ghostly discharge he fasted so many days before the feast began that when the day arrived he was too weak to walk. When the people had assembled, he had himself carried out and set down at the edge of the open space where the dancing would go on. All the men there knew that there was one of them he meant to shoot ; no one knew whether it was himself. There he sat as the dancers rapidly passed him circling round, a fearful object, black with dirt and wasted to a skeleton with fasting, his *tamatetiqa* within his closed fingers stopped with his thumb, his trembling arm stretched out, and his bleared eyes watching for his enemy. Every man trembled inwardly as he danced by him, and the attention of the whole crowd was fixed on him. After a while, bewildered and dazed with his own weakness, the rapid movements of the dancers, and the noise, he mistook his man ; he raised his arm and lifted his thumb. The man he aimed at fell at once upon the ground, and the dancers stopped. Then he saw that he had failed, and that the wrong man was hit, and his distress was great ; but the man who had fallen and was ready to expire, when he was made to understand that no harm was meant him, took courage again to live, and presently revived. No doubt he would have died if the mistake had not been known.

There is a strange method of magical attack used at Savo, and known at Florida, called *vele*, a word which means to pinch. The man who has the secret of this takes in a bag upon his back the leaves and other things in which *mana* for this purpose resides, and seeks to find the man alone he goes to injure. When he finds him, he seizes him, bites his neck, stuffs the magic leaves down his throat, and knocks him on the head with an axe, but not so as to kill him. He then leaves the man, who goes home, relates what has happened, and dies after two days. If the attack is made in the night, the man cannot tell who his assailant was ; but the *vele* is used also in broad daylight, and the assailant does not conceal himself, but tells his name and bids his victim make it known. As he goes home the charm makes him forget it. A strong man will not

be attacked in this way. The same thing is done in Guadalcanar, and the people of Saa at the extremity of Malanta hear
of it at Marau Sound by the name of *hele*. At Lepers' Island,
in the New Hebrides, the *vequa* very much resembles this.
The wizard overcomes his victim with his charms, so that the
man cannot distinctly see him or defend himself; then he
shoots him with a little bow and arrow made of some charmed
material, and strikes him with the arrow. The man does not
know what is done to him, but he goes home, falls ill, and
dies; he can remember nothing to tell his friends, but they
see the wound in his head where he was struck, and in his
side where he was shot, and know what has happened
to him.

The practice of magic arts for mischief is in the Banks'
Islands and in Lepers' Island called *gaqaleva*, and is always
dreaded in case of sickness. In Lepers' Island the wizards
who practise it are believed to have the power of changing
their shape. The friends of any one suffering from sickness
are always afraid lest the wizard who has caused the disease
should come in some form, as of a blow-fly, and strike the
patient; they sit with him therefore and use counter-charms
to guard him, and drive carefully away all flies, lest his enemy
should come in that form. Some men by *gaqaleva* can turn
into a shark and eat an enemy, or more commonly some one
whom his enemy has hired the wizard to destroy. The story of
Tarkeke shews this belief in Aurora also, where, as in Lepers'
Island and in Pentecost, magicians turn into eagles and owls
as well as sharks. This power is not always used for malicious
ends, as was shewn by Molitavile at Lepers' Island. A vessel
'recruiting labour,' called by the natives a 'thief-ship,' had
carried away some people from the island, and their friends
were very anxious to know what had become of them. Molitavile, who had the power of changing his form, undertook
to turn himself into an eagle and fly after the vessel. He
told all the people of the village in the first place to keep
away from that side of the open space between the houses
from whence he would take his flight. Then he entered

into a house decorated with cocoa-nut fronds, and they saw no more ; but they knew that he drank the kava he had prepared, and then lay down till his soul went out of him in the form of a bird and followed the ship. After a while he emerged from the house, and told the people that all who had been carried away were well but one, who was dead. Long afterwards, when some of those who were then on board returned, they said that he had brought back the truth, one of them by that time had died.

(4) *Dreams.* The native belief as to the nature of dreams, and as to the part played by the soul of men in dreams, is a subject of enquiry which belongs rather to the general question as to the conceptions the people have of the nature of the soul itself and of human life ; but the use of dreaming as a branch of the practice of magic comes appropriately into view in this place. In Maewo, Aurora, in the New Hebrides, the dreaming-man, *tatua qoreqore*, who may be also in other ways a *gismana* in his use of supernatural power, is in request in cases of sickness. In an ordinary case, when it is supposed that a ghost is the cause of the complaint, the friends of the sick man send for the professional dreamer and give him now tobacco, as formerly they gave mats, to find out what ghost has been offended, and to make it up with him. He sleeps, and in his dream goes to the place where the sick man has been working ; there he meets some one, like an old man it is likely, of small size, who really is a ghost, and he learns from him what is his name. The ghost tells him that the sick man as he was working has encroached upon his ground, the place he haunts as his own, and that to punish him he has taken away his soul and impounded it in a magic fence in the garden. The dreamer begs for the return of the soul, and asks pardon on behalf of the sick man, who meant no disrespect ; the ghost pulls up the fence in which the soul is enclosed, and lets it out ; the man of course recovers. These dreamers are able also to visit Malanga, an abode of the dead. Sometimes if a child is sick it is supposed that there is some one in Malanga drawing away its soul. The conjecture is that the soul of the infant is

in fact that of some one who has died and gone to Malanga,
but has afterwards desired to come back to earth, and has been
born as the infant that now is sick ; and, moreover, that the
mother in Malanga, not wishing to lose the society of her
child there, is drawing back the re-born infant's soul. The
dreamer having received his fee goes in a dream to Malanga,
and intercedes with the mother there ; he gets back the soul,
and the child recovers. In Saa also in the Solomon Islands,
if a child starts in its sleep it is believed that some ghost is
snatching away what must be called in translation its shadow.
A wizard doctor undertakes to go in sleep and bring it back ;
he dreams and goes ; if those who have taken the 'shadow' let
him take it back the child recovers, but if the child dies the
dreamer reports that they would not let him come near them.
In the same place when a thing is lost a wizard is engaged to
find it in a dream. In Lepers' Island in case of theft or of any
hidden crime some wizard who understands how to do it drinks
kava, and so throws himself into a magic sleep. When he
wakes he declares that he has seen the culprit and gives his
name.

(5) *Prophecy.* The knowledge of future events is believed
to be conveyed to the people by a spirit or a ghost speaking
with the voice of a man, one of the wizards, who is himself
unconscious while he speaks. In Florida the men of a village
would be sitting in their *kiala*, canoe-house, and discussing
some undertaking, an expedition probably to attack some
unsuspecting village. One among them, known to have his
own *tindalo* ghost of prophecy, would sneeze and begin to
shake, a sign that the *tindalo* had entered into him ; his eyes
would glare, his limbs twist, his whole body be convulsed,
foam would burst from his lips ; then a voice, not his own,
would be heard in his throat, allowing or disapproving of what
was proposed. Such a man used no means of bringing on the
ghost ; it came upon him, as he believed himself, at its own will,
its *mana* overpowered him, and when it departed it left him
quite exhausted. Still a man to whom this happened, when
he had a reputation as a prophet, would be employed to assist

in the council and make that a branch of his profession as a
wizard.   The description of prophecy given in San Cristoval
is identical with the foregoing.   In Saa, men who are possessed
with a *lio'a* prophesy of things to come.   In Lepers' Island
it is believed that the spirit Tagaro puts his power as a spirit
into a man, *manag*, so that he speaks what otherwise he could
not, in the way of foretelling things to come, as well as of
making known what is concealed.   These prophets are consulted when a new *gamali*, the house of the Suqe Society,
is to be built, to know if there will be peace or war; because
a number of people assemble for such a purpose, and if there is
danger of fighting they will not leave their homes.

(6) *Divination.*   There are many methods by which ghosts
and spirits are believed to make known to men who use them
the secret things which the unassisted human intelligence
could not find out; and some of these hardly need perhaps the
intervention of a wizard.   These methods of divination differ
very little in the various islands.   In the Solomon Islands,
in Florida for instance, when an expedition has started in a
fleet of canoes, there is sometimes a hesitation whether they
shall proceed, or a question in what direction they shall go.
A *mane kisu* divines; he declares that he has felt a *tindalo*
come on board, for one side of the canoe has been pressed down;
he asks therefore the question, ' Shall we go? shall we go
there?'   If the canoe rocks the answer is in the affirmative, if
it lies steady it is negative.   When a man is sick and it is
desired to know what *tindalo* is eating him, the *mane kisu* who
knows how to divine by *paluduka* is sent for.   He comes,
bringing some one with him to assist, and the two sit down,
the wizard in front, the assistant at his back, and they hold a
stick or bamboo by the two ends.   The wizard begins to slap
with one hand the end of the bamboo he holds, calling one
after another the names of men not very long deceased; when
he names the one who is afflicting the sick man the stick of
itself becomes violently agitated.   Another method of divination is called *gogondo*.   The operator who knows this art takes
leaves of the dracæna equal in number to the *tindalo* ghosts he

knows, and with them other leaves, vines of creepers, and bark
belonging to each *tindalo*, in which the *mana* of each resides.
With these he goes to the place sacred to his *gogondo*, and the
people interested assemble. Then he ties the leaves to his
own body, and begins to split each dracæna leaf down the
middle. Each leaf answers to a *tindalo*, and if a leaf splits
crooked it is the *tindalo* answering to it that is eating the
sick man. The same *gogondo* is used to see whether a sick
man will live or die; if the leaf representing the patient
splits clean he will recover, if crooked he will die. In Motlav
and the other Banks' Islands they divined by means of a bamboo into which a ghost had entered, and which pointed of
itself to the thief or other culprit to be discovered. A common
method of divination in the Banks' Islands is called *so ilo*, and
is used to enquire where a lost person or thing is to be found,
who is the thief, whether an absent friend is alive or dead.
The hands are lifted over the head and rubbed together with
a magic song calling on a ghost. The sign is given by the
cracking of the joints; when the question is of life or death,
if the thumbs or shoulders crack the man still lives, if the
elbows crack he is dead. So if a man sneezes he will *so ilo* to
know who it is that curses him; he revolves his fists one over
the other and then throws out his arms; the revolving is the
question, and the answer is given as he asks, ' Is it So-and-
So ? ' and his elbows crack. Another method of divination was
occasionally in use at Motlav in the same group. After a
burial they would take a bag and put *make*, Tahitian chestnut,
and scraped banana into it. Then a new bamboo some ten feet
long was fitted to the bag and tied with one end in the mouth
of it, and the bag was laid upon the grave, the men engaged
in the affair holding the bamboo in their hands. The names
of the recently dead were then called, and the men holding
the bamboo felt the bag become heavy with the entrance of
the ghost, which then went up from the bag into the hollow of
the bamboo. The bamboo and its contents being carried into
the village, the names of dead men were called over to find out
whose ghost it was: when wrong names were called the free

end of the bamboo moved from side to side while the other
was held tight, at the right name the end moved briskly
round and round. Then questions were put to the enclosed
ghost, 'Who stole such a thing? Who was guilty in such a
case?' The bamboo pointed of itself at the culprit if present,
or made signs as before when names were called. This bamboo they say would run about with a man who had it lying
only on the palms of his hands; but, it is remarked by my
native informant, though it moved in men's hands it never
moved when no one touched it.

(7) *Ordeals.* To clear or to convict a man accused of guilt
there are ordeals managed by men with whom the magic instruments, and the knowledge of the charms by which they
can be used, remain. There are several ordeals used at Saa
which may stand as examples from the Solomon Islands. One
is called the *dau he'u,* stone working, the knowledge of the
use of which is passed down from man to man with the magic
stone which is employed. An accused person goes to the man
who has the stone and engages him to undergo the ordeal.
The people assemble and the accused denies the charge, and
he submits to the ordeal through his compurgator. The
latter heats the stone and throws it from hand to hand; if
his hands are not burnt the accused is pronounced innocent,
and pays a porpoise-tooth fee. There is much preparation
with a very young cocoa-nut, the flower of sugar-cane and
chanted charms to make the proceeding *saka,* hot, with supernatural power. It is probable that sometimes the accusers
make their preparations also with a bribe. Another consists
in the application of a lighted bundle of cocoa-nut fronds to
the legs of the accused, who stands up for it or is tied between
two posts. This is done with charms by the man who manages
it, and also gets his fee. In another the accused swallows a
charmed stone heated by the wizard employed, and is innocent
if he takes no harm. In a fourth the accused eats a bit of a
cocoa-nut which has been made very *saka* for the purpose,
and broken in pieces; if he is guilty he falls afterwards from
a tree or some other accident befalls him, or he pines away.

Another method is to take almonds from a sacred place and mash them with a charm ; the accused eats and is judged guilty if he is the worse for it.   There is again a very ancient spear at Saa, very *saka*, full of magic power, called *usu*, dog, because it has dogs' teeth upon it.   This is placed on the head of the accused and he says, ' If I did the thing, may I die with this spear ; ' if he is guilty he sickens and dies with the power of the spear.   There is also a very sacred song, very *saka*.   The wizard who knows it sings it, and the accused man says, ' Well, that song is for me ; if I did that let me and my children suffer.'   Finally, there is the alligator ordeal, used in the passage between Mala Paina and Mala Masiki, where the reptiles are very numerous.   A man accused of serious crime is taken there ; the wizard who manages the ordeal calls the alligators with his charms, and the accused who is confident in his innocence and in the wizard's power dares to swim across.   No one will hold him guilty if he escapes.   In this ordeal also it is sometimes not the accused, but the man who knows the charm who submits himself to the test.   In Lepers' Island a man to prove his innocence will submit to be shot at with arrows ; if he be hit he is of course guilty ; if he be innocent, Tagaro will protect him, just as he protects in fighting any young man whom he preserves that he may be prosperous and great.   The favour of Tagaro in either case is sought for with the appropriate charm.

(8) *Poison*.   To the best of my knowledge the Melanesian people were not acquainted with the use of any substance which, when taken with food or drink, would be injurious by its natural properties, until they learnt the use of arsenic from Queensland.   Returned ' labourers ' brought that back with them, and used it with fatal effect in the same way in which native poisoners used their own magical preparations, by mixing it in food ; and it is more than probable that the certain and fatal effect was believed then to be due to the powerful magical and not natural powers with which it was endued.   At any rate, if what native magicians employed in poisoning food had any naturally noxious qualities (which is

not denied), it was not any naturally noxious property which
was expected to produce the injurious result; nor when
mischief followed was it ascribed to the natural quality of
what had been administered; the magic charms had in native
belief the power of poisoning, and communicated it to the
preparation which was mixed with the food. No doubt the
materials over which the poison charm was sung were such as
seemed to have a certain congruity with the effect to be
produced. The secrets of poison-making have not become
known; but in Florida it is believed by the people that the
liver of a black snake dried in the sun or over a fire was the
chief ingredient in the poisons which were used there. There
were certain persons who knew the art, and were hired to
poison with *maomao*, made with the *mana* power of the *tindalo*
ghost belonging to the sorcerer employed, and mixed in the
food of the man whose life was aimed at. The Savo people
were great poisoners; Florida men who visited them were
careful what they ate. The effect of the poison was that one
who had taken it fell sick, vomited, and afterwards died.
The practice of this art was dangerous to the poisoner; a
known poisoner was put to death in Florida, and so were
many innocent persons suspected or accused. In the Banks'
Islands to poison was to *vangan pal*, to feed by stealth. The
Ureparapara people in that group had the repute of being
poisoners, others would get poison from thence; in Mota no
one knew the art. In Lepers' Island poison is called, by a
parallel expression, *aruwana*; all that I have learnt of it is
that the preparation of it is very secret, and that it is made
with charms in the same way with the *garata* above described.
In fact the correspondence between the native poison and the
charm that works destruction through a fragment of food is
complete: in the one case a portion of the food already eaten
by the person to be injured is mixed with certain magically
powerful substances; in the other the magically powerful
substances are mixed in the food to be eaten. In either case,
according to the native belief, the mischief was caused by
magic. A man eating away from his closest friends was in

equal fear lest he should be charmed through a fragment of his food or poisoned by what might be put into his food. The poisoned arrows, of which more hereafter, have never been found to have been prepared with anything which could be properly said to be poison ; and undoubtedly the dreaded power of such arrows to give fatal wounds was by the natives believed to be due to the magic charms with which they were made, and to the dead man's bone with which they were pointed.

(9) *Tapu* and *Curses*. The word taboo is one of the very few that the languages of the Pacific Ocean have given to the English language ; and something of its meaning therefore may be supposed to be understood. But the *tapu* or *tambu* of Melanesia is not so conspicuous in native life as the *tapu* of Polynesia ; and it differs also perhaps in this, that it never signifies any inherent holiness or awfulness, but always a sacred and unapproachable character which is imposed. This is not strictly accurate as regards the word in the Solomon Islands, where everything connected with a ghost of worship, *tindalo*, *lio'a*, or *'adaro*, is *tambu* of itself ; it is accurate as concerns the Banks' Islands and New Hebrides, where what is inherently sacred is *rongo* or *sapuga*. But still in cases where the English word taboo can be employed there is always in Melanesia human sanction and prohibition. Some thing, action, or place is made *tambu* or *tapu* by one who has the power to do it, any one whose standing among the people gives him confidence to lay this character upon it. The power at the back of the *tapu* or *tambu* is that of the ghost or spirit in whose name, or in reliance upon whom, it is pronounced ; for the *tapu* is a prohibition with a curse expressed or implied. Thus in Florida a chief will forbid something to be done or touched under a penalty; he has said, for example, *tambu hangalatu*, any one who violates his prohibition must pay him a hundred strings of money; it seems to the European a proof of the power of the chief; but to the native the power of the chief, in this and in everything else, rests on the persuasion that the chief has his *tindalo* at his back. The sense of this in the particular case is remote, the apprehension

of angering the chief is present and effective, but the ultimate sanction is the power of the *tindalo*. If a common man were to take upon himself to *tambu* anything he might, people would think that he would not do it unless he knew that he had the power to do it; they would watch, and if any one who violated his *tambu* were to fall sick, he would be recognized at once as one who had a powerful *tindalo*, and he would rise. Each *tindalo* has his special leaf, and a man will set his *tambu* with the leaf of his *tindalo* as a mark; men do not always know whose leaf it is, but they know that they have to deal with a *tindalo*, not only with a man, if they disregard the mark. The *tambu* is too convenient an institution to drop when the original sanction of it has ceased to operate; a native Christian teacher therefore does not hesitate, as a man of position in society, to set a *tambu*; thieves he says are afraid of a man if not of a *tindalo*. In the Banks' Islands there is a minor prohibition, *soloi*, as well as the more solemn *tapu*, in which probably there is no direct reference to a supernatural sanction. But a man by virtue of the supernatural *mana* which accrues to him through his association with a spirit will *va-tapu*, separate from common use, a path, trees, part of the sea-beach, a canoe, a fishing-net, and no one would be surprised if sickness fell at once upon any one who should break the *tapu*. A person of no particular distinction would set his *soloi* before the trees or garden, the fruit and produce of which he wished to reserve for some feast, and intruders would know at any rate that he carried his bow and arrows. Stronger than any individual sanction was that of the secret societies called *Tamate*; each had its leaf, and any member of one could set the leaf of his society as a mark, to disregard which would stir the anger of all the members. The payment of a pig or money would appease the individual or society whose prohibition had been despised.

It is evident that a *tambu* approaches to a curse, when it is a prohibition resting on the invocation of an unseen power. Thus at Saa, a few years ago, the chief forbade the young people of the place to go to school, with a curse by the name

of a *lio'a*, a ghost of power.   In such a case if native ideas
only had prevailed, money, pigs, or valuable gifts would have
been sufficient to *toto*, make it up with, the chief, and he
would have been willing to *toto 'akalo* (page 137), set the
matter right by a sacrifice to the *lio'a*; but in this case the
Christian teachers, though really in some danger of their lives,
refused to acknowledge the power of the *lio'a* and of the curse,
and would give nothing to the chief, who thereupon professed
himself quite unable to remove the curse.

A curse by way of asseveration is very common in Florida,
and no doubt in the other Solomon Islands.   A man will deny
an accusation by his forbidden food, *butonggu!* by some *tindalo*,
Daula, the ghostly frigate-bird, or Bagea, the ghostly shark.
The Florida people, and their neighbours probably, were
sufficiently advanced to garnish their conversation with profane
and filthy swearing, even before 'contact with civilization' put
into their mouths those words which are too often the first
they learn of English.   I am not aware of the existence of this
habit in the Banks' Islands.   The more serious curse there is
to *vagona*, to make into a tangle, to prohibit easy access
or procedure, under the sanction of a spirit's power; to swear
therefore by the name of some ghost or spirit is to *vava vago-
gonag*, that is, to speak making a supernatural power to
intervene, the withdrawal of which can only be effected by a
sufficient offering to appease the layer of the curse, who will
proceed to satisfy the being invoked.   To curse in the sense
of expressing a wish for mischief, with a mental if not a verbal
reference to a supernatural power, is to *vivnag*.   Such may be
called the formula used in pouring water into the native oven
(page 147), and such a curse is supposed to be the cause of
sneezing.   The milder forms are those whereby a troublesome
or impertinent request or remark is met; '*Iniko o suri tamate*,
you are a dead man's bone'; and by what they call sending off,
varowog, to certain trees which have something of a sacred
character, *vawo mele!* on a cycas, *vawo aru!* on a casuarina,
vawo poga! forms which mean not much more than 'you be
hanged!'

CHAPTER XIII.

POSSESSION. INTERCOURSE WITH GHOSTS.

It is difficult to separate the practice of magic arts from the manifestation of a ghost's or spirit's power in possession; because a man may use some magic means to bring the possession upon himself, as in the case of prophecy, and also because the connexion between the unseen powerful being and the man, in whatever way the connexion is made and works, is that which makes the wizard. Yet there is a distinction between the witchcraft and sorcery in which by magic charms the wizard brings the unseen power into action, and the spontaneous manifestation of such power by the unseen being; even though there may be only a few who can interpret, or to whom the manifestations are made. In a case of madness the native belief is that the madman is possessed. There is at the same time a clear distinction drawn by the natives between the acts and words of the delirium of sickness in which as they say they wander, and those which are owing to possession. They are sorry for lunatics and are kind to them, though their remedies are rough. At Florida, for example, one Kandagaru of Boli went out of his mind, chased people, stole things and hid them. No one blamed him, because they knew that he was possessed by a *tindalo* ghost. His friends hired a wizard who removed the *tindalo*, and he recovered. In the same way not long ago in Lepers' Island there was a man who lost his senses. The people conjectured that he had unwittingly trodden on a sacred place belonging to Tagaro, and that the ghost of the man who lately sacrificed there was angry with him. The

doctors were called in ; they found out whose ghost it was by
calling on the names of dead men likely to have been offended,
they washed him with water made powerful with charms, and
they burned the vessel in which the magic water had been
under his nose ; he got well. In a similar case they will put
bits of the fringe of a mat, which has belonged to the deceased,
into a cocoa-nut shell, and burn it under the nose of the
possessed. There was another man who threw off his *malo* and
went naked at a feast, a sure sign of being out of his mind ; he
drew his bow at people, and carried things off. The people
pitied him, and tried to cure him. When a man in such
condition in that island spoke, it was not with his own voice,
but with that of the dead man who possessed him ; and such
a man would know where things were hidden ; when he was
seen coming men would hide a bow or a club to try him, and
he would always know where to find it. Thus the possession
which causes madness cannot be quite distinguished from that
which prophesies, and a man may pretend to be mad that he
may get the reputation of being a prophet. At Saa a man
will speak with the voice of a powerful man deceased, with
contortions of the body which come upon him when he is
possessed ; he calls himself, and is spoken to by others, by
the name of the dead man who speaks through him ; he will
eat fire, lift enormous weights, and foretell things to come.
In the Banks' Islands the people make a distinction between
possession by a ghost that enters a man for some particular
purpose, and that by a ghost which comes for no other
apparent cause than that being without a home in the abode
of the dead he wanders mischievously about, a *tamat lelera*, a
wandering ghost. Wonderful feats of strength and agility
used to be performed under the influence of one of these
' wandering ghosts ' ; a man would move with supernatural
quickness from place to place, he would be heard shouting at
one moment in a lofty tree on one side of a village, and in
another moment in a tree on the opposite side, he would utter
sounds such as no sane man could make, his strength was such
that many men could hardly master him. Such a man was

seized by his friends and held struggling in the smoke of
strong smelling leaves, while they called one after another the
names of the dead men whose ghosts were likely to be abroad;
when the right name was called the ghost departed, but
sometimes this treatment failed.   It was a different thing
when, as used to happen in former days, a ghost from Panoi,
the abode of the dead, would come for a certain purpose into a
man and speak with his voice.   This did not happen to all
men alike, but to some who were subject to this possession.
Such a man would somewhere see a ghost, come home and lie
down sick.   People would come to see him, and calling him by
his name would ask what was the matter.   He would answer,
'It is not he, it is I,' that is, not the sick man, but the ghost
who answers by his voice.   Then they would call over the
names of the lately deceased to see whose ghost it was, and
when they hit on the right name he would answer, 'It is I.'
Then he would begin to weep, and tell them that he had come
back because he knew in Panoi that his wife and family were
not duly cared for, or that his property was being wasted.
He would scold his relatives for their misconduct, and he would
tell them of things they did not know, such as where lost
property would be found.   Some one would then bring in a
bunch of strong-smelling leaves to drive him away, and he
would immediately perceive its presence ; they would hide it
and deny in vain that they had brought it in.   They caught
hold of him struggling and howling, and put the leaves to his
nose ; he seemed to die, the ghost departed from him as the
soul departs from a dying man.   After a while his senses
would return, and he would declare that he knew nothing of
what had been said or done since he saw that ghost and
sickened.   Such a medium as this, though not a wizard by
profession, no doubt found it worth his while to receive these
ghostly visits.

An Omen is a spontaneous manifestation or warning given
by supernatural power, and not obtained by the arts of
divination.   The sign given to a Florida party, when they
start upon their voyage and wait for the rocking of their

canoe, might be such if the sign were not given in answer to
the wizard on board. True omens are observed at Saa. There
is a small bird named *wisi* from its cry, which means ' No.'
It has other notes which resemble the voice of a man talking.
If men starting on an expedition hear the cry *wisi !* it is not
enough to turn them back perhaps, but if they fail they
remember the warning ; if they hear the other notes they are
confident of success. A man working in his garden hears the
bird, and he asks, ' Is there fighting ? ' The bird answers
wisi, No. He asks again, ' Is it a stranger come from far ? '
The bird answers *wisi*, or chatters to give an affirmative reply.
This is, however, not seriously thought of. If a frog, or some
other creature that does not usually come indoors, is seen in a
house it is an omen. They will go and enquire of a wizard
what it means. If the creature comes and cries they know
that soon there will be crying for a death. There is in that
island a remarkable kind of snake rarely seen, called *mati e
sato* ; it is about ten inches long, glistening like gold, and
when full grown, the natives say, so resplendent that nothing
of it can be clearly seen but its eyes and snout ; when it is
taken into the hand it is exceedingly smooth and slippery.
If one of these is seen in a house it is a sign of death ; if
running, of violent death ; if quiet, of death by sickness. If
the venomous snake *a'u* is seen in a house it is a sign of death
or fighting or misfortune ; if coiled up it is a sign of quiet
death ; if running, there will be violence. When a beginning
is made of building a house or canoe, or of clearing a garden,
a man will call aloud, and then if something remarkable
appears it is a sign that the work will be interrupted by
death or war ; if nothing comes, all will be well. The sacred
character of the *sigo*, kingfisher, in the Banks' Islands has been
mentioned, and that its cry is ominous. It is the same in
Lepers' Island, where, if a party is going to battle and a kingfisher, *higo*, cries to the right, it foretells victory ; if it cries to
the left, it bodes failure.

There is a belief in the Banks' Islands in the existence of a
power like that of Vampires. A man or woman would obtain

this power out of a morbid desire for communion with some ghost, and to gain it would steal and eat a morsel of a corpse. The ghost then of the dead man would join in a close friendship with the person who had eaten, and would gratify him by afflicting any one against whom his ghostly power might be directed. The man so afflicted would feel that something was influencing his life, and would come to dread some particular person among his neighbours, who was therefore suspected of being a *talamaur*. This latter when seized and tried in the smoke of strong-smelling leaves would call out the name of the dead man whose ghost was his familiar, often the names of more than one, and lastly the name of the man who was afflicted. The same name *talamaur* was given to one whose soul was supposed to go out and eat the soul or lingering life of a freshly-dead corpse. There was a woman some years ago of whom the story is told that she made no secret of doing this, and that once on the death of a neighbour she gave notice that she should go in the night and eat the corpse. The friends of the deceased therefore kept watch in the house where the corpse lay, and at dead of night heard a scratching at the door, followed by a rustling noise close by the corpse. One of them threw a stone and seemed to hit the unseen thing ; and in the morning the *talamaur* was found with a bruise on her arm which she confessed was caused by a stone thrown at her while she was eating the corpse. Such a woman would feel a morbid delight in the dread which she inspired, and would also be secretly rewarded by some whose secret spite she gratified.

A certain mysterious power was believed to attach to some men in the Banks' Islands, which the natives find it difficult to explain. There is something belonging to a man called his *wuqa* or *uqa*. If a stranger sleeps in some one's habitual sleeping-place in his absence and afterwards finds himself unwell, he knows that the *uqa* of the man in whose place he slept has struck him there ; or if one leaves an associate and goes elsewhere to sleep, the *uqa* of the man he leaves will follow him and strike him ; he will rise in the morning weak and

languid, or if he had been unwell before he would be worse.
Although this is not done by witchcraft a man is held responsible for what his *uqa* does, and is made to pay money to
the injured man, and by an act of his will to take off the
malignant influence.

Here may be mentioned also certain tricks which ghosts or
spirits play on men, or which men know how to make them
play. At Mota in the Banks' Islands a little boy named
Peitavunana, heavenly water, was frightened and chased by a
ghost up the mountain. He was sought for in vain, and a
fight was threatened. They divined for him, *so ilo*, by cracking of the fingers (page 211), and a man from Vanua Lava
announced that he would be found in a certain very inaccessible
place. There he was found by Somwaswas at the root of a
tree crying and calling on his mother, his body covered with
excrement, the food of ghosts, and streaming with blood from
the thorns through which he had been forced, and in his
hand an unripe fruit of the mammy-apple. He said that his
dead mother had come to him and given him the food.
Another little boy, Nungwia, sleeping on the beach at night,
was conveyed by a ghost into a very small cavity beneath a
rock, into which it was impossible for him to have climbed.
In Lepers' Island they have a way of playing with a ghost.
They build a little house in the forest near their village and
adorn it with leaves and cocoa-nut fronds. It has a partition
dividing it in two, and a bamboo twelve or fifteen feet long
is put within, half on one side of the partition, half on the
other. The men assemble in the night to try the presence of
a ghost, and sit in the house on one side only of the partition
with their hands under one end of the bamboo. They shut
their eyes, and call the names of the lately dead. When they
feel the bamboo moving in their hands they know that the
ghost is present whose name was the last they called. Then
they ask, naming one of themselves, ' Where is Tanga ? ' and
the bamboo rises in their hands and strikes him, and then
sinks back. They are sure then of the presence of the ghost,
and tell him they will go outside ; and they go out, singing,

823142

with one end of the bamboo in their hands. Then the bamboo leads them as the ghost within it chooses. They make known what they wish by singing, and the bamboo makes them do the contrary to what they say they want; if they sing that they will go up hill it drags them down. Finally, they sing that they wish not to return into the path, and they are led out of the bush into the path ; they sing that they do not want to go into the village, and they are taken there. In the same way a club is put at night into a cycas-tree, which has a sacred character, and when the name of some ghost is called it moves of itself and will lift and drag people about. In Mota a few years ago they tried again a practice of this kind long disused, with a success that caused alarm. A basket was fastened to the end of a bamboo and food put in it ; a man took the bamboo upon his shoulder and walked along, the basket at his back ; presently he felt a heavy weight in the basket as much as he could carry, a sign that a ghost had come into it. The bamboo then would drag people about, and put up into a tree would lift them from the ground. This resembles a good deal a method of divination used at Motlav, and described above, but there is no divination in these tricks.

There was, and perhaps still is, in the Torres Islands something similar to this, when ghosts influenced and took possession of people with the use of sticks. This has been described by a native under the name of *Na tamet lingalinga*, by which name those who are subjected to the ghostly influence are called. It is done, he writes, on the fifth day after a death. There was a certain man at Lo who took the lead, and without whom nothing could be done ; he gave out that he would descend into Panoi, the abode of the dead, and he had with him certain others, assistants. He and his party were called simply ' ghosts ' when engaged in the affair. The first thing was to assemble those who were willing to be treated in a *gamal*, a public hall, perhaps twenty young men or boys, to make them lie down on the two sides, and to shake over them leaves and tips of the twigs of plants powerful and magical

with charms. Then the leader and his assistants went into all
the sacred places which ghosts haunt, such as where men
wash off the black of mourning, collecting as they went the
ghosts and becoming themselves so much possessed that they
appeared to have lost their senses, though they acted in a
certain method. In the meanwhile the subjects lying in the
gamal begin to be moved ; those who bring as they say the
ghosts to them go quietly along both sides of the house without, and all at once strike the house along its whole length
with the sticks they carry in their hands. This startles those
inside, and they roll about on the ground distracted. Then
the ' ghosts' enter in with their sticks, and in this performance
each is believed to be some one deceased, one Tagilrow, another
Qatawala ; they leap from side to side, turning their sticks
over to be beaten by the subjects on one side and the other.
The subjects are given sticks for this purpose, and as they
strike the stick the ghost ' strikes,' possesses, them one after
another. In this state the sticks draw them out into the
open place of the village, where they are seen. They appear
not to recognize or hear any one but the 'ghosts' who have
brought this upon them, and who alone can control them and
prevent them from pulling down the houses ; for they have a
rage for seizing and striking with anything, bows, clubs,
bamboo water-vessels, or the rafters of the houses, and their
strength is such that a full-grown man cannot hold a boy in
this state. After a time the ' ghosts ' take them back into
the *gamal*, and there they lie exhausted ; the 'ghosts' go to
drink *kava*, and as each drinks he pours away the dregs calling the name of one of the possessed, and the senses of each
return as his name is called. It is five days, however, before
they can go about again. This was done once after a
Christian teacher had come to Lo, and two of his scholars
whom he let go to prove that it was a deception were
possessed.

People in the Banks' Islands have certain tricks which
those who do not understand them believe to be the work of
ghosts. A man will hear a voice from the ground beneath

his feet, calling him by his name. This is said to be done by letting an open bamboo some foot or two into the ground in some place not far from the person to be addressed, where the operation will be unseen, and then speaking into the end of the bamboo, and directing the voice in the way the sound is meant to travel. Again, a family party working in their garden will see smoke and sparks ascending in the direction of their village; they hear the hissing of the flames and the popping of the bamboo rafters; they are sure that it is their own house burning, and run to save what they can. When they reach the village all is quiet, the houses are all standing with fastened doors, as in the hours of work. The trick has been played by a party who somewhere in a line with the house have made a fire, and exploding green reeds which fill with steam when heated in the fire, and beating with the tips of dry cocoa-nut fronds upon the ground, have imitated with wonderful exactness the noises of a house on fire.

It will hardly be inappropriate here to introduce the Melanesian superstition about sneezing, to which some reference has been already made. In Florida when a man sneezes they think that some one is speaking of him, is angry with him, perhaps cursing him by calling on his own *tindalo* to eat him; the man who sneezes calls upon his *tindalo* to damage the man who is cursing him. In the same way at Saa if a man sneezes when he wakes, he cries, 'Who calls me? If for good, well; if for evil, may So-and-So (naming a *lio'a*) defend me.' In the Banks' Islands also some one is supposed to be calling the name of a man when he sneezes, either for good or evil. In Motlav if a child sneezes, the mother will cry, 'Let him come back into the world! let him remain.' In Mota they cry, 'Live, roll back to us!' The notion is that a ghost is drawing the child's soul away. It has been said that at Mota a man enquires when he sneezes by a certain divination who is cursing him; he will also stamp with his foot and cry, 'Stamp down the mischief from me! Let it be quiet! Let them say their words in vain;

let them lay their plots in vain!' [1]. There is a special form of words used when one's step-father sneezes (page 40). The native notions in the New Hebrides are much the same; but in Lepers' Island, if an infant sneezes, it is a sign that its soul has been away, and has just come back; the friends present cry out with good wishes. They judge in the same island by the character of the sneeze what is the motive with which the sneezer's name is being called; if it be a gentle sneeze no harm is meant, a violent paroxysm is warning of a curse.

---

[1] *Tara sur o lea nan nau—ni masur—nira vetvet wora, nira sorsora wora!*

CHAPTER XIV.

BIRTH. CHILDHOOD. MARRIAGE.

IN attempting to trace the course of a Melanesian life from birth to burial we soon meet with practices connected with the Couvade. A proper Couvade has perhaps been observed in San Cristoval alone, when the young father was found lying in after the birth of his child; and it should be observed that this was where the child follows the father's kindred. There is much however which approaches this. At Saa it is not only the expectant mother who is careful what she eats, the father also both before and after the child's birth refrains from some kinds of food which would hurt the child. He will not eat pig's flesh, and he abstains from movements which are believed to do harm, upon the principle that the father's movements affect those of the child. A man will not do hard work, lift heavy weights, or go out to sea; he keeps quiet lest the child should start, should over-strain itself, or should throw itself about as he paddles. In the Banks' Islands also, both parents are careful what they eat when the child is born, they take only what if taken by the infant would not make it ill; before the birth of her first child the mother must not eat fish caught by the hook, net, or trap. After the birth of the first child, the father does no heavy work for a month; after the birth of any of his children, he takes care not to go into those sacred places, *tano rongo*, into which the child could not go without risk. It is the same in the New Hebrides; the expectant Araga father keeps away from sacred places, *ute sapuga*, before the child's birth, and does not enter his house ; after the birth, he does work in looking after his wife and child, but he must not eat shell-fish and other produce of the beach, for the infant would suffer from ulcers if he did. In Lepers' Island, the father is very careful for ten days ; he does no work, will not climb a tree, or go far into the sea to bathe, for if he exerts himself the child will suffer. If during this time he goes to any distance, as to the beach, he brings back with him a little stone representing the infant's soul, which may have followed him ; arrived at home, he cries, 'Come hither,' and puts down the stone in the house ; then he waits till the child sneezes, and he cries, 'Here it is,' knowing then that the soul has not been lost.

Abortion and Infanticide were very common. If a woman did not want the trouble of bringing up a child, desired to appear young, was afraid her husband might think the birth before its time, or wished to spite her husband, she would find some one to procure abortion either by the juice of certain plants taken in drink or by twisting and squeezing the fœtus. Infanticide was more prevalent in some islands than others ; since Christian teaching has been introduced a great change is visible in Maewo, Aurora Island, and at Wango in San Cristoval, where the birth of an infant was of late years indeed an unusual thing, and all the children in the villages had been bought from inland. In those parts the old women of the village generally determined whether a newborn child should live ; if not promising in appearance, or likely to be troublesome, it was made away with, its mouth perhaps stuffed with leaves and the body cast into a hole and covered with a stone. In the Banks' Islands, if of the wrong sex or otherwise unwelcome, the infant was choked as soon as born. Male children were killed rather than female in that group ; if there were female children already, another would not be desired ; but the females were rather preserved, as it is important to observe, because of the family passing through the female side, as well as with the prospect of gain when the girl should be betrothed and married.

There is nowhere in the groups generally the practice of

killing one of twins, nor is there anywhere any dislike to the birth of twins further than from the trouble they entail. In some places, as at Saa, twins are liked ; at Motlav the people of a village are proud of their twins, and the parents and relations make much of them ; no one would adopt one of them, because it would spoil the pleasure of seeing them together, and deprive them of their natural right to be together ; the only sad thing about them is that they give much trouble, and that the parents will be so sorry if they die. In Florida alone there seems to be something of a suspicion that two fathers may be concerned ; but they take it that the woman has trespassed on the sacred place, *vunuha*, of some ghost, *tindalo*, whose power lies that way. In Lepers' Island also it is thought that twins may be a gift of Tagaro. Women who want a child will go to a sacred place in hope that the spirit will give them one, and sometimes he gives them two.   There is now in the island one Malavaiboe, Pig-twin, the survivor of twin sons of Arusese ; the people believe he will turn out a great man, not so much because he is a twin, as because Tagaro gave the twins of which he is one to their mother when she went to ask a child.

At Saa, when a newborn infant is eight or ten days old a sacrifice, *'unu qo* (page 137), is made to the family *lio'a* to provide against misfortune. In Lepers' Island when the infant is ten days old the mother is well again, and the father goes down to the beach to wash the things belonging to the child. As he goes he scatters along the path little toy bows, if it be a boy, a sign that he shall be a strong bowman ; if it be a girl, he throws down bits of the pandanus fibre out of which mats are made, for the mats which count as money are to be her work. In case the child dies after eating for the first time the parents will not eat that food afterwards themselves. At Araga, Pentecost Island, a first-born son remains ten days in the house in which he was born, during which time the father's kinsmen take food to the mother. On the tenth day they bring nothing, but the father gives them food and mats, which count as money, in as great quantity as he can afford. They,

the kin of the father and therefore not kin of the infant, on
that day perform a certain ceremony called *huhuni*; they lay
upon the infant's head mats and the strings with which pigs
are tied, and the father tells them that he accepts this as a
sign that hereafter they will feed and help his son.   There is
clearly in this a movement towards the patriarchal system, a
recognition of the tie of blood through the father and of duties
that follow from it.   Another sign of the same advance of the
father's right is to be seen in the very different custom that
prevails in the Banks' Islands on the birth of a first-born son ;
there is raised upon that event, a noisy and playful fight, *vagalo*,
after which the father buys off the assailants with payment of
money to the other *veve*, to the kinsmen that is of the child
and his mother.   It is hardly possible to be mistaken in
taking this fight to be a ceremonial, if playful, assertion of the
claim of the mother's kinsfolk to the child as one of themselves,
and the father's payment to be the quieting of their claim and
the securing of his own position as head of his own family.

As children grow they remain in their tender years in the
women's care within the house.   They are commonly weaned
when they can crawl.   Their first advance in life when they
are boys depends very much upon the custom of the place
concerning clothing.   In the Banks' Islands, where males of
any age wore nothing, boys as they grew bigger were sent to
sleep in the *gamal*, the public club-house ; the parents said
' He is a boy, it is time to separate him from the girls.'
They took their meals at home until sooner or later they had
their place bought for them in the Suqe Club.   In the
Torres Islands the nose is bored on the third day for the
future ornament.   In Florida and its neighbourhood boys of
six or seven put on the little wrapper worn by males, and are
very particular about it.   At Santa Cruz the boys go at first
to the chief's *mandai*, canoe-house and public hall, in the
daytime and go home to sleep ; after a while they cease to
return at night.   Before dress in that island comes the indispensable nose-ring ; the hole for this is made in infancy and
a little ring inserted.   When the ears are bored it is a great

occasion and a pig is killed, and so always when an additional
hole is made, and a Santa Cruz boy may be seen with more
than thirty ear-rings. The Santa Cruz dress is ample, and is
assumed with a feast and killing of a pig. The boy's as-
sumption of a dress depends therefore on the ability and
willingness of his friends to provide the feast, and some big
boys go naked. The dress in the New Hebrides, at Lepers'
Island, and Pentecost differs little from that of Santa Cruz.
The boy puts on his *malo* dress when his parents think him
big enough, and sooner or later as they can afford to make a
feast. Before this he has lived at home, but now he eats and
sleeps in the *gamali* club-house, and now begins his strange
and strict reserve of intercourse with his sisters and his
mother. This begins in full force towards his sisters; he
must not use as a common noun the word which is the name
or makes part of the name of any of them, and they avoid
his name as carefully. He may go to his father's house to ask
for food, but if his sister is within he has to go away
before he eats; if no sister is there he can sit down near the
door and eat. If by chance brother and sister meet in the
path she runs away or hides. If a boy on the sands knows
that certain footsteps are his sister's, he will not follow them,
nor will she his. This mutual avoidance begins when the
boy is clothed or the girl tattooed. The partition between
boys and girls without which a school cannot be carried on is
not there to divide the sexes generally, but to separate brothers
and sisters. This avoidance continues through life. The
reserve between son and mother increases as the boy grows
up, and is much more on her side than his. He goes to the
house and asks for food; his mother brings it out but does
not give it him, she puts it down for him to take; if she calls
him to come she speaks to him in the plural, in a more
distant manner; 'Come ye,' she says, *mim vanai*, not 'Come
thou.' If they talk together she sits at a little distance and
turns away, for she is shy of her grown-up son. The meaning
of all this is obvious. At Santa Cruz and the neighbouring
islands the separation of the sexes in daily life is carried far,

but has not this character. At Santa Cruz the men and women never work together promiscuously or assemble in one group; men with their wives and children only, and men with their mothers, work in the gardens; when a crowd assembles the women collect aloof. In Nufilole, one of the Swallow group, the separation is complete; men and women are never out together; in the morning the men go out first and come back, after that the women go and fetch water, when they return the men go out again.

It has been said in Chapters V and VI that there is not known in these Islands of Melanesia any initiation or 'making of young men'; there is only the entrance into the various societies. The nearest approach to such initiation seems to be found at Saa. A chief's son in that part of Malanta goes early to the *oha*, canoe-house and public hall, while common children still eat and sleep at home; he may go there when he is twelve years old. Before that they are very careful about him; he must not go under the women's bedplace, his mother must never use bad words in scolding him, he must not consort with big boys who will teach him bad ways; he is kept apart lest he *lo'u*, fall, be low [1]. At first he goes only in the daytime to the *oha*, and comes back to his mother to sleep. When the time comes he is put with boys of his own age to undergo a sort of noviciate. The custom is dying out; boys used to stay in the *oha* sometimes for years. First of all there was a *toto* sacrifice (page 137) to purify the boys. Afterwards they went out every morning early in a canoe to catch the bonito-fish, till each boy had caught one. Men paddled with the boys, a boy sitting behind a man; when the man had a bite the boy behind him came forward and helped to haul it in; the fish counted as the boy's, he had caught a fish which one must be *saka*, be possessed of a certain mysterious power, to

---

[1] It is curious that the word *lotu*, commonly used for the profession of Christianity in Polynesia and in Fiji, should occur in this sense in the Solomon Islands. The meaning from which its use to describe the new religion came was that of bowing down as in prayer. To go where women may be above his head is degrading to a chief; hence the refusal to go below on board a vessel.

catch ; and he had reached a certain stage in life. A boy did not come out when he had caught his fish, he remained for the time fixed for him at his entrance, according to his father's rank, or that in which his father had aspired to set him ; for the length of his stay depended very much upon the expense to which his father proposed to go. One might come out before his time, as Wateaado did when his brother died and he was wanted to take his place. At certain intervals during this seclusion feasts were made, and a great one when a boy came out. There was no secret initiation, nothing whatever was taught the boys, the only thing they learnt was how to fish for bonito. They came out young men and strangers to the people of the village, out of whose sight they had grown up. This custom has now ceased at Saa.

Circumcision is unknown in almost all the islands which are here in view ; it has come up from Ambrym to the lower end of Pentecost, as a prevailing custom, and not very lately. It is done at any age, whenever the boy's friends choose to make the feast. It is not a mark of initiation and has no religious or superstitious character ; it is a social distinction. It is known but not yet practised in Lepers' Island, but is said to have been already introduced into the southern part of Aurora. A sharp bamboo is used. There is no doubt that the custom, for it is not a rite, has come across from the eastwards to the Southern New Hebrides, and has been for some time in common use, the dress in some of those islands, if it may be so called, being adapted to it.

The childhood of a girl can hardly be marked except by her advance towards matrimony, to which her being clothed and tattooed is in some places at least a necessary step. In Florida and the neighbouring parts, in Santa Cruz, in Pentecost Island, and most of the New Hebrides, the women's dress is a petticoat of strings of fibre or of leaves. In the south-eastern Solomon Islands and the Banks' Islands the women wear a band with tufts or fringes, to which in Lepers' Island there is added out of doors a mat which envelopes the person. The moral character and training of the girls may well be

noticed before their betrothal and marriage are taken in hand.
Considerable laxity of intercourse between boys and girls
undoubtedly existed, and unchastity was not very seriously
regarded ; yet it is certain that in these islands generally
there was by no means that insensibility in regard to female
virtue with which the natives are so commonly charged.
There is but too good a cause generally for the natives to
present at once their unchaste females to white visitors, and
these then speak from experience little creditable to those of
their colour who have preceded them.   There is a considerable
difference however to be observed between one island and
another in this matter, an example of which appears in the
presence or absence of a word signifying a harlot.   In Florida
such a woman is called *rembi*, and occupied not long ago a
recognized place in native life ; but it was in consequence
generally of misconduct, such as adultery or fornication within
the *kema* kin, that a woman was condemned by the chief of
her place to such a life.   She belonged to the chief, lived in
one of his houses, and most of her earnings were his.   When
she had accumulated porpoise teeth and money she would be
allowed to marry, being well worth having, and then reference
to her former career would not be proper.   While *rembi* she
was not particularly despised ; no one would step over her legs,
go too near to her, or talk to her without cause.   At Wango
in San Cristoval and in the neighbourhood girls were very
loose before marriage, getting money for themselves privately
by prostitution ; and besides, there are harlots, *repi*, there, some
girls not yet married, and some widows.   They considered
themselves much stricter at Saa in Malanta ; a girl of family
found pregnant before marriage would be killed, unless the
paramour could pay enough to save her and make her his wife.
A girl of no family, that is, not of the chief's family, would
not be killed, but might be allowed to become a harlot if not
married by her lover.   Sometimes a man allows his daughter
to become a harlot to gain money ; and a chief at Ulawa will
buy a girl from her father and keep her to earn money for him
as well as for herself ; but such a *repi* in either island is not

respected, is thought a low character, and will have but little given for her if she is married. The good families in Ulawa also are strict, and mothers look well after their girls. At Santa Cruz, where the separation of the sexes is so carefully maintained, there are certainly public courtesans. In the Banks' Islands there is no such thing known[1]; it was always in old times the duty of parents to look well after their children both boys and girls, and to scold and correct them if they should see them going wrong; girls were never allowed to go about alone without their mother or elder friend; however common irregular intercourse may have been it was never allowed, never respectable, public feeling was on the side of virtue. There were respectable families where the girls were known or presumed to conduct themselves perfectly well, to *toga mantag*, and a girl from such a family would as a rule be chaste up to the time of her marriage. Bastards were very rare in the Banks' Islands[2]. A woman living without a husband would indeed sometimes be seen with children; but then it was known in the place that she had been taken to wife by a man whose previous wife was jealous and had driven her from the house. In the Northern New Hebrides, as Pentecost and Lepers' Island, harlots are unknown, though there are unmarried girls and married women who are known to receive mats and ornaments in prostitution secretly. There is a story in Lepers' Island of a man with two wives who when he went from home hung a bag in his house which he expected to be filled with mats by the time he came home. In these islands also a reputation for chastity is valued for its own sake, and in respectable families care is taken of the girls. In every island it may be said that there are households in which it is understood that the family is generally

[1] To translate the word harlot in Mota, it has been necessary to use the phrase *tavine vilevile som*, a woman who gives money, with a singular inversion of meaning. In fact the women of bad character are those married women who give secretly money to youths by way of invitation. The youth gives back food by way of pledge.

[2] A bastard was called *nat gaegae*, a child of the thicket, and was said to be *wota vanameag*, born without belongings, as a desert place is *vanua vanameag*.

well conducted, and which are respectable accordingly, and everywhere there are families which are not respectable. Bastards are generally very rare.

Betrothal comes very early in the life of many Melanesian girls ; a man with a son born to him looks out for the birth of a suitable girl to be his son's wife. This is especially the case with persons of consequence and wealth, and upon this begins the long series of payments and negotiations which come to their end at the marriage. The general character of these transactions may be understood from the ways in which matrimonial affairs are managed in the various islands. The first marriage of the young man may be taken to be in view ; wives are added to the first with less to do about it, but not without a good deal of bargaining on the part of the men concerned, and a great deal of business and talking on that of the women. In Florida the girl who has been engaged as an infant, and for whom some payment has been made on the engagement, is tattooed when she comes to the proper age for it. This, *uhuuhu*, is done by a man whose profession it is to do it, and who receives much money, pigs, and food in the exercise of his art ; a feast is made for him and for the company assembled of friends and relations, who help to bear the expense. The pattern is first marked out in circles with a bamboo, and the skin is cut with the bone of a bat's wing. The amount of tattooing varies, but the pain and swelling is always considerable. No girl would be considered marriageable unless tattooed, and the operation performed is a sign that the time is come when the father of the young man to whom one is engaged should pay something down with a view to the marriage. Further advance, however, may be delayed for months or even years before the future father-in-law goes with his party to pay down the whole sum of money agreed upon. Then after staying two days at least, with endless difficulties interposed, the girl is given up, and an extra sum of money has to be paid, *na rongo ni nggoti kekesa*, the money to break the post near the door used to take hold of in going in and out of the house, to finish her going in and out of her old home. This is given to the women of the bride's party, who then take her by the hand and give her up. They lift her from the ground and carry her on the back of one of them out of the house to the other party, who then take her away. The bridegroom does not yet make his appearance. The bride then stays in her father-in-law's house two or three months waiting for her parents to bring their present of pigs and food. When they arrive with this they make a feast which is the wedding banquet, but neither they nor the young couple partake of it. This is the final ceremony; the young man takes his wife to his father's house or his own ; he is married, *taulagi* [1]. The amount given by the bridegroom's party varies according to the wealth and position of the families ; from fifty to a hundred *rongo*, coils of native money. When fifty is given, the bride's party give in return five pigs ; and when a hundred, ten pigs ; and they say that the money buys the pigs and not the damsel. It is the duty of the young man's relations to help him in this matter, and they are very willing to do it, if he on his part has been active and willing in garden-work and other duties.

At Saa in Malanta when little children have been betrothed, the girl, still very young, comes bringing her food with her to spend a month or two in her future father-in-law's house, and to become acquainted with the family. The betrothed children converse and play together at their ease, knowing what is proposed ; and this visit is repeated while the children are little from time to time, and part of the money porpoise teeth, and dogs' teeth to be paid to the girl's

---

[1] 'During the morning of the feast, whilst the bride's relations are waiting about for the acknowledgment of their contributions to the wedding breakfast, it is the custom of the boys of the village to take their bows and arrows and prowl amongst these watchers, and so to irritate or alarm them by shooting amongst them, that they are glad to buy immunity from this dangerous amusement by paying a fish's tooth. They shot over their heads and past their ears, and between their feet, and through their hair, till one heard exclamations of disgust and annoyance on all sides.'—Rev. J. H. Plant. It should be observed that this is in the bridegroom's village, and that the boys' object is to get bought off.

father is handed over [1]. In consequence of this familiarity, when the girl is marriageable and all is arranged she goes willingly enough to take up her abode in her new family, without any real or affected reluctance on her part, or lifting and carrying by her friends. It is sometimes, however, a long time before the marriage is consummated, through the shyness of the bridegroom, though the parents encourage the young couple to be friendly, and give them opportunities of talking and working together. The virginity of a bride is a matter of much concern to her friends, not only because the boy's friends will not pay what they have promised if her character in questionable, but because they value propriety. This all refers to the good families in the main; among inferior people early betrothals are unusual; the young people have not always made friends, and the taking of the bride to her new home is a greater affair. At Santa Cruz in the same way engagements of marriage are often made in infancy. The father looks out a suitable girl sooner or later, and the boy is not told. Presents and feather-money are interchanged between the parents on both sides. In course of time the boy is told that a girl is engaged for him, but is not told who she is; he is warned only not to go near a certain house, and guesses who it is. The youth when the time comes is often very reluctant to marry, he cries and asks why they want him to go away. However, when he marries he brings his wife to his father's house, until he builds one for himself [2].

In the Banks' Islands arrangements are made by the friends, and the payment to be made agreed upon; the young man, or his friends for him, *la goro o tavine*, give money and pigs to secure the woman, and her friends again *tango goro o nago lagia*, ' lay hold on the face of the marriage,' by an answering present.

---

[1] On one occasion, when Bishop Selwyn was present, eighteen porpoise teeth, fifty strings of money, twenty pigs.

[2] I have been told by a Loyalty Island teacher living on the island that a young married couple do not cohabit, but meet secretly for a time. This however was not allowed to be correct by Santa Cruz boys of whom I enquired.

When the matter is settled the bridegroom's friends make a feast, and the tail of the pig is given to the bride's father. After due payment of the money the girl is taken to wife without ceremony. If a girl were engaged to an old man or one she dislikes she might run off into the bush with the youth of her choice, and a pig given by his friends might settle the matter. The payments for a wife are not very heavy in this group, but vary in the different islands. A girl betrothed as a child is here often taken to her future home to be brought up there to know the people and, if she belongs to another island, the language of the place. Boys and girls, and young people generally, who are engaged are very shy about it, and will hardly look at one another; but as the time for marriage draws on it is correct for the youth to make little presents and otherwise shew attention.

In the Northern New Hebrides a girl betrothed in child-hood is taken to her future father-in-law's house and brought up there; the boy often thinks she is his sister, and is much ashamed when he comes to know the relation in which he stands. This however is not the common way, for it is only the children of great people who are betrothed as infants. When the girl is old enough to be married in Araga she is sometimes tattooed, and always assumes her petticoat. There is some ceremony there when the marriage day arrives; people assemble in the middle of the village, and the father of the bride or some friend of consequence makes a speech. The bridegroom sticks a branch of a dracæna into the ground and brings up the pigs, food, and mats given for the bride. Then the orator exhorts him to feed his wife properly and treat her kindly, and not to be sulky with her, and he hands over the young woman, who is attired in a new petticoat and wrapped in a new mat. There follows a feast, and the bridegroom goes round about his father-in-law or the orator, stroking him, to thank him. A sort of sham-fight takes place on the occasion, in which sometimes men are hurt, the two sides being the kinsmen of the bridegroom and of the bride; if one of the bridegroom's

brethren is hurt, it is his business to make it up with him by
a present. Whether this can be called capture is very
doubtful; but no doubt it represents the feelings with which
the bride's kinsmen regard the loss of her services; it cannot
be the loss of any rights of intercourse, since she was unapproachable by any of them. The bride is taken by female
friends to the bridegroom's house or his father's, sometimes
crying, and dragged along if she dislikes the match. An
unwilling bride will refuse intercourse with her husband, or
run away to some one she likes better; in that case, if her
return seems hopeless, a pig is given and she stays. Sometimes, again, the young couple are so shy of one another that
they will not speak after marriage, as it has not been proper
to speak before; the friends and neighbours do not approve
of this, and it is on this account that it is thought wise
to ensure mutual acquaintance and liking by bringing the
engaged couple together as children. At Lepers' Island
among people of consequence infant betrothals are the proper
thing; when a chief has a girl born to him another will
come and secure her for his boy, giving a present and
making a feast. If the boy is old enough at the time of the
feast he is made to take a young drinking cocoa-nut, put a
dracæna leaf into the eye of it, and give it to the infant's
mother for the child to drink. This is called *huhu vuhe goroe*,
to give her suck with a drinking cocoa-nut and secure her[1].
When the betrothed girl is about ten years old, the boy's
mother takes her to her own house to teach her household
ways, and the children are for the time brought up together.
When she is growing big her parents take her back for her
tattooing, which is done in lines all over her body, with
nothing on her face. Hitherto she has worn nothing except
on great occasions; now she is always clothed; in the house

---

[1] ' When a female child is born, the father or mother of some male child
brings him into the house with a bamboo of water, and the male child proceeds
to wash the female, who henceforth becomes his betrothed, and they grow up
together recognizing each other as man and wife.'—Rev. C. Bice; at Maewo,
Aurora Island.

she wears only the *para*, a fringed band, and out of doors she is wrapped in mats. At this time the women on both sides are very busy talking over the price to be paid by the bridegroom's friends, which varies much; if the youth is the son of a great man, a tusked pig and a hundred mats are not too much, for common people two or three ordinary pigs and fifty mats will do. These arrangements often take a long time, for the women delight in them; and while they go on the young couple are encouraged to converse and not be shy. At last the wedding day arrives; the young man's friends take the pigs, mats, and uncooked food, and set them down in the middle of the bride's village. The bride's friends have already prepared cooked food, and the two parties eat together; the marriage is thus complete. The bride is carried on someone's back to her new home, wrapped in many mats, and with palm-fans held about her face, because she is supposed to be modest and shy. Formerly there was always a house built beforehand, and food prepared for the young couple, who ate together as a sign of union. Here, as elsewhere, a girl will run away to one she loves, and he may keep her if he can satisfy her friends; but sometimes he is afraid of the disappointed bridegroom's friends, sometimes he is too poor to make it up with hers; he is obliged then to decline to receive her, and she must go back, unless indeed she had rather strangle or hang herself.

The reserve exercised between those who have been brought near by marriage, and the mutual avoidance of some, has been already mentioned, and must be understood to begin as soon as the engagement of the young couple is complete. There is a singular example of this kind of reserve at Florida, where there is no difficulty in meeting or using the names of persons connected by marriage. In case of a woman having had a lover before her marriage she will never after marriage mention his name, calling him *a hanu*, that person, and she will never meet him in the path. Her husband looks out for this, and observing who it is demands money of the former lover, and when that is paid no more notice is taken of the matter; but if satisfaction were refused a quarrel would ensue. A newly-married husband, without waiting for observations, would often beat his bride to make her confess who her paramour had been.

The old habits of the people in all the islands were very strict in regard to adultery. The punishment of the man was death; but the punishment was very generally mitigated on payment of a fine. Thus in Florida an injured husband would give money to the chief to have the adulterer killed, and he, if he could, would make satisfaction in money to both chief and husband, and so save his life. The woman, however, would probably be made a *rembi*, harlot, for the profit of the chief. At Saa an adulterous wife is dismissed, and the adulterer is punished with death, exile, or fines. In case of adultery in a chief's family he will have the adulterer killed, or receiving a large fine will let him go to Ulawa and live; a man's friends will sometimes hide him for a time, hoping that the chief will consent to take a fine, and if they find him implacable, will kill the man themselves or give him up. When the wrong has been done among lesser men, the friends of the husband and of the adulterer will often fight about the damages to be exacted; and from this cause indeed most of the fighting throughout all the groups proceeds. A chief of Saa, Ulawa, Ugi, or San Cristoval, who has had the adulterer killed, makes a *bea*, a stage from which speeches are made, and rewards those who have killed him; and for himself at Saa he makes the sacrifice *toto 'akalo* (page 137), to clear away any danger that may happen to him as the cause of death. In the Banks' Islands and Northern New Hebrides the treatment of adultery is very simple; the man is shot or clubbed by the husband or his friends in their first indignation, and the woman is beaten, scolded, and threatened with death, but the matter is compromised very generally by payment of money and pigs. A wife jealous of her husband, or in any way incensed at him, would in former times throw herself from a cliff or tree, swim out to sea, hang or strangle herself, stab herself with an arrow, or thrust one down her

throat ; and a man jealous or quarrelling with his wife would
do the like ; but now it is easy to go off with another's wife
or husband in a labour vessel to Queensland or Fiji.

Divorce is easy and common, and may be said to be effected
at the will of either party, though it is naturally more easy
for a man to dismiss his wife than for a woman to leave her
husband. The great difficulty is the property given for the
wife ; a man does not wish to lose this, and will try many
times to get back a runaway wife before he gives her
up, giving presents to her relations. If the separation is
amicable, the father of the woman will give back what he
has received, having in view another son-in-law. After some
time spent in wedlock the woman has worked out a good deal
of what was given for her, and a pig or two on one side or the
other settles all claims. It may be said that generally man
and wife get on well together, and are united by their great
fondness for their children.

The Levirate obtains as a matter of course. The wife has
been obtained for one member of a family by the contributions
of the whole, and if that member fails by death, some other is
ready to take his place, so that the property shall not be lost ;
it is a matter of arrangement for convenience and economy
whether a brother, cousin or uncle of the deceased shall take his
widow. The brother naturally comes first ; if a more distant
relation takes the woman he probably has to give a pig.
In Lepers' Island if a man who is a somewhat distant cousin
of the deceased wishes to take the widow, he adds a pig to the
death-feast of the tenth or fiftieth day to signify and support
his pretensions, and he probably gives another pig to the
widow's sisters to obtain their good-will. If two men contend
for the widow she selects one, and the fortunate suitor gives a
pig to the disappointed. In fact a woman, when once the
proper payment has been made for her, belongs to those who
have paid, the family generally ; hence a man, as in the story
of Ganviviris, will set up his sister's son in life by handing
over to him one of his own wives ; not because the young
man has a right to his uncle's wives, but because the woman

is already in the family. It is a rare thing that a woman should remain a widow long, but there is a period and sign of mourning. In San Cristoval men and women wear large tassels of grey shells as ear-rings for a mark of widowhood; to cut the hair short and daub the person with soot and ashes is very common. In the Banks' Islands the widow or widower refrains from some article of food, such as yam, for a year or lesser time, and wears a rope round the neck, a *ganaro*, as a sign of it. To *val* or *naro* in this way is a sign of mourning for any loss.

Polygamy is the rule, though a considerable number of wives is found only with rich and elder men. One wife is commonly enough for a Florida man, who says that he can neither manage nor afford more than one. When a great man like Takua had seven it was thought a great many. At Visale in Guadalcanar Tekaunga has, or had, sixty wives; in Florida a wife costs much, in Guadalcanar but little. At Saa ordinary men have two wives, great men eight or ten. In the Banks' Islands a well-to-do man has ordinarily two wives, and may have three. A Vanua Lava man was not long ago believed to have thirty. As a man advances in life and survives his maternal uncles, his brothers, and his cousins, the widows of these tend to accumulate around him; they are called his wives, live in houses round him and work for him, but he lives practically with two or three younger women whom he has taken for himself. In Lepers' Island, where men generally have two wives, a singular arrangement is approved of, whereby a man who has a young wife takes an elder woman, a widow, for a second, to look after the first. Some men there have three or four wives; a great man lately had fifty wives, and his son and successor has already thirty; a chief inland is credited with a hundred. Polygamy in all the islands is a fruitful cause of quarrels and bloodshed.

Anything properly called Polyandry is unknown, nor is it easy for natives to conceive of it as a possible marriage state. Still cases are known in the Banks' Islands where two widowers live with one widow, and she is called wife to both, any child she may have being called the child of both. Such cohabitation, however, is not so much marriage as a convenient arrangement for people who find themselves alone in later life. In Lepers' Island, also, there has been a case lately in which two young men, brothers, returned from Queensland, have taken a young woman as a wife for both. The two men have their *gamali*, and she has a house; there are two children. This is a new and unheard-of thing, brought, as the natives say, from Queensland [1]; the young men could only get one woman to marry, and in their absence had lost all care for propriety. In the Banks' Islands also cases occur where a husband connives at his wife's connexion with another man; this is not counted adultery because it is allowed; it is not polyandry, for the second man is not a husband; the thing is thought discreditable.

[1] 'Polyandry is to be seen under our eyes here in Fiji among the "imported labourers."'—Rev. L. Fison. The women being very few in proportion to the men become something like communal wives to those of their island, or group, one of whom they could have married at home.

CHAPTER XV.

DEATH. BURIAL. AFTER DEATH.

THAT death is the parting of soul and body, and that the departed soul continues in an intelligent and more or less active existence, is what Melanesians everywhere believe; but what that is which in life abides with the body, and in death departs from it, and which, speaking of it in English, we call the soul, they find it very difficult to explain. Like people very much more advanced than themselves, they have not in the first place a perfectly clear conception of what it is; and in the second place, like other people, they use words to represent these conceptions which they acknowledge to be more or less figurative and inexact, when the precise meaning of them is sought for. Nor is it any wonder that, believing that such a thing as what we call a soul exists in connexion with the body which they see, they speak of and conceive of the soul when separate from the body as if it were in some form and shape visible to the eyes. Thinking, to Melanesian natives at any rate, is like seeing; what is thought of must have some form to be thought of in; and a visible thing that has a likeness to that which is thought of offers its name as a convenient means of expression. 'Suppose that there are people who call the soul a shadow, I do not in the least believe that they think the shadow a soul or the soul a shadow; but they use the word shadow figuratively for that belonging to man which is like his shadow, definitely individual and inseparable from him, but unsubstantial. The Mota word we use for soul is in Maori a shadow, but no Mota man knows that it ever meant that. In fact my belief is that in the original language this word did not definitely mean either soul or shadow, but had a meaning one can conceive but not express, which has come out in one language meaning shadow, and in the other meaning something like soul, i.e. second self[1].' So Mr. Fison writes. 'The Fijian word for soul is *yalo*, that for shadow *yaloyalo*. I have not been able to find any trace of the belief that shadow and soul are indentical. I believe that Williams' remark about the " two spirits" was the result of a confusion in his mind concerning *yalo* and *yaloyalo*.' The civilized observer is always ready to assume that the savage takes a childish view and has absurd beliefs, when all the while, if the savage could put him to a close examination, his own conceptions would be found very indistinct and his expressions mainly figurative. Many a voyager, not an observer, carries away as a sort of joke the story that the natives think their shadows are their souls, who could not tell exactly what he means by the word 'soul' which he uses himself. It may suffice to make the statement that, whatever word the Melanesian people use for soul, they mean something essentially belonging to each man's nature which carries life to his body with it, and is the seat of thought and intelligence, exercising therefore power which is not of the body and is invisible in its action. Further understanding of their conceptions cannot well fail to follow from the study of the words they use.

It has been shown (page 121) that among Melanesians there is a universal belief in the existence of personal intelligent beings of power superior to that of men, and without bodies such as are the bodies of mankind; and that these beings, whom we call spirits, are distinct from the disembodied spirits or souls of dead men which we call ghosts. It is not surprising, therefore, that the same word which is used for spirit should be used also to describe the soul of man while it is clothed with and animates his body. The soul of a living

---

[1] Quoted in Professor Max Müller's Hibbert Lectures, p. 88.

man in Florida is a *tarunga,* a spirit, individual, not corporeal, separable, though not in fact often separated during life from his body. So also is such a spirit as a *vigona* a *tarunga,* though they are not very ready to acknowledge the existence of such a *tarunga.* During life a man's *tarunga* goes out of him in dreams and returns; at death the *tarunga* departs finally from the body; the corpse is simply a dead man, *tinoni mate* ; the separated soul is no longer *tarunga,* a spirit, but *tindalo,* a ghost. But *tarunga* is not equivalent to soul any more than spirit is equivalent to soul ; a soul is a *tarunga,* and no other name is given to it. Pigs have *tarunga* ; when a man sells a pig he takes back from it its *tarunga* in a dracæna leaf, which he hangs up in his house ; thus he does not lose more than the fleshly accidents of the pig, the *tarunga* remains waiting to animate some pig that will be born. A pig is an animal of distinction and has a *tarunga* ; yams and such things have none ; they do not live with any kind of intelligence. Is it then to be said that a man and a pig are alike as regards the *tarunga,* that each has a soul ? The native to whom the question is put intelligibly will laugh ; such a thing cannot be ; when a man dies his *tarunga* is a *tindalo,* a ghost, and who ever heard of a pig *tindalo*[1]? In the Banks' Islands the spirit that never was a man, but was always superhuman in intelligence and power, and, as far as could be conceived of a personal being, was incorporeal, was called a *vui* (page 124). It would not be surprising, therefore, if the word *vui* were used to describe the soul ; and it is impossible to say that it would be incorrectly so used, for the nature of a *vui* and of a soul is the same (page 124)[2]. The words accepted in use to represent the English soul are in Motlav *talegi,* in Mota *atai.* A man's *talegi* goes out of him in sleep, not in all dreams, but in such as leave a vivid impression of scenes and persons visited when the man awakes.

---

[1] The word *taluna,* another form of *tarunga,* is found in Santa Cruz, but I am unable to assign to it any more particular meaning than ' spirit.'

[2] In fact I have known a native of Mota writing of his inward feelings to speak of his *vui, na vuik.*

When a man fainted the *talegi* had gone out, but life remained.
Life depends on the presence of the *talegi* in the body, health
depends upon its sound condition. A ghost can damage the
talegi, either spontaneously or moved by magic charms, and
then the man falls sick, and his body is weak, or the ghost
takes the *talegi* away, and the man lies just breathing in his
chest ; but it would not be said that all disease is the result
of the *talegi* being taken or damaged ; it would not be said of
ulcers for example. The *talegi* has no form, but it is like a
reflection or a shadow. The Mota *atai* is no doubt the Maori
ata, which means a shadow, but *atai* never means shadow in
Mota, nor is *niniai*, which means shadow and reflection, ever
used for soul. At the same time damage was thought to be
done to the body by means of the shadow or reflection, as
when the shadow fell upon a certain stone (pages 182, 4), or a
man's face was reflected in a certain spring of water (page 186).
The power of the spirit, *vui*, belonging to the stone or the
spring could lay hold on the man by his shadow and reflection,
as the power of a ghost could get a hold on a man by a
fragment of his food, the shadow being in a way another
person of the man. But that the shadow was the soul was
never thought. So in Saa they talk of a ghost snatching
away the shadow of a child that starts in sleep, and a
doctor undertakes to bring it back ; but, says Joseph Wate,
who tells the tale, ' they say shadow and they mean something else, for the shadow of the child is seen all the while.'
The use of the word *atai* in Mota seems properly and originally to have been to signify something peculiarly and
intimately connected with a person and sacred to him, something that he has set his fancy upon when he has seen it in
what has seemed to him a wonderful manner, or some one has
shewn it to him as such. Whatever the thing might be the
man believed it to be the reflection of his own personality ;
he and his *atai* flourished, suffered, lived and died together.
But the word must not be supposed to have been borrowed
from this use and applied secondarily to describe the soul ; the
word carries a sense with it which is applicable alike to that

second self, the visible object so mysteriously connected with
the man, and to this invisible second self which we call the
soul. There is another Mota word, *tamaniu*, which has almost
if not quite the same meaning as *atai* has when it describes
something animate or inanimate which a man has come to believe to have an existence intimately connected with his own.
The word *tamaniu* may be taken to be properly 'likeness,' and
the noun form of the adverb *tama*, as, like. It was not every
one in Mota who had his *tamaniu*; only some men fancied
that they had this relation to a lizard, a snake, or it might be
a stone; sometimes the thing was sought for and found by
drinking the infusion of certain leaves and heaping together
the dregs; then whatever living thing was first seen in or
upon the heap was the *tamaniu*. It was watched but not fed
or worshipped; the natives believed that it came at call, and
that the life of the man was bound up with the life of his
tamaniu, if a living thing, or with its safety; should it die, or
if not living get broken or be lost, the man would die.
Hence in case of sickness they would send to see if the *tamaniu*
was safe and well. This word has never been used apparently
for the soul in Mota; but in Aurora in the New Hebrides it
is the accepted equivalent. It is well worth observing that
both the *atai* and the *tamaniu*, and it may be added the
Motlav *talegi*, is something which has a substantial existence
of its own, as when a snake or stone is a man's *atai* or *tamaniu*;
a soul then when called by these names is conceived of as
something in a way substantial. There is another word used
in Mota, never applied to the soul of man, but very illustrative
of the native conceptions, and common also to Aurora, where it
is used with a remarkable application; this word is *nunuai*.
In Mota it is the abiding or recurrent impression on the
senses that is called a *nunuai*; a man who has heard some
startling scream in the course of the day has it ringing in his
ears; the scream is over and the sound is gone, but the *nunuai*
remains; a man fishing for flying-fish paddles all day alone in
his canoe with a long light line fastened round his neck; he
lies down tired at night and feels the line pulling as if a fish

were caught, though the line is no longer on his neck ; this is
the *nunuai* of the line.   To the native it is not a mere fancy,
it is real, but it has no form or substance.   A pig, therefore,
ornaments or food have a *nunuai* ; but a pig has no *atai*, or
may hesitatingly and, carelessly be said to have one.   This
word is no doubt the same as *niniai*, shadow or reflection,
meaning not shade, which is *malumalu*, but the definite figure
cast by the interception of rays of light upon the ground, or
formed by reflection in the water.   There is no confusion in
the native mind between a shadow and a reflection, but they
use the one word to describe that definite individual something
which, itself insubstantial, is so closely connected with the
substance that gives it form.

This word, in the form *nunu*, is used in Aurora to describe
the fancied relation of an infant to some thing or person from
which or from whom its origin is somehow derived.   A woman
before her child is born fancies that a cocoa-nut, bread-fruit,
or some such thing has some original connexion with her
infant.   When the child is born it is the *nunu* of the cocoa-nut,
or whatever it may be, and as it grows up it must by no means
eat that thing, or it will be ill ; no one thinks that there is
any real connexion in the way of parentage, but the child is a
kind of echo.   There is another way in which a child is the
nunu of a person deceased.   Thus Arudulewari is the *nunu* of a
boy whom his mother brought up and who was much beloved
by her.   This boy died not long before Arudulewari was born,
and then the mother believed that her foster-child had wished
to come back to her, and that the infant was his *nunu*.   But
Arudulewari is not that person, nor, as he says, is his soul
supposed to be the soul of the dead boy; he himself is the *nunu*,
the echo or reflection of him.   So Vilemalas, a name which
means ' Bring-the-day-after,' was born after an adopted child
of his mother's had been killed and not brought back till the
day after, and he is the *nunu* of the slain person come in his
place.   In Mota there is no such use of *nunuai*, but there is a
notion that a man may have something, not exactly his *atai*
or *tamaniu*, with which he is originally connected.   A man

will scatter money into a deep pool among the rocks on the
shore into which the tide is pouring, a sacred place ; he will
call on his near forefathers, dive in, and seat himself upon the
bottom. If he sees anything there, a crab or cuttle-fish
perhaps, he fancies that is his real origin and beginning ; he
gets *mana*, supernatural power, from it, and pigs will multiply
to him. At Maewo, Aurora, *nunu* is never the soul ; that is
tamaniu ; and it is a very remarkable thing that the body
is thought to be the integument of the soul. It is a strange
thing that in the islands of the New Hebrides nearest to
Aurora, in Pentecost and Lepers' Island, the word *tamtegi*
is used for soul, for this is no doubt the Mota *tamate*, dead
man ; the natives, however, have persisted in their assertion
that they have no other word.

We are now prepared to follow the corpse of the dead
Melanesian to his burial, and his soul after its separation from
the body to the abode of the dead ; and it is probably better
to do this by taking the funeral customs and the beliefs
concerning the state after death together as they are found in
the various islands. It will be seen that there is a considerable
agreement both in customs and beliefs, and a universal consent
about some particulars, such as in belief in the continued
existence of the separated soul, and in the practice of com-
memorating the dead by feasts at which some portion of food
is offered to them. In the Solomon Islands the ghost, being
the principal object of worship, occupies, as has been shewn, a
much higher place in the religious world of the natives than
it does in the islands which lie to the eastward, and on that
account it is desirable, before entering upon details, to draw
the distinction between the two classes of ghosts which is
generally recognized in the former islands. The distinction is
between ghosts of power and ghosts of no account, between
those whose help is sought and their wrath deprecated, and
those from whom nothing is expected and to whom no observance is due. Among living men there are some who stand
out distinguished for capacity in affairs, success in life, valour
in fighting, and influence over others ; and these are so, it is

believed, because of the supernatural and mysterious powers
which they have, and which are derived from communication
with those ghosts of the dead gone before them who are full
of those same powers.   On the death of a distinguished man
his ghost retains the powers that belonged to him in life, in
greater activity and with stronger force ; his ghost therefore
is powerful and worshipful, and so long as he is remembered
the aid of his powers is sought and worship is offered him ;
he is the *tindalo* of Florida, the *lio'a* of Saa.   In every society,
again, the multitude is composed of insignificant persons,
'numerus fruges consumere nati,' of no particular account for
valour, skill, or prosperity.   The ghosts of such persons continue their insignificance, and are nobodies after death as
before ; they are ghosts because all men have souls, and the souls
of dead men are ghosts ; they are dreaded because all ghosts are
awful, but they get no worship and are soon only thought of
as the crowd of the nameless population of the lower world.

   In the Solomon Islands, in Florida, when a man dies, his
spirit, *tarunga*, becomes a ghost, *tindalo*, and the body is
spoken of as a dead man, *tinoni mate*.   Some ghosts are worshipped and exercise much spiritual activity in the world as
tindalo (chaps. vii, viii) ; some pass at once out of the consideration of all but members of the family.   The corpse is
usually buried.   Common men are buried in their garden
ground, chiefs sometimes in the village, a chief's child sometimes in the house.   The grave is not deep ; it becomes
sacred in so far as no one will tread upon any grave, while
the burial-place of a man whose *tindalo* has become an object
of worship is a sanctuary, *vunuha* ; the skull is often dug
up and hung in the house.   Men and women are buried
alike, their feet turned inland ; the return from the funeral
is by another road than that along which the corpse was
carried, lest the ghost should follow.   A man is buried with
money, porpoise teeth, and ornaments belonging to him, his
bracelets put on upside down ; and these things are often
afterwards secretly dug up again.   Sometimes a man will
express a wish to be cast into the sea ; his friends then

paddle out with him, tie stones to his feet, and sink him.
In Savo, near by, common men are thrown into the sea as a
rule, and only great men buried.   In Florida the funeral of a
chief, or of one who is much esteemed, is delayed for two
days after death; and after the funeral the relatives and
friends assemble to *kilo dato na tinoni mate,* that is to say, to
partake of a funeral feast, and to hang up on the dead man's
house his cloth, his axes, spears, shield, and other properties,
heaping yams and other food upon the ground.   At the feast
a bit of the food is thrown into the fire for the deceased, with
the call, 'This is for you.'   As the mourners eat, they are
anxious about swallowing the food well down; if a morsel
sticks in any one's throat, it is a *butuli,* a portent, the man
will die.   When they hang up the dead man's arms on his
house, they make great lamentations; all remains afterwards
untouched, the house goes to ruin, mantled as time goes on
with the vines of the growing yams, a picturesque and
indeed, perhaps, a touching sight; for these things are not
set up that they may in a ghostly manner accompany their
former owner, they are set there for a memorial of him as a
great and valued man, like the hatchment of old times.
With the same feeling they cut down a dead man's fruit-
trees as a mark of respect and affection, not with any notion
of these things serving him in the world of ghosts; he ate of
them, they say, when he was alive, he will never eat again,
and no one else shall have them.   There is a certain notion
that burial is a benefit to the ghost; if a man is killed anywhere and his body is not buried, his ghost will haunt the
place; when a man's head has been taken, and his skull added
to some chief's collection, the ghost for a time, at least,
haunts about; and so it is also when the arms and legs of
men murdered or executed for crimes are sent to distant
places to shew what has been done.   Ghosts of men whose
heads have been taken are seen without their heads.   The
abode of the departed is Betindalo; but yet ghosts not only
haunt their burial-places and come to the sacrifices offered to
them, but they are heard at play by night blowing panpipes,

dancing and shouting. Betindalo is apparently situated in
the south-eastern part of the great island of Guadalcanar, to
which the ghosts pass over through the district of Florida
nearest to it, Gaeta. Here appears a ship of the dead, almost
alone in Melanesia. The Gaeta people used to believe that
all the ghosts of Florida passed along a path through their
gardens leading to a point of land where they assembled ; as
they passed along nothing was seen, but a twittering sound
was heard ; while they were waiting at the point their
dancing was heard at night. From time to time a canoe
came over from Guadalcanar and took the ghosts across to
Galaga, opposite to Gaeta. They landed first upon a rock
near to the shore, and there for the first time became aware
that they were dead. Arrived upon the shore, they met a
certain *tindalo* with a rod, which he thrust into the cartilage
of their noses to see if they were pierced ; if that were so,
there was a good path the ghosts could follow down towards
Marau at the extremity of Guadalcanar ; ghosts who could
not pass this test were not allowed to follow the path, but
had to make their way as they could with pain and difficulty.
Living men in canoes when nearing the shore at Galaga have
seen the forms of the dead and recognized the persons, but
on near approach they disappeared. A man not long ago
alive at Gaeta once appeared to die, but revived to tell
the story how he had passed with others along the path of
ghosts, and had gone to take his place in the canoe which
came for them at night ; but a tall black *tindalo*, he said,
whom he recognized, forbad him to come aboard, and sent
him back into the world again.

At Bugotu, in Ysabel, the spirit, *tarunga*, leaving the dead
man, *tinoni dhehe*, becomes a ghost, *tindadho*; the place of
ghosts is the little island of Laulau, but they haunt their
graves, and are seen at night, disappearing when approached.
The ghosts, as they fly through the air and near Laulau, light
first on certain rocks where they become aware of their sad
condition. Living men visit the island, as in the story of
Samuku, and see these rocks ; they see also forms as of men

which vanish as they are approached ; they find paths round
the island neatly kept, and bathing-places cleared of stones ;
if they hang up fish in the trees, they seek for them in vain
in the morning ; marks made to shew a road are taken away.
On the top of the island is a pool of water, Kolapapauro, and
thither the ghosts, when they arrive, repair to present themselves to Bolafagina, the *tindadho* who is the lord of the
place.   Across the pool is a narrow tree-trunk lying, along
which the ghosts advance ; Bolafagina examines their hands
to see if they have the mark cut upon them (a conventional
outline of the frigate-bird ; page 180) which admits them to
his company ; those who have it not are thrown from the tree
into the gulf beneath, and perish out of their ghostly life.
When a chief dies, they bury him so that his head is near
the surface, and over it they keep a fire burning, so that they
may take up the skull for preservation in the house of the
man who succeeds to power.   An expedition then starts to
procure heads in honour of the deceased, now become a
tindadho to be worshipped.   Any one not belonging to the
place will be killed for the sake of his head, and the heads
procured are arranged upon the beach, and believed to add
mana, spiritual power, to the new *tindadho* ; until these
are procured the people of the place do not move about.
The grave is built up with stones, and sacrifices are offered
upon it [1].

At Wango in San Cristoval the soul, *'aunga* (another form
of *tarunga*), departed from the body becomes a ghost, *'ataro*, and
the ghost on leaving the body is believed to make its way to
three small islands near Ulawa.   On his first arrival there the
ghost feels himself still a man, and does not realize his condition ; he finds friends, and gives them the news of the place
he has just left.   After some days a kingfisher pecks his head,
and he becomes a mere ghost (page 190).   The existence of
the ghosts in these islands, Rondomana, is shadowy and

---

[1] ‘ The dead man’s wife and child were then dragged to the open grave and
strangled there, and their bodies thrown in, together with his possessions, guns,
rifles, money, and valuables of all kinds.’—Rev. A. Penny.

inactive ; they range aimlessly about and lodge in caves. Men
landing on the islands in stress of weather see them on the
beach ; but they dread living men, and disappear when closely
approached. It must be taken that these *'ataro* which abide
in Rondomana are but the ghosts of common men who while
they lived had no power, *mana* ; for there are *'ataro* also which
are active and powerful, feared, invoked, and propitiated,
present in full activity in the places in which they dwelt as
living men. Here, as elsewhere, a man's ghost has in greater
force the power which the man had in his lifetime, when he
had it from his communication with the ghosts that went
before him ; and those who have lately died have most
power, or at least are the most active sources of it. The
ghost of the great man lately dead is most regarded ; as
the dead are forgotten their ghosts are superseded by later
successors to the unseen power. The bodies of common
people are cast into the sea, but men of consequence are
buried, and some relic of them, skull, tooth, or finger-bone,
is taken up and preserved in a shrine in the village.
There are, therefore, land ghosts and sea ghosts. The former
are seen about the villages and heard to speak, haunting their graves and relics ; their appearance that of men
lately dead, their voice a hollow whisper. Their aid can be
obtained by those who know them, and they are believed to
fight among themselves with ghostly weapons. The ghosts
that haunt the sea have a great hold on the imagination of
the natives of the south-eastern Solomon Islands, and as these
people love to illustrate their life in sculpture and painting,
they show us clearly what they conceive these ghosts to be.
There was many years ago at Wango a canoe-house, *oha*, full
of carvings and paintings representing native life ; it had
along its wall-plates and lower purlins a series of pictures
illustrating the principal affairs of life as naturally as may be
seen in Egyptian tombs ; a feast from the first climbing after
cocoa-nuts through all the processes of preparing and cooking
food ; a fight upon the beach (the sea shewn to be so by the
fishes depicted in it), with all its various action ; voyages and

accidents at sea, and among them a canoe attacked by what
appeared at first sight demons hornèd and hoofed. These were
the ghosts that haunt the sea, their forms having suffered a sea
change, and composed as much as possible of fishes, their spears
and arrows long-bodied garfish and flying-fish. If a man on
returning from a canoe voyage or from fishing on the rocks
falls ill, it is because one of these sea ghosts has shot him
(page 196). These ghosts are therefore propitiated in any

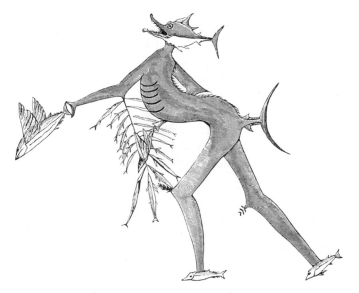

SEA-GHOST, FROM A NATIVE DRAWING.

danger at sea with areca-nuts and fragments of food cast to
them among the waves, and their anger is deprecated in
prayers. Sharks also have *'ataro* in them, the ghosts of
those who have foretold their future appearance in that form.
In these islands, as elsewhere, the death-feast is held, and
a morsel of food is thrown upon the fire as the dead man's
share. A great man also was commemorated by an image of
him in a canoe-house or on the stage put up at feasts, and
before it food was placed.

At Saa, and in the neighbouring parts of Malanta, the same word is used for the soul of a living man and the ghost of an ordinary person, *'akalo*, which is another form of the *'ataro* of San Cristoval. The *'akalo*, which goes out of the body in dreams and returns again, goes out finally in death, leaving the body after a natural death *ra'e*, after a violent death *lalamoa*. The ghosts of ordinary people are *'akalo*, and nothing else ; those of chiefs, valiant fighting men, men of conspicuous success in life, of men who are *saka*, have spiritual power, are expected to become *lio'a*, ghosts which again are *saka*, have spiritual power, and are worshipful accordingly; as the ghost of a warrior when found by proof to act becomes *lio'a ni ma'e*, a ghost powerful for death. The origin of death is ascribed, as in the Banks' Islands and New Hebrides, to the old woman who having changed her skin afterwards resumed the slough, which had caught upon a reed. All ghosts upon leaving the body swim first to a point of land at Saa, then to a point of Ulawa, then to the Three Sisters, *'Olu Malau*, then to a point of San Cristoval near Hada, and lastly to Marapa, two islands lying off Marau in Guadalcanar. While the body is rotting the ghost is weak ; when the smell has ceased the ghost is strong, it is no longer a man. The ghostly inhabitants of Marapa live something like a worldly life ; the children chatter and annoy the elder ghosts, so they are placed apart upon the second island ; men and women ghosts are together, they have houses, gardens, and canoes, yet all is unsubstantial. Living men cross to Marapa and see nothing ; but there is water there in which laughter and cries are heard ; there are places where water is seen to have been disturbed, and the banks are wet as if bathers had been there. A dead chief makes his canoe and his house there, like those which his living son is building, but they are built of the soft esculent hibiscus, and come to nothing ; it is like the play of children. This ghostly life is not eternal ; the mere *'akalo* soon turn into white ants' nests, which again become the food of the still vigorous ghosts; hence a living man says to his idle son, ' When I die I shall have ants' nests to eat, but then what will you have ? ' The

lio'a ghosts of power last longer because they are *saka*, and the
more *saka* they are the longer they last ; they are remembered
and worshipped on earth, and so long their strength remains ;
but when men forget them and turn to worship some more
lately dead, and when no sacrificial food is offered them, their
power fades away, and they turn into white ants' nests like
the others. There are two rulers of Marapa, who are called
lio'a, though not strictly so, because they were never men and
never pass away—the chief Kari'eu, and inferior to him, Kikiriba'u, the cutter—off of heads. These two go about in their
canoes, one collecting ghosts, the other heads; in times of
sickness at Saa if trunks of trees are seen floating by at sea
they are said to be the canoes of Kari'eu and Kikiriba'u. The
ghosts whose abode is in Marapa can return to Saa to visit
their village and their friends again. They are seen like
shadows, having a certain form fleeting and indistinct, some
hideous, some not unpleasant. If one who sees a ghost is
not frightened he can discern the features and know who
it is ; but if he is frightened he sees only a dreadful something. A man who for some reason wishes to see a ghost,
puts lime from his betel-box upon his forehead, and then he
plainly sees.

The burial of common people at Saa is a simple affair ; an
ordinary man is buried the day after death, a very inferior
person at once. There is a common burial-place which does
not get filled up because the bones are from time to time taken
up, after the flesh has decayed, and heaped on one side. Men
of some rank and consideration are not buried for two days ;
women sit round the corpse and wail, *i'o pe'i rae*, and people
assemble to see the dead man for the last time and to eat the
funeral feast. If a very great man dies, or a man much
beloved by his son, the body is hung up in his son's house,
either in a canoe or enclosed in the figure of a sword-fish, *ili*.
Very favourite children are treated in the same way. The
figure of the sword-fish is cemented like a canoe and painted ;
no smell whatever proceeds from it. If the body is put into
a canoe they make fine raspings or chippings of a certain tree

to spread under and above it, and lay over that certain large
leaves, and planks above all. The canoe is not closed over
with cement, but there is very little smell. Sometimes the
corpse is kept in this way for years, either in the house or in
the *oha*, the public canoe-house, waiting for a great funeral
feast [1]. When a year of good crops arrives a man will say,
'Now we will take out Father.' The corpse is taken then, if
that of a comparatively inferior person, to the common burial-
ground, if of a chief, to the family burying-place, where
sacrifices are made as above (page 137) described. The skull
and jawbone are taken out, and these are called *mangite*, which
are *saka*, hot with spiritual power, and by means of which the
help of the *lio'a*, the powerful ghost of the man whose relics
these are, can be obtained. The *mangite* is enclosed in the
hollow wooden figure of a bonito-fish, and set up in the house
or in the *oha*, where it remains till the *lio'a* goes out of
memory or credit. In the *oha* on the beach at Saa they lately
made a boat-like receptacle, and put in it all the old *mangite* of
forgotten *lio'a*. A man will sometimes hang up his wife in
this way, and when she is taken out to the burying-place her
jaw will be kept in a basket, or one of her teeth in a bit of
bamboo, and hung up in the house as a memorial. It can
be nothing more, for no woman's ghost can be a ghost of
power, *lio'a*, nothing but a mere departed soul, *akalo*. Men
will put food as an offering of affection and memory to
these *mangite*, and to the figures and canoes containing
corpses.

Burial, however, is not universal at Saa. It often happens
that the corpse of a chief or lesser man is thrown into the sea
(to do which is called *kulu rae*), either at the request of the
deceased, or to save trouble. The friends tie a bag of sand to
the feet of the corpse, paddle out, and sink the corpse in a
certain place where are hollow rocks below ; it never rises to
the surface. When this is done a *mangite* is preserved, hair or
nails, tied in a bundle and hung up. Sometimes, but rarely,

[1] A similar custom was observed by Mr. Forbes at Timor. Naturalist's
Wanderings in the Eastern Archipelago, p. 435.

a corpse is burnt, at the wish of the deceased [1]. When this is done they preserve a *mangite* by wrapping the head about, or enclosing it in a hollowed stem of banana, to keep it from the fire. The place where a corpse is burnt is sacred. Some corpses, again, are laid in a canoe or on a stage beside a place of sacrifice, holes being made in the bottom of the canoe, and bamboos set to carry away rain-water and the liquor of the corpse into the ground. At one time they did at Saa what now they do in Bauro; they poured water on the corpse until the flesh was consumed, and then took the skull as a *mangite*. In these methods of disposing of the distinguished dead, whose ghosts are expected to be *lio'a* possessed of power, there may be seen very probably the effect of the belief, of which mention has been made, that the ghost continues weak while the corpse continues to smell; the *lio'a* of the dead man sunk in the sea, burnt, enclosed in a case, or rapidly denuded of flesh, is active and available at once.

The ornaments of a dead man are buried with him, or are kept in remembrance of him. A man's cocoa-nut and bread-fruit-trees, and others, are cut down by his friends after his death, out of respect to him as they say; and they deny that they think that such things follow a man in any ghostly form, since it seems ridiculous to suppose that even pigs can have a soul, *akalo*. To cut trees down in this way is to *ngoli*; for a dead chief they *ngoli-ta'a*, they fence round a certain plot of ground and put his canoe in it in memory of him, with his bowl and weapons; his friends add such things of their own in honour of him, and decorate the fence with leaves and flowers. For a man of no great position they content themselves with throwing yams and other food upon the roof of the dead man's house in memory of him.

At Santa Cruz the corpse is buried in a very deep grave in the house, wrapped in many mats. For two days they cry over a man and then bury him; on the fifth day the funeral

---

[1] This is the only example within my knowledge of the method of disposing of the dead which Dr. Guppy found to be common in the chiefs' families about the Bougainville Straits.

meal is eaten and all is over. Inland they dig up the bones again to make arrowheads, and take the skull to keep in a chest in the house, saying that this is the man himself, and setting food before it. The departed souls are *duka*; they assemble after death at a place called Natepapa, and from thence go on to the great volcano Tamami (called Tinakula), in which they are burnt and renewed, and where they stay. Nevertheless they haunt the bush in Santa Cruz, and are seen at night, and when it is wet and dark; men see them like fire, with fire under their armpits like fire-flies, and are much afraid of them.

The abode of the dead has in all these examples been shewn to be above ground, in islands more or less remote from those in which the living dwell, and all known and visited by living men. It is probable, however, that a certain belief in an underworld is also present, the Turivatu of the Florida invocation in sacrifice (page 131), a region beneath the earth corresponding to that country above the sky where Kamakajaku or Vulaninggela visited the sun. The belief in Santa Cruz that ghosts pass into the great volcano implies something of a descent below, as does the parallel belief at Savo that the volcanic crater there is the receptacle of departed spirits. When we pass, however, to the eastward the ghosts no longer have their abodes upon the surface of the earth, but underground. From the Torres Islands to Pentecost in the New Hebrides, the name of the nether-world is, with variations, Panoi, to which all the openings—whether by volcanic vents or unknown mouths—throughout all these neighbouring islands lead. In all alike the ghosts assemble at certain places and go down to what is their proper place, though they can return again to earth. The locality of Panoi is unknown, save that it is underground; and Panoi is one, not a separate receptacle for the ghosts of each separate island. The people of the Torres Islands, however, and those of Pentecost, do not know that they have a common belief and use a common word.

In the Torres Islands the word used for soul is a form of

the Mota *atai, nete.* The departed soul goes down to Panoi near a rock called Vat tugua, not far from Lo, where a very ancient casuarina-tree growing at high-water mark overhangs the sea, and endures the heaviest storms and highest tides unmoved. In these islands the practice has prevailed of laying out the bodies of the dead on stages near the houses, to putrefy and decay; but they now begin to bury.

The story of the Origin of Death noticed in the account of Saa (page 260), has its parallel in the Banks' Islands and again in the New Hebrides. At first men never died, but when they advanced in life they cast their skins like snakes and crabs, and came out with youth renewed. After a time a woman growing old went to a stream to change her skin ; according to some she was the mother of Qat, according to others Ul-ta-marama, Change-skin of the world. She threw off her old skin in the water, and observed that as it floated down it caught against a stick. Then she went home, where she had left her child. The child, however, refused to recognize her, crying that its mother was an old woman not like this young stranger ; and to pacify the child she went after her cast integument and put it on. From that time mankind ceased to cast their skins and died. In another Banks' Island story this woman is Iro Puget, Bird's-nest Fern, the wife of Mate, Death [1]. There are many others. In one the cause of the introduction of Death was the inconvenience of the permanence of property in the same hands while men changed their skins and lived for ever. Qat therefore sent for Mate, who dwelt in Panoi, or by the side of a volcanic vent in Santa Maria, and assured him that he would only have to go to Vanua Lava and not be hurt. Death therefore came forth ; they laid him on a board, killed a pig, and covered him over ; then they proceeded to divide his property

---

[1] There is a saying at Mota, when any one is observed not to have his ears bored, *Iro Puget te nine wora o pue ape qatuma,* ' Puget will break her bamboo water-carrier on your head.' The meaning is that Ro Puget will be met at the entrance to Panoi, and will so treat any one who has not followed the custom. This is parallel to what has been noticed at Florida and Bugotu.

and eat the funeral feast.   On the fifth day when the conch was blown to drive away the ghost, Qat opened the covering over Mate and found him gone; nothing but bones remained. In the meanwhile Tangaro the Fool had been set to watch the way to Panoi, where the paths to the lower and upper worlds divided, lest Mate should go below; the fool sat in front of the way to the world above, and let Mate go down to Panoi; all men have since followed Death along that path. Another story makes the same fool—under his name of Tagilingelinge—the cause of death, because when Iro Puget set him to guard the way to Panoi in prospect of her own death, he pointed out that way to her descending ghost instead of the way back to the world, and so she, and all men after her, died and never came back to life.   In Lakona, part of Santa Maria, the story goes that Marawa stole a woman whom Qat had made (page 157); and in the night while he and she were sleeping Qat came quietly, pulled out their teeth, and shaved their heads.   Then he took the hairy plexus of the tree-fern and put it on their heads, giving the names of baldness and of the 'second hair,' as gray hair has since been called.   Then he spread spider's web over their eyes, so that when they woke in the morning dimness was over their sight.   The woman refused to go back to him; so in a song he called for baldness, blindness, toothlessness, old age, and death, because she had disobeyed his word.

The soul, *atai* or *talegi*, goes out of the body in some dreams, and if for some reason it does not come back the man is found dead in the morning; when a man faints, *mate mule*, dies and goes, his soul really starts on the way to Panoi, but is sent back; the other ghosts hustle him away from the mouth of the descent, or his father or friend turns him back, telling him that his time is not yet come; so he relates when he returns.   In true death the separation of soul and body is complete, the *atai* or *talegi* becomes *o tamate* or *natmat*, a dead-man, and the corpse also is spoken of by the same word. The ghost, however, does not at first go far, and possibly may be recalled; the neighbours therefore bite the finger of the dead

or dying person to rouse him, and shout his name into his
ear, in hope that the soul may hear it and return. The soul
possibly may be caught. A woman at Mota some years ago
who knew that a neighbour was at the point of death heard
something rustling in her house, like the fluttering of a moth,
just when cries and wailings told her that the soul had flown.
She caught the fluttering thing between her hands and ran
with it to the house of death, crying that she had caught the
atai ; she opened her hands above the corpse's mouth to restore
the soul, but there was no recovery. The ghost does not at
once leave the neighbourhood of the body, it hangs about the
house and the grave five or ten days, and shews its presence
by noises in the house and lights upon the grave. It is not
generally in the Banks' Islands thought desirable that the
ghost should stay longer than the fifth day, and there is a
custom of driving it away with shouts and blowing of conchs;
in some places bull-roarers are sounded. It will be convenient to take the proceedings which follow after death in
the various islands of the group, before describing the course
of the departed ghost into the lower world and its condition
there. These proceedings consist of the mourning, the
funeral, and the funeral-feasts.

In the Banks' Islands the dead are generally buried. It is
the duty of the members of the other *Veve*, of the other 'side
of the house,' to dig the grave. The burial takes place earlier
or later, according to the estimation in which the deceased is
held. In an ordinary case it is on the second day; the friends
cry round the corpse, and women are hired to wail meanwhile.
The place of burial is in the bush not far from the village;
but a great man, or one whose death was remarkable, was
buried in the village near the *gamal*, and a favourite son or
child in the house itself. In the latter case the grave was
opened after fifty or a hundred days, and the bones taken up
and hidden in the bush, or some of them hung up in the
house. Some bodies were not buried, but laid up in the bush
outside the village in a chest, *pugoro*, such as those in which
dry bread-fruit is kept, and there left to decay. This is called

to *salo*; as is also the laying of the corpse in a shallow cave
under a projecting rock. There was, however, and still remains,
a custom in some places of keeping the body unburied and
putrefying in the house as a mark of affection. At Gaua, in
Santa Maria, it was the women's business to watch the corpse,
laid on a mat over cross sticks between two slow fires in the
house for ten days or more, till nothing but skin and bones
was left ; during which time they drank the drippings of the
corpse. The same was done in former days at Mota. The
description of the funeral of a man of rank at Motlav will
hold good generally of any of the Banks' Islands. The corpse
of a great man was brought out into the open space in the
middle of the village, loosely wrapped in a mat, with his
malosaru dress of ceremony on, his *som ta Rowa* necklace round
his neck, his forehead smeared, *il*, with red earth, *mea*, his
armlets, and bracelets of pig's tusks reversed, but no bow
at his hand, on his breast a cycas leaf, *no mele*, the mark of
his rank in the Suqe, and the leaves of the crotons, *sasa*,
belonging to his Tamate societies. By his side were heaped
bunches of cocoa-nuts tied together, and plenty of old dry
cocoa-nuts, yams of various kinds, caladium, and all kinds of
food, with a bunch of the leaves of a particular dracæna stuck
upon the heap, the *karia garame tamate*, the ghost's tongue
dracæna, all of which were afterwards heaped upon the grave.
Then a man ready of speech made an address to the ghost,
telling him, when they asked him in Panoi whether he were
a great man, to say what was heaped beside him. The orator
would not spare his faults[1] ; if he were a man of bad character
he would say to him, ' Poor ghost! will you be able to enter
Panoi? I think not.' Then the burial took place. Upon
the grave was set a bamboo vessel of water with a cocoa-nut-
shell cup, and a little dish with a roasted yam in it; as the
food was eaten by rats they renewed it, for the rat might be
the deceased himself, at any rate during the five days that the
ghost remained about the place. At Gaua they hang up pigs

---

[1] ' I myself heard Parut at Mota abuse I Mala, because he had died without
having completed his *suqe* for him.'—Rev. J. Palmer.

that they have killed, or parts of them, at the grave; when the man goes down to Bono, Panoi, the ghosts there will see him come down with these, and think much of him. The Gaua people, however, deny that pigs have ghosts[1]. It is interesting to observe how a judgment upon a dead man's merits was pronounced. Not long ago when a corpse was being buried at Motlav, a man whom the deceased had ill used followed with a stone, and threw it on the body, crying out, 'You have ill used me, and persecuted me to kill me— you have died first.' At Gaua when a great man died his friends would not make it known, lest those whom he had oppressed should come and spit at him after his death, or *govgov* him, stand bickering at him with crooked fingers and drawing in the lips, by way of curse. Relatives in Motlav watch the grave of a man whose life was bad, lest some man wronged by him should come at night and beat with a stone upon the grave, cursing him. Sometimes the friends will have a sham burial, and hide the grave in which the corpse is really laid; because if a man in his lifetime has had *mana* to shoot and kill, to charm with the *talamatai* and in other ways, there will be *mana* for the same purpose in his corpse; men will want to dig up his bones for arrows and for charms, and his skull to roll the string upon wherewith to tie their *talamatai*. So at Gaua when a body has been wasted over the fire, they bury the bones in the village under some large stone, and cover it with another stone, lest the bones should be taken up for arrows. At Ureparapara[2] as soon as a man dies his

---

[1] If the pigs that have been killed are seen in Panoi, it may be thought that they must have souls to be seen there, since their bodies are at the grave. But this is not the native notion; of a pig or an ornament there is a certain something, shadow, echo, of itself that can be seen, but there is not that which man has, the intelligent personal spiritual part which separates from the body in death. When a ghost is seen what is seen? Not the soul, the *atai*, but the dead man, the *tamate*; for the *atai* can never be seen, the *nunuai*, echo, of the body, its *taqangiu*, outline, can be seen, but indistinctly. When an English ghost appears in the dead man's habit as he lived, is it thought to be his soul that appears?

[2] For this and for what follows concerning Lakona, I am indebted to the Rev. J. Palmer.

friends bring a quantity of food of all kinds to hang up on
white peeled *palako* sticks round the corpse when it is laid
out in the middle of the village.   Then the orator makes his
speech to the deceased, giving him messages to take to the
dead, bids him carry the news of the place, especially what
has been done and is intended to be done in the various
societies, and tells him for whom in Panoi besides himself
the food hanging round him is intended.   When the speech
is ended, two small yams or caladium roots are roasted over a
fire of cocoa-nut fronds lighted for the purpose; the cooking
is only in show, and the food is scraped with the left hand
instead of the right.   A small joint of bamboo is filled with
water, and put with the food into a new clean basket for the
ghost.   At the same time a pig is killed.   When all this is
done, the body is tied up in a mat and followed to the grave by
all the men and women, the children remaining in the village.
All the food is buried on the body; or if there be too much,
some is hung above the grave, whence the bolder people take
it secretly and eat it.

The ghost is driven away in the same island five days after
death with a peculiar ceremony.   Bags of small stones and
short pieces of bamboo are provided for the people of the
village, and are charmed by those who have the knowledge of
the magic chant appropriate for the purpose.   Two men,
each with two white stones in his hands, sit in the dead
man's house, one on either side.   These men begin to clink
the stones one against the other, the women begin to wail,
the neighbours—who have all assembled at one end of the
village—begin to march through it in a body to the other end,
throwing the stones into the houses and all about, and
beating the bamboos together.   So they pass through till
they come to the bush beyond, when they throw down the
bamboos and bags.   They have now driven out the ghost,
who up to this time has been about the house, in which the
widow has for these five days never left the dead man's bed
except upon necessity; and even then she leaves a cocoa-nut
to represent her till she returns.   At Motlav the ghost is not

driven away unless the man who has died was badly afflicted with ulcers and sores, either a *gov* covered with sores, or a *mama-nigata* with a single large ulcer or more. When such a one is dying the people of his village send word in time to the next village westwards, as the ghost will go out following the sun, to warn them there to be prepared. When the *gov* is dead they bury him, and then, with shell-trumpets blowing and the stalks of cocoa-nut fronds stripped of some of the leaflets beating on the ground, they chase the ghost to the next village. The people of that village take up the chase, and hunt the ghost further westward; and so on till the sea is reached. Then the frond stalks are thrown away and the people return, sure that the ghost has left the island, and will not strike another man with the disease.

The series of funeral-feasts or death-meals, the 'eating the death' as they call it, follows upon the funeral, or even begins before it, and is the most important part of the commemoration of the dead; it may be said, indeed, to be one of the principal institutions of the islands. The number of the feasts and the length of time during which they are repeated varys very much in the various islands, and depend also upon the consideration in which the deceased is held. The meals are distinctly commemorative, but are not altogether devoid of the purpose of benefiting the dead; it is thought that the ghost is gratified by the remembrance shewn of him, and honoured by the handsome performance of the duty; the living also solace themselves in their grief, and satisfy something of their sense of loss by affectionate commemoration. It is not easy to determine how far there is now any feeling that friendly association of the living and dead is continued by their both partaking of the meal, when a morsel of food is thrown aside with a call to the deceased. At ordinary meals when the oven is opened a bit of food is put aside for the dead, with the words 'This is for you, let our oven be well cooked.' At a death-meal the words are 'This is for thee.' It is readily denied now that the dead, either dead friends generally in the one case or the lately deceased in the

T

other, are thought to come and eat the food, which they say
is given as a friendly remembrance only, and in the way of
associating together those whom death has separated; but it
can hardly be doubted that the original intention at least was
a common participation in the meal. It is not altogether
consistent, however, with the conception of an underground
abode of the dead, that they should be conceived of as present
at the later feasts, though the first of all is held while they
are still believed to be about. The eating the death, *gana
matea*, begins with the burial; they eat first, as they say, his
grave; after that they 'eat his days.' The days are the fifth
and the tenth, and after that every tenth day up to the
hundredth, and it may be in the case of a father, wife, or
mother even so far as the thousandth. At Nembek, a part of
Gaua, where they lay the corpse between fires, they bury the
remains and finish the death-meal on the fifth day. At
Tarasag, near by, when a great man dies the people from all
the villages around bring mashed yams the next morning to
the place where the dead man lies, and eat them there. The
people of the place begin the death-meals that day with a
large ovenful, and continue on the tenth, and on every
successive tenth day. Sometimes for a very great man they
eat every day up to the fiftieth, and then start with the fifth
and tenth day feasts. For counting the days so that the
guests from distant villages may arrive on the proper days,
they use cycas fronds, one in the hands of each party, on
which the appointed days are marked by the pinching off or
turning down of a leaflet as each day passes. At Ureparapara
the first fire for the death-meal is lit on the day after the
burial; after that on each fifth day to the hundredth, and if
they go beyond that every tenth day to the thousandth. At
Lakona, in Santa Maria, immediately after the death the pigs
of the deceased which he has left as legacies are distributed to
his relatives, and one or two more are killed and the meat
given to the people of the place. In the evening he is buried,
or laid out in a chest or in a cave, and no food or water is
put with him. Next morning begins the counting of the

death-days. If the deceased was a great man, a *tavusmele*, there will be a drum brought out and they will dance, to drive away their grief, as they say, so that they may eat the death-meal with cheerfulness; visitors come to dance and are paid for it. The death-feast lasts only five days for a woman, six for a man. The concluding action is peculiar to Lakona; on the sixth day after death each man kills a sow, and the women come and buy the meat, from which the last death-meal, called the *Vulqat*, is supplied. The next morning all is finished with a meal ' to clear away the *Vulqat.*'

The ghost when it leaves its former dwelling-place makes its way to Panoi, to which there are many entrances, called *sura*, in the various islands, some underground and unknown, some well known, like the rock Aliali on the mountain at Mota, volcanic vents on the burning hill Garat over the lake at Gaua, and the great mountain of Vanua Lava, the Sur-lav, great *sura*. The ghosts congregate on points of land before their departure, as well as at the mouth of the *sura*, where they are heard dancing, singing, shouting and whistling with land-crabs' claws on moonlight nights. To these points of land and the *sura* entrances to Panoi it was possible for ghosts who had already descended to return, and it was thought by some that they would come out to receive, sometimes with dancing, the freshly dead, shew them their various haunts, and conduct them to the underworld. There is also the notion that there are *sura* appropriated to particular classes of ghosts; as the *sure lupa*, where simple harmless people congregate, and the *sure lumagav*, where youths go who die in the flower of their age, a place more pleasant than the rest, where all kinds of flowers abound and scented plants. This fancy was mostly that of women, who thought much of all who died young, and above all of those who had been shot for them, who had died on their account, *me matewolira ti*, paid for them the price of their death.

A precise and consistent account of the condition of ghosts after they have arrived at Panoi, and of that place itself, is difficult indeed to obtain from the natives of this group; nor perhaps is it reasonable to expect it. But the stories of descents to Panoi shew in their relation what are the common conceptions in the native mind. It does much to reconcile the varying accounts to recognise the truth that Panoi is not a single receptacle the same for all, and that there is a corresponding distinction between one class of ghosts and another. This is clearly believed at Motlav, where they say that when a ghost goes down the *sura* it is met by another ghost, and according to the character of the man in life is allowed to enter into Panoi, or sent back to another place, dreading which it goes to wander on the earth. The true Panoi is a good place, and there is a bad place besides which is sometimes meant when the word Panoi is used. Thus, if a man has killed another by treachery or witchcraft, when after death he descends the *sura* he finds himself withstood at the entrance to Panoi by the ghost of the man he has wronged; he sees another path leading to the bad place he dreads, and so he turns back to earth. If one has killed a good man without cause, the good man's ghost withstands his murderer; if one man has killed another in fair fight he will not be withstood by the man he slew; if a bad man slew a bad man both would be together, but not in the true Panoi. This division is very important—that there are some ghosts who enter Panoi, and some who are not allowed to enter, these last being of bad character. Very important indeed also is it, as shewing native notions of moral right and wrong so often denied to them, to observe what sort of men were admitted and who were refused. Who was the man of good character in life? It is answered that he was one who lived as he ought to do, *me toga mantag*, an answer that may have no moral meaning. But who was the man of bad character? It is answered, one who killed another without due cause, or had caused a death by charms, one who used to steal, to lie, one given to adultery. Thus those who enter into the true Panoi still live as they ought, *we toga mantag*, they live in harmony, in a good way of living; those who remain in the bad place quarrel and lie in misery, not in physical pain indeed, but restless, wandering back to earth, homeless, malignant, pitiable ; these are they who eat excrement and open their mouths for wind ; these are they who do harm to the living out of spite, who are dreaded as eating men's souls, who haunt the graves and woods. There is a singular belief at Lakona concerning this kind of judgment after death. The ghost's path leads him to the volcanic vents of the burning hill Garat, and as he runs along the ghosts assemble to receive him. They beat him, ghost as he already is, to death, then cut him to pieces, and each ghost will take a piece. They then put him together again, and if he has in his lifetime wrongfully shot the father, brother, or *sogoi* relation of any of the ghosts into whose hands he has fallen, or done any other wrong, the ghost who has the grievance will hide the piece of him that he has taken ; he will remain with some part of him deficient, and when he goes down to Panoi and the ghosts ask him what has become of that bit of him, he will tell them that some one has kept it from him because he had done him wrong.

The ghost of a *vasisgona*, a woman who has died in childbed, cannot go to Panoi if her child lives, for she cannot leave her child. They therefore deceive her ghost by making up loosely a piece of a banana trunk in leaves, and laying it on her bosom when she is buried. Then, as she departs, she thinks she has the child with her ; as she goes the banana stalk slips about in the leaves and she thinks the child is moving ; and this in her bewildered new condition contents her, till she gets to Panoi and finds that she has been deceived. In the meanwhile the child has been taken to another house, because they know that the mother will come back to take its soul. She seeks everywhere for the child in grief and rage without ceasing ; and the ghost of a *vasisgona* therefore is particularly dreaded.

Panoi is near, under the land of living men, as death is near to life. If a man is nearly killed he says, 'I have been close to Panoi, and have returned.' There is much there that is like the upper world, villages, houses, trees with red leaves,

and there is day and night; it is even a beautiful place, for
at a great festival when the village place is bright with
flowers and coloured leaves, and thronged with people dancing,
drumming and singing, the saying is that it is 'like a *sura*,
as if the mouth of Panoi were opened.' When a ghost first
descends, he waits at first outside the ghostly village; he is
weak, and he stops till he has recovered strength. The
ghosts make a dance in his honour. When he arrives they
ask him, 'Have you come to stay?' If he has only fainted,
it is then discovered, and he returns. The fresh ghost finds
there something like an earthly life, but it is hollow and
unreal. There is nothing that they do but talk and sing and
dance; there is no *gamal*, the indispensable club-house of
earthly life; men and women live together, without sexual
intercourse; there is no fighting, there is no one in authority,
no *vui*, spirits, other than ghosts of men. A great man goes
down like a great man, in all his finery of ornament. The
pigs killed for his funeral feast, the food heaped upon his
grave, do not go down as he does; he is a *tamate*, a dead man,
a ghost; he has as a dead man the *atai*, soul, that he had under
different conditions as a living man; his ornaments are on his
person as a ghost, but the shadow, *niniai*, of them only, for
no such things, not even pigs, have *atai*. There is a further
belief that there are compartments, enclosures fenced apart, in
which those who have died violent deaths keep together; those
who have been shot are in one place together, those who were
charmed to death in a second, those who have been clubbed
in a third together. Those who have been shot keep rattling
the reeds of the arrows they were shot with; hence if a rat is
heard in a house making that kind of noise the saying is that
it is a reed-rattling ghost, *tamate ninginingi togo*. Ghosts in
Panoi have not knowledge of things out of their sight and
hearing as the *vui*, spirits, have; nevertheless they are invoked
in time of need and distress, as if they could hear and help.
They come upon earth when they please, and see how their
friends and property are faring, and they hear the news from
new-coming ghosts. These ghosts, as distinguished from

those who have no home in Panoi, are in a general way kindly
to living men ; though if their friends and property are
damaged, they are angry and revengeful. It is true that men
are afraid of these and all other ghosts, because a ghost is of
itself a dreadful thing to a living man. They are seen, but
not distinctly—only their eyes like phosphorescent fungi, or
something red. Life in Panoi is eternal, unless indeed, as
some say, there are two Panois, one below the other, and the
dead die from the upper to the lower, as living men die from
earth ; from the lower they never die, but turn into white
ants' nests, *te wog qatete nia.*

Descents to Panoi have been by no means uncommon.
There was a woman, who died not many years ago, who once
much desired to see her lately dead brother ; she perfumed
herself with water in which a dead rat had been steeped, to
give herself a death-like smell, pulled up a bird's-nest fern, a
puget, and descended by the hole she had opened. She had
no difficulty in finding Panoi, and she saw friends there who
were surprised to see her, and never discovered that she was
alive. She found her brother lying in a house, because as a
recent ghost he was not strong enough yet to move about.
He cautioned her to eat nothing there, and she returned.
This descent was in the body, as was that of one Molborbor
of Valuwa, who went down and saw his wife ; but a man in
Motlav, more lately dead, used to go down in sleep, his soul
descending, and his body remaining as in a trance. He could
do this at will, and received money for doing it, professing to
visit the recently dead, about whom their friends were un-
happy, and even to be able to bring them back. He never
did in fact bring any back ; he said he had seen the persons
and talked with them, but was prevented from bringing them
back. He, too, prepared for his soul's descent by washing his
body with water in which a putrid rat, snake or lizard had
been steeped. There was a man in former days at Motlav,
Vanvanvegirgir by name, who going down to Panoi in his
talegi, soul, took once another man with him in his body.
This man had lately lost his wife, and went to Vanvanvegirgir

to enquire about her. He was instructed to give himself the
appropriate smell with the liquor of a putrid black gecko, and
was given a stick. The two then descended, and reached
Panoi; the ghosts detected the living man, and cried out,
'The smell of that world!' The two declared that they were
really dead, and to try them the ghosts brought out dead
men's bones, to see if they would rattle them as ghosts do,
by one, by two, by three; they did this rightly and were
allowed to go on. Vanvanvegirgir went forward to find the
man's wife, and brought her to him; they talked together,
and the man begged her to go back to the world with him.
That she said was impossible, and she gave him a shell
armlet by which to remember her. He took her by the
hand and began to drag her; her hand came off, and her
body came to pieces. For, as the story is explained, ghosts
in Panoi have something more of body and substance than
they have when they come back into the world; else the
man could not have taken hold of his dead wife's hand.
When a ghost comes into the world, it is but a *taqangiu* that
is seen, a something circumscribed by an outline like a
shadow; but the ghost in Panoi, of which the other is probably again the ghost, has a *tarapei*, a body, which has not
only form and colour, but a certain consistency. There is
still living in Vanua Lava a woman who turned her descent
to Panoi to a useful purpose. Her husband, a Gaua man,
died, and she herself was very ill and appeared to die. She
recovered, however, and told the people that she had followed
her husband to the hill Garat, and had seen him there bound
hand and foot. The ghosts told her, she declared, that this
was done because he had not paid his debts; ' Go back,' they
bade her, 'to the Gaua people, and say to them, Pay your
debts, don't kill one another; this is how we shall treat such
men.'

The manner of burial in Ma wo, Aurora, in the New
Hebrides, and the belief of the people there concerning the
dead, is fully described in an account written by a native, of
which what follows is generally a translation. In the first

place, he says, they think that when the soul, *tamani*, leaves
the body in death, it mounts into a tree in which is a bird's-
nest fern, and sitting among the fronds, laughs and mocks at
the people who are crying and making great lamentations
over him. There he sits, wondering at them and ridiculing
them. ' What are they crying for ? ' he says ; ' who is it they
are sorry for ? Here am I.' For they think that the real
thing is the soul, and that it has gone away from the body
just as a man throws off his clothes and leaves them, and the
clothes lie by themselves with nothing in them ; (the Maewo
word *gavui* applies in such a case, the white of an egg is the
gavui of it, the yolk the real thing ; the word for clothes is
gavu, integument). Then the soul goes through his gardens
and along his customary paths, and finally leaves the place.
He runs along the line of hills till he reaches the end of the
island, and there he comes to the place of recollection, the
Maewo name for which is *vat dodoma*, the stone of thought ;
if he remembers there his child or his wife or anything that
belongs to him, he will run back and come to life again. In
the same place also are two rocks with a deep ravine between
them ; if the ghost clears this as he leaps across he is for
ever dead, but if one fails he returns to life again. The ghost
pursues his course running along the mountain range to the
end opposite to Raga, Pentecost, at the *mate tasi*, land's end,
or brink of sea, and when he arrives safely all the ghosts of
those who have died before assemble and receive him joyfully.
They believe also that as he runs the ghosts of those whom he
has wronged in this world, whom he has foully slain by club
or arrow, or has killed by charms, take a full revenge upon
him, beating him, tearing him, and stabbing him with dag-
gers, *mataso*, such as men stick pigs with ; one of them will
say to him, ' While you were still in the world you thought
yourself a valiant man ; but now we will take our revenge
upon you.' Another path of the ghosts takes them to the
northern point of Maewo, where there is a deep gully and
three leaping-places, one for men, one for women, and one for
ulcerous persons. It is a curse to wish a man may fall down

there ; if a ghost falls in leaping he is smashed to pieces, but runs on and comes to the hill Tawu, which is very sacred to ghosts. Here is the mouth of the hollow which leads to Banoi, and here the newly-arrived ghost is beaten by those whom he has wronged, and they cry to him, ' Down already ! ' Here is Gaviga, a *vui*, the chief of Banoi, and Matamakira, or Salolo as the Tanoriki people say, a quarrelsome and ill-tempered man on earth ; these stand with large and sharp spears and try to stab the new-comers. There is a huge fierce pig also there, which will devour all who have not in their lifetime planted the *emba*, pandanus, from which mats are made. If one has planted such he can climb up out of the reach of the devouring beast, and for this reason every one likes to plant that tree. Here also, if a man's ears are not pierced, he is not allowed to drink water; if he is not tattooed, he must not eat good food.   Here the ghosts of those who have not joined the Suqe hang like flying foxes upon the trees (chap. vi). In order that his child may have hereafter a good house in Banoi, a man, when the child is a year old, makes a little *gamal*, club-house, in his garden for a boy, and puts in it a bow and arrows and a club ; for a girl he builds a little house, and plants an *emba*, pandanus, to make mats with beside it. The writer has not mentioned how the ghosts congregate at the entrance to the lower world, and wait there, and are heard by men, some at play and some crying with grief and pain ; the latter, the lately dead who had just become aware of their condition ; he allows that it is so believed, but says that the people of his place, Tanoriki, are not so well acquainted with these stories as the Tasmouri people, who live near this gulf down which the ghosts descend.   It is believed also that the ghosts in Banoi are black, and feed on excrement, some of them at least ; and that the trees there have red leaves, and that the fowls there are also red.

The writer goes on to describe the funeral and the death-meals.   ' The first thing after the death of a man of some rank, is to cut in the bush certain vines which are called corpse-binding vines.   Then they bring together many mats (such as those which pass as money) to wrap the corpse in. Women bring out mats, such as are used for sleeping on, and spread them in the open place in the middle of the village, and over these good clean mats. When these are ready, those who have been at work sit on the heap of mats and begin the wailing, so that people at a distance may know that the time has come to swathe the corpse. Then, all having assembled by the heap of mats, men and women carry out the corpse wrapped in a single mat from his house to the weeping crowd; and when they lay him on the mats spread as a bed the crying is wonderful, nothing can be heard at all but that. They put on his belt and his *malo* dress, and smear him with red earth, and dress his hair with a cock's feather or pigs' tails. His mother, or wives or sisters, throw ashes over their heads and backs. When they have swathed the corpse in mats and bound all round with the vines, some man of the dead man's kin sits upon the bundle, and is carried with it by many men to the grave, which has been dug by the side of the *gamal*. After this the wives of the deceased, or his father and mother, do not go about as usual for a hundred days, they spend the day at home. Men may walk about, but the female mourners cannot go into the open, and their faces may not be seen; they stay indoors, and in the dark, and cover themselves with a large mat reaching to the ground. In the early morning the widow goes out of the house covered over with a mat, to weep at the graveside; every day she does this till the hundredth day, and also in the afternoon; and not she only, many people of the village weep. All the women put on a mat, "as large as a single plank," which remains on their head as a sign that they are in mourning for the death, and refrain from certain food; but the immediate relatives of the deceased may not eat yam, caladium, bananas, or other good food; they eat only the gigantic caladium, bread-fruit, cocoa-nuts, and mallow, and other things; and all these they seek in the bush where they grow wild, not eating those which have been planted. They count five days, and then build up stones over the grave; great heaps of stones, much larger than are now made, are seen where men of old times were buried. After that, if the deceased was a very great man with many gardens and pigs, they count fifty days, and then kill pigs on the day called the *Ulogi* or *Sawana*. On the *Ulogi*, the howling, at mid-day there is wailing at the grave-stones, which have been dressed and adorned with leaves and flowers ; some cry, and some begin a song sacred to the dead. When the ovens are opened the assembled crowd departs ; and the people of the village kill pigs, and they cut the point off the liver of each pig, and the brother of the deceased goes near the bush and calls the dead man's name, crying "This is for you to eat."

'Upon this all cry again ; and all their body and face they smear over with ashes ; and they wear a cord round their necks for a hundred days, to shew that they are not eating good food. If they kill many pigs like this they think it is a good thing; but if not, they think that the dead man has no proper existence, but hangs on tangled creepers, and to hang on creepers they think a miserable thing. That is the real reason why they kill pigs for a man who has died ; there is no other reason for it but that[1].'

'Meanwhile,' he continues, 'the ghosts have known the number of days since the last comer has died ; and the relatives of the dead man have counted the days to eat the death-meal for him, the fifth day or the tenth, and a crowd has

---

[1] Bishop Selwyn witnessed a singular practice at Tanoriki in Aurora on the hundredth day after a woman's death, while the feast was being held. 'Pigs were killed and yams mashed and distributed, and then the men began to go into the bush and get long rods of a sort of ginger that tapered to a point. These they brandished with both hands, and looked anxiously down the path leading to the next village. Then the cry arose, "They are coming," and down came some ten or twelve men, mostly young, carrying on their heads baskets which they held with both hands, leaving their bodies completely exposed. Long before they came in sight one heard cracks like a whip, and saw the cause. If a smiter was ready he threw his rod back, and the sufferer instantly stood still and received an unmerciful thwack delivered with both hands, which shivered the rod to atoms. The point came right round the man's body, and I could see the long wheals afterwards, though the back was somewhat protected by the string girdle they wear.'

come together to eat and to remember him and weep. Then
they think that the ghosts and he who has lately died come
back to the world for this, and that the ghosts call this the
great feast of the man who died. They believe that they come
and carry away food and pig's flesh for themselves to eat; but
men are not aware of their taking anything away, they speak
figuratively. It is just as when a little mash, or cocoa-nut, or
bit of pig is put upon a dead man's grave for him to eat; they
do not think that the ghosts take the things as men do; not
at all, the things remain all right; but they think that they
take away the *tamani* of the things. And if a little is given
they think that they carry it away as if it were a great deal,
and go down rejoicing to Banoi with shouting and with songs.
Thus they do to the hundredth day, and after that they think
no more about it.'

The Origin of Death was ascribed at Lepers' Island, both to
the disuse of the power of changing the skin, and to the defect
of nature which had not given men that power. Once upon
a time a woman and a crab disputed the point, the woman
maintaining that the crab was better than men, changing its
shell, becoming young again, and living long. She wanted
the crab to change bodies with her; and she blamed Tagar
because he did not make men rightly. But in accordance
with the story which is told in varying forms in the Solomon
Islands, the Banks' group, and the New Hebrides, men had
in former times the power of changing their skin. There was
an old woman who had two grandchildren. These two boys
were one day playing at blocking back the water of a little
brook, when the stream brought down a Tahitian chestnut. One
of the boys took it, and gave it to his grandmother to roast.
Afterwards the other boy, who had at first despised the chestnut,
ran home unobserved and ate it, so that when the first boy went
for it the chestnut was gone. The boy scolded his grandmother
for neglect, and she, angry in her turn, said to the boys, ' You
two don't wish to live for ever, but would rather that we should
not live.' She had just come back from changing her skin in
the water higher up in the stream which the boys were blocking

back; and they had seen the cast-off skin, picked it up with a
stick, and thrown it out of the water. The old woman in her
anger followed the stream down to the place where her skin
was lying on the bank, and put it on again. Since that
time mankind has lost the power of changing skins, and all
have died.

At death the soul, *tamtegi,* departs from the body. When
it is certain that it is gone the wailing for death begins.
At first the *tamtegi* does not go far away, and there are
sounds which shew its presence; they never drive it away,
it is only the soul of one who has been eaten that is driven
off with the blowing of conchs; when the time comes it goes,
and the time is a hundred days. The corpse is buried
wrapped in the mats which serve as money. When Mairuru
died they wrapped him at once in mats, and added more
next day, till the corpse with its wraps was so large that it
took two days to dig a grave for it, and on the third day
they buried him. He was swathed in one hundred short mats
and ten rolls of a hundred fathoms each; but Mairuru was
a very great man; with common people fifty mats would be
enough for a man, five for a boy. After the funeral pigs are
killed, and five fowls, and the fowls are roasted over the fire.
When the meal is ready the chief mourner takes a piece of
fowl and of yam and calls the name of some person of the
place who has died, saying, 'This is for you.' This he does
till he has called all those whose death is remembered in the
place, including the lately dead, and has given each a bit of
fowl and yam. What remains he eats himself, and then the
assembled mourners eat; this is to 'eat the grave.' Counting
five days from the death, they prepare the oven for 'eating
the death,' and when it is opened give morsels to the ghosts,
as on the day of burial. The same is done on the tenth day,
which is a great day with a large assemblage, and the same
again at a similar feast on the fiftieth day. Every fifth day
also there is a death-meal, and the hundredth is the last. On
that day for a very great man there will be a hundred ovens.
The last solemnity is remarkable. On the evening of that

day all the people assemble in the middle of the village; a man of the *waivung* division to which the deceased did not belong, one near to him by male descent, mounts a tree and calls all the names of the deceased one after another, for a great man has many names (page 114); there is a solemn silence as the names are called, all listen for a sound; if any sound is heard they take it for the answer of the dead, and all raise the wailing cry because it is the last time they will hear his voice. They have no thought of driving away the ghost; they call to him to come and take all their food and all they have, and go with it to Nggalevu. If no sound answers to the last call they think he has already gone. A man is buried with his bow and arrows and his best ornaments; but his pigs'-tusk bracelets are put on upside down. Nggalevu will know him to be a great man by what he sees with him and upon him, for he will be seen as a man is seen though he be a ghost, a *tamtegi*; what it is of the ornaments and other things that will be seen they have not considered, but certainly not a *tamtegi*, nor a soul; it raises a smile to ask whether there be the *tamtegi* of a bow. When a man dies his cocoa-nut-trees, fruit-trees, and things in his garden are cut down and destroyed. This is done, they say, out of a feeling of tenderness and sorrow; no one but he shall enjoy them.

The dead man's soul when it leaves his dwelling-place makes its way along the mountain path to Manaro, to the lake which fills the crater of the island. Sometimes men notice recent footsteps on the path, and go down to the villages to ask who has died and just gone up. The abode of the dead is Lolomboetogitogi, and the descent to it is by a volcanic vent near the lake. There ghosts assemble, and there has always been Nggalevu, a *vui*, a spirit not a ghost, who is the master of the place, and receives the new-comers. There is also a pig by which they have to pass. Beside the lake, on the farther side, which no man has been known to reach, there is a volcanic vent which sends up clouds of steam. Men go up to the nearer side of the lake and climb a tree

which overhangs it ; they cry aloud to Nggalevu to give
a sign that he is there, and a column of steam goes up. In
Lolomboetogitogi are trees and houses where the dead have
their abode ; though they are thought to come out, and are
seen like fire at night, or a man in the dusk sees something
like a dead tree-fern trunk standing before him in the path,
and fears to go on further. In Lolomboetogitogi the dead
are thought to live a happy if an empty life, free from pain
and sickness ; but there are those that come out for mischief,
hunting men to add them to their company ; and if a man
has left children when he died, one of whom sickens afterwards, it is said that the dead father takes it.

Two descents to Lolomboetogitogi are well remembered.
A young man lost his wife and much desired once more to see
her ; he took a friend and mounted to the lake ; they swam
to a certain rocky islet, and the widower, giving one end of a
clue to his friend, dived into the water ; as long as he was
alive, he said, he would keep pulling at the line. He arrived
at a village, and found an old friend, who warned him to keep
by himself, and by no means to eat. His wife he could not
see ; he took some sweet herbs growing in the village, and
returned through the water to the rock. Another man still
living went down by a banyan root in the forest, and found
the village of the ghosts ; they gave him food, which he
brought back with him without eating any, bananas old and
black. Another descent is the subject of a story not seriously
told or believed, a sort of parody on the above, which relates
how a man made his way to an underworld of pigs, *ureuremboe*,
the pig-world, of which a snake, Tamatemboe, dead-man-pig,
was the master ; the snake had stones in a lump at its neck,
and these stones were powerful for wealth in pigs ; so the man
said who brought the stones with him, and had them for sale
or hire.

At Araga, Pentecost, there are two stories as to the Origin
of Death. In one a man and a rat dispute, the rat saying
that the man would die outright, but that himself would live
again. The man and rat meet again in the path and quarrel,

and the man kills the rat; it begins to putrefy: 'How it stinks!' cries the man. 'You will be as bad,' says the rat. 'But I shall live again,' says the man. 'No! like me,' says the rat. The other story is a variant of the common one about changing the skin. There was a man who had two boys living with him, and used to change his skin every day and come out to work with them. One evening he put on his old skin again, and the boys killed him because he had deceived them. If he had lived, all men would have changed their skins and never died.

A ghost after death is *atmat*, dead-man, but, as in Lepers' Island, the same word is used to designate a man's soul when he is alive. At death the *atmat* leaves the body, but lingers near it for five days. It is not driven away, but goes off itself to the abode of the dead called Banoi ; in case of fainting, the man on recovering says he was not allowed to enter. The corpse is watched till it is buried ; in the case of a great man for three or four days ; it is then rolled in the mats valued as money and taken to the *gamal* ; if a great man, the mats are many, and the swathed corpse is set up between two stakes. After a time it is buried ; a great man is buried in the village place in a *qaru*, with stones set up and with dracænas and other coloured shrubs planted round. After the burial the fire is lighted for the death-meal, and they go on 'eating the death' for a hundred days, which are counted on a cycas leaf. By way of mourning the relatives smear themselves with smut and ashes. The ghosts, going away, or being let go, make their way down the coast, along the beach, to Vatang-gele, where they are heard singing, shouting, and drumming. The place of assembly before the descent into Banoi is a point of land opposite Ambrym, where there is a stream the ghosts cannot pass, and a tree from which they leap into the sea ; a shark waiting below bites off the noses of those who have not killed pigs in accordance with the customs of the island. There is a town in Banoi, with houses, trees, sweet-smelling plants, and shrubs with coloured leaves, but no gardens, because there is no work. The new-comer is weak at first, and rests

before he begins to move about the place. A new arrival is
greeted by a dance; for the husband, wife, or friend of one
already there they *raparahi bolo*, go through an elaborate
performance. The ghosts of those who have died violent
deaths keep together; those who have been shot with the
arrow sticking in the body, those who have been clubbed
with the club fixed into the head; those also who have died
of cough keep together. When a ghost comes down with
the instrument of death upon him, he tells who killed him,
and when the murderer arrives the ghostly people will not
receive him; he has to stay apart with other murderers. To
the question how one is received who has killed another in
fair fight no certain answer can be given. As to the food of
ghosts in Banoi there is a difference of opinion; some say
they eat nothing, some thàt they eat excrement and rotten
erythrina wood; probably the ghosts rejected by the happier
crowd have the dismal food. Ghosts haunt especially their
burial-places, and revenge themselves if offended; if a man
has trespassed on the grave-place of a dead chief the ghost
will smite him, and he will be sick. Ghosts seen appear like
fire. My informants tell me that no fragment of food is
offered to a ghost, a doubtful statement; but if they see
bananas or other food rotting in a dead man's garden, they
say it is the ghost's food, not meaning so much that the
ghost eats this, as that as is the man so is his food [1].

It remains to notice what practice there appears to be in
these islands of burying the living with the dead. A case is
remembered at Saa, where the wife of a chief killed in fighting
asked for death that she might follow her husband, and was

---

[1] At Ambrym they bury in the house; after five months they dig up the
bones, take the skull, jawbone and ribs and put them under the root of a hollow
tree. The small bones they bury again in the house, the long bones they tie
up in baskets with yams and other food and put up in a tree. The body of
a great man is not buried; it lies in the house in a canoe or in a drum, women
and children sleep round it to watch and remove the worms; after ten months
they take up the skull, jawbone, and long bones of arms and legs and
hang them in the house; the other bones are wrapped together and sunk
at sea.

strangled accordingly. At Maewo it has often happened that a woman has demanded to be buried with her husband or a beloved child. Not long ago a woman insisted on it ; they dug a grave, wrapped her in mats, and buried her alive with her child. In Lepers' Island lately when Mairuru was buried, the people, accusing his wife of having poisoned him, wanted to bury her alive with him ; she consented, but the presence of a Christian native prevented this being done. The killing or burying alive of sick persons is another matter.

CHAPTER XVI.

THE foregoing chapters have been, mainly at least, concerned with subjects to deal with which such knowledge of the thoughts and ways of Melanesian people as can only be gained by personal acquaintance with them, and familiarity with their language, is most required. The present chapter will contain notices of such matters as lie much more upon the surface of native life, and are open to the observation of the visitor and traveller; the arts, namely, in which the culture of the people expresses itself, by which they build and decorate canoes and houses, plant and cultivate their gardens, furnish themselves with weapons and implements for war and work, catch fish, prepare their food, furnish themselves with clothing and ornaments, make and use money as a medium of exchange. So long a catalogue of their arts of life shews that Melanesians do not take a very low place among the backward peoples of the world. To deal fully and adequately with these matters would require much space; it is the less necessary to do so since much information has been already made public, as by Dr. Guppy for example, concerning the Solomon Islands; but there is certainly room for additions, and even in these matters there is much value in what natives say about themselves.

(1) *Canoes.* The inhabitants of groups of islands are likely to be seafaring people, and canoes are naturally among the first objects that present themselves to a visitor. Hardly anything seems in my remembrance to have been more striking

than the difference between the canoes of the natives when
for the first time we passed from the New Hebrides and
Banks' Islands to the Solomon Islands, and exchanged the
clumsy outriggered tree-trunks of the Eastern groups for
the elegant forms and brilliant ornaments of the plank-built
craft of the West. But upon consideration, the outrigger
canoe that sails must be thought to take a higher rank than

NEW HEBRIDES CANOE.

one propelled by paddles only; and certainly the outrigger
canoe is the one characteristic of Melanesia. It is only in the
Solomon Islands that plank-built canoes are seen; but there
also small canoes with outriggers are used, and these are in
fact the same with those of Santa Cruz, the Banks' Islands
and the New Hebrides; all alike are hollowed trunks of trees
with outriggers. Double canoes are nowhere seen in these

islands as in Fiji; but the *aka, angga, wangga,* of the Banks'
Islands and New Hebrides, is doubtless the same thing with
the *wangga* of Fiji. The large sailing canoes, which in the
New Hebrides will carry forty men, are also single trunks
dug out and shaped for the hull, with sides built up and
decks laid with planks tied on with sinnet. Before the time
when the labour trade made the natives afraid to move
about, and 'recruiting' meant destruction of canoes for the
capture of their crews, red 'butterfly' sails were the common
and pleasing ornament of an island scene in the New Hebrides and Banks' groups.

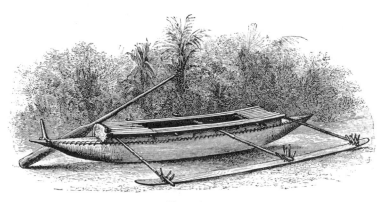

MOTA CANOE.

To take the example of a Mota *aka.* The sail, *epa,* was
formed of mats, woven by women, and sewn together by men
with needles of tree-fern wood, or the bone of a ray's sting.
The mast, *turgae,* with a forked butt, was stepped upon the
midmost of the three yoke-pieces, *iwatia,* which connected the
outrigger, *sama,* with the hull. The yoke-pieces were fastened
to the outrigger by being lashed to wooden pegs fixed into it.
Upon the foot of the mast was stepped again the forked end
of a boom, *panei;* both were stayed with ropes, *tali,* and in
the triangular space between the mast and boom was spread
the sail, lashed to both, and sinking in a graceful curve
between the two. A large paddle for steering, *turwose,* was

tied to a horn, *tiqa-taso*, at the stern. The whole safety of
the vessel depended on the strength and elasticity of the
attachment of the outrigger to the hull. In former times the
work of shaping the body of the canoe and adzing out the
planks with which the sides were raised was done with shell
adzes; and the holes for the lashings were bored with the
columella of a volute shell. A large canoe was owned in
common by several men, or by one very important person;
money was paid for hire and freight. All canoes of any size

SANTA CRUZ CANOE.

had names; when a new canoe came for the first time to
land away from home the crew was pelted in a friendly
way [1].

The Santa Cruz canoes, of better workmanship and form,
are substantially the same as these; the large sea-going
canoes, *loju*, carry a large stage on either side above a very

[1] In the Torres Islands of late years there were no canoes; the people were
reduced to use catamarans of bamboo, if they wished to cross from one to
another island. Their canoe-makers had died out, and they, very characteristically, acquiesced, as at Lakona also they did for a time, in going without.

narrow hull, and have a house upon one of them for the crew. In these canoes, with the large sail rising into curved horns, they make long voyages to Vanikoro and other islands that they know, steering by the stars. The Solomon Island plank-built canoe has probably not been developed in ignorance of the outrigger [1]. In the straits between long islands like Malanta and Guadalcanar the natives have prided themselves on the skill with which they build and paddle their canoes. Ulawa was once a famous centre of manufacture and of sale [2]. Canoes from Saa would make a six days' voyage for trade and pleasure, to Owa, Santa Anna and Santa Catalina, in one direction, steering by the stars at night, and to Alite in the other. Large canoes again cross from Alite to Guadalcanar to exchange money and ornaments for food, and as they return heavily laden throw out floats of dry cocoa-nuts at night, to rest and sleep. The moon in her second quarter lying on her back is called in Florida a 'canoe of Mala.' A very graceful little catamaran is used within the reefs of San Cristoval; five or six stems of the fronds of the sago-palm lashed together, the tips of them brought back by lines towards the butts, and the end of the high curved prow so formed decorated with a crimson streamer. A war canoe of the first rate is a long while in building; for three successive years I had the opportunity of seeing one at Ha'ani, from the *bea* set up to gain funds when the work began to the last ornamentation with shell carvings and streamers. Such a canoe forty-five feet long would carry ninety men. The form of a Florida *peko* is more graceful than that of the Ulawa build; the large one in Takua's great *kiala* at Boli was sixty

---

[1] Dr. Guppy mentions Bishop Patteson's notice of an outrigger canoe at San Cristoval, said to have been built after a Santa Cruz model. Within the last few years again it has been said that at Ulawa they have lately learnt to catch sharks after a Santa Cruz fashion in outrigger canoes. But they certainly caught sharks in that way more than twenty years ago; and it is likely that if they had copied Santa Cruz canoes they had done so long before Bishop Patteson observed the outriggers. Such small canoes are not uncommon.

[2] A large Ulawa canoe is preserved in the Brenchley Museum at Maidstone; another is in the British Museum.

feet long by six feet wide, and the stem and stern turned up
to the height of fifteen feet[1]. These canoes are all constructed of planks adzed out so as to leave cleats by which
they are lashed to curved rib-pieces of mangrove wood, which
give the necessary stiffness to the vessel; the edges of the
planks being sewn together with sinnet, and the seam

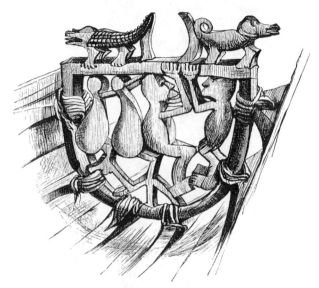

SPEAR-REST IN FLORIDA CANOE.

covered with cement. In a war canoe a rest for spears and
other weapons is set up amidships[2], and various *tindalo*

[1] Every kind of canoe has its own name; as in Florida, where the general
name is *tiola*, the *peko* is the war canoe, with stem and stern running up to
high flat ends, and long in proportion to its breadth; *mbinambina*, with stern
turned up as in a *peko,* but with the head straight, with a guard of planks
against the wash of the waves, and broader than a *peko* in proportion to its
length; *tola*, with both ends turned up not very high; *roko*, with ends not
turned up at all.

[2] In Mr. Brenchley's 'Cruise of the Curaçoa' is reproduced a native picture
of a canoe from Ugi, now at Maidstone, in which the spears are seen in their
rest; upon them is a bent bow set up upon its back, which is described as a
bowl for propitiatory libations. Though the explanation is incorrect in this
particular, sacrifices are commonly offered in canoes. The woodcut above shows

charms are fixed and hung on to the stem to secure quiet seas
and a favourable result to expeditions [1]. Canoes of importance
in these islands also have names, and festivities follow their

FIGURE-HEAD OF FLORIDA CANOE.

completion; one made at Olevuga was named Biku, after
a relation of the owner; it would carry thirty paddlers and

a rest for spears forming part of a rib-piece cut out of a slab of wood and used
to stiffen a canoe amidships. The figures represent a crocodile and a dog
above, two men and two cockatoos below. To this rib-piece the cleats on the
planks are seen to be lashed.

[1] In the woodcut above not only are the head, which represents that taken
when the canoe was first used, and the hanging board, which swings above
the waves with a soothing motion, full of *mana*, but the bamboo tubes above
wound round with red braid are stuffed with *tindalo* relics and leaves for
protection and success.

as many sitters; when it was cemented with *tita*, a hundred
pigs were killed for the feast. Such a canoe required a life
for its inauguration[1].

In the Eastern Solomon Islands, if no victim was met with in
the first voyage of a new canoe, the chief to whom the canoe
belonged would privately arrange with some neighbouring
chief to let him have one of his men, some friendless man
probably, or a stranger, who would then be killed, perhaps as
he went out to look at the new canoe. It was thought
a kind thing to come behind and strike him without
warning. Further west also captives were kept with a
view to the taking of their heads when new canoes were
launched.

It is remarkable that while the paddles used in the Eastern
Solomon Islands as far as Florida are pointed, some very
narrow and pointed indeed, those used in Ysabel have an
obtusely pointed, short, and broad blade with a comparatively long shaft, the latter having a crescent-shaped handle,
and the former a crutch, for the upper hand. The paddles of
the Banks' Islands and New Hebrides are comparatively
shapeless and heavy.

A custom common to the Solomon Islands and the Eastern
groups is that of taking a new canoe about to show it with a
large party who receive presents wherever they visit. A great
deal of trading is carried on between the various islands of
each group; in two places the people live by commerce and

---

[1] For example, Dikea, the chief of Ravu in Florida, bought his *peko*, named
Lake (fire), at Olevuga in the same island, for sixty *rongo*, a large sum of
money. It was brought over secretly and put into a *kiala*, canoe-house,
built out of sight, till a head should have been procured. Dikea sent to his
brothers Sauvui and Takua for help, and when he saw their fire-signal at the
mouth of the Vula passage in the night joined them there, bringing the
new canoe, and as they passed through other canoes joined the expedition.
Before daylight they had ambushed at Hagalu; and in the morning a single
man, Tibona, came by them in his canoe. They hid till he was past, and then
drew down the new *peko* to chase him; he dived to escape, but they caught
and killed him, set up his head at the prow of the canoe, and paddled back to
Ravu with shouting and blowing conch-shells; the women and children however would not go out to see.

manufactures. Rowa, one of the Banks' group, has but a
tiny population on one of the islets of its reef. They still
mainly obtain their food from Saddle Island and Vanua
Lava, carrying over in exchange fish and the money that
they make at home. Not many years ago it was believed
that if food were grown at Rowa there would be a famine in
Vanua Lava, and also that if a sow were taken there it would
devour the people ; but the Christian teacher of the place,
himself a Rowa man, has boldly met both dangers. The
other seat of commerce is on the Alite islets close to the
Malanta coast near Florida, the inhabitants of which are
enemies to their neighbours of the mainland, and have no
gardens there ; they buy their chief subsistence from
Guadalcanar with the money and the ornaments that they
make.

(2) *Houses.* The typical Melanesian house requires very
little description ; a roof of bamboos bent over a ridge-pole,
which is supported by two main posts, very low side walls,
and the ends filled in with bamboo screens. The dwelling-
houses in the New Hebrides and Banks' Islands are poor,
and contain little that can be called furniture ; a chest on
legs, cleverly made, to contain dried bread-fruit, a fire-place
sunk into the ground, a hole and pile of stones for an oven ;
wooden hooks, cut from branching trees, hanging from the
roof with bags of food to protect them from the rats ; large
wooden platters with their pestles, bowls, bamboos for water,
and wicker dishes leaning against the side walls ; a few
wooden knives and tools stuck between the layers of thatch ;
mats spread upon the floor ; these may be seen everywhere ;
and often there is an inner chamber, screened off with reeds.
The door is nothing but a number of stalks of sago fronds
run through the middle by a stick which is thrust down
between the double threshold of the doorway, and tied above,
when the house is empty, from outside through an opening
left above the doorway for the purpose [1]. The *gamal,* club-

[1] 'It seems to be the custom here (at Ureparapara), as well as in some
parts of Vanua Lava, for three or four families to occupy a single house. These

house, is in construction the same, but larger, stronger, and furnished with openings in the sides as well as doorways at the ends. The roofing is thatch of the smaller sago-palm, which makes an excellent roof, and the preparation and fixing of which is the chief work of house-building. The palm frond, with its midrib removed, and the leaflets doubled over a reed, and pinned together with wooden skewers, or spikes from the base of sago fronds (the Malay *atap*), is in all the islands what a tile or slate or shingle is else-where. In the Solomon Islands the cocoa-nut frond is also used, the lesser sago being apparently unknown. The roofing there, however, is very fine, the ataps being laid very close together, and the thatch extremely thick in the large buildings such as the canoe-houses. These, *oha* in Malanta and San Cristoval, *kiala* in Florida and Ysabel, to which the Santa Cruz *madai* and *ofilau* correspond, are fine and spacious buildings; the *kiala* at Kolakamboa in Florida was a hundred feet long by fifty wide, and fifty high; an *oha*, in Ugi and San Cristoval at least, was decorated with all the skill of the noteworthy native artist [1]. In these the large canoes are kept, men congregate and young men sleep, strangers are entertained, the huge wooden bowls used in feasts are kept, the jawbones of pigs eaten or killed in such feasts are suspended, and the skulls of men killed in war, and sometimes no doubt also eaten in the place, are hung up; in the *oha* also are the *mangite* of the dead (page 262). The posts which support the ridge-pole and the purlins of an *oha* are carved into figures of men, crocodiles and sharks; a *kiala* is much less ornamented. A Solomon Island dwelling-house is certainly superior to one in the Eastern groups; its walls are higher, it is more generally partitioned into chambers, and it is furnished with

are built very long, and have slight divisions in them, seldom more than two feet high.'—Bishop Selwyn, Journal, 1882.

[1] Brenchley's ' Cruise of the Curaçoa,' chap. xvi; Guppy's 'Solomon Islands,' chap. iv. I have never seen any ornamentation so elaborate and interesting as that of an *oha* at Wango, long since fallen into decay.

bedsteads which lift the sleeper from the ground ; its higher
and better-finished ridge-piece gives it a more picturesque
appearance. When the visitor from the eastward reaches
Florida he finds houses built on piles ; when he reaches Ysabel
he sees tree-houses for the first time. The pile-houses are
excellent dwellings, the side walls and the floor formed
of split bamboos flattened and interlaced, and the face of the

HOUSE AT YSABEL.

house handsomely ornamented with interlacing patterns of
bamboo stained black. The dwelling-houses of chiefs are
sometimes noble buildings ; a new one at Honggo measured twenty-four paces long by nine wide, and was thirty
feet high. The floor of this, of interlaced bamboo, was
raised some height above the ground, and the hearth upon
the ground occupied a sunken space. Inside such a house
small houses for several wives are sometimes ranged against

the walls, and sometimes a tiny house on piles is built in the middle. In former days when a chief's dwelling-house or canoe-house was finished a man's head was taken for it as for a new canoe ; a boy or woman was sometimes bought to be killed. It is a matter of tradition that men were crushed under the base of the great pillar of such a house, when it was set in its place. The tree-houses, *vako*, are not seen till Ysabel is reached, where they are needed as a refuge from the head-hunters. One of these to which Bishop Patteson mounted, was built at a height of ninety-four feet from the ground, and was approached by a ladder from a fortified rock below which the tree was rooted ; the house, which had a stage outside it, was eighteen feet long, ten feet broad, and eight feet high. The houses at Santa Cruz, according to the account given of the first discovery, were round ; they are now square, though round houses are said to be built. The only round house that has come under my notice was at Ha'ani in San Cristoval, one built to contain and shelter the village drums, and an excellent building. Sometimes in the Banks' Islands a *gamal* may be seen the rafters of which are curved. It may be well to notice here how the two words for house run through the islands ; one, which in Malay is *ruma*, varying from that form in San Cristoval to *'ma* in the Loyalty Islands and Santa Cruz ; the other, which is *whare* in New Zealand, not by any means so common, but *vale* and *hale* in the New Hebrides, *vale*, *vathe* and *va'e* in the Solomon Islands[1]. The absence of ancient house-mounds has been observed (page 48), and accounted for by the little permanence of village sites. When a ruinous house is demolished to build another on the same site, it is found that the constant sweeping of the

---

[1] In Maewo, Aurora, ' the *ima* is the married man's residence. Within this house the cooking of the food for the family is done, and the married couples live. This house is known from the rest by having the front and back ends worked with cane, and more pains are expended on the building of it. The *vale* has no fire-place for cooking, and is mostly used as the apartment of the young females before marriage, and for stowing anything that may be inconvenient in the *ima*.'—Journal of Rev. C. Bice, 1886.

floor has sunk it below the outside level, and that this again has been raised close round the house by accumulation of various rubbish. When the new house is to be built, the hollow inside is filled with the outside accumulation, and the result is a little elevation of the site. If then an ancient site is seen some four or five feet high, it must represent a pretty long occupation of the ground.

In two islands far apart, in Ysabel and in Santa Maria, there are very remarkable structures to be seen. In Bugotu, Ysabel, Bishop Patteson slept in 1866 in a fortified place thus described. 'The site for the village has been chosen on a hill surmounted by steep, almost perpendicular coral rocks; the forest has been cleared for some space all round, so as to prevent any enemy from approaching unperceived; there is a wall of stones of considerable height on that side where the rock is less precipitous, with one narrow entrance, approached only by a smooth slippery trunk of a tree, laid at a somewhat steep inclination over a hollow below.' So also at Tega the people built a *toa*, 'an impregnable fort on a rocky knoll in the midst of the village.' These forts are made for protection against head-hunters. The stone buildings in a village in Gaua, Santa Maria, are very extraordinary; nothing like them has been seen elsewhere in these islands. There are three small *gamal* houses on platforms about ten feet high, built up with stones untouched by any tool, and some of them three feet long by two deep. The building is wonderfully square and regular; the style quite Cyclopean, the large stones ingeniously fitted, and the interstices filled with small stones. Besides these platforms there are two or three obelisks about four feet high, and a little dolmen of three stones. There are also two *wona* platforms, such as are always seen near a *gamal* (page 101), but much larger, and built of large stones very squarely put together. In one of these is a passage for pigs with a stone lintel. These remarkable works are shown in the frontispiece. That such stone-work exists elsewhere in these islands cannot be positively denied, but none has been heard of, and in the neighbouring islands there is nothing at all resembling it. It would naturally be thought, therefore, to belong to former times and to a different population; but it is indeed recent, and has proceeded from the ambition or the fancy of a single man but lately dead [1]. When he reached the rank in the *suqe* in which he had no equal, and had to eat alone, he determined to build his *gamal* unlike those of other men. When he took further steps, and made his *kolekole* feasts (page 110), he did the same. For this he hired men from Lakona in the same island, where they build their *wona* with small stones; they selected the stones that suited Vagalo's design, and worked under his direction. This example of originality, and of the individual enterprise which has produced a work single of its kind, seems most valuable. It may help to explain the strange trilithon at Tonga.

(3) *Cultivations.* The Melanesians are a horticultural people; the skill and care with which gardens were kept and planted could not from the first fail to strike their visitors, and marked them off by a distinction that cannot be mistaken from the natives of Australia. The Melanesian 'labourer' carried off to Queensland was amazed to find men who, though black, had no garden, and did not bring back very flattering accounts of white men's cultivation either. A garden of yams carefully trained on reeds, kept absolutely clear from weeds, and beautiful in the leafage of the vines, is a fine sight indeed; gardens, in San Cristoval as an example, with the various plots within a common fence neatly marked and divided, shew the exact regard for individual rights; gardens raised and worked in steps on the steep sides of Meralava have been formed with much skill and labour; the irrigated gardens [2] of the esculent caladium or arum in Aurora and

---

[1] The death of this man Valago shewed his remarkable character. Finding himself weak with advancing years and wasted by disease, he compelled a young man to fight with him at close quarters. Having received an arrow wound he died, forbidding vengeance, but expressing satisfaction that men should say that 'Valago was shot, and did not die like a woman.'

[2] 'Every inch that was available was used for irrigation, by means of one little streamlet which is made to do a vast deal of work before it can

Vanua Lava (if any survive the ruin caused by the labour
trade in the latter island), are a proof of considerable and very
ancient skill in cultivation. The esculent caladium is grown
for food in Egypt and in Syria, and its use stretches in an
unbroken chain from China throughout the islands of the
Indian and Pacific Oceans; it is not by any accident that a
dry garden, as opposed to an irrigated one, is called *uma* in
Sumatra and in the New Hebrides [1]. The respective shares of
men and women in garden work is settled by local custom.
Cultivation has produced a wonderful variety in yams, bananas, bread-fruit, and no doubt other common food-producing
plants; I have a list of eighty names of varieties of yams, and
sixty of bread-fruit, grown in the little island of Mota,
most of which an experienced native recognizes and names at
once. It may be said generally, that the natives are fond
of planting flowering shrubs and sweet herbs about their
villages, but this is much more seen in the Banks' Islands
and New Hebrides than in the Solomon Islands. The beauty
and variety of hibiscus, croton, dracæna, acalypha, amaranthus,
are surprising; no village is without its ornamental plants
and flowers. In the Banks' Islands they know how to graft
the various kinds of croton; taking two young branches of
equal size and breaking the end off each, removing an inch of
the bark from the stock and the same length of the wood from
the scion, bringing the bark of each to meet exactly; this is
done in damp hot weather only.

(4) *Weapons.* The use of the bow is universal in the islands
with which we are concerned; but the bow is not universally
the chief war weapon. The spear is in some islands so
conspicuously the fighting weapon that it is easy for one who

reach the sea in a course of about two miles.'—Bishop Selwyn, Maewo,
1878.

[1] 'This is now the first month of their preparation for yam planting, which
they perform in different stages. After a man has marked out the range of
his garden that is to be, he determines upon the day when they shall " umwa"
it, that is clear out all the scrub and undergrowth. Here his friends make a
" bee " for him, and get the business over in one day.'—Rev. C. Bice, Maewo,
1883.

has seen a good deal of native life to deny that the bow is
used in war, though, as in Florida for example, the use of
it is not so very rare. In Florida, Guadalcanar, Ysabel, San
Cristoval, and to a less degree in Malanta, the proper thing
is to fight with spears; and the fashion may not be of very
long standing, if at least we may take the narrative of the
first discoverers to be correct. With the spear comes the use
of the shield; yet the San Cristoval spearmen use no such
defence, but turn off spears thrown at them with long curved
glaives, and the shields in use in Florida are not made in
that island. Spears are generally made of palm wood, in
Ysabel of ebony; they are mostly barbed, but in Florida the
kona are headed with human leg-bones, cut and broken into
jagged points. The fighting with spears in the open, as on
a beach, is not attended with much mortality, and comes
very much to a series of duels; when one was hit, his enemy
would run in on him with his club. There are occasions on
which a combined attack is made upon a village by enemies
who have by payment and by promises secured the assistance
of numerous allies, and such an attack, if not at once
successful or defeated, becomes something like a siege; but
an open spear fight, the mutual spearing, *vei totogoni*, of
Florida, is not common [1]; ambushes set round a village in
the night, or for a single man in the path, are more common
and deadly; in these the tomahawk is now the effective
weapon. When a young warrior in Florida killed his first
man, he would let the blood run from the weapon into his
mouth. The bows of Malanta, powerful weapons, are
commonly used in war in that island. Slings are not
unknown in the Solomon Islands, and are said to have been
brought into use for attacking the tree-houses. Men never
like to go about without something in the hand, to be used

[1] According to Takua's account of the famous fight to which he owed his
place in Florida, 200 canoes came together from the neighbouring parts to
attack Ta-na-ihu. Their first onset being unsuccessful, because anticipated,
they fought with spears on the slope of the hill for three days. The assailants
then withdrew, without much loss on either side.

in a sudden quarrel perhaps ; in Florida and thereabouts a
paddle-shaped club is a favourite walking weapon, *rau ni Aba*,
the leaf, so called, of Aba, a place in Guadalcanar where they
are made. The spears, shields, clubs, bows and arrows of the
Solomon Islands are common in museums. The spear [1] is
practically unknown as a weapon in the Banks' Islands, it
comes into use, in company with the bow, in Ambrym ; the
Espiritu Santo spear, with its triple point and graduated
barbing of human bone, is perhaps the most fearful of all
these weapons. Where they fought with bows, as in the
Banks' Islands, an open battle was not common; much
shouting of defiance, cursing, abuse and boasting, stamping
with the heel, and grasping of the ground with the toes, a
great sign of valour, resulted in little bloodshed [2]. Slings,
talvava, in the Banks' Islands were used chiefly in defence
against a night attack ; when such was expected, men would
from time to time sling stones down the paths by which the
enemy would approach ; but skilful slingers would do good
service in a fight. Clubs in the Banks' Islands never seem
to have been the carefully, and indeed beautifully, shaped
weapons used in the New Hebrides ; with these latter arrows
are warded off in fighting.

The Melanesian weapons, however, which demand most
attention, and require most explanation, are the poisoned
arrows, as yet so little understood. The belief in the deadly
virulence of the poison used, and in the hideous methods of
preparing it, is too firmly fixed to readily give way. Yet
a careful examination of poisoned arrows and of their effects,
by English and by French medical officers, has resulted twice

[1] Old men in the Torres Islands carry a heavy wooden pointed staff which
may be called a pike. In the Banks' Islands a spear is called *isar*, stabber,
but is only known in use, as in Aurora also, to stab pigs.

[2] About thirty years ago a combined attack was made by about 600 men from
the southern parts of Vanua Lava upon the people of Port Patteson, who with
their allies numbered about half their assailants. Their women backed up
the attacked party, encouraging them with cries and beating upon the trees.
There was no great loss of life, and the assailants retired. Not half the
number could be brought together now.

over in the declaration that the reputed poison-stuff on the
arrows is not poisonous, and that therefore the fatal effects of
wounds from the arrows are not due to the preparation which
is reputed poisonous[1]. From the scientific side, then, the
view is clear; and if the matter is approached from the
native side, it appears with equal plainness that the deadly
quality which they believe to attach to these weapons does
not belong to what can properly be called poison. It has been
said (page 213) that the Melanesian preparations wherewith
deadly property was believed to be conveyed to food were not
properly poisonous, that the effect was not thought to be
produced by the natural properties of the substance used, but
entirely by supernatural properties imparted by magic arts;
and this although there might be deleterious qualities in the
stuff employed. Most certainly this is the native view of
what is called poison on their arrows; what is sought, and as
they firmly believe obtained, is an arrow which shall have
supernatural power, *mana*, to hurt, in the material of which it
is made, and in the qualities added by charms and magical

---

[1] 'An Enquiry into the Reputed Poisonous Nature of the Arrows of the
South Sea Islanders, by Staff-Surgeon A. B. Messer, M.D., R.N., published
by the Authority of the Lords of the Admiralty,' 1876, has, with others, the
following conclusions. 'That in the numerous cases in which men have been
wounded by these arrows, no recorded instances are known of poisonous effects
following.' 'That the "locked-jaw" is not the result of poison on the arrows;
and as this disease is the only cause of fatal results after these wounds, the
arrows themselves are not in any way dangerous beyond the severity of their
wounds, and the conditions under which they are received.' The Report of
the Commission appointed by the Governor of New Caledonia in 1883 is
quoted by Mr. Romilly in the chapter on Poisoned Arrows in 'The Western
Pacific and New Guinea,' as completely dispelling 'the vulgar notion of the
fatal nature of these weapons.' As Mr. Romilly refers to myself, I may say
that in the two cases mentioned the man who died had been little influenced,
and the one who survived much influenced by Mission teaching, to which
indeed it is reasonable to ascribe a good deal of the absence of alarm and
distress from his mind. His constant exclamation was 'My mind is easy, I
have heard the Bishop.' In that year, 1870, I obtained without difficulty the
information concerning these arrows in the Banks' Islands which is here set
forth, and which all that I have learnt since from other islands has shown to
be correct. I do not remember to have heard of the renewal of the poison,
which is likely enough.

preparations. That a punctured wound in the tropics is often
followed by tetanus, that the breaking off of a fine point of
bone in a wound is sure to be dangerous and likely to be
fatal, that an acrid or burning substance introduced by the
arrow into the wound will increase inflammation in it, are
facts altogether outside the native field of view. The point
is of a dead man's bone, and has therefore *mana*, it has been
tied on with powerful *mana* charms, and has been smeared
with stuff hot and burning, as the wound is meant to be,
prepared and applied with charms ; that is what they mean
by what we, not they, call, poisoned arrows. And when the
wound has been given, its fatal effect is to be aided and
carried on by the same magic that has given supernatural
power to the weapon.

Poisoned arrows, as they are called [1], are used in the Solomon
Islands, Santa Cruz, the Banks' Islands, and New Hebrides.
In the Torres Islands and Lepers' Island arrows are used for
fighting which are not poisoned, yet belong entirely to the
same class with those that are, being as much valued,
trusted and feared as the others ; a very instructive fact : in
Lepers' Island both kinds are used. There is a great difference in the size and weight of the arrows of various islands,
and in the proportion of the parts, but the structure is everywhere the same. There is a shaft of reed, a foreshaft of hard
wood, tree-fern or palm, and a point of human bone ; the
point is let into the foreshaft, and that into the shaft, and
the joinings are firmly bound with fine string or fibre.
Santa Cruz arrows are uniformly nearly four feet long,
and weigh about two ounces ; Banks' Island arrows are
about three feet nine inches long, and weigh about an
ounce ; Torres Island arrows are only two feet ten inches
long, weighing three-quarters of an ounce. The bone point
of a Santa Cruz arrow is seven inches long, and the foreshaft of hard wood, curiously carved and coloured, is sixteen
inches long. The bone head of a Torres Island arrow is

---

[1] Natives would never use the same word for the preparation with which
their arrows are smeared and for that which they mix with food.

a foot long, the fore-shaft eight inches, the reed-shaft twenty inches. The one is a heavy and powerful weapon, requiring a large and powerful bow; the other is slight and weak, little more than a human bone fitted for the bow; one is poisoned, the other is not; both are in native estimation equally deadly. Some of the New Hebrides and Solomon Island arrows have a very small point of bone. It is the human bone first of all that in native opinion gives the arrow its efficacy; the bone of any dead man will do, because any ghost has *mana* to work on the wounded man; but the bone of a man who was powerful when alive is more valued [1].

Though it is the human bone that gives in the first place the deadly quality to the arrow, yet the bone must be fitted into the shaft with the magic charms which secure supernatural power to the weapon. The maker sings or mutters charms as he ties the bone to the foreshaft; hence, as I have been told, the *mana* is put in where the bone joins the foreshaft. These charms are known but to a few whose business it is to make the arrows; but still if one should, as did the young man at Omba who made arrows of his brother's bones, take the bones of one he knew in life and call upon his ghost, as he would be sure to do, in binding on the head, no doubt his arrows would be perfectly well prepared. The 'poison,' again, is an addition to the power of the bone; the magical efficacy of this preparation is added to the supernatural power residing in the dead man's bone. When the bone had made the wound, the dead man's power, which had been brought by incantations to the arrow, would make the wound fatal. The preparation of burning juices mixed with charms, and smeared

---

[1] The true Lepers' Island arrow, *liwue*, is made with a broad white head of human bone with jagged edges, nine or ten inches long, and without any preparation in the way of poison; and they use also poisoned arrows made and bought in Maewo. To make the *liwue* the leg-bones of men of no particular consideration are taken up out of their graves. Not long ago there was a man in that island, who out of affection for his dead brother dug him up and made arrows of his bones. With these he went about speaking of himself as 'I and my brother;' all were afraid of him, for they believed that his dead brother was at hand to help him.

upon the bone with charms, carries to the wound what is
itself like inflammation, and the ghost will make it inflame.

The treatment of the wounded man proceeds on the same
principle. If the arrow, or a part of it, has been retained, or
has been extracted with leaf poultices, it is kept in a damp place
or in cool leaves ; then the inflammation will be little and soon
subside. Shells, which have been made efficacious for the purpose by charms, are kept rattling above the house where the
wounded man lies, to keep off the hostile ghost. In the same
way the man who has inflicted the wound has by no means
done all that he can do. He and his friends will drink hot
and burning juices, and chew irritating leaves ; pungent and
bitter herbs will be burnt to make an irritating smoke ; a
bundle of leaves known to the shooter or bought from a wizard,
a *qesis*, will be tied upon the bow that sent the arrow, to secure
a fatal result; the arrow-head, if recovered, will be put into
the fire ; the bow will be kept near the fire to make the wound
it has inflicted hot, or, as in Lepers' Island, will be put into a
cave haunted by a ghost ; the bow-string will be kept taut
and occasionally pulled, to bring on tension of the nerves and
the spasms of tetanus to the wounded man.

The preparation of the poisoned arrows in Aurora, New
Hebrides, is thus described by a native writer : ' When they
have dug up a dead man's bone they break it into splinters
and cut it properly into shape, and sit down and rub it on a
stone of brain-coral with water. After that it is fixed into a
bit of tree-fern wood; everyone cannot do that, it is some one
who knows (the charms). When that is done, the thick juice
of *no-to* (excævaria agallocha) is put upon it. Then it is put
in a cool place on the side wall of a public hall, and no fire is
made there, so that the cold may strike upon it and it may
turn like mould. Then they dig up the root of a creeper they
call *loki*, and come back and strip off the bark and scrape the
inner fibre into a leaf; and that, wrapped in another leaf,
is put upon the fire. When it is cooked this is wrapped in
the web from the spathe of a cocoa-nut, and squeezed into
a leaf of the nettle-tree. Then with a piece of stick they

smear it on the point of bone to help the *toto*.   After this it
is put again into a cool place, and it swells up in lumps, which
as it dries become smooth again.   Then it is
fastened to the reed, and bound round with
fine string.   After that they take a green
earth, which is only found in one place, and
paint it over [1].   When it has been painted,
they take it to the beach and dip it into the
sea-water till it becomes hard ; then the *toto*
(poisoned arrow) is finished.'   In the neighbouring island of Whitsuntide they finish
off with stuff found on rocks on the shore,
thought by them to be the dung of crabs, and
believed to have much magic power [2].

In Mota, in the Banks' Islands, the poison
is made from the root of the climbing plant
loki, cooked over the fire with the juice of
pandanus root.   This mixture is black and
thick, and is smeared on the points of human
bone, which are put in the sun to dry, and
then kept five days indoors wrapped up, when
the stuff turns white.   Another mixture which
is thought to cause more inflammation and to
act more quickly is made with the juice of
toi, an euphorbia.   The points of these arrows

[1] I was once assured by a young naval officer that he
had seen putrid flesh upon the natives' arrows.   Asked
whether he had taken one into his hand to examine it, he
replied with disgust that he would not have the thing
near him.   He probably to this day believes that he has the
witness of his own eyes to the truth of the common belief.

[2] For the origin of these arrows at Maewo see the
story of Muesarava.   The writer of that story adds, ' And
this Maewo *toto* is exceedingly *mana* ; if it hits any one
by chance, without being shot at him, he dies.   If it hits
any one like that they always take care of salt-water; any
one who has eaten what is salt cannot go near the house
where the man lies.   And there is a filthy custom ; if
any one has been with a woman he cannot possibly go
near ; if he goes to-day, the man will die to-morrow.'

SHAFTS.   SANTA MARIA.

are protected with caps, and the arrows themselves carried in a quiver. The man in a rage who is ready to shoot pulls off the caps and thrusts them into his hair, and grasps a number of arrows in his bow hand. The shafts of these *toto* arrows are most elaborately ornamented in Santa Maria. No arrows are feathered.

At Santa Cruz the foreshaft is of palm wood, carved with shark's tooth or shell, and painted red and white. The

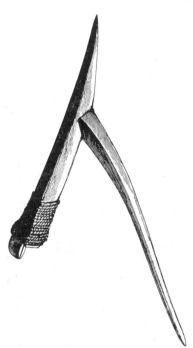

bone head is covered with a preparation of vegetable ashes, which gives great supernatural power. The foreshaft is bound at intervals with a string of fibre, which is covered with the same sort of preparation which covers the bone point; and this binding is no doubt done with charms to fasten supernatural qualities on the arrow.

The common result of a wound from any of these arrows, whether 'poisoned' or of bare bone, is certainly tetanus, which is expected. Even if, however, the *loki* be, as has been supposed, some kind of strychnine, it is well established that

SHELL ADZE.   TORRES ISLANDS.

this is not the cause of the disease. If it be asked how the very common belief has arisen that these arrows are poisoned with putrefying human flesh, if the preparation be wholly vegetable as above described, I can but conjecture that natives answered 'dead man' to early traders' enquiries. The native meant that the deadly qualities of the weapon came from the dead man of whose bone the head was made;

the European, thinking of poison, not magic, supposed that the poison was from a corpse. If it be asked again why, if the arrows be not really poisoned, the natives are so much afraid of them and careful not to touch them, it is enough to say that they firmly believe that they are deadly, and that this belief will outlast the belief in the power of the charms with which they are made.

(5) *Tools and Implements.* Before the introduction of metal, the adzes with which most of native work was done were in some islands of stone, in some of shell. The division is very clear: the Solomon islanders, except in Rennell and Bel-

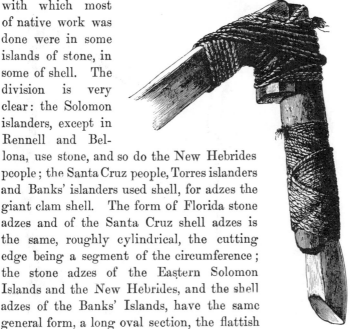

lona, use stone, and so do the New Hebrides people; the Santa Cruz people, Torres islanders and Banks' islanders used shell, for adzes the giant clam shell. The form of Florida stone adzes and of the Santa Cruz shell adzes is the same, roughly cylindrical, the cutting edge being a segment of the circumference; the stone adzes of the Eastern Solomon Islands and the New Hebrides, and the shell adzes of the Banks' Islands, have the same general form, a long oval section, the flattish sides meeting to form the edge. The shell adzes of Santa Cruz are beautifully finished, those of the Banks' Islands often very rough.

SHELL ADZE.
SANTA CRUZ.

When iron was introduced the Banks' Islands people, seeing it in the form of hoop iron, were inclined to call it heaven-root, *gar tuka*, supposing ships to come from beyond the horizon, and to have brought some of the strong and hard base of the firmament; when axes were seen they settled into the use of the word *talai*, clam shell, for iron. In Florida, Solomon Islands, a stone adze was *gila*, the *ira* of San Cristoval, and whence they took *halo* for iron is not explained. It is interesting to observe that in Lepers' Island, the stone adzes were called *talai maeto*, black clam shell, a name now given to iron; the native adze was evidently at first of shell, *talai*, and when stone was used the old name was retained. They still use the *til*, a volute shell,

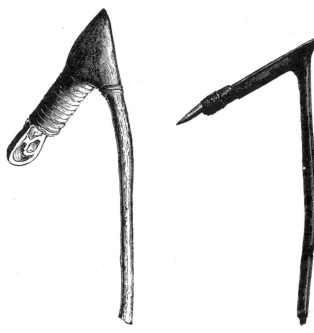

SHELL ADZE.   LEPERS' ISLAND.   STONE ADZE.   SAN CRISTOVAL.

for working the inside of their canoes. Another shell, the *tire*, was used in the Banks' Islands for a chisel. The rapidity with which the shell and stone implements give way to iron is surprising. Santa Cruz was very little visited, almost un-visited, ten years ago, and it was difficult to get any shell specimens even five years ago. The crookedness and slight-ness of the wooden handles used in the Solomon Islands is surprising. For cutting threads, shaving, and fine carving,

obsidian, chert, and sharks' teeth were used. The bamboo
knife has hardly been superseded by steel or iron; the edge
will not stand long, but while it stands it is far sharper than
a common steel knife in hands that know how to use it [1].

Pottery is unknown in the islands which are here in view,
being present in well-known forms in Fiji, and in ruder
unglazed dishes in Espiritu Santo. There may be room for
question whether the wide circular wooden dishes, *tapia*, of the

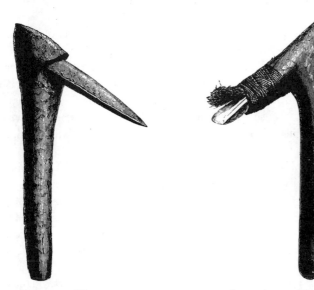

PALTARA. MOTA.   SHELL ADZE. MOTA.

Banks' Islands, and the deep wooden pots, *popo*, bought by
the Florida people from Guadalcanar, carry with them any
reminiscence of fictile ware. The *paltara*, used to chop bread-
fruit open in the Banks' Islands, is an interesting representation
in wood of the shell adze.

Stone-boiling, in Mota *salo*, was known all through the
islands, though not very much practised for cooking, at least

---

[1] A saw is made in the Banks' Islands by rolling up a strip of bamboo in a
spiral form. The name given to this implement, *saosao*, casts a doubt upon
its native origin.

in the Banks' Islands, where the cream squeezed out from grated cocoa-nut was often cooked over the embers in the shells. The bowls of the south-eastern Solomon Islands, remarkable some of them for their enormous size, some for their fantastic shape, all for their really beautiful ornamentation, represent stone-boiling in purpose if not often in use. The oval wooden bowls, *wumeto*, of the Banks' Islands sometimes stand on legs. The pestles in very active use there for making mash, *lot*, in the broad wooden dishes are wooden, sometimes ornamented with the figure of a bird at the upper end, an almost solitary instance of carved figure ornament on the implements of those people. It need hardly be said that all Melanesian people are mat-makers; the remarkable thing is that in Santa Cruz alone is found a loom with which beautiful mats are woven with the fibre of a banana cultivated for the purpose; these looms are identical with those in use in the Caroline and Philippine Islands and in Borneo.

(6) *Fishing.* A large part of the subsistence of Melanesians is generally and naturally derived from the sea, though the character of the shore modifies the extent of fishing industry. Something to eat with vegetable food is always looked for; and shell-fish, octopus, and such things from the reefs are in daily request. Fish are caught by angling from the shore or from canoes, by nets, by shooting or spearing, in woven pots, by poison, and with the use of torches at night. Hooks, now generally superseded, were most commonly made of tortoise-shell; in the Solomon Islands the hook common in the Pacific was beautifully made; a piece of mother-of-pearl, with or without a wooden back, with a tortoise-shell hook lashed to it, and a few beads on a short string, requiring no bait. The very small fish-hooks of mother-of-pearl and tortoise-shell, of either material alone, or of some shell which might imitate a bettle, at Savo, San Cristoval, Ulawa, were among the prettiest and most skilful products of native handiwork. The flying-fish is caught not with a hook, but with a double prickle of tortoise-shell, or spines from palms.

To fish for these from a canoe a very long and
light line is required; in Santa Cruz and the
Solomon Islands a
float is used, a short
stick, or wooden
shaft shaped like a
bird atop, weighted
with a stone, a
contrivance which
must also be known
in the Banks' Is-
lands, since it has
a name, *wo-uto*,
there [1]. The stitch
in netting is that
familiar in Europe,
and nets are made

SANTA CRUZ FLOAT.

extremely fine, and very large and strong. In the
Solomon Islands no mesh is used for a very large
net, but for a pig-net the loop is measured by
the knee, for a turtle-net by a man's shoulders.
Nets, sometimes fifty feet square, are used as seines,
and are let down between stages in shoaling
water; they are cast by the hand, or sunk by the
side of a canoe. An ingenious contrivance is where
a square net has its four corners kept apart by two
diagonal elastic rods, at the intersection of which
the line by which it is lowered is attached; when

[1] With reference to the remarks of Dr. Hickson (Naturalist
in Celebes, p. 200) and Dr. Guppy (Solomon Islands, p. 151), it
should be observed that these floats are used to catch only
flying-fish, and that on account of their extreme shyness. In
the Solomon Island floats, on which the figure of a bird occurs,
the line is wound round the hollow of the bird's back and a
projection below made for the purpose. For this the shape of
a bird is certainly convenient, and the genius of those people
leads them to ornamental forms. The Celebes floats seem
certainly to represent those of the Solomon Islands in a remarkable and instructive way.

MALANTA
FLOAT.

a fish is seen above the net the line is hauled up, the ends of the rods come together, and the net forms a bag containing the fish. Fishing with a kite is practised in the Solomon Islands and Santa Cruz; the kite is flown from a canoe, and from it hangs a line with a tangle of spider's web or of fibre, which it drags along the water, and in which a fish with a projecting under jaw entangles its teeth. In Lepers' Island small fish are caught in nets made of spider's web; in the Banks' Islands they are driven by children into barricades of dead coral. A singular method of catching sharks is practised at San Cristoval, which is said to have been borrowed from Santa Cruz; an outrigger canoe is used with a bamboo stage on the outrigger; one man paddles the canoe, another on the stage shakes cocoa-nut shells strung on a loop of bamboo to attract a shark; when a shark comes near, the man substitutes a fish, and has a noose ready into which the shark swims; when caught and hauled on to the stage the shark is despatched with a club. This goes on some way out from shore, to be clear of man-eating sharks, for those caught in this way are eaten. The dugong is taken, but rarely, at the Bugotu end of Ysabel. The reef and lagoon between Ra and Motlav is at times the scene of an exciting chase of fish, when a shoal is driven into the shallow of the reef by a long line of natives shouting and beating the water with their hands. I have seen at Lakona in Santa Maria, and no doubt the same thing is seen elsewhere, a large fish-trap in which reed fences lead the fish as the tide retires into circular enclosures from which they cannot retreat. Walls of stone to shut back fish as the tide ebbs are common in the New Hebrides. Fresh-water fish are abundant wherever there are streams and lakes; some the natives recognise as peculiar to fresh-water, some they say live also in the sea, *sale rua tasi*; in the mud of the irrigated gardens of Aurora an eatable fish is found. Eels are abundant, but in some places are not eaten. In the *tas*, the lake of Santa Maria, they are very large; when the water is low the natives dig pits by the margin of the lake, and into these the eels find their way when the water

rises; when it recedes again the eels are left behind and are
shot and speared. Names of rank are given to the very
largest eels, after the names of the Suqe; it is the fashion to
measure anything remarkable for size, and to hang up the
measuring line in the *gamal*; I have seen a measure of
thirty inches the circumference of an eel not of the highest
rank.

(7) *Food and Cooking.* The yam no doubt takes the highest
place as the staple food of Melanesians, though in some
places what is commonly known as taro, the esculent caladium, is much more grown. The number of varieties of
yams in a single island has been noticed; there is much difference also in the general character of the tuber in eastern
and western groups of islands, the Solomon Island yams
being round and compact, and of no great size, while in the
New Hebrides one at least has been measured by the height
of a man of more than six feet. A species with a prickly
vine, the *tomago* of the Banks' Islands, *mitopu* of Santa Cruz,
pana of Florida, *hana* of San Cristoval, is very commonly
grown; and another prickly kind is sometimes cultivated,
which grows wild in the Banks' Islands, the *qauro*, and is
eaten there grated and washed in sea-water when food is scarce.
The caladium is only called *taro* by the natives when they
think they are speaking English; there are many varieties
grown in dry ground on the hills, as well as in the skilfully
irrigated gardens of Aurora. The giant caladium, *via* alike in
the Banks' Islands and Madagascar, is eaten in the New Hebrides and the Solomon Islands. Bananas supply much food
in numerous varieties; in Lepers' Island the fruit seems to be
eaten in larger proportion than elsewhere. The bread-fruit is
scarce in the Solomon Islands, most abundant perhaps at Mota
and the other Banks' Islands, where it forms an important
part of the food supply when dried over a fire, wound round
with strips of leaves, as is done also in the Solomon Islands,
and preserved in chests. The making of anything like the
madrai of Fiji from fermented bread-fruit is not practised. In
the Banks' Islands the pith of the sago-palm is washed into

starch in a trough of the stem, and cooked in cakes, but it
hardly ranks as an article of common food.   In Santa Cruz it
has an important place; sago pith cooked whole was the main
provision of canoes from Tikopia which visited the Banks'
Islands one year during my stay.   Melanesian natives are
very fond of mashing yams, taro and bread-fruit, and eat the
puddings so made with sauce of the cream-like juice squeezed
out of scraped cocoa-nuts, and cooked by stone-boiling or in
the shells upon a slow fire.   The leaves of an hibiscus like the
manihot and of many trees are cooked in the ovens.   Tapioca
has been introduced.   The nuts of the canarium have a very
important place in native cookery.   Though a good deal of
cookery is done by roasting upon the fire such things as fish,
mash, eggs, wrapped in leaves and laid upon the embers, and
thin yams continually scraped and turned, all the substantial
meals are prepared in the native oven.   There are differences
in detail, but the method generally is the same, and the
result admirable, the food being cooked by steam in its own
juices.   The hole in the ground which forms the oven is
mostly permanent, with its heap of stones that will bear the
fire lying by it; the fire lighted in the hole which has been
lined with stones heats those and others heaped upon it;
when the fire has burnt down, these latter stones are taken
out with wooden tongs, the food wrapped in leaves is
arranged within, hot stones are laid between the larger
parcels, and the rest of the hot stones above all; the whole is
shut in with leaves, or may be covered in with earth; water,
salt or fresh, is poured in to make steam, and every escape of
the steam is watched and closed.   The process is lengthy, and
gives much of the day's occupation to the native men, who
cook for themselves; it is a pity, perhaps also because it
takes less time, that the introduction of iron pots and sauce-
pans is changing the native cooking for the worse.   A good
deal of care is taken about washing the hands before cooking,
and to eat *panlepa*, dirty-handed, is a discredit in the Banks'
Islands.   Fire is produced by the stick and groove.

(8) *Clothing.*   Bark-cloth, *tapa*, hammered out from the

bark of paper mulberry is made, but roughly, in Ysabel, and
worn in Florida; it was made till lately in Ulawa and San
Cristoval; a rough kind, made perhaps always from the bark
of banyan figs, is used in the New Hebrides. When such
cloth was in use the name of it, e.g. *tivi* in Ysabel and Florida,
sala in Ulawa, was ready for European cloth. In Aurora *gavu*,
and in the Banks' Islands nearest to Aurora *gagavu*, is used for
cloth, no doubt identical with the Maori *kahu* and *kakahu*.
In Mota the word *siopa* was applied at once to European
clothes, which, as the natives knew nothing of tapa, was surprising. The native explanation is that the Tongans, who for
two years visited the Banks' Islands and made a short settlement on Qakea, were clothed with *siopa*. They have in fact
shifted the vowels in *siapo, hiapo* (the Maori *hiako*, bark), the
name of bark cloth in Tonga and Samoa. In Motlav, again,
the word *malsam* was applied to cloth, of which the first
syllable is no doubt the common *malo* of Fiji and elsewhere.
It was strange that among the people of the Banks' Islands,
where the men were content to go without any covering at all,
the art of making a very handsome and elaborate dress was
known; this was the *malo saru*, the *malo* put on over the head,
of variegated matting work in four pieces joining at the neck,
worn in dances by those of sufficient rank to do so. The art
expired some years ago with the last two men who practised
it. Two *malo saru*, probably the only existing examples, are in
the British Museum, one of which is shewn on page 108. To
all appearance the work, which much resembles that in the
Santa Cruz mats, must, like those, have been produced in a
kind of loom.

The dress of women varies remarkably, and does not vary
quite in accordance with the changes in the dress of men. In
Florida and its neighbourhood in the Solomon Islands, where
the male dress is scanty but perhaps sufficient, the women
have short petticoats of fibre. In the south-eastern Solomon
Islands the male attire is very scanty, and the women are
contented with a fringe. The men again at Santa Cruz are
amply clad in what may perhaps be called the dress of the

Polynesian colonies, and the women wrap their bodies and
cover their heads with mats.   In the Banks' Islands the men
wore nothing, and the women had a little double band, *pari*,
ending in fringed tufts, of platted fibre, sometimes well ornamented with a crimson dye.   In Lepers' Island the dress

BELLONA.   SOLOMON ISLANDS.

of the men is the same with that of Santa Cruz; the women
indoors wear the *pari*, and out of the house wrap themselves in
ample mats.   But whereas the man's dress is the same in
Pentecost as in Lepers' Island, the petticoat of the women
again appears there, and continues southwards in the group.

In Lepers' Island a crimson dye is applied to mats through a stencil of banana leaf.

(9) *Money.* There is some recognized medium of exchange in all the islands now in view, but the shell currency of the Banks' Islands and of the Solomon Islands is perhaps alone worthy of the name of money. It is probable that the ornaments of the person most in vogue have everywhere a certain relative value, and pass in exchange for food and other necessaries, and the general apparatus of native life. Besides these there are products of industry which are made for the single purpose of exchange, and which may be called Mat-money, Feather-money, and Shell-money. The *Mat-money* is in use in the Northern New Hebrides, Aurora, Pentecost and Lepers' Island. The mats are long and narrow, made for no other purpose than to represent value, and are in Aurora and Lepers' Island valued the more, the more ancient and black they are. Women plait them; either those of the family, or women hired for the purpose. In Aurora the name is *malo*, the name of the dress which is worn by some men there, as by all at Lepers' Island. The mats are kept in little houses specially built for them, in which a fire is kept always burning to blacken them; when they hang with soot they are particularly valued. Their value, however, is estimated by the number of folds, which are counted in tens; a mat of twenty folds is called double, one of thirty folds treble. Though these mats will buy anything of sufficient value to equal a mat, they are mostly used for buying the steps in the *Suqe* Club. If a man wants to raise funds for this, he sends a pig into a village where he knows mats are to be had, and he receives mats less in value than his pig; when he can repay the mats he recovers his pig. In Lepers' Island and in Pentecost these mats are called *maraha*. In the latter island red ones, *bwana*, a word which in San Cristoval means pandanus, are of most value; in Lepers' Island the ancient and rotten ones which have long hung in the house are very choice, though the value still goes by the number

of folds. There are three lengths of mats in common use; some mats are a hundred fathoms long, some when folded ten fathoms; the width is about two feet. A middle-sized mat will buy a tusked pig. A rich man will keep fifty mats and more in his house, hung up and decaying, a proof of ancient wealth. Mat-money is also lent at interest, and so becomes a source of wealth; there is no fixed rate of increase, the lender gets what he is able to insist upon, up to a double return. In these three islands the discs of shell, *som*, *hom*, are beautifully prepared and worked up into armlets and necklaces, which are much valued, but there is no use of them as money. *Feather-money* is peculiar to Santa Cruz; it is·made of the red feathers from under the wings of a parrot, Trichoglossus Massena. The birds are caught in the deep bush, where they are very tame, with bird-lime smeared on a rod which a man carries in his hand, and on which they perch; he must take care not to eat anything hot or fat, or they will not come near him. The small red feathers are first gummed on to pigeon's feathers, and these are bound on to a prepared foundation in rows, so that only the red is seen. A length of this feather-money, called *tavau*, about fifteen feet long, is coiled up and packed with peculiar ornaments. Short pieces are made for convenience in arranging about prices. On festive occasions the dancing ground, *nava*, fenced round with huge discs of coral, is hung with the uncoiled feather-money of those who make the feast. The people say that formerly they had also shell-money. Though this feather-money is peculiar to Santa Cruz, there is in the Banks' Islands, in Santa Maria and Meralava, where the *som* shells are not found, a medium of exchange of the same character. The little feathers near the eye of fowls are bound on strings, and generally dyed a fine crimson; these are used as necklaces or anklets, by way of ornament and distinction (*kole wetapup*, p. 110), but also pass very much in the way of money. A braid not unlike this was formerly used in the Loyalty Islands as a medium of exchange, the red fur under the ears of the flying-fox being used in the same way as the feathers. *Shell-money* in the Solomon Islands and the Banks' Islands differs widely in one respect; in the former it is in some places carefully and evenly made, and is of two sorts of less and greater relative value[1], while in the latter it is all alike rough and unfinished, only quantity being cared for; but in the Banks' Islands the character of money is more clearly marked, and money-dealing surprisingly developed. In the Solomon Islands, porpoise teeth in San Cristoval and Malanta, dogs' teeth in Florida and Ysabel, are current with a tolerably fixed value; of the dogs' teeth only that immediately behind the canines is valued, and these to be worth much must be very white and sound[2]. The shell-money used in Florida and at Saa is made at Alite, and is taken in exchange mostly for pigs. The discs are carefully and accurately made from certain shells broken and rubbed into shape, the holes for stringing being drilled with a pump-drill, in Florida *puputa*, in San Cristoval *nono*, armed with a point of flint or obsidian. These discs are used for ornaments as well as money. The money is either white, *turombuto*, or red, *rongo*; all is generally called *rongo*, and there does not appear to be a definite proportion of value between the two kinds. Six coils, about ten fathoms, is called a *rongo*, and ten *rongo* of red or white is an *isa*. Anything can be bought with shell-money; and the money is lent, but without interest. In this last particular the Banks' islanders are so advanced that it is hard to believe them in other ways so much uncivilized. The material is rude enough, but the forms and terms of money-lending are most elaborate. To make the money, the body of a shell, *som*, is broken, and the tip rubbed on a stone by means of a pointed stick inserted in the broken end till the inner

---

[1] The Florida money is smoothly finished; that used in Ysabel and Ulawa is much more rough; a very small and finely-finished kind of great value is made at Haununu in San Cristoval; about 50 discs of this, $\frac{1}{16}$ of an inch in diameter, can be strung upon an inch of thread.

[2] In Florida 1 dog's tooth is equal in value to 5 porpoise teeth; in San Cristoval 1 dog's is worth 1 or 2 porpoise's, according to quality.

hollow of the shell is reached ; into the hole thus appearing
at the tip of the shell the stick is then inserted, and the
broken base ground smooth on the stone. There is thus
a shell used for each disc, and no drill is needed, as indeed
none is known. The shell discs are strung upon a slender
strip of the bark of a hibiscus. The shell-money, *som*, thus
made is good for any kind of purchase, but the great use
of it is in buying steps in the *Suqe* Club. The *som* is
arranged and counted in coils ; two sticks are fixed in the
ground and the *som* is wound, *siga*, upon them ; a turn from
the one stick and back again is *tal* ; ten rounds, *tal sangavul*,
is a hank or coil, *qatagiu* ; when the quantity is less than
the *qatagiu* it is counted as so many *tal*. The full length
of the turn is a full fathom, the measure of a man's arms
stretched out, *rova togtogoa* ; if a smaller measure is used the
qatagiu is named accordingly. Rich men accumulate large
quantities of this money; a hundred *qatagiu*, however, is
enough to make a man rich. Accumulation results from
the system of the Suqe and Tamate Clubs above described
(chapters v, vi), and also from the practice of money-lending ;
but according to native ideas the unseen spiritual influence
called *mana* was the cause of wealth. The rate of interest
is cent. per cent. without regard to time. A man borrows,
avu, and the owner lends, *tawe* ; a debt, *pug*, is thus
established. A debt is not only contracted by borrowing,
but a rich man upon occasion imposes a loan, which his
friend for his own credit is bound to accept, and to discharge with a double return. The pressure put on a debtor
who does not pay when payment is demanded is admirably
effective. All the men of the creditor's place come and sit,
bringing their wives with them, in the debtor's premises ;
the debtor lights his fire and cooks food for them ; if the payment is not forthcoming they stay over night, go home next
morning, and after a while repeat the visit. The debtor's
neighbours and friends pity him and help him with food and
money, till he scrapes enough together to pay the debt.
A man borrowing money of a friend to pay a debt asks him

to shield him, *ti goro*, to stand between him and his creditor. If a man borrows money and lends that again to another, he is said to *tul* the lender, to treat him unfairly; if a man uses money he has borrowed of one man to satisfy another creditor, he is said to divert the payment, *viro goro*, into another course. When a man borrows, say ten strings of money, from another, he will make the creditor his debtor also, by lending him say four strings of his own money; this smaller loan is called a *tano ravrav*, a drawing-place, and to make it is said to put down rollers in the way as if to draw up a canoe, *lango goro*, because it is thought to make the transaction more easy for the borrower, who becomes the creditor of his creditor, and cannot so well be dunned by him. To pay a debt is to close it up, ·*wono*. Money transactions play a great part in native life : social advance is secured by possession of shell-money, because the steps in the Suqe Club cannot be taken without it ; social eminence is maintained by it, because the moneyed man has his debtors under his thumb, and by the power he has of imposing a loan he can make rising men his debtors and keep them back. By the Suqe institution money was kept in continual circulation, alike in large and small quantities. The little reef island of Rowa supplies common money, and also the finer sort, which is used only as ornament. This is sometimes extremely small and finely made, and with it, before the introduction of beads, was sometimes strung a bit of remarkable stone or a concretion from some shell [1]. In the Torres Islands, where the material for shell-money is absent, they now buy with beads, which indeed have in the Banks' Islands to some extent superseded money for small purchases ; formerly their very pretty arrows were used in the way of

---

[1] The discs of Banks' Island money, which differs little in size from that of the Solomon Islands, are about ⅛ of an inch in diameter. The length of ten upon the string is about an inch. The fine *som ta Rowa* is not more than $\frac{1}{15}$ of an inch in diameter, and as many as 60 discs go on an inch of string. A *puto lakai*, rough pearl from a giant clam, when bored with a rat's tooth for stringing, will buy a large pig.

money, and in a lesser degree mats, and boars' tusks; the head of the peculiar pig *rawe*, with its tusks, is still very valuable there.

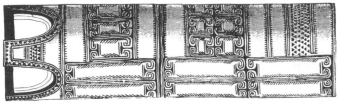

LIME-BOX. YSABEL.

(10) *Decorative Arts.* There appear to be four distinct groups into which the languages of the Melanesian islands

PATTERN ON COCOA-NUT WATER-BOTTLE. YSABEL.

here in view naturally fall; and each of these groups has a distinctive style of decoration. The Western and Eastern

Solomon Islands must be divided into two groups; San
Cristoval, Ulawa, and Eastern Malanta have their own style
of art. Santa Cruz stands per-
fectly distinct; the Banks' Islands and the Northern New
Hebrides must go together.

1. Beginning in the west, if
there be anything distinctive it
may be found in such ornament
as appears on the lime-boxes of
Ysabel. But there is and has
been so much intercourse with
islands further west that the
style of New Britain ornament
is represented in the paddles,
for example, of Bugotu. The
beautifully made and ornamented shields and clubs which
have been common at Florida
were made in Guadalcanar; the
discs of clam-shell covered with
a plate of tortoise-shell cut into
an open-work pattern belong to
all these islands to the west.
Patterns of lines and circles in
tattooing or incised on cocoa-nut
bottles are also characteristic.

2. The carvings, paintings and
representations of scenes of
native life executed in San Cristoval and its neighbourhood have
been mentioned. Drawings by
native boys, such as those on
pages 196, 259, would not be
found in other islands. The
decoration and fantastic shapes
of bowls cannot fail to strike

BANKS' ISLAND EAR-ORNAMENT.

attention; the nautilus-shell inlay on bottles, cups, spoons, is
really excellent. The artistic faculty of these people is
remarkable. From Malanta come combs which shew extraordinary beauty of decoration as well as neatness of make;
but they are the work of the inland people rather than of
those whose skill is shewn in the ornamentation of canoes and
canoe-houses.   3. The change of character in decoration when

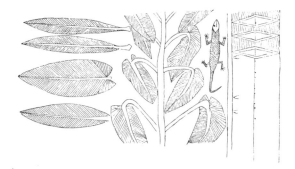

ORNAMENT.   AURORA ISLAND.

Santa Cruz is reached is unmistakeable. The
ornamental bands in the mats shew perhaps
nothing distinctive; but while the fancy of the
natives shews itself in the shapes into which
their bowls and pillows are carved, there is a
fixed determination of painted ornament to
lines, crosses, and stars of black and red upon a
white ground.. Their love of turmeric as a dye
for ornamented bags connects them with the
Polynesian colonies, such as that in Mae in the
New Hebrides. They stand alone in their love
of tags and loose ends by way of ornament.   4. In the Banks'
Islands and New Hebrides mats, baskets, bags are skilfully
made and well ornamented; the decoration of reeds, as the
shafts of arrows (page 311), and ear-ornaments with incised
line patterns, is characteristic. It is remarkable that there is
a style of pattern belonging to each island or neighbourhood;
in a handful of ear-ornaments, natives can pick out each one

and determine with certainty where it was made. In the
patterns of tattooing, where it is used in these groups, and
in the stencilled figures used on the mats in the New Hebrides,
the character of the ornamentation shewn in the ear-ornaments is reproduced; just as tattoo on the cheeks of the
women of the Florida neighbourhood follows the pattern
incised on the cocoa-nut bottles.

With this conventional character of the ornament of each
group or region there appears also upon occasion a remarkable freedom of ornamentation. The part of an ornamented
walking-stick here shown was cut with a common knife in
Norfolk Island by a native of Aurora, who was not at all
aware that he was executing a work of art. A comparison of
the graceful foliage ornamentation incised on the back of a
nut-shell used as a casket with the lined pattern on the cocoa-
nut bottle above, shews again an unexpected freedom in the
art of Ysabel.

CHAPTER XVII.

DANCES. MUSIC. GAMES.

(1) *Dances*. It may be confidently asserted that in the Melanesian islands here in view dances have absolutely no religious or superstitious character, although visitors find 'devil dances' and 'devil grounds' enough. Men and women always dance apart; the songs which accompany the dances are undoubtedly some of them indecent, and I would by no means deny that there are indecent dances, though I never heard of them. There might be thought to be a superstitious character in those dances in which the performers are supposed to be 'ghosts,' if it were not that ghosts were believed to amuse themselves with dancing as well as men; it might be thought that when the members of *tamate* ghost clubs dance in masks representing birds or fish they are dancing in honour of what may be called their totems, if there were the least reason to believe that the emblems of the clubs had any character of the sort. An Ambrym drum set up when a death-feast is celebrated, and carved into a representation of a face, is no doubt meant to represent the deceased, so that it may be said that dances are performed before the images of ancestors, and the deceased may be called either 'god' or 'devil,' according to the terms employed; but after all it is but a festival in memory of some lately dead member of the community, and the dancing and drumming are parts of the festivity. Women's dances are everywhere ungraceful and uninteresting; in the *rorohi* of Florida they sway their bodies

and stamp their feet in a circle; in the *lenga* of the Banks'
Islands they stamp, and scream a song. In a Banks' Island
feast while the men sing and dance round the drum, the
women, two and two, with the arms of each over the other's
neck, tramp round the dancing-ground with short heavy
steps, shaking as they go. The most graceful men's dance
I have seen is one in which in San Cristoval and Saa performers wave dancing clubs as they represent fighting scenes,
with the accompaniment of a very soft and tuneful song. The
general term for men's dancing in Florida is *gavai*; in the
silaru they sit as if paddling; in the *hauhamumu* there is a
concert of many bamboo pipes blown in certain tunes,
without a song; this is a performance learnt by men from
ghosts, and brought over from Laudari in Guadalcanar.
Parties of men practise these dances till they are perfect,
and then start on a voyage about the neighbouring islands,
going a-dancing, *gavai tona*, exhibiting their performance
everywhere, and receiving hospitality and handsome presents
wherever they go. After the return of such a party they will
divide from two to five hundred *rongo*, a large sum of money,
among them. In Santa Cruz every great man has near
his house his dancing-ground, *nava*, fenced with huge discs
of coral; the great aim in dancing is to stamp the feet all
together with the utmost exactness and the loudest shock.
Many of the Banks' Island dances, in elaborate figures carried
out with the greatest precision, are really beautiful and interesting; the performers, with their heads wonderfully adorned,
and their limbs decorated with shining fringes of unopened
palm-fronds, advance and retire in two lines, interlace in curves,
cross and recross in ranks, waving their arms and stamping
their feet, on which rattling anklets of empty nuts are hung,
to the beat of a bamboo drum carried by a leader, or beaten
by a seated performer. To keep them right in their steps
they repeat to themselves the words of the song belonging
to the dance. In Maewo, Aurora, clapping of hands plays a
great part in common dancing and singing. In Lepers'
Island, when a hundred or more men dance and sing round a

drum or drums in a *bue*, 'the earth shakes under their feet, and the land resounds about them;' and indeed it is no wonder that such dances give excitement and delight. The favourite time for dancing is a moonlight night, if the dance is the chief thing in view; the dancing and drumming of the common feast goes on in daytime.

(2) *Songs.* Words fitted to music are the songs and poetry of the people; the character of the tunes differing more in the various groups and islands than the general character of the words. There is no conception of poetry without a tune, though tunes without words are not unknown. In songs certain words or forms of expression, which are not used in common speech, are everywhere thought poetical and appropriate, and words are lengthened or shortened to fit what must be called the metre. In the Banks' Islands the use of a distinct song-dialect is very remarkable, in which not only are words used which are never used in speech, some probably archaic and some borrowed from a neighbouring island, and not only are words contracted or prolonged to suit the tune, but in each island the song-language is so different from that of ordinary speech that the two have the appearance of two dialects, as completely as in the Dialogue and Chorus of a Greek play. The difference is least conspicuous in Gaua, Santa Maria, most conspicuous probably in Mota. On one side of Mota songs are composed in something like the language of Gaua, on the other in something like that of Motlav; yet the language of no Mota song is the spoken language of Gaua or Motlav, nor is a Mota song quite in the song-dialect of Gaua or Motlav. Every one of the Banks' Islands has at least one form of speech for songs and another for common use, while some, like Mota, are not content with two. In Santa Maria, however, while the spoken language of Lakona is very different from that of Gaua, the songs are almost if not quite the same. A poet or poetess more or less distinguished is probably found in every considerable village throughout the islands; when some remarkable event occurs, the launching of a canoe, a visit of strangers, or a feast, song-

makers are engaged to celebrate it and rewarded, or the occasion produces a song for which, in the Banks' Islands at any rate, a complimentary present is made. In Florida a song is *linge*; a song about some one, in honour of him, is his song, *na lingena*; in the Banks' Islands a song is *as*, and is called the song of the person celebrated, *na asina*; to compose a song in Florida is to fit it, *kanggea na linge*, in Mota it is to measure it, *towo as*. New words are thus fitted to old tunes, but new tunes are invented, as well as old ones modified. In the Banks' Islands a song has certain regular successive parts with distinctive names, each introduced by a vocalic prelude which marks the *qau-as*, the knee, or turn, of the song. Some songs are led off by a single voice, *we put*, some begin with many voices together, *we saru*; sometimes the party of singers is divided, some start the song, *we tiu*, the rest follow with an answering part, *we sarav goro*. Songs are no doubt often indecent and obscene, but there are many which are perfectly harmless, some pretty in tune and words, some in which poetry may be recognized, though much is conventional. The following song is surely not devoid of poetry, and might be so translated as to give a very favourable impression of native powers. It was composed at Lakona, in Santa Maria, in honour of Maros in his absence at sea, whose song it therefore is, and who speaks in the exordium. ' *Leale! ale!* I am an eagle, I have soared to the furthest dim horizon. I am an eagle, I have flown and lighted at Mota. I have sailed with whirring noise round the mountain. I have gone down island after island in the West to the base of heaven. I have sailed, I have seen the lands. I have sailed in circles, I have been strongly set. An ill wind has drifted me away, has drawn me away from you two. How shall I make my way round to you two? The sounding sea stretches empty to keep me away from you. You, Mother, you are crying for me, how shall I see your face? You, Father, are crying for me, how shall I see your face? I only long for you, and weep; it is irksome to me; I go about as an orphan, I alone, and who is my companion?

Roulsulwar (his little daughter), you are crying after me without the house.' (Repeat this first part ; then the poet speaks to Maros.) ' Youths ! My friend, you have lingered ; I have lingered over your song. I have measured it, and lengthened out my voice, the sound of it has spread down hither to my place. Ask, hear ; who was it that measured the song of Maros ? It was the song-measurer who sits by the way to Lakona.' Repeat the last part. The songs of Aurora strike visitors as more musical than most. The following is a translation of a song used in flying a kite in Lepers' Island. ' Wind ! wherever you may abide, wherever you may abide, Wind ! come hither ; pray take my kite away from me afar. E-u ! E-u ! Wind ! blow strong and steady, blow and come forth, O Wind !'

(3) *Musical Instruments.* The drum, in many forms, may be said to be the characteristic instrument of Melanesia, yet there seems to be no use of such a thing in Florida, and perhaps no knowledge of a native drum in Santa Cruz. The common form of drum is represented by a joint of bamboo with an open longitudinal slit ; this may be seen in various sizes from the largest to small bamboos, and is followed in the form of the drums which are made of logs of trees. In these the trunk of a tree of a suitable kind and size is hollowed from a long and narrow opening at the side, the lip of which, cut thin, receives the beat of the drum-sticks. These drums are very resonant and well toned, and can be heard at a great distance. The skill of the drummers and the pieces they perform are not contemptible, when two or even three performers sit down to one drum and play some piece of native drum-music in the Banks' Islands, or when three drums of different size and tone, as I have heard at Saa, are played together with surprising precision and variety. At Saa and in San Cristoval there are large houses for the drums ; the story of the settlement at Saa (page 49) shews how good drums are valued. In the Banks' Islands a drum is *kore*, in Lepers' Island *singsing*; a large *singsing*, and some are very large, has a handle left in the wood when the end is squared

to help in moving it, and has a little house built over it to keep it from sun and weather.   In all these islands the drums lie horizontally upon the ground, but in Ambrym and the Southern New Hebrides they stand erect, the butt buried in the earth and the tapering top shaped into a face.   The bamboo drums if large are held by an assistant as the performer beats, small ones can be carried in a dancer's hand.   Such instruments as these are no doubt im-properly called drums.   I have seen the hollow trunk of a tree-fern set up in the ground, and a mat tied over it to form a drum-head, beaten with the fists, and also a thin broad slab of wood, probably cut from the buttress of a tree, laid over a hole dug in the ground and struck with a rammer ;   these, however rude, may be called true drums.   Panpipes, *vigo* in Mota, *galevu* in Florida, *luembalambala* if of seven or eight pipes, *nggovi* if of three, in Lepers' Island, are common ;   it is the

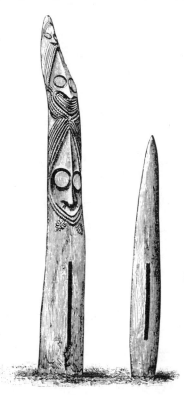

AMBRYM DRUMS.

proper thing in some places to assist the instrument with a vocal sound.   Some *galevu* have a double row of pipes, one of each pair open at the bottom, the other closed.   Single bamboo pipes are blown in the Florida *hauhamumu* dance, two with each performer, or one of the largest size; with these certain tunes, which have each their names, are played in concert with considerable musical effect.   The reed, or

FLORIDA GALEVU.

(The treble and bass, with other notes between occasionally thrown in:
written down by Mr. G. BAILEY of Norfolk Island.)

bamboo, pipes of the Banks' Islands, *wegore*, produce a plaintive
little music. The corresponding *nggore* of Lepers' Island is
longer, some three feet, and has four holes, so that native
songs can be played. The *waru*, double flute, of the same
island consists of two lengths of slender bamboo with the
knot between them ; on either side of the knot on the upper
side is a hole, and at both ends two holes above and below.
When the instrument is played the knot with its two holes
goes into the performer's mouth, his outstretched hands
support the bamboo, and he modulates the sound with his
fingers and thumbs on the holes at the ends. The bamboo
used is not more than two-thirds of an inch in diameter, for
a strong sound is not liked ; the music of the *waru* is 'excellent
to hear' in native ears. In the Solomon Islands the bamboo
jew's-harp, the *nene* of Florida, is common, which is unknown
in the Eastern Islands. A stringed instrument is known in
the Solomon Islands, the *kalove* of Florida. It is made of a
piece of bent reed or bamboo a foot long and of half an inch
diameter. From end to end of this two strings are stretched,
passing over little bridges which are pushed up towards the
end to tighten them ; the strings are tuned to one note.
The performer holds the curved back of the instrument in his
mouth, and strikes the strings with a little plectrum of reed
held in his right hand ; with the fingers of his left hand he
holds the *kalove* so that he keeps one of the strings per-
manently stopped, and to produce higher notes can stop the
free string as the tune requires it. The music thus produced
is not very audible to any one but the performer, to whom it
gives great delight. Among musical instruments must be
included the castanets, of shells of nuts and seeds, worn upon
the ankles in dancing, upon the wrists, and, as in Santa Cruz,
hung upon dancing-clubs, for these are important accessories,
especially in a stamping dance such as the Banks' Island *qat*.
In the preparation for a feast in San Cristoval men sit
together to scrape the cocoa-nuts [1], and as they scrape follow

---

[1] To scrape the nut conveniently they use a seat like a quadruped, the body
and head being the trunk of a small tree and the legs four branches ; the head

the song they sing with the motion of their hands, rattling the castanets on their wrists together with admirable precision and variety to beguile their task. In the Banks' Islands, to add to the din of the multitude of drums big and little at a feast, I have seen a man shaking dry shells from the beach in a bag of matting. In Aurora they fasten bamboo rods pierced with holes to the tops of trees, and so contrive an Æolian flute, such as those mentioned by Dr. Tylor in his 'Early History of Mankind.'

(4) *Games.* A game which belongs to the Banks' Islands and New Hebrides is *tika*, the Fiji *tiqa*, played with reeds dashed in such a manner upon the ground that they rise in the air and fly to a considerable distance. In some islands, as Santa Maria, a string is used to give impetus, and in some the reed is thrown also from the foot. The game is played by two parties, who count pigs for the furthest casts, the number of pigs counted as gained depending on the number of knots in the winning *tika*. There is a proper season for the game, that in which the yams are dug, the reeds on which the yam vines had been trained having apparently served originally for the *tika*. When two villages engage in a match they sometimes come to blows. There are marks on the *tiqa* to shew to whom they belonged. It is remarkable that in Mota a decimal set of numerals is used in this game, distinct from the quinary set used on every other occasion of counting; in Florida also there are numerals used in a game, but only the common numerals in an altered form. In the Banks' Islands boys play at hide-and-seek, *rurqonaqona*; there are two sides, and if the boy who is hiding is not found by the seekers, he suddenly jumps up and counts a pig against them. There is also a kind of prisoners' base, *taptapau*; each party has a cooking-place, *um*, in which they are safe, and outside which they may be caught. In Lepers' Island they have football, played by men and boys in two sides between two fences, with a native orange, bread-fruit, or cocoa-nut; the goal is gained when the ball is driven out at

is armed with a shell scraper. In the Museum at Batavia is a similar seat with the tail of a horse, and the scraper of iron.

either end from between the fences ; a pig is counted for each
goal.   In the same island in *waliweli tambagau* two parties sit
opposite to one another in the moonlight; a man or boy from
one side comes forward holding the door-shutter of a house,
tambagau, before him, and the other side guess who he is and
call his name ; if they fail a pig is counted against them ; if
they succeed one of their party takes the door.   The women
play the same among themselves.   They have also a game
like hunt-the-slipper, and play at hiding canarium almonds,
counting pigs in success. Cat's-cradle,in Lepers' Island *lelegaro*,
in Florida *honggo,* with many figures, is common throughout
the islands.   I have seen in Florida a game in which two
parties of boys tossed backwards and forwards a rough ball on
the points of sticks, the object being to keep it from the
ground as long as possible.   In the Solomon Islands the great
game is throwing and dodging spears, or sticks instead of
spears.   This is to some extent represented in the Banks'
Islands by two parties throwing native oranges at each other.
At Lakona they used in a friendly way to resort to the *sarevnate,*
the shooting-ground, and practise at one another with their
bows and arrows.   In the Banks' Islands and Torres Islands,
and no doubt in other groups, they use the surf-board, *tapa.*
In Mota, *taptapui* is racing to get first to a certain object ;
tititiro is throwing at a tree or some other mark.   Archery is
practised with banana trunks set up as targets.   Counting is
made into a kind of game ; in the Banks' Islands strokes are
arranged on the sand, or on a board, in a certain figure
representing numbers, and these are counted with the finger
accompanied by a whistled tune; something of the same kind
is done in Florida, sticking fingers into the sand in number
according to a counting song brought from Alite.   Boys
sitting together in a narrow ring toss from side to side another
who stands among them, and holds himself as stiffly as he can,
so that he is thrown like a log of wood.   Children in the
Banks' Islands, when a rainbow is seen, play at cutting off its
end, *toto gasiosio*; if they can cut it short there will be no more
rain.   There is in the Banks' Islands a certain approach to

acting ; a man will imitate the voice and gestures of another, the gait of a cripple, the fury of a man in a rage, or will pretend to be a woman, for the amusement of a crowd.

(5) *Toys.* Kites, used in fishing in the Solomon Islands and Santa Cruz, are used as toys in the Banks' Islands and New Hebrides, though not commonly of late years. They have their season, being made and flown when the gardens are being cleared for planting. The kite is steadied by a long reed tail, and a good one will fly and hover very well. The name is in the Banks' Islands *rea*, in Lepers' Island *mala*, an eagle. The use of the bull-roarer, *buro*, in the Mysteries at Florida, has been mentioned. It is there only that any superstitious character belongs to it. There is no mystery about it when it is used in the Banks' Islands to drive away a ghost, as in Mota, where it is called *nanamatea*, death-maker, or to make a mourning sound, as in Merlav, where it is called *wo-rung-tamb*, a wailer, and used the night after a death. It is a common plaything ; in Vanua Lava they call it *mala*, a pig, from the noise it makes; in Maewo it is *tal-viv*, a whirring string ; in Araga it is merely *tavire bua*, a bit of bamboo. Rattles are merely toys; in the Banks' Islands the dry seed-pods of a cassia are tied in a row between two strips of bamboo. In the same group the name of a toy, *taplagolago*, has been adopted for the English wheel, and after that for any wheeled vehicle or machine. Children used to make a broad hoop of a sago frond, and set it running down hill, with the cry *taplagolago*! 'it runs of itself!' Tops are made in the Solomon Islands of the nut of a palm and a pin of wood, the whole visible length of which, between two and three inches long, is below the head. To spin the top a doubled string is wound round the shaft, and the two ends are pulled smartly asunder. A similar top was used in Pitcairn Island by the half Tahitian children of the Bounty Mutineers.

Whistling was hardly in native use as a way of producing a tune, though a song might be whistled without words. In the Banks' Islands there is a way of whistling a man's name to call him, *woswos-loglog*.

CHAPTER XVIII.

(1) *Cannibalism.* It may be safely asserted that in the Banks' Islands and Santa Cruz there has been no cannibalism, though the natives were not ignorant of the practice of it by others. When some fifty years ago a party of men from Tonga, as it is remembered, left the little island of Qakea, on which they had for a short time settled, the proofs that they had eaten those whom they had killed in the fighting which preceded their departure caused such horror and rage against them that a party returning a year after to the same place was immediately attacked. In the Solomon Islands it is strange that the practice has recently extended itself. It is asserted by the elder natives of Florida that man's flesh was never eaten except in sacrifice, and that the sacrificing of men is an introduction of late times from further west. The coast people of Bugotu say the same of themselves; but they freely accuse the inland people of the same island, with whom they have a good deal of free intercourse, and whose speech is not very different from their own, of being cannibals, and of killing men for the sake of eating them. A few years ago one Nunu, an inland chief, was believed to say that pig's flesh was bad and man's flesh sweet to him; a man who had mounted to his place and found himself in a sweat would sit down to cool before he showed himself; Nunu took the sweat as a sign of fatness, and would desire to eat him. In Ulawa, again, there

is no eating of men; it is thought that the *lio'a*, the ghosts of power, do not like it; and at Saa it was not the old custom of the place, the elder men even now will have nothing to do with it. The younger men have taken to it, and eat the bodies of men killed in battle; they have followed the custom of men from the eastern coast who have lived with them, and of the Bauro men of San Cristoval whom they have visited. The natives of San Cristoval not only eat the bodies of those who are slain in battle, but sell the flesh. To kill for the purpose of eating human flesh, though not unknown, is rare, and is a thing which marks the man who has done it. This is a subject on which stories which come from traders are not very trustworthy. In the Northern New Hebrides there is no doubt cannibalism. I know nothing about it in Aurora, but have been told by an eye-witness of what is done in Pentecost. After a bitter fight they would take a slain enemy and eat him, as a sign of rage and indignation; they would cook him in an oven, and each would eat a bit of him, women and children too. When there was a less bitter feeling, the flesh of a dead enemy was taken away by the conquerors to be cooked and given to their friends. In the neighbouring islands, and at the back of his own island, said my informant, they kill for the sake of eating. In Lepers' Island they still eat men. It was not the common fashion, however, to eat enemies killed in fair fighting, it was a murderer or particularly detested enemy who was eaten, in anger, and to treat him ill; such a one was cooked like a pig, and men, elder women and boys ate him. The boys were afraid, but were made to do it. It is the feeling there that to eat human flesh is a dreadful thing, a man-eater is one afraid of nothing; on this ground men will buy flesh when some one has been killed, that they may get the name of valiant men by eating it. A certain man in Lepers' Island mourned many days for his son, and would not eat till he bought a piece of human flesh for himself and his remaining boy; it was a horrid thing to do, appropriate to his gloomy grief.

(2) *Heads.* Head-hunting is not practised by any of the natives eastwards from Ysabel; that is to say, they do not make expeditions for the sole purpose of obtaining heads.   In Bugotu, the south-eastern extremity of Ysabel, the people have suffered and still suffer most seriously from the attacks of the head-hunters from beyond, whose expeditions, following the coasts from a great distance, and sometimes for months, have reached Malanta and Guadalcanar, in one most disgraceful instance the head-hunters being brought to Florida in an European vessel.   The practice, however, of taking heads and preserving them as signs of power and success belongs to the Solomon Islands generally.   The heads of enemies killed in fight are preserved as trophies, and set out on stages as in Florida, or hung up under the eaves of the canoe-house as in San Cristoval.   When a chief in the exercise of his authority had a man killed for an offence, or had him murdered out of revenge or hatred, or for a sacrifice, he added the head to his collection; it was a sign of his power and greatness.   Hence, as the more heads he could show the more his power was in view, he was ready on every opportunity and on any pretext to take a life and a head.   When a chief had a man killed, he would keep the head, but sent the legs and arms to his neigh-bours, to shew what he had done.   If, for example, an accused man got away from Mboli in Florida to Savo, the Mboli chief would send a request, backed by a present of money, to the Savo chief to have him killed; the Savo chief would keep the head and send a leg or arm to Florida, where the chief would hang it up to shew his power.   The heads thus taken and preserved are distinct from those of deceased relatives, which are kept as memorials of affection.   Skulls may be seen suspended equally at the entrance of a Solomon Island *oha* and a New Hebrides *gamal*, but the signification is, in all cases probably, distinct.

(3) *Castaways.* A stranger as such was generally through-out the islands an enemy to be killed.   Thus at Florida a stranger who had escaped from a wreck on to an islet was killed when seen, and spoken of as a cocoa-nut that had floated

ashore. There was a common belief that a stranger would bring with him disease or some other mischief. But it was often a question whether a castaway was a stranger. If he were recognised as belonging to an hostile district, there was no doubt of his fate; but if he fell into the hands of those to whose division, *kema* or *veve*, he belonged, he would probably be saved. It is a not uncommon thing that canoes should be blown from Santa Cruz and the Reef Islands to Malanta and Ulawa; the men on board them were not wholly strangers, though personally unknown; they were men and from known lands, not strange beings like white men from without the world. They were therefore received as guests, sometimes establishing themselves after a while by marriage, sometimes waiting an opportunity to return. Many single canoes from time to time have been blown away from Polynesian islands, and have drifted to the Banks' Islands; in many cases the castaways have been kindly treated, and have added a strain to the native race. Within the last forty years men from Tikopia have twice been most kindly received at Mota.

(4) *Slaves.* There is no such thing as slavery properly so called. In head-hunting expeditions prisoners are made for the sake of their heads, to be used when occasion requires, and such persons live with their captors in a condition very different from that of freedom, but they are not taken or maintained for the purposes of service. In the same islands when a successful attack and massacre enriches the victors with many heads, they spare and carry off children, whom they bring up among their own people. Such a *seka* will certainly be killed for a head or for a sacrifice before any native member of the community, but he lives as an adopted member, shares the work, pleasures, and dangers of those with whom he dwells, and often becomes a leading personage among them. A refugee or a castaway is not a slave but a guest; his life is naturally much less valued than that of a man of the place, and useful services are expected from him, while he mixes freely and on equal terms with the common people.

(5) *Burying alive.* Nothing seems more inhuman than the practice of burying sick and aged people alive, yet it is certain that when this was done there was generally a kindness intended.   It is true that sometimes the relatives of the sick became tired of waiting upon them, and buried them when they thought they ought to be ready for it; but even in such cases the sick and aged acquiesced.   It was common for them to beg their friends to put them out of their misery. Some years ago a man at Mota buried his brother, who was in extreme weakness from influenza ; but he heaped the earth loosely over his head, and went from time to time to ask him whether he were still alive.   Of late years, though old people ask for it, their friends will not consent.   Not long ago in Pentecost, a woman after a lingering sickness in a time of famine was buried, and was heard for three days crying in her grave.   In Lepers' Island the patient was sometimes strangled, with his own consent [1].

(6) *Burning alive.* This has only been heard of at Araga, Pentecost Island.   In fighting time there, if a great man were very angry with the hostile party, he would burn a wounded enemy.   When peace had been made, and the chiefs had ordered all to behave well that the country might settle down in quiet, if any one committed such a crime as would break up the peace, such as adultery, they would tie him to a tree, heap firewood round him, and burn him alive, a proof to the opposite party of their detestation of his wickedness. This was not done coolly as a matter of course in the execution of a law, but as a horrible thing to do, and done for the horror of it; a horror renewed in the voice and face of the native who told me of the roaring flames and shrieks of agony.

[1] In the same island, in the bush country, there was a great man who had a poor brother.   In a time of famine the poor man stole food, not asking food from his brother, or taking it from him.   The chief buried his brother alive, in spite of his own wife's entreaties, and the poor man's supplications ; he bound him, dug a grave, put mats in it, threw him in and buried him.   The act was shocking to the opinion of the islanders, but it marked a great man who would do what he chose.

(7) *Heavenly Bodies.* There is no appearance of a belief
that any heavenly bodies are living beings; in the Banks'
Islands the Sun and Moon are thought to be rocks or islands.
In Lepers' Island the story is told that the Sun and the
Moon quarrelled while the Sun was making a mash of wild
yam, and that he threw the mess in a rage at the Moon's face,
on which the splashes are to be seen; but this is told without
any serious belief. It is commonly believed that there is a
human being, male or female, in the Moon. The stories of
Vulaninggela and Kamakajaku shew the belief in Florida and
Ysabel that there is a person who goes with the Sun and
whose name is Sun, rather than that the Sun is a person. In
Florida the name of the Man in the Moon is Ngava; when
the Moon rises full they cry 'There is Ngava sitting.' Every
new moon is thought to be really new. No cause is supposed
for eclipses, unless it be the magic of some weather-doctor;
an eclipse is a wonder, a portent, bringing an appalling sense
of danger, which finds expression in shouting, blowing conchs,
and beating house roofs, with no very distinct purpose of
driving the fearful thing away. Eclipses of the sun are not
recognised as occurring at Mota. When a remarkable comet,
called in the Banks' Islands a 'smoking star,' appeared in
the year 1882, the Lepers' islanders blew conchs to drive it
away, or at least to divert the mischief. A falling star is
the same sort of portent; some great man will die, there will
be an attack of enemies. The appearance of two stars
close together, *warue* in Lepers' Island, signifies war. The
Solomon Islands people are more concerned about the stars
than their Eastern brethren, perhaps because of their longer
voyages; the Santa Cruz people and Reef islanders excel all
the rest in their practical astronomy. The Banks' islanders
and Northern New Hebrides people content themselves with
distinguishing the Pleiades, by which the approach of yam
harvest is marked, and with calling the planets *masoi*, from their
roundness, as distinct from *vitu*, stars. In Florida the early
morning star is called *gama ni votu*, the quartz pebble for
setting off to sea; when it rises later it is *gama ni ndani*,

the shining stone of light; the Pleiades are *togo ni samu*, the company of maidens; Orion's belt is the *peko*, the war canoe; the evening star is *vaovarongo diva*, listen for the oven, because the daily meal is taken as the evening draws on; stars are called dead men's eyes. At Saa the Southern Cross is *ape*, the net, with four men letting it down to catch the palolo, and the Pointers are two men cooking what has been caught, because the palolo appears when one of the Pointers appears above the horizon; the Pleiades are *apurunge*, the tangle; the Southern Triangle is Three men in a canoe; Mars is the Red Pig.

(8) *Months and Seasons.* The moon is naturally the measure of time; there is no native notion of a year as a period of fixed time; the word, *tau* or *niulu*, which corresponds most nearly to the word year, signifies a season, and so now the space of time between recurring seasons; thus the yam has its *tau*, its season of five moons from the planting, when the erythrina is in flower, till the harvest after the palolo has come and gone; the bread-fruit has its *tau* during the winter months; the banana and the cocoa-nut have no *tau*, being at all times in fruit. The notion of a year as the time from yam to yam, from palolo to palolo, has been readily received; it is very doubtful if such a conception is anywhere purely native. It is impossible to fit the native succession of moons into a solar year; months have their names from what is done and what happens when the moon appears and while it lasts; the same moon has different names. If all the names of moons in use in one language were set in order the periods of time would overlap, and the native year would be artificially made up of twenty or thirty months. The moons and seasons of Mota in the Banks' Islands may serve as an example. The garden work of the year is the principal guide to the arrangement, the succession of (1) clearing garden ground, *uma*; (2) cutting down the trees, *tara*; (3) turning over and piling up the stuff, *rakasag*; (4) burning it, *sing*; (5) digging the holes for yams, *nur*, and planting, *riv*. Then follows the care of the yam plants till

the harvest, after which preparation for the next crop begins again. At the same time the regular winds and calms are observed, the spring of grass, the conspicuous flowering of certain trees, the bursting into leaf of the few deciduous trees. When a certain grass, *magoto*, springs, the winter as it must be called is over ; when the erythrina, *rara*, is in flower it is the cool season ; *magoto* therefore and *rara* are names of seasons in native use, and answer roughly to summer and winter. The strange and exciting appearance of the well-known annelid, the palolo, *un*, sets a wide mark on the seasons. The April moon coincides pretty well with the time of the *magoto qaro*, the fresh grass ; clearing, *uma*, of gardens goes on, the trade wind is steady. This is followed by the *magoto rango*, the withered grass ; both are months of cutting down trees in the gardens, *vule taratara*, and in the latter the stuff is burnt. In July the erythrina, *rara*, begins to flower, it is the *nago rara*, the face of winter ; gardens are fenced, it is a moon of planting yams, *vule vutvut.* Planting continues into August, when the erythrina is in full flower, *tur rara*, the *gaviga* Malay apple flowering at the same time ; the south-east wind *gauna* blows ; the yams begin to shoot, and are stuck with reeds. In the next month the erythrina puts out its leaves, it is the end of it, *kere rara* ; the yam vines run up the reeds and are trained, *taur*, upon them ; the reeds are broken and bent over, *ruqa*, to let them run freely ; the ground is kept clear of weeds ; the tendrils curl, and the tubers are well formed. Then come the months of calm, when three moons are named from the *un* palolo, first the *un rig*, the little *un*, or the bitter, *un gogona*, when at the full moon a few of the annelids appear. It is now the *tau matua*, the season of maturity ; yams can be eaten, and if the weather is favourable a second crop is planted. The *un lava*, great palolo, follows, when at the full moon for one night the annelid appears on the reefs in swarms ; the whole population is on the beach taking up the *un* in every vessel and with every contrivance. This is the moon of the yam harvest ; the vines are cut, *goro*, (in old days this was done with a shell), and the tubers very carefully taken up with digging sticks to be stored. A few *un* appear at the next moon, the *werei*, which may be translated the rump, of the *un*. In this moon they begin again to *uma*, clear the gardens; the wind blows again from the west, the *ganoi*, over Vanua Lava. It is now November or December, the *togalau* wind blows from the north-west; it is exceedingly hot, fish die in the shallow pools, the reeds shoot up into flower; it is the moon of shooting up, *vule wotgoro*. The next month is the *vusiaru*, the wind beats upon the casuarina trees upon the cliffs; the next again is called *tetemavuru*, the wind blows hard and drives off flying fragments from the seeded reeds; these are hurricane months. The last in order is the month that beats and rattles, *lamasag noronoro*, the dry reeds; the wind blows strong and steady, work is begun again, they *rakasag*, to dry the rubbish of their clearings, and make ready the fences for new gardens. By this time the heat is past, the grass begins to spring again, and the winter months return.

(9) *Narcotics.* The use of the areca nut *mbua*, chewed with the betel leaf, with the addition of coral lime, is universal in the Solomon Islands and Santa Cruz, and extends to Tikopia; to the eastward it is unknown. Solomon islanders on their way to Norfolk Island look wistfully at a species of areca-palm in the Torres Islands, the nuts of which the natives of that group sometimes chew to quiet hunger, but which will not do for those who know the *mbua*, and they can replenish their stock of betel leaves in the New Hebrides, where that pepper grows naturally, but they feel that they have passed into a foreign region. In the Banks' Islands and New Hebrides they drink the infusion of the root of the *Piper methysticum* well known as kava, called *gea* at Mota, *malowo* in Aurora. This is in the Banks' Islands so recent an introduction that the use of it had not spread to Santa Maria a few years ago. The difference in the mode of preparation seems to point to two distinct sources or times of introduction. In the Banks' Islands drinking the *gea* is called *woana*; the

root is chewed by the drinker; when the fibres are separated a little water is taken into the mouth to assist in squeezing out the saliva, water is added again in the cocoa-nut-shell cup, and the fibres being removed and well squeezed over the cup the potion is ready. In Aurora the *malowo* is pounded with a rough coral pestle and mortar. The moderate use of this narcotic has no bad effect; excess, which is more common perhaps in the New Hebrides, makes a man listless and stupid. The plant used is not indigenous; there is indeed a pepper of the same species very common, but it will not do for the *woana*. There is a certain sacred character about the plant, as has been shewn, and the use of it is confined to men. The introduction of tobacco into common use in the Northern New Hebrides and Banks' Islands is quite recent, but the people are now given up to the use of it. Smoking was universal in the Solomon Islands, at Florida, Ysabel, and San Cristoval, thirty years ago, with men, women, and infant children, and the tobacco was grown and prepared by the natives; yet it was not known at Saa at that time, where it has since been introduced from Arosi in San Cristoval, and the elder men at Florida remember when it was a new thing in their childhood. There has been for many years a good deal of intercourse with whalers at San Cristoval; they have no native name for tobacco there, and I believe never grew it; its introduction then is readily accounted for. In Florida the native-grown tobacco, now discarded for the far stronger *tambaika*, was called *vavuru*, and the dried leaves were made up in twists; the pipe, formerly made of a shell and a reed in evident imitation of the European pipe, is still *pipiala*; the old people say that the seed had come from a ship[1].

---

[1] Logana at Florida, whom I should not take to be more than 60 years old, was grown up when he first saw a ship. The first he saw had two masts; the people on board traded well and fairly, giving a piece of iron for a big yam, a hatchet for a cockatoo. This was probably the Southern Cross. The name given at first was *ungaungau*, not *vaka* as now. Ships were thought to belong to *tindalo* ghosts, and to portend a famine; those who saw them ran away and hid themselves in their houses. Tobacco appears to have been introduced

(10) *Counting. Measures.* The systems of numeration in use among Melanesians might well here be exhibited and explained, but I have treated the subject elsewhere. It will be however reasonable to say something as to methods of counting. The fingers are the natural counters ; in the use of them there is curious variation. In the Banks' Islands the right thumb is turned down first, and is followed by the fingers of the right hand and then of the left, both hands with closed fists being held up together to shew the completed ten. It is the number of fingers turned down that is to be noticed, not of those that stand up. In Florida they begin with the little finger. In Lepers' Island they begin with the thumb, but having reached five with the little finger they do not go on to the other hand, but throw up the fingers they have turned down, beginning with the forefinger and keeping the thumb for ten. The use of the cycas leaf for counting (page 272) is common to the Banks' Islands and New Hebrides. A string with knots to mark the days is used in the Solomon Islands. In Florida stones and canarium shells are used to help in counting ; at a feast a man will go round with a basket, and every one present will put some small thing into it, that so the number entertained may be known. At Saa when yams are counted two men count out each five, making ten, and as each ten is made they call out ' one,' ' two,' and so on. A man sits by, and when ' ten ' is called making a hundred, he puts down a little yam for a tally.

The natural measure of length may be said to be the fathom, the width of the outstretched arms, the Florida *goto*, Mota *rova*. Examples of more particular measurements may be taken from Mota ; the taut fathom, *rova togtogoa*, is the line stretched as far as possible with the arms thrown back ; *rova ate lue*, the fathom of looking out, is that of a line stretched away as far as possible by the left hand, but held by the right upon the shoulder, where the face turns round to

to Florida and Bugotu by Europeans who were not whalers ; their pipe in form, and perhaps in name, does not allow of a connexion with the tobacco-smoking of New Guinea.

meet it; another is *avawo sus*, from the outstretched left hand
to the right nipple; *alo masale pei*, at the watercourse, from
the left hand to the breast bone. Lesser measurements are,
alo vivngai, from the arm pit; *alo maluk*, from the hollow of the
elbow to the fingers' end; *sogo siwo*, from wrist to finger end.

(11) *Salutations.* People living in small communities and
always in view of one another have little need for salutations,
and there is little to be said upon the subject in regard to
Melanesia. If any one passes through a village he will be asked
whence he comes, and bid to go on, as a kind of salutation;
he will say on leaving, 'You stay.' There is, however, in the
Banks' Islands a friendly action called *varpis*; two men insert
each the middle finger of his right hand between two of his
friend's fingers, grip them tight together, and then quickly
pull them asunder with a crack. This is a greeting, a mark
of fellowship and of approval. Kissing is not indigenous; to
punpun is analogous to it, snuffing with the nose, not rubbing
noses, and this is not thought proper or becoming to be done
except to children. Rubbing noses is practised in the Polynesian settlements only. It is not the custom to say
anything by way of thanks; it is rather improper to show
emotion when anything is given, or when friends meet again;
silence with the eyes cast down is the sign of the inward
trembling or shyness which they feel, or think they ought to
feel, under these circumstances. There is no lack of a word
which may be fairly translated 'thank'; and certainly no one
who has given cause for it will say that Melanesians have no
gratitude; others probably are ready enough to say it.

(12) *Wild Men.* In Florida they believe that on the
mountains of Laudari, the part of Guadalcanar upon which
their own island looks out, there are wild men whom they call
Mumulou. They are men, and have language; the hair of
their heads is straight and reaching down their legs, their
bodies are covered with long hair, and they have long nails;
they are large and tall, but not above the size of men. One
was killed not long ago, the coast people of Laudari say, and
so they know very well what they are like. They live in

caves in the mountains; they plant nothing, and eat snakes and lizards. They eat any coast man they can catch; they carry on their backs bags filled with pieces of obsidian, with which to pelt men whom they see, and they set nets round trees to catch men who have climbed them; they use spears also. In Saa they say there are Mumu in the forest, human, very small in stature, but very strong and swift; they have very long hair, and long nails, with which they tear the coast men to devour them; they go about in threes, a male, a female, and a child. Lastly, Saa men who have been in the 'thief-ships' have seen the Australian natives like the Mumu. In the New Hebrides, similar creatures are seen basking on the rocks of the slopes of the great volcano of Ambrym; even in the little island of Mae they used to be seen—for they are now extinct—on the Three Hills. In Lepers' Island the wild men are called Mae; they have long hair, long teeth, they dwell in caves, carry off pigs, and if they meet a man alone will seize and eat him. In the night they are heard crying in the valleys, and it is then said that the Mae is washing her child. The name shows some connexion with the superstition described (page 188), but they call no snake a *mae*, and these are men. However much these stories vary, the belief may be said to be general from Ysabel to Mae, just as stories of wild men have been current in New Zealand. Descriptions very much like these have their place in grave treatises on mankind. It may be said to be certain that the Melanesian belief has no foundation in present fact in the existence either of ape-like men or man-like apes; it may be a question whether the belief is founded on the memory of large simians in former seats of the Melanesian people. To myself, so far as it has any foundation at all in fact, it appears to be a fanciful exaggeration of the difference, which the coast people are much disposed to exaggerate, between themselves and the men of the *uta*, the inland tracts, who have no canoes and cannot swim, the true 'orang utan' or man of the woods, the 'man-bush' of pigeon-English.

CHAPTER XIX.

THE native Stories or Folk-tales which follow are all of them, with the exception of the first, translated from the manuscripts written for me by natives of the various islands in which the stories are told. The first example was written down by the Rev. A. Penny at Florida, in the native language as he heard the story told. The translation is as accurate and literal in each case as I could make it; the detailed prolixity of a native narrative is very characteristic; and it is possible that, with the varying quality of the story-telling of the individual writers, there may appear something also of the different narrative style of the eastern and western groups of these islands of Melanesia. The value of truly native stories is beyond all question; they exhibit native life in the particular details which come in the course of the narrative, they are full of the conceptions which the native people entertain about the world around them, they show the native mind active in fancy and imagination, and they form a rich store of subjects for comparison with the folk-tales of other parts of the world. To the question how far those who tell and those who hear these stories believe them to be true it is hard to give an answer. To some extent they are believed, and to a great extent they are treated as flights of fancy. A story-teller warming to his subject, and with all that he relates pictured in his mind, very likely believes it all as he tells the tale; a story will be quoted to explain or confirm some statement,

and would have little effect if not brought forth as true ;
a story, because it has always been told and heard, is not open
to much doubt or criticism.   But it may be safely said that to
the natives a story is not a piece of history; the marvels are
not very seriously taken, however much they are enjoyed ;
anything seems possible of course when magic is at work and
when spirits are the agents; that there are such spirits as
Qat, for example, is not doubted, and the story goes that he
performed certain feats.   I cannot, however, think that the
natives seriously believe that birds and fish talk; I have
never discovered from them that they do not distinguish
between animate and inanimate things, between birds and
beasts and men.   When an owl in a story talks and cooks food,
both actions are on a level, not of supposed fact but of fancy.
The native mind is full of lively intelligence, and is by no
means to be judged incapable of the invention of marvels and
enjoyment of the flights of fancy ; though in the highest flights
it moves in accordance with generally accepted beliefs.   There
is in Florida and in Mota a title for a story to tell, *tugu ni
pitu, kakae lea*, which marks the character of the narrative.

These stories are here divided into three classes : I. Animal
Stories, concerned mostly with birds and fishes, as is natural
in islands were mammals are very few; II. Stories containing Myths and Tales concerning the origin of things;
III. Wonder Tales.

I. *ANIMAL STORIES.*

1. THE HERON AND THE TURTLE.   FLORIDA.

One day a *Soo*, Heron, caught his foot fast in the coral ;
the tide came in, but his neck was long.   When the tide
reached to the top of his neck there came along a Shark
Come and save me, says the Soo.   Wait a bit, says the Shark.
There comes a *Boila* ; Come and save my life, says the Soo ;
and the *Boila* says to him, Wait a bit, says he.   There comes

the great Garfish; Come and save me, brother, says the Soo; the Garfish says, Wait a bit. There comes a Rock-cod; Come and save my life, says the Soo; Wait a bit, says the Rock-cod. There comes a Crocodile; Come and save me, says the Soo; Wait a bit, says the Crocodile. In the end all the fish came, and nothing could be done. Then comes a Turtle. Brother! come here and save my life, says the Soo. And the Turtle says, You will pay me of course. And the Soo says, I have nothing with me to pay you with. And there was a sea-urchin alongside the Soo, and he says, I will pay you with money, says he. But the Turtle says, No. And the Soo says, Dog's teeth, and porpoise teeth; but the Turtle says, No, I don't want it. Then he offers him the sea-urchin, and the Turtle eats it up with great delight, and says joyfully, Now I will save you, you have given me my pay. So he smashes to fragments the stone (that held the bird's foot) and the Soo is saved. And the Soo says, Now you have saved my life; if ever hereafter you are in need, in case you are going to be killed and I should hear you call, I will come and save you, says he.

After this the people of Hagelonga went to fish, and they let down their net and sat holding the corners of it on their tripods of poles. There comes a shark; A fish below! shall we pull up the net? say some; Not that, say the others. There comes a rock-cod; A fish below! shall we pull up? say some; No, say the others. In the end all the fish in the sea come along, and they don't pull up the net. Then comes round the turtle, and comes into the middle of the net, and they cry, Here he is! we will see what he is worth. And the turtle comes right up into the net, and they take him, and tie him, and carry him ashore, and make a fence round him. And the chief of Hagelonga says, To-morrow we will split wood for him, and get leaves for him, and dig up yams for him, this turtle of ours, says the chief. So as soon as it was light they went off, and they split wood, and they gathered leaves, and they dug food; and they appointed the boys to watch the turtle and went away. And when they

were far away the Soo comes along, and the boys say to him,
Where have you come from? and the Soo says to them,
I am just idling about; and he says to them, Should you
like me to dance for you? says he. And the boys say, Yes,
we should like you to dance for us. And the Soo says, Bring
me the porpoise teeth and dog's teeth ornaments of your
fathers and mothers, that I may dress myself up in the best.
And they brought him the best ornaments, and he dressed
himself out in them, and then he danced for them. So
he danced along to the fence in which the Turtle was, and
the Turtle saw him coming, and cried out, Now I am to die,
my brother, cries he. And the Soo says to him, And now I
shall save your life, because you saved mine before. And the
Soo came into the house where the boys were, and there he
danced for them. And he says, *Kerembaembae! Kerembaembae!*
Loosed is your leg that they have tied! and his leg is loosed.
Kerembaembae! Slipped out is your head! and his head
slipped out. *Kerembaembae!* Clear the forepart! and the forepart of him was clear. *Kerembaembae!* Clear the hinder part!
and his hinder part was clear. *Kerembaembae!* Clear the rest
of you! and the rest of him was clear. *Kerembaembae!*
Follow the path! *Kerembaembae!* Reach the sand! *Kerembaembae!* Down with you into the sea! *Kerembaembae!* Dive out
of sight! *Kerembaembae!* Go a fathom's length! *Kerembaembae!*
Go two fathoms! So he escaped with his life. And the
people returned from inland and came out into the open,
and looked at the fence. But the Soo was gone; and they
said, Some one has stolen our turtle; and they asked the
boys, and said, Who has been here now? And the boys said,
There was only a Soo came here and danced for us, and we
gave him all your things, and he deceived us so that we
did not go and look after the turtle, said the boys to them.
And bad were the feelings of the people of the village; and
they went and looked at the path, and there they saw the
traces of the turtle, and they said, Yes, he has saved himself
for certain, nobody has stolen him, said they.

2. THE THREE FISH. UREPARAPARA.

The story of the *Watwata* (an Ostracion) and the Sole. The two were scratching one another, and the Sole said to the Watwata, Scratch me. But the Watwata said, No, you shall scratch me first. And the Sole scratched the Watwata, scratched him well. And the Watwata said, Brother, you have scratched me badly, but the Sole said, No, it is all right. And the Watwata said, Well! now I shall scratch you in my turn. After that he scratched him, scratched him extremely thin. And the Sole said, Well! you have scratched me badly, but we two will play hide and seek. And the Sole said, You shall hide first. After that the Watwata hid, and got out of sight under a stone. The Sole sought him and found him. After that the Sole hid in his turn, and buried himself in the sand; and the Watwata sought him in vain. But the *Song* (a fish which shews its teeth) stood and laughed at it; and he has grinned so ever since. It is finished.

3. THE RAT AND THE RAIL. UREPARAPARA.

A Rat and a Rail (Porphyrio) were taking a walk together, and they found a gaviga-tree (eugenia) with ripe fruit. They stood under it and disputed as to which of them should climb up. The Rat said, Rail, climb up! The Rail said, You! So they disputed till the Rat climbed up. Then the Rail begged of the Rat, Brother, give me that black ripe one; but the Rat ate it, and threw him down the stone. Then said the Rail again, Brother, give me that one, it is very ripe indeed; but the Rat ate it all, and again threw down only the stone. Thus the Rail begged again and again for fruit, and the Rat treated him in the same way. At last the Rail made one more petition to the Rat, Brother, give me that one that is red ripe; and the Rat took it and threw it down upon the forehead of the Rail, and there it stuck fast. Eh! brother, said the Rail, you have made game of me, my brother; but make haste and come down, be quick about it. Then the Rail took the unfolded leaf of a dracæna; and as the Rat was coming down the stem of the tree, he was standing ready, and thrust it hard into the rump of the Rat, and there it stood fast. So the tail in the Rat's rump is the unfolded leaf of a dracæna that the Rail fixed firmly there; and on the forehead of the Rail is the *gaviga* fruit, still red, that the Rat threw down upon it.

4. The Birds' Voyage. Mota.

A Story to tell. They lived in their place. The *tawan* was in fruit at Qakea; the wind began to blow; then said they, Well, now at last we will paddle over and eat tawan. So they make a start and go, and come from here and there. And the *renga*, Green Parrot, says, I go with you; but they say, O-o-o! You just go back, lest your father should be angry with us about you. And he sings 'I go and tell my daddy! the wind has blown hard against you; beat against you, beat, beat!' Ah, well! come along! and he gets on board. Then says the *Wasia*, You fellows, where are you going to? And they say, To Qakea, to eat tawan. So says he, I will go with you; and they say, Stay where you are, lest your father and mother scold us on your account. Then he sings, 'I go and tell my daddy! the wind has blown hard against you, beat against you, beat, beat!' Ah, well! come along! and he gets on board. Then the Pigeon says, You fellows, where are you going? And they say, For a voyage. And he says, I will go with you; but they say, Not you; lest your father should scold us about you. And he sings, 'I go and tell my daddy! The wind has blown hard against you, beat against you, beat, beat!' Ah, well! come along! and he gets on board. And when all were on board there was a Hermit Crab sitting there, and he said, You fellows, just let me come. But they said, You just stay there to look after our island. And he said, Nay, my brothers, you won't make me miserable. And they said, No! It is only we who can climb that are going, not you who crawl. And he says, Take me over! I will sit under the tawan-trees, and you will eat making the fruit fall, and I will eat on the ground. So they said, Very well! you have argued against us, but come along; and he gets on board. Then the *Weru* says to the Crab, Friend, sit up this way near me; and he crawls along and sits near him. Then the Weru says to him, Friend, while we two are sitting here, don't shuffle about, lest you make a hole in the canoe. (The canoe was the leaf of a giant arum.) And he says, Yes, I know all about that. But the Weru keeps an eye upon him, and if he shuffles with his claws the Weru says to him, Friend, I keep telling you, don't be shuffling about; eh! you will soon have made a hole in the canoe! But he says, Eh! Friend, I know all about it. The wind had come down into their sail, and they were already in the open sea; and the Crab shuffled about, and his claw pierced right through the canoe, and the water came pouring quickly in. (In another version the Crab was set to bale the canoe, and scratched a hole.) And they cried out, Be quick! our canoe has a hole in it, the Crab had trodden it through. And they said, Well, let us leap overboard; and they all of them leapt overboard, and the Crab leapt overboard, and sank right out of sight to the bottom of the sea; but they all of them swam, and he crawled along on the bottom. And they all swam and came out upon the shore, but not he you may be sure. Then they said, Fellows! are we all men alive or not? And some one said, No, there is one poor fellow our friend missing. So they said, Ah! but who will swim after him, and dive in search of him? And they spoke to one, and he refused, and to another, and he refused; then said the Weru (eulabeornis), Here am I, I will go and look for him. So she swims, and dives, and does not find him, and comes up to the surface; and dives again, and goes on diving, and her body turns black, and dives, and dives, and dives, and her eyes turn red. But the Crab had already crawled up ashore before them all; and there he was quietly sitting. And they were on the sand in a clump of *wislawe*, when the Weru swam up; and they said, Hallo! Have you seen him, or not? And she says, Ah!

my brothers, you know that I have sought him, and have not
seen him at all; and I have dived and dived, and my body is
black and blue, and my eyes are red; and so I have swum up
ashore. But as they are still together, they see the Crab
crawling out into the open, and they say, Hallo! where did
you swim up from the sea? And he said, Indeed when we
became pieces of the wreck, you know, I sank right down, you
know, to the bottom of the sea, and then I crawled here. And
they said, *Ewe!* we said you were the missing one of our
number, but it is not so, we are all safe. Come, let us tidy
ourselves up. Then said the *Tasis* to the *Tagere*, Friend, come
here and make me tidy; and the *Qatman* said to the Green
Parrot, I will tidy you, and the *Tatagoras* said to the *Wasia*, I
will tidy you; and they all of them sat down in pairs. Then
said the Rat to the Owl, Friend, come here, let me make you
tidy; so he sits down and the Rat begins to make him tidy;
and as he combs his head he keeps saying, 'Comb-comb-dung-
dung, comb-comb-dung-dung'; and he dungs upon the head
of the Owl. Then says the Rat, My paws are tired out, let
some one else take my place. I will, says the *Mes*, the
trichoglossus parrot; so the Rat runs off, and the *Mes* sits down
in his place. And the *Mes* parrot combs the Owl's head, and
perceives that it smells, and *Is-is!* cries the Parrot. And the
Owl asks, Eh? what is the matter, friend? Oh! nothing, he
says. But he says, Speak out; and the Parrot says, Oh! your
friend the Rat has played you a trick, he has played you a
trick in tidying you; he has made a pig of himself upon you.
Then said the Owl, Really! is that true? and he flies off and
chases the Rat; and the two go round and about. But the
Rat saw a hole and ran into it, and the Owl sat by helpless.
Then says he, What shall I do to this fellow who has made a
mock of me? and he cracks a cocoa-nut and sets it up opposite
the mouth of the hole; but the Rat did not come out. Then
says he, What shall I do to deceive this Rat? and he sought
what he might do. Then says he, If I roast this red *wasia*
caladium and try, will that do or not? So he roasts it right
off; and as he scrapes that root the smell goes out and reaches

·the Rat in the hole. And when it was cooked he broke it, and put it at the mouth of the hole. Then the Rat creeps out to eat the *wasia*, and the Owl is staring hard at the mouth of the hole, if perchance he may see the Rat creep out. And he says, That will do; and now be sure you die this minute! And the Rat came out to eat; but the Owl swooped down upon him, and killed him you may be sure with his talons, and ate him up.

5. The Shark and the Snake. Lepers' Island.

This is about the Shark and the Snake. They quarrelled, and the Shark told the Snake to come down into the sea, that the Shark might eat him. The Snake said to him, They will kill you, and I shall eat a bit of you. Now when they killed the Shark, the Snake went down into the sea and ate the Shark.

6. The Hen and her Chickens. Lepers' Island.

This is about a Hen that had ten Chickens. So they went about seeking their food, and they fell in with the tuber of a wild yam, a *gigimbo*. After a while the tuber got up and ate one of the chickens. They called to a Kite, which said to the Hen, Put them under me. So they got there and stayed. Presently the Tuber came and asked the Kite, Where are they? *He-i*, said he, I don't know. So the Tuber scolded the Kite; and the Kite flew down and took it up from the ground, and hovered with it in the sky, and then let it drop down to the ground. Then another took it up, and hovered in turn in the sky, and dropped it, and it fell down and broke in two. So the two Kites divided the Tuber between them; therefore some of the tubers are good, and some are bad. We call the name of the good tuber *nggeremanggeggneni*.

II. *MYTHS AND TALES OF ORIGINS.*

1. The Story of Kamakajaku. Bugotu, Ysabel Island.

He dwelt upon the hill at Gaji ; and he was mending his
nets, and he looked down upon the ocean, and saw it dark
exceedingly. And his grandchildren went down to the sea to
fish upon the reef, and Kamakajaku said to them, Go and
dip salt-water for me in the place I see the sea like that, said
he to them. And his grandchildren went forth and down and
fished on the beach, and fished with nets ; and afterwards
they dipped the salt-water, and came up and arrived at the
village, and went and gave it to him. And he said to them,
Give the dish hither, and I will pour it down and see if the
blackness of it is like what I looked down upon, said he.
And he poured it down, and looked and did not find it like
what he looked down upon from his place upon the hill.
And it was morning, and he took the salt-water-vessel, and
went forth down, and put in his ear a bit of obsidian, and
went down and came to the sea, and put down on the beach
his bag and club and shield ; and so he took in his hand the
vessel and waded, and went down from the shore, and looked
up to the hill where he dwelt, and did not yet get sight of it,
and swam still out from the shore till he saw the hill at Gaji,
and then he dipped. And the surface of the sea sounded and
bubbled, and he heard coming-to-him a *Kombili* (King-fish),
a very great fish ; and it came and swallowed him, and went-
off with him eastwards to the rising up of the sun, and went
off with him till it arrived with him at a shallow place, and it
threw itself about so that Kamakajaku perceived that there
was a beach probably. Here am I, says he, and he thought
of the obsidian in his ear, and felt for it and found it, and cut
asunder the belly of the Kombili, and leapt out, and saw a
brightness. And he sat down and pondered, Where I wonder
am I ? he said. So up rose the Sun with a bang, and rolling
from side to side. And the Sun says, Don't stand in my way,

you will die at once; stay on my right, says he. And he drew aside till the Sun rose away, and then he followed; and they two went up towards heaven, and went on and arrived at the village of the Sun's children. And he said, Here you stay, said he; so he stayed with them, with his children and grandchildren, and the Sun went off. And Kamakajaku stayed; and they asked him, Whence did you come hither? And he said, From the earth; I dwelt in my place, and I dipped salt-water, and a big fish swallowed me, and so I arrived here at your good town. So they remained in company; and they ate only raw food, those people above; and he shewed them fire, so that they ate cooked food. And they said to him, Don't go to that place, it is taboo, said they to him; and they went their way. And he kept house, and thought what that was they had said; Don't you go, they said, said he. And he went over, and opened up a stone which was the covering of a hole in the sky, and he looked down on his place at Gaji, and he cried. They brought him food, but it was not for him (he would not have it); so they asked him, Have you gone over by the further end of the house there? We forbade you to go there. Yes. And do you want to go down? And he said, Yes. And they made a house, and gave him a banana, and gave him seed of *pau* (to dye with), and they took a cane and tied it to the saddle-piece of the house, and he Kamakajaku sat in it. And they let it down. And they said, When the birds and such things cry, don't look out, but when the cicalas and the things that live on the earth cry, then you may look out; and they let him down, let him down. And when one cane was too short, they tied another to it, and it reached down to the hill and rested. And his friends had been seeking him, because they thought that he was dead already. And on the day that he came down again from heaven, they rejoiced because they saw him again, and good was their heart. And he lived a long while, till he died on his hill Gaji. And it is finished; yes, it is just this, the Story of Kamakajaku.

2. The Story of Samuku. Bugotu, Ysabel Island.

Samuku lived in his village, and built his house, and worked, and good and many were his affairs; so he took a wife and married, and they two lived well, and agreed perfectly well together, and worked, and much was their food. And Samuku came home and asked for food, because he was hungry, and his wife had not prepared any food, and Samuku was angry with his wife, and scolded her greatly. And his wife said to him, I am tired of making food for you, your father and mother are dead, who is to make you food? Go and see them in Tuhilagi, says she. And Samuku was angry, and he sat and thought; and he said, Good, I will go and see them. So he hauled down a canoe and put out to sea to Tuhilagi, and landed at Lelegia tarunga, the Ghosts' Mangroves, and stepped up the beach and went in shore, and found the company of ghosts. And they asked him, Why have you come here? You are not dead yet, said they to him. And Samuku answered, My wife scolded me, and sent me here, said he. And at night he stayed in a house, and when it was morning the house disappeared. So he played them a trick and made a net, and they went to fish with it, and he saw the forms of the ghosts, and the net caught in the coral. And when it was light all the company of ghosts departed from him, and he went down and slept on the sand. And the people of a certain place found him and took hold of him, and took him to be with them till he died. Finished is the story of Samuku, not a very long one.

3. The Mim. Torres Islands.

They say that the Mim people dragged the yams from place to place, having brought them ashore at Hiw, and then dragged them to Tugua, for which reason the yams at Hiw and at Tugua are very large and long. But when they dragged them along here to Lo, all the people were down on the reefs fishing and heard nothing of it; nor

did they know anything till they found the rind of the
yams sticking to the roots of the trees along the path.
These they picked up and planted; and on that account
the Lo yams are not very large, but plentiful enough.
Because the Mim people sliced their yams in half for the
men of Hiw and of Tugua, and then passed on to Toga,
and sliced again for them there, on which account the yams
there are very large and long. Afterwards they crossed to
Ureparapara, where the people sliced the yams in half and
planted them. They did the same in all the islands that
way; it was only at Lo that the people did not see and hear
what was going on. The crowns of the yams remained and
were planted somewhere. The Mim people went dragging
the yams through all the islands, shouting and calling to the
men of every place to come and slice the yams, and take their
burden from them.

4. The Origin of Poisoned Arrows. Aurora Island.

I have often heard them telling the story about it in this way.
They say that in old times there was no fighting. But there
was an old man whose name was Muesarava, who was blind
and used to stay doing nothing in the house; and he heard a
pigeon calling, and took a bow and broad-headed arrow and
went under the tree; and the pigeon let drop a bit of the
fruit it was eating, and that blind man shot at a venture into
the tree, and hit the pigeon without seeing it. And he took it
up, and went and put it into the oven together with the
yams, and sat down and sang a song. But two young fellows
came along and quietly opened that old man Muesarava's
oven, and ate up his pigeon with some of his yams. Then
they went to another place, and sang back a song to him;
and he heard it, and went back to eat his pigeon, but found
when he uncovered the oven that it was eaten up, and that
something not good had been put in its place. Then he
was exceeding angry, and plotted a fight against the people
of the place whence the two young men had come who had

stolen and eaten Muesarava's food. And now Muesarava
began to make fighting arrows of men's bones. Muesarava
went and grubbed up with his hands a boy who had died, and
took his bones, and beat them to splinters and rubbed them
sharp. But his enemies on their side knew nothing of that,
they only cut wood into shape, or bones of fish or birds, and
fixed them in their arrows, while Muesarava on his side
prepared men's bones. And when they fought they shot at
him and hit, but he did not die ; and he shot them and they
could not live, but died outright all of them. And they
fought again and shot at him, and hit him and he did not
die ; but Muesarava shot at them and hit, and they all died.
So it often happened, and they saw that they died in very
great numbers ; and they asked Muesarava why it was that
they shot him and he did not die, while he shot them and
they all of them died. Therefore he told them and said,
' Go and grub up one of the dead men I have shot, and scrape
his bones, and point your arrows with that.' Upon this they
listened to his counsel and did as he had said to them ; and
when they fought again they shot him, and he straightway
died.

And that thing, the dead man's bone that Muesarava
ground to a point for himself with his own hand, still
remains, and has not yet been spoilt ; the reed-shaft has been
spoilt and replaced over and over again, but that dead man's
bone still remains ; I have seen it myself in my brother's
possession ; it still remains. The people think a great deal of
it, thinking that there is supernatural power, *mana*, in that
toto arrow. If there is heard a rumour of fighting, and that
is pointed in the direction whence it comes, the fighting
comes to nothing.

5. Tagaro's Departure. Aurora Island.

There was a man looking for his wife, and he came to
Tagaro's village when he was not there ; and he wished
to steal Tagaro's pig, a *rawe*, so he caught the pig and

tied it with the vine of a wild yam. And Tagaro was still
in the forest when he heard the noise, and he came back
and found where the vine had been broken off, and he was
exceedingly angry. So he cut out a canoe for himself, and
carried all the things of this world into it, and put out the
fire, but threw back a fire-brand. All the good things, they
say, he took clean away. This is the story about Tagaro.

6. How Tagaro made the Sea. Aurora Island.

They say that he made the sea, and that in old times the sea
was quite small, like a common pool upon the beach, and that
this pool was at the back of his house, and that there were fish
in the pool, and that he had built a stone wall round it. And
Tagaro was gone out to look at the various things he had
made, and his wife was in the village, and his two children
were at home, whom he had forbidden to go to the back of
the house. So when he was gone the thought entered into
the mind of those two, Why has our father forbidden us to go
there? And they were shooting at lizards and rats; and
after a while one said to the other, Let us go and see what
that is he has bid us keep away from. So they went and
saw the pool of salt-water with many fish crowding together
in it. And one of the boys stood on the stones Tagaro had
built up, and he sees the fish, and he shoots at one and hits it;
and as he runs to catch hold of it he threw down a stone, and
then the water ran out. And Tagaro heard the roaring of the
water and ran to stop it; and the old woman laid herself
down in the way of it, but nothing could be done; those two
boys who had thrown down the stone took clubs like knives
and prepared a passage for the sea, one on one side and the
other on the other side of the place, and the sea followed
as it flowed. And they think that the old woman turned
into a stone, and lies now on the part of Maewo near
Raga.

7. How Tagaro the Little found Fish.
Lepers' Island.

They say that he drew down his canoe and paddled out in
search of fish; and he saw a great rock standing in the sea, and
he floated gently without paddling to see whether he would find
fish or not. And he saw many fish rising up to the surface
from under his canoe, and he fed them with the food he had
in his hand, and he perceived that these fish knew how to
eat the food of the land. Then said he, I am going to leave
you, but the day after to-morrow I shall grate some *loko* for
you to eat, and shall pour cocoa-nut sauce over it, and bring it
here to you. So he left them and stayed, they say, one day
at home. And when the second day came for him to go
he took that *loko* which he had sauced with cocoa-nut juice,
and launched his canoe, and paddled out to the place where
those fish were. And he called them with a song, which he
sang like this, *Bulenggu sava ige! ige wuweu, mo gaigei woworoa,
mo gaigei woworoa sobe,* My fish, whatever you are, nice little
fish, here is your food with sauce, your food done with cocoa-
nut sauce. But there was another person, whose name was
Merambuto, who stood on the beach, and heard Tagarombiti
calling his fish with a song like that, and next day Merambuto,
having made haste to prepare food in the night, drew down
the canoe in the early morning, Tagarombiti's canoe, and
paddled out till he came to the place where Tagarombiti had
floated before. And he sang again that song, *Bulenggu sava
ige!*—Then those fish heard his voice that it was loud, and
did not rise, because they knew it was a different person by
his loud voice. And Merambuto perceived that they did not
rise, and he altered his voice so as to be small like Tagarombiti's. And he called them with a small voice singing
that song, *Bulenggu sava ige!*—Then those fish heard that the
voice was small, and they rose all of them to the surface, and
he caught every one of them with a hook. And he made
haste to paddle ashore, and went back into his village, and

made up a fire, and put the fish in the oven. But when it was broad daylight Tagarombiti went himself, and they were all gone ; and he understood that this thief Merambuto had caught all the fish, and paddled quickly back and hauled up his canoe. And he looked for footprints to know which way he had gone round ; and he found footprints and followed them, following on till he came to Merambuto's place ; and there he went into the house to him, and sat down with him in a friendly way. Then said Tagaro, What is that in the oven ? I am hungry. And Merambuto said, That is my food, but it is very bad, you cannot eat it. Then says Tagarombiti, Indeed ! is your food so very bad ? But those are my fish, and you have caught them all. And he struck him, and killed him in his house, and set fire to the house, and it was burnt and destroyed. And Tagarombiti took back the fish from the oven, and went back and put them into a little pool of salt-water, and the fish revived ; one side of them was gone, one side still remained. And we call them, *tavalui ige bulei Tagaro,* Tagaro's half-fish—soles.

8. Story of the old Woman, how she made the Sea. Lepers' Island.

Nobody knows what her name was, but she was an old woman. And there were two children who lived with her in her house, but nobody knows what their father's and mother's names were ; the story about them is that the mother of these two was the daughter of this old woman. Her house was a good one, fenced about with reeds ; there was a fence all round the house, and there was a fence also made against the back of the house, and those two children were forbidden to go into it, because she would be there by herself. And in that little fence at the back of the house she put carefully a leaf of the *via* (gigantic caladium) ; and they say that in that leaf she always made water, and was always very strict in forbidding those two to go there, lest they should see it. And these two were both boys, and they were always shooting lizards. So one day when the old woman went into the garden to work and to bring back food for the three of them, she said to those two, Don't you go there! and they answered, Very well, we shall not go. And she went out of the house, and went into the gardens, and those two brothers played with their bows, shooting lizards. After a while one said to the other, It would be a good thing to go and see what it is where the old woman has forbidden us to go. Very well, said the other, let us go; so they went, and they saw that via leaf and the water in it. Then they saw a lizard sitting on a part of that leaf, and one of them shot at it, but missed the lizard and hit the leaf, and the water that was in it burst quickly forth. And the old woman heard it, and perceived that those two had probably shot the leaf. And she stood up and cried with a loud voice, *Horodali bulu, horodali bulu!* and twice again, *Dali ure, dali ure!* (Pour round about and meet! Round about the world!) And thus the sea for the first time stood full around the whole world, for before that they say there was no sea. So the old woman you may say made the sea herself.

III. *WONDER TALES.*

1. The Story of Dilingavuv. Torres Islands.

They were living in their place, and his companions made a garden, and planted bananas in it. When the bananas bore fruit and ripened Dilingavuv went every day and ate bananas in their garden, not eating on the ground, but climbing into the trees and eating. After a while he was discovered; one of the party went into the garden and saw him up in a banana-tree eating; so he ran and told the others. Says he, You fellows, I have seen the one who steals and eats our bananas. Then said Maraw-hihi, Hew out bows for us to go and shoot and kill him. But they said, Marawhihi, no one will be able to shoot and kill him. I will shoot him and kill him, said Marawhihi. It is wholly impossible, said they. However they hewed out bows, each for himself, and put points to their arrows; and when that was done Marawhihi said, Let us go after him one by one. So one went first, and came to the garden, and saw him sitting up in the banana-tree, and went on tiptoe towards him to shoot him. But Dilingavuv stretched out his arms like a bat, and the man was afraid, and ran back and told the others. It can't possibly be done, said they. But Marawhihi said that one must go again, and another went, and the same thing happened again. Thus they all went in turn, and came back and disputed with Marawhihi, saying, It can't possibly be done. Then said Marawhihi, I shall do it myself, I shall shoot him and kill him. And this Marawhihi they say was more clever than them all; and he went last and saw Dilingavuv sitting in the banana-tree, and he stepped along on tiptoe under the banana, and when Dilingavuv stretched out his arms he was not frightened at him; but he shot him with a bird arrow of casuarina wood, and hit him on the ear, and shot it right off; and he fell headlong to the ground. So Marawhihi ran and told his friends; but Dilingavuv got up from under the banana and went home to his mother. When he reached his mother's house, he called to her within, and she answered him and said, What is it, my son? And he said, Give me an axe. And his mother said, What are you going to do with it? But he deceived her, and did not tell her that Marawhihi had shot his ear off. Then he went and cut another ear for himself out of the root of a tree, and the name of that tree is the *Raw*, and as he was chopping the Raw root, he said, Chop in pieces! chop asunder! But Marawhihi had sent one of his men who went and listened, and heard him saying this, Chop in pieces! chop asunder! and he ran back and told Marawhihi that Dilingavuv was chopping himself out an ear in place of the other. After this Marawhihi and his men made a feast and danced, and danced every day. And when Dilingavuv heard of it, he said, I will go and have my revenge. So he gathered a great quantity of Tahitian chestnuts, and took fire, and collected stones, and took a dancing cloak of leaves, and went to them. But he did

not go right up to them into the open, but stayed beside the
village.   Then he made up a fire and roasted his chestnuts,
and heated the stones, and dug a very deep hole and covered
over the mouth of it with the dress of leaves ; and so he sat
and watched them dancing.   Before long as they were
dancing one of them fell out to take breath ; and when he
saw Dilingavuv sitting and eating chestnuts, he called to him
to give him one.   Run over here, says Dilingavuv ; so he runs
over to him, and sits down on this dancing dress ; and as he
throws himself down to sit he goes clean down into the hole.
And Dilingavuv played the same trick to all the company at
that dance, and let them all down into that one pit, and
Marawhihi last of all.   Then he took the stones that he had
heated over the fire, and threw them down into the hole to kill
the men with heat ; but as he threw them down Marawhihi said
to his companions, Come round over to this side of the pit, and
they did so, and not one of them was killed.   But Dilingavuv
went home thinking he had killed them all.   Then Marawhihi said to his men, Do you know how we shall save our
lives ? and they answered, We are all dead already.   Not at
all, said he, I know very well that we shall not die.   Then
Marawhihi cast up his eyes out of the mouth of the pit, and
saw a banyan branch bending over the pit ; and he said, Let
us *ker galgalaput* at that banyan branch (shoot one arrow
after another, making each one strike and fix itself into the
one before it).   And they did so ; and the reed-shafts of the
arrows they had shot reached down to them into the pit.
Then said Marawhihi, Climb up along the shafts ; and they
said to him, You first, and we after you.   So he climbed
up on the line of arrows and got out of the pit, and so they all
saved their lives.

2. A Story about an Eel.   Vanua Lava.

They were living in their place, and they were planting
their gardens ; and one day when they went to plant, a boy
said to his father and mother, To-morrow when you go again,

you will put by a yam for me. Next morning his father
and mother went, and put by a yam for him ; and he roasted
it and ate it, and then went and asked some other boys for
more. But they scolded him, and said to him, What! has
your father gone and not left you anything to eat? They
gave me some, he said, but I have eaten it all up. Why
then do you ask for our food too? they asked ; but he cried
and said, Very well! I will tell mother and father by and
bye that you have scolded me. When his father and mother
came back, he said to them, When you both left me I ate
up all my food, and went and begged some of theirs, and
they were very angry with me ; so to-morrow when you go
again to plant you are to put two yams for me. Next
morning they two went planting again, and put two yams
for the boy; and when he had roasted them he went and
followed a stream, and found a nice place, and sat down to
eat. As he was eating, crumbs of food fell into the water,
and an Eel came out and ate, and turned into a man, and
rose up and came to the boy. When they two had eaten
all the yam, the Eel said to the boy, To-morrow you will
roast two yams again, and bring them here, and we two will
eat them. After that the boy went home, and the Eel went
back into the water ; and the boy said to his father and
mother, To-morrow when you go you must put two yams for
me ; and in the morning they put for him two yams. He
roasted them, and took them in his hand, and went to his
place and ate ; and the Eel came out again. When they
had finished eating the Eel said to the boy, Let us anoint our
heads. So they dressed their heads and adorned themselves,
and went into the garden, and helped the people who were
digging the ground. But when that Eel dug the ground all
the people crowded to see him do it ; some went back to their
digging, but the women would not do their work, and their husbands were exceedingly angry with the Eel, and rushed upon
him, and would have killed him ; but the boy who came with
him poured water on him, and he turned into an Eel again.
And they caught hold of him, but he escaped ; and they

missed their hold upon him over and over again, and he
jumped into the water. So they said, All right, we will
make rain for him ; and they made a great rain, and the
water swelled into a flood and carried the Eel to the beach.
When the flood subsided they went down and found the Eel
lying on the beach, and they cut him into short pieces, and
left him. But the boy, his brother, ran down and saw the
Eel lying there, and wept ; and his tears fell upon the Eel,
and he turned into a man again, and stood up and said to
his brother, You are to go up inland and tell your father and
mother that you three are to go and take up your abode
in another island. The boy therefore said to his father and
mother, We three are to move to another island. After they
had gone, one day an old woman was sitting, and she heard
the Eel singing a song ; and she said to the people, Listen
to that singing a song like the Eel ; but some of them
answered, It is not that, the Eel is dead ; but they heard
plainly the Eel's voice, and said, It is true, it is the
Eel's voice. And when he had finished singing they heard
a loud report ; and as they were sitting a very great surf
rose and swept them away, all of them ; and they all died,
and that island was entirely lost.

3. MOLGON AND MOLWOR. VANUA LAVA.

The father and mother of these two brothers, who lived at
Gaua, said to the elder of them, Molgon, you are to look well
after him, the younger one, and feed him well. All right, he
said ; and then their father and mother died. They two lived
on ; and one day they drew down a canoe, and paddled up the
course of a stream, and came upon a *palako* fruit floating down it.
They broke it in two and ate it. They paddled on and there
came floating down two, one for one of them to eat, one for
the other ; they paddled on and three came floating down,
one for one, one for the other, and one they broke in two ;
they paddled on and four came floating down, two for one,
two for the other ; they paddled on and five came floating

down, two for one, two for the other, and one they broke in
two; they paddled on and six came floating down, three for
one, three for the other; they paddled on and seven came
floating down, three for one, three for the other, and one they
broke in two; they paddled on and eight came floating down,
four for one, four for the other; they paddled on and nine
came floating down, four for one, four for the other, and one
they broke in two; they paddled on and ten came floating
down, five for one, five for the other; they paddled on and
saw the source from which the fruits had floated down.
Then the first-born said to the younger, You sit here, and I
will go and gather for us both to eat. So he went and
gathered fruit. But a woman, Roprialal, came out of her
house, and looked down to where he was standing, and
called him. He went to her, and she said to him, We two
will cook food in the oven; and they two cooked food in the
oven, and afterwards they ate. He could not eat all the *qeta*,
caladium, and he said to her, I will go with this to my
brother, that he may eat it; but the woman said, If you can't
eat it all, throw it outside for the pigs; and he cried. Then
they made a mash, and he could not eat it all, and said to her,
I shall take this for my brother to eat. But the woman said,
Throw it outside to the pigs; and he cried. Then she asked
him, What is your name? and he said, Molgon. And what
is the name of that fellow over there? and he said, Molwor.
And she said, *Aia!* true enough! your name is Molgon,
Go-catch, and you have come here and have caught on to the
pigs which belong to you and me, and the house, and the
gamal, and the food, and the money; but he, his name is
Molwor, Go-clear, and he has come here to be clear of all the
goods of you and me. And he cried and cried. Then the
woman said, Get up, let us go and see him; and they went
over and found him dead, lying in the canoe, for the sun had
smitten him dead with its rays. And he cried and cried, and
his tears dropped on his brother's breast, and he came to life
again, and said to him, Brother, our father when he died told
you to take care of me, but you have gone away to eat and

have not thought of me; and he went on talking. But the
woman stood and urged him, saying, Come here! we two
will go up away from him again. Then as Molwor spoke to
him, Molgon wept wonderfully; and when he had finished
speaking, Molwor sang a song to him, and got down from the
canoe, and put his legs into the water, and began to turn into
an eel ; and when he had quite finished his song he plunged
into the water, and his brother who had been standing by
leapt down also into the water. And the woman stood and
looked down, and blood came up from the water. And they
two turned into stones lying in the water-course ; and the
woman stood and wept greatly, and went back again up the
hill.

4. THE GHOST-WIFE. MOTA.

A story to tell. They were living and living in their
place; a famine prevailed. And there was a woman and her
son, and they both were hungry. After a time the mother
went to dig *qauro*, wild yams, for them to eat, and when she
had finished digging the *qauro* she would return to her son in
the village ; and as she went she found a *gaviga* (Malay apple)
tree in fruit, in a deserted garden, and she put down her
basket, and took a stick with a crook and pulled down the
branches of the gaviga with it, and then she gathered with her
hands and ate. And when she had finished eating she put
some seeds into her basket; and as she went along she broke
the tips of the branches to mark the path. And when she had
arrived at the village she said to her son, Take the things out
of our basket ; and he took them out one by one, and as he
took them out he found the gaviga seeds in the basket which
his mother had put there. Then says her son to her, What
is this you have been eating, and have put the seeds in the
basket for me to see ? And his mother says, Where ? And
her son takes out the gaviga seeds. Then says his mother to
him, *Esi !* I don't know; somebody I suppose has put them
there. But he says, No! you have been eating them to-day,

because I see plainly that the seeds are still moist. So he presses his mother hard to tell him ; and his mother tells him. And it was already evening, and she says to him, As you go along you will see a little path where the branches have their tips broken down, and you will pass through there and come out (upon the tree). So he follows the word his mother gave him ; and as he goes along the sun is setting, but he arrives at the gaviga-tree and climbs up. And when he had climbed up to eat it was dark. Then he sees something flying to him on the gaviga and settling. Then says the ghost to the living man, Where do you come from ? And the man says to him, It is not as you suppose. Mother came here to dig *qauro* and she found this gaviga, and then she went home and told me, and after that I came here. Then said the ghost to him, She is my sister to be sure, and my own nephew are you ; come here and let me hide you, because we are many of us now coming here to eat gavigas. So he takes him and makes him sit down in the hollow of the gaviga ; and his uncle sat over the mouth of the hollow of the gaviga in which the man was. Then while he is in the hollow he hears a whirring sound coming, like birds, and settling on the top of the gaviga. Then says the man to the ghost his uncle, What is this ? And he says to him, They are here already, some ghosts who are come to eat gavigas, and if you hear them buzzing in talk together don't be afraid, and don't let your bones quake, here am I with you. So he sits within ; and his uncle looks about, and sees two gavigas in a bunch, and says to another ghost, Pluck those two for me. And he gives them to him, and he eats one and gives the man the other. And he went on doing so for him till daylight ; and when the day was dawning and some of the ghosts were taking flight he says to a damsel among them, Don't be in a hurry to fly off, you and I will fly together ; and she says, Very well. But when they had all the lot of them taken flight, and it was clear daylight, the ghost says to the man, Well now, come out ; and he comes out from the hollow of the gaviga-tree. Then says the ghost his uncle to him, Well, here is a damsel for

your wife.   And the man says to the ghost, Ah, I don't
know! will she be agreeable or not?   And his uncle says,
She agrees.   Then the female agreed with the man, and they
two went back into the village.   And when the two arrived
at the village his mother asked him, Where is that woman
from?   And he says, She is my wife ; Uncle gave her to me.
And she says, Who is Uncle?   And he says, Your brother of
course, who died long ago ; when I went to eat gavigas and
it was night I saw him fly first to me, and he put me in the
hollow of the gaviga.   Then says his mother, Very well, we
three will live here, and she may live with you ; so the three
lived together.   And as the three lived together those two
worked for yams and taro and *tomago* and hibiscus ; and as
they were working so her husband appointed the time for his
suqe, and appointed five days.   And they waited counting
the days, and when it came to the fifth day he went off, and
he said to his wife, You two are not to come, you and our
child ; you two go into the garden and weed away the grass
from the taro, and when you have finished weeding go to the
other part where it is ripe, and pull up for yourselves, and
come back here.   And she did so ; and when she had finished
weeding she took up their child on her back ; but as the two
came near the taro the woman stretched out her hand to pull
some up, and there was a bunch of taro already in her hand ;
and she put it aside ; and if she touched a hibiscus plant to
pluck the leaves, behold, a bundle of hibiscus leaves again in
her hand ; and if she essayed to lay hold on sticks for fire-wood,
there was a faggot of fire-wood already in her hand ; and the
two went home.   And they two come back into the village,
and light a fire for their oven, and do the necessary work
about it, and cover it in.   And she opens it, and then her
husband comes back and asks her, Where have you two been?
And she says, In our garden.   Then he says, But who gave
you taro? And he says, But I have seen that belonging to us
still untouched.   Then she says, Not so ; it was taken in our
garden.   Then he says again, *Esi!* perhaps I did not observe
exactly.   So they waited again five days for the rank of Qoro-

qorolava ; and when it comes to that day he goes away again
from those two ; and he makes the same arrangements and
goes away.   After that she takes her child up on her back,
and goes with it to the yam garden; and when they have arrived
there she puts down her child and works at weeding.   And
when she has weeded all the place she does again as before ;
if she essays to dig a yam for their food, and she lays hold on
the leaf of the yam, there is a tuber already in her hand ; and
if she essays to pluck hibiscus leaves, they are in her hand
already; and if she essays to take a cocoa-nut, there is a cocoa-
nut already in her hand.   And the evening draws on, and the
two go home ; and her husband comes home and sees them, and
asks them, What have you two eaten ?   And she says, We two
have been in our garden working, and have dug a yam for
our food, and plucked hibiscus leaves, and taken cocoa-nuts.
But her husband says to her, Not so ; I have been into our
garden and have seen one thing, but I have not seen at all
that a yam has been dug, not at all ; and no cocoa-nut has
been taken.   And the woman says to him, Not so ; we two
certainly have got the food in our garden.   But the man
says, Not so ; there is some one else probably who has given
it to you.   And she says, Who is there that will trouble
himself about us? he will be a ghost, I suppose !   And he
says, Tell me who gives these things to you.   Who should it
be that would give me anything? says she.   And the man
says, No! tell me the truth.   Then the woman says to him,
Well! come along, we three will go into our garden.   So the
three set out and went and arrived ; and the woman says to
him, Well! look here, you are angry with us, but you may
see for yourself.   Then she touches taro, and it was as before,
and yams, and it was so.   Then the man says, Not so ; some
one else has been giving you things.   But as he says thus he
lays hold on a stick and beats her, and says, You don't belong
down here below, you belong above the sky.   What have
you been doing here?   Get back into your own country.
And she says, Very well, I will soon go back into my own
country.   And one day after again he beat her and went off.

And when she has seen that he is gone she gathers banyan
leaves into a heap, and sets fire to them, and they burn.
Then she says to her child, Sit here, and I will go to the
other side of the fire; and she goes to the other side of the fire,
and the smoke goes straight up into the clouds, and the
child's mother goes up in it; and her child cries beside the
fire, and she goes on up into the clouds [1].

5. GANVIVIRIS. MOTA.

The story about what Ro Som did for Ganviviris is not an
old one; he was a man whom my father's grandfather and
his friends had seen; he was an orphan, his father was dead,
and his mother too was dead, and he lived with his mother's
brother.   And his uncle did nothing for him in the *suqe*
club, he still remained an *avlava*, because he was an idle
fellow, and whenever they called him to go to work he would
refuse, and when they were all gone inland to the gardens he
would go down to the beach to shoot fish, and do nothing
else day after day.   But one day when they had called him to
work and were all gone, he took his bow and went down to
Ngerenow, and there he saw a *sauma* slowly swimming along
and rolling from side to side quite close to him; and he took
an arrow tipped with casuarina wood, and drew his bow to
shoot.   And just as he was releasing the string he heard a
voice inciting him and saying, Let fly! Let fly! And he
drew down his arrow from the bow-string, thinking it was a

---

[1] Here the MS. ends. The story goes on to relate that the man found
his child crying for its mother beside the fire, and refusing to be comforted.
He sought help from all the birds and living creatures, but none would listen
to him till he came to the Spider, *marawa*, who readily undertook to bring
the child to its mother. He spun a line from earth to heaven, took the man
and the child on his back and carried them safely up. A feast was going on
in heaven, and the two sat down in the circle of spectators. The men were
dancing round the drum, and the women tramping round in pairs. Each
time the mother passed the child it cried out Mother! She stopped at last
and asked, Who is that cries Mother! to me? Recognizing her child and
husband she agreed to return, and the Spider carried all three of them safe back
to the earth.

man, and he turned his head again and again to look behind
him to see who it was, but there was no man. And he drew
again, and heard again the voice inciting him ; and he looked
again, for he still thought it was a man. And the third time
he drew his bow, and heard the voice, and loosed the string
and hit the sauma. And he ran down and caught the fish by
the tail, and threw his arms round it ; but the fish struggled,
throwing itself about, and carried him off into a dry cave,
which was, they say, the dwelling of Ro Som (Money). And
Ganviviris cried aloud, but the sauma turned into a woman, and
said, Don't cry, it is I who have had pity on you. I have
seen you every day, and now I am going to do you a service.
You shall go back ; and when you go home you are to tell
your uncle to bid his wives plait bags for you, and let them
be ten, and make a chamber for yourself parted off from the
house, and hang up all the bags in the open ; and don't eat
anything to-day. So Ganviviris dived out of the cave, and
went back into the village, and said to his uncle, *Tata*, tell
those three to plait me ten bags. And his uncle said to him,
What have you got belonging to you to stow in them ? You
are a penniless fellow, and one who never plants or gathers.
But he says, *E !* just let me have them plaited. So his
uncle said to his wives, You are to plait bags for Ganviviris.
And they three cried, *E-o-o !* who is to listen to him, an
avlava, a fellow who does nothing at all? But his uncle said,
Plait them just to try what his nonsense means ; then we
shall see what sort of property he has got to stow in them.
So the three women plaited the bags. And in the night Ro
Som came to Ganviviris and said, Make haste to hang up
your bags. And next day he hung up the bags ; and in the
night as he was lying down to sleep he heard the rafters
creak again because of the money which was filling the bags ;
and he got up and felt one after another those ten bags,
every one quite full. And Ro Som said to him; Tell your
uncle to give you his third wife. So he spoke out to him
about it, and his uncle let him have one. And he said again,
Tata, let us break up fire-wood for the day after to-morrow.

But his uncle said to him, What property have you got to
give for us to buy your rank with, you a penniless fellow
with nothing coming in? And he says, Lend me some
money and a pig to make the first payments with ; but this
he said to try him. And his uncle said to him, I shall not
consent to let you have any property of mine ; why should I?
you are an idle fellow. But he says, *Tata*, let us break up
fire-wood the day after to-morrow, and to-morrow we will go
into your gardens, and I will look for some taro there. So
they went to the gardens, and he said to his uncle, Put up a
palako as a warning against taking anything from these
gardens. And his uncle said to him, You are putting a mark
upon a great quantity ; what have you got of your own to pay
so great a price with? And he says, You will pay the great
price. But he says, I shall not listen to you about my money
and my food. So they went back again into the village, and
all the people then heard of what had been done, and they
laughed at Ganviviris, saying that he would never be able to
eat his *suqe* rank. But next day they broke up fire-wood, and
he bought taro with a great price, with ten coils of money for
each garden. And his uncle said to him, You have bought
food with a great price ; you have succeeded in that, but you
have to give money all round for your *suqe*, where have you
got anything for that? And he says, That will be your doing
of course. But his uncle had no wish to let him have his
money; so he says, Let us bring the taro to-morrow, and
crack almonds for the feast. And he said again to his
uncle, *Tata*, let your children twist some cords. So his two
children twisted, and his wives twisted ; and the neighbours
asked his uncle saying, They are twisting cords, but where is
the pig there tied up by the house? And he says, *Esi!* we have
never seen any belonging to him, he is a pauper. But in the
evening he went and got four pigs, and tied them up near the
village. And he ate on one day the *avirik* and the *qatagiav.*
And in the night Ro Som said to him, You are to take all
your ranks in the *suqe* here at Qakea ; you are not to take
any at Mota ; if you disobey my word in this you will die.

And on the day he bought his rank he said to them, Have
you made all the return for my money? And they said, When
you have completed your distribution of property we will
make an end of our return; lest we should crush ourselves
into poverty. So he went and loosed and brought out two
rawe pigs and two boars, and he went into his house and
carried out his money-bags on his back, and with that he
made distribution; and they were amazed at those *rawe* and
boars, all of them with their tusks curled round till they met,
that Ro Som had given to him. And after five days again
they broke up fire-wood, and on the tenth day again he bought
his steps of rank, the *avtagataga* and the *luwaiav*. And on
the fifth day again they broke up fire-wood, and on the tenth
day he bought his steps, the *tamasuria* and the *tavai suqe*;
and on the fifth day again he said, Let us break up fire-wood,
and on the tenth day he bought the steps *tavasuqelava* and
kerepue. And always he was buying food with large payments, and he paddled over to Vanua Lava and bought with
large sums there, and to Mota and bought with large sums
there: and he went on in the *suqe* till he reached the *weme-
teloa*. Then he desired to make his *suqe* also at Mota, and he
went and built his house at Tasmate, and they broke up fire-
wood and danced the *taqesara*. But he appointed the tenth day
for a *sawae*, and on the ninth day he prepared mashed yams;
and at the *sawae* he appointed the tenth day for a *kolekole*.
And at the *kolekole*, when the noise of the *sawae* was sounding
like thunder, and the feast was at its height, they saw a
woman walking up the sloping ground below the cliff, using
a spear for a walking stick, with bracelets on her arms reaching to the elbow, and on her right arm a boar's tusk, and her
head smeared with red earth, and pigs' tails fastened to her
hair; and they thought that some visitors had just landed
from a canoe. And she went straight to the house of Ganviviris and passed out of sight within it; and they went to
see who it was and found no one there. And they told Ganviviris, We have seen a woman go into your *kole* house, with
bracelets and boars' tusks on her arms; and he said, Don't

mention it in the village. And he went up there to bring
out his money-bags on his back, and he saw that his ten bags
had nothing in them; and he went outside and saw that all
his pigs were gone; his distribution of property came to
nothing at all. And when the evening was dark, and Ganviviris was sleeping in his house, they heard him cry out,
and they asked him, What ails you? And he said, *Esi!*
there is something, but I don't know what it is, that has
happened to me. And he began to sicken on that very night,
and on the fifth day he died.

6. THE LITTLE ORPHAN.   MOTA.

A story to tell. They were living in their place, the boys
were growing up, and their father and mother said to them,
Go down to the beach, and catch fish with hook and line for
us, and we two will go inland and get vegetables for us all
to eat with them. And they said, Very well; and the two
went up to the garden, and they went down to the beach.
And as they were going along the path the Little Orphan said,
Let me go with you. But they said E-o-o! not you, a little
orphan, we will go by ourselves alone, we who are children of
fathers; if you were to go with us what would you eat?
You have no father, you have no mother, who will give you
food to eat with your fish? And they went first, and the
Little Orphan behind. And those the children of fathers
went down to the beach, and the Little Orphan went down
a steep place eastwards to the landing-place at Sanwawa;
and there he fishes for himself with a line and hook. And
when he sees those others mounting back into the island,
he also strings his fish together and mounts back himself;
and he comes near to them, and they say, Don't come together
with us, you have no father and no mother to give you
vegetable food to eat your fish with. So they mount up,
and they before and he behind. But they go on the way
homeward, and he stops short, and goes into his cave
and roasts his fish. And when he has roasted them he takes

his fish up together and goes out, and goes out down to the
beach, and sits down, and dips his fish into a little pool of
salt-water, and eats them by themselves without any vegetable
food.   After this on another day they went again ; and the
Little Orphan says, I will go with you ; and they say, No, we
have already said that you the Little Orphan are not to come.
If you come with us, and you catch fish, what have you to
eat with them? you have no food to eat your fish with.   And
they went before and he went after ; and they went to their
place, and he to his.   And he fishes with his hook and line
and keeps his eye upon them ; and when he sees them
mount up inland, he also mounts up himself.   And they say
to him, Don't, we tell you, be coming along with us ; if you
come here who is there to give you food ? you have no father
and no mother to give you food to eat your fish with.   And
they go on into the village, and he stops short, and roasts
again his fish and eats them without vegetable food.   After
this on another day again they went ; and he said, Let me .
go with you ; but they said, You are not to go, we only
shall go who have fathers and have mothers, you are not
to come, a little orphan.   And they went again before, and
he behind, and they to their place and he to his.   And as he
stood down there, a fish comes on his hook first, and he runs
up on the rocks and takes it off the hook ; and runs and
lets down his hook into the water, and a *tapanau* is caught,
and he takes it up, and runs up and puts it down into a little
pool.   And he runs over again and lets down his hook and a
nongpitpit is caught ; and he runs up and puts it down into
the pool ; and runs over and lets down his hook and a *gavaru*
is caught, and he goes with it and puts it down into the pool,
and runs over and lets down his hook, and a plaited hibiscus
line (*gavaru*) is caught by him ; and he goes up with it and puts
it down.   And he runs over to let down his hook, and a woman
and her child come up out of the sea to him ; and their name
is Ro Som (Money), and he puts them down on the reef.
Then Ro Som says to him, Let us three go together.   And
the Little Orphan says, E-o-o ! not you two ; I will go by

myself. But she says, No, we three. But the Little Orphan
says, No, you two must not ; I shall go by myself, because
I have no food to feed you with. But she says, Never mind,
string our fish together and we three will go. So the three
went along and arrived at the Little Orphan's dwelling-place ;
and he looks and sees a house and a *gamal*; and he asks her,
Whose house is this ? and whose *gamal* is this ? And Ro Som
says to him, It is the house of us three, and your *gamal*. So
they three enter into the house, and sit down. And Ro Som
says to the Little Orphan, Come now, cook the fish for us
three to eat. But he says What is there ? What are we
going to eat the fish with ? I told you that you two must
not come with me ; I have no food. But she says, Cook
the fish, we three will eat them with some vegetable food
presently. So he makes up a fire for the fish, and puts hot
stones inside them and wraps them in leaves, and puts them
on the fire, and the three sit down and wait. Then Ro Som
says to him, Now then, take down our fish. And he says,
What are we to do ? What are we going to eat them with, I
mean ? And she says, Look, there is a heap of cooked food
there for us to eat the fish with. So he goes over to the fish,
and takes them off the fire, and they three ate. And when
they had finished eating he goes out of the house into the
village and sees gardens, a banana garden, and a *tomago* garden,
and a yam garden, a *wowosa* garden, a *weswes* garden, a
sugar-cane garden ; and the bananas were beginning to rot,
and the *tomagos* were sprouting afresh, and the yams were
sprouting, and the reeds were throwing up flower stalks, and
the *qeta* were beginning to rot. Then he said to his mother,
Oh, mother, whose gardens are these here ? And Ro Som
says, They belong to us three only ; and she says to him,
To-morrow you will make up fires in the *gamal* in every oven,
and we two will be here in the house, and we three will make
mixture of cooked food and scraped cocoa-nut for food for pigs.
And says the Little Orphan, Very well, but what are we to
feed with it ? But she says, Just get to work about it. So
they two cooked a quantity of food in the oven inside the

house, and he also cooked a quantity in the *gamal*; and the
pigs' food made by the two in the house was a hundred baskets-
full and that in the *gamal* a hundred. And as soon as they
covered in the ovens the food was cooked. And the Little
Orphan mixed the food for his part in the *gamal*, and
Som and her child mixed for their part in the house;
and when the three have finished mixing, they take the food
out into the village place, and the Little Orphan puts his
down on a stone, and Som and her child put theirs down
at the door of the house. And Ro Som says, Well now, call
the pigs, *sumsum*; and the Little Orphan gets up and *sumsums*,
and he hears continued squealing, and he sees boars with
tusks that curl and meet, and *rawe* with tusks that curl
and meet, and sows; these all come rushing out to the three,
and the three feed them and they eat. And while they are
eating, Ro Som says to him, Have you got any uncle on your
mother's side? And he says, I have an uncle, but he does
not come to look after me, and he gives me no food. Then
said Ro Som, Run and say to him, *Tata*, come and make the
payments for my steps in the *suqe*. So the wife of the uncle
of the Little Orphan saw him coming, and she said to the
people, Drive that boy away that is coming here; who is
there to attend to him, and give him food? Then says the
Little Orphan, *Tata!* And his uncle says *O-e!* what is it?
And he says, Come out here. So his uncle came out to him;
and he says, *Tata*, pray come to me to pay, *sar*, for my steps.
And his uncle says, Oh, but if I pay that, what will you *vile
pulai*, return payment, with? And his nephew says, Come let
us go. So the Little Orphan led the way, and his uncle
came behind, and they went on. And when they arrived
beside the Little Orphan's village, his uncle sees a place where
pigs have been rooting, and he says, Ah! these pigs' rootings,
whose are they? And he says, Mine to be sure. But he says,
Oh, I dare say! Where are you going to get pigs from to
be your property? Then he sees also a garden, and he says,
Whose is this yam garden? and he says, Mine. And his uncle
says, I'll beat you for saying it; but he looks about and

the bananas are rotting, and the caladium is rotting, and
the tomagos are sprouting. And then he sees a house and
says, But whose house is this? and whose *gamal* is this?
And the Little Orphan says, My house and my *gamal.* And
his uncle says, But how is it that you have got these? Who
is there who will assist you and give you thatch? And the
Little Orphan says to his uncle, Well, let those people give
the first money, *vene,* for the *avrik.* And his uncle says to
the people, Come, give in your money to begin with, I will
sar, pay back, to you. And all the people say, You fellows!
how is it? What has he got to return with? He has no
money. But his uncle makes the first return, *sar,* payment
to them, and when he had paid them all, the Little
Orphan gives money for his uncle's property; and he says
again, *Tata,* make payment again to them for the *qatagiav.*
And they *vene* to his uncle, and he makes the full return
to them all, and his nephew returns his property to him,
pigs and money. And he says to his uncle again, Pay,
sar, them again for the *av tagataga,* and he pays; and
when he has paid them all, his nephew makes the return of
his property, gives pigs and money   And he says again to his
uncle, *Tata,* let those people again make, *vene,* their contribu-
tion of money for the *luwai av*; and they make it; and his
uncle repays them; and when he has paid them all, his
nephew runs up into the house, and brings money out on his
back, and makes the return of his property to his uncle. And
that food that they ate would never come to an end; they
made one cooking of it, and they still went on eating it for
rank after rank in the *suqe*; they eat, and they stay at it
right through like that. Afterwards he says again to his
uncle, Well now, pay them again for the *tamasuria,* and he
pays them again; and his nephew runs up again, and brings
out again on his back bags of money, and gives pigs, and
makes return of his property to his uncle. And the people
still remain; and he says again to his uncle, *Tata,* pay them
again for the *tavai suqe*; and he pays again; and when he
has paid them all, his nephew runs up and goes into the

house, and carries out money again on his back, and gives
pigs and *rawe*s, and makes return of his uncle's property.
And he says, *Tata*, pay again for the *kerepue*; and he pays,
and his nephew brings money, and pigs, and *rawe*s, and gives
them to his uncle.　And he says again, *Tata*, pay them for the
mele; and he pays; and his nephew runs up and goes into the
house and carries out money, and gives pigs and *rawe*s, and
makes return of his uncle's property.　And that money will
never come to an end, because his mother was Ro Som (i.e.
Money); and she sits in the house and is hard at work multi-
plying that money.　And he says again, *Tata*, pay them again
for the *tetug*; and he pays; and his nephew runs up and goes
into the house, and carries out money, and gives pigs and
*rawe*s, and makes return of his uncle's property.　And he
says again, *Tata*, pay them again for the *lano*; and he pays
them; and his nephew makes return of his property again.
And he says again, *Tata*, pay them for the *qorqorolava*; and
he pays; and his nephew makes return of his property, brings
pigs, and brings *rawe*s, and makes return again to his uncle.
And thus it went on till he rose to the top, till he ate right
through all the ranks of the *suqe*.　After that he says to his
uncle again, *Tata*, let us two make a *kolekole*; and his uncle
says, Very well.　And he makes a *kolekole* for a stone, a *sewere*,
makes one for an image, *nule*, makes one for a *gamal*, makes
one for a *wenereqoe*, pig's tail, makes one for a *wetapup*,
chicken's feathers, makes one for a *sarlano*, a hat, makes one
for a *liwan tamate*, figure of a ghost, all those *kolekole*s of
every sort and kind he accomplished.　After that his nephew
made a return of his property; he returned, went on returning, returned to the uttermost his uncle's property.
And his uncle killed pigs for him; killed for the *sewere*,
killed for the *nule*, killed for the *gamal*, killed for the *wenereqoe*, killed for the *wetapup*, killed for the *kolevat*, the stone,
killed for the *qatqatmemea*, the red head, killed for the *sarlano*,
killed for the *liwantamate*.　And when he had finished killing,
his uncle commanded the people of his village to take his
pigs, and his *rawe*, and his money, to carry away; to carry

away his pigs, and to carry away his *rawe*, and to carry away
his money.   And his uncle went up to the door of the house,
and said to his wives, Come along, get up you two, we three
will go home ; one of you will lead a pig with a line, one of
you will carry a bag of money on her back.   But they said
to him, No ! go home yourself, we two are going to stay and
marry your nephew, the Little Orphan.   And he says, Not
so, you two cannot marry him because formerly you used
contemptuous language to him ; has he become good again ?
no, he is bad.   I wanted to give him food, but you two
forbade it, and I was prevented giving him food ; and I
wanted to go and look after him, but you two forbade it, and
my going to see him came to nothing ; and if you two are
to make advances to him, is he good again ? no, he is bad.
You two could not eat, when you saw him it made you sick,
and you two can't live with him.   But they said, Not at all,
you go home by yourself, we two are going to stay with him.
Then his uncle says, No, get up both of you, we three are to
go home.   But they two say, No, you go home by yourself.
Then says he, Who is it you two here are going to marry ?
You two can't live with him, the object of your scorn.   Then
they two get up and the three go home together.   And the
Little Orphan goes into the house, and makes a fire, and puts
pig's flesh into the oven to make it keep.   And when he has
finished with his pig, then comes a report of a voyage, that
the Motalava people with the Losalava people are going to
paddle over to Gaua.   Then says the Little Orphan to his
mother, Oh, mother, those people are going to paddle over to
Gaua to-morrow, and may I ?   And his mother says, You
must not ; stay and look after your meat in the oven.   But
he says E-o-o ! not so, mother, I shall go on the voyage with
them ; I am going to them, and you two will cook my pig
for me.   So it was night and morning ; and when morning
was come he goes up inside the house and speaks to his
mother and says, Well, mother, as I am going away from you
two, and you two stay here, there is that heap of food you are
to eat ; but these you are not to touch.   And he goes off, and

they start on their voyage. And when he reaches the landing-place, he sees that those people have already dragged down the canoe and set it afloat on the edge of the sea; and he runs and jumps up and climbs right up on board the canoe, and they paddle off. But they all of them had taken pigs with them, but the Little Orphan had not taken one for himself, and he had brought nothing but a cockle-shell in his hand, and that shell-fish was not opened. And when they brought the canoes to shore at Gaua, the people there came down to meet them, and one of them runs over and cries, Friend! and touches his friend's hand, and the two go up the beach together; and some other runs down and cries, This is my friend, and touches his hand, and they two walk up together; and some other runs down and cries, This is my friend, and takes him, and they two walk up ashore; but that poor Little Orphan, they don't want to be friends with him. And they stay and stay, and the wind rises, and they are to start on their voyage; and they set off and paddle, paddle on, and go out at Losalava. And when those people drag up their canoe (at Mota), he runs back, runs and runs, and reaches the house where they three lived, and goes straight inside the house, and sees the heap of yams still remaining as it was; and he says, What have you two been eating? this food still remains untouched. And they two say, We have been eating it to be sure, that food. But he says, No, there is some other man I think has been bringing you wild food of the forest. Now he makes a fool of himself in this, supposing that it was as if his mother were living with a man. But that female Ro Som wept exceedingly because he had been angry with her, and she and her child wept till the sun went down. Then the Little Orphan goes near to them, and lies upon their legs, and tries to console them, but can't succeed; and they cried on, till they heard the nose of the Little Orphan whistling in sleep, and then they removed softly their legs, and put down his head on the ground; and they run to the money-bags, and unloose the pig, and the two run off. And as they went out that village turned into a deserted garden. But as they ran away the old woman sat down, the bags of money were very heavy upon her, and one of the bags fell down. And a pig with tusks remained tied at that landing-place at Sanwawa, and that money-bag remained lying where it fell. And that Little Orphan woke and jumped up, and there he was in a deserted garden, and he ran looking for those two, and he came out upon the shore, and sees an old woman sitting there and asks, Oh! have you seen anybody at all here just now? And she sings, Look, look over there! *Ioio! ialo!* the two are plunging back into the sea at the place where the Little Orphan had fished them up. It is finished.

NOTE.—Two more Stories from Mota in native MS. are too long for insertion in full.   One is the Story of *Wowut-ta-Taragaviga*, whom his parents kept in the house till he was grown up, and then advanced to the highest *suqe* rank. Another man of the same island taking the same step sent a portion of his feast to Wowut-ta-Taragaviga by an orphan, all others being afraid of approaching the *gamal* of so high a rank. Wowut takes a liking to the orphan, and pays him with money. He goes again and again with food till he has ‘ thousands of money, thousands of boars, thousands of pigs with curled tusks,’ and with these advances himself to high *suqe* rank.   Then Wowut dies, and directs that when his friend comes to mourn over him he is to be given his wife in memory of him. The other is the Story of *Qat-wuruga*, who was born of a mother who had been killed by a fall from a tree, and grew up in the forest like the children in the Story of Taso. His maternal uncle finds him and takes him home, where his uncle’s wives neglect him and ill-use him, and give him his name of Scurfy-head. The boy begs his uncle to take him back to the forest, and he carries him out of the sight of the sea into the midst of the island, Vanua Lava. Then he settles himself, and after a while snares birds.   One day the fat of a bird roasting over the fire fell through on to the head of Wetopunpun beneath the earth, and he comes up above ground. This is the boy’s father, the ghost of his dead father, or a *Vui* spirit. With the charm ‘ *Soso-punpun, Soso-punpun* ’ (like the *Kerembuembae* of Story No. 1) he makes food, gardens, a village, a *gamal*, pigs, fowls, a drum—all native wealth. Qat-wuruga’s uncle comes to see him, and undertakes his advance to the highest ranks of the *suqe*, receiving his due payment of pigs. His wives, incredulous at first, go to a *kolekole* and see the youth they have despised in all his splendour. They desire to stay as his wives, and make him cut open his breast and give them some of his liver to eat. A canoe from Maewo comes over, and they find the fresh emblems of his rank ; they challenge comparison with their own, and see open-mouthed with astonishment the number of jawbones of the pigs he has killed in his feasts. They beguile him to sleep, and carry him off to their own island to kill and eat him. While they are

7. THE WOMAN AND THE EEL. AURORA.

A woman went to lay pandanus leaves to weave mats with in the water, and she laid them there in the evening and went home. In the morning she went to take the leaves from the water; and when she went to take them out, behold, they were turned into an eel. Then she ran back and told it to some men who were engaged in the *suqe*, and they ran down and tied a cord to the eel and dragged it up to the village. But there was a lame man who could not go with them, and he lay in the *gamal*, club-house; and by the side of the *gamal* there was a croton-tree; and as they dragged up that eel it curled its tail round the croton, and the croton was nearly broken, and the lame man saw it. But they dragged hard at the eel and it loosed its tail from the croton, and they brought it into the village, and laid it at the entrance of the *gamal*. So when they ran off for fire-wood and banana leaves to cook it with, the eel said to the lame man, When they are eating don't you eat; they shall eat by themselves. Consequently the lame man did not eat; but they put the eel to be cooked in the oven of the *suqe*, and covered in the oven. And when they opened the oven they all took up pieces of the eel, every one of them a piece, and when the great man said to them, Now put them ready, then they all put them ready; and after that he said again, Now let us eat, and they all took a bite at once. But as they bit once their legs turned into eels; and they bit a second time and the bodies of them all turned into eels; and they bit again, and they were all eels; and the great man glided away first, and they all followed him into the water.

making preparations for their dance and feast, one of their party takes pity on him, unties and delivers him; the two paddle back to Vanua Lava. But when they reach Qat-wuruga's place all has disappeared. When he was captured his father Wetopunpun had gone to the beach and sat there grieving. The Qakea people, seeing him there day after day, paddled over and took him to their place, where there was a famine. There with his charm ' *Soso-punpun* ' he makes gardens full of food to appear. They envy him and he leaves them, and seeks a solitary place, where he sits down by the side of Ro Som with all his possessions round him. A stone there representing him is a place of sacrifice to this day.

8. The Little Owl. Aurora.

This is about two women who were getting fire-wood, and
found a young owl, a bird with white feathers and very large
eyes; it was a young bird of this kind that they found.
And one day the two women went to look at their little bird,
and found that he was turned into a man ; so they took him
into the village, and he became their husband. And the
three lived always in perfect harmony together, and built
their house, and worked in their garden, and so remained
many years. But after that he took to beating them when
they quarrelled, and they scolded him for it, saying, You
there are a bird, and our property because we found you ;
why do you beat us like this ? So he said he would leave
them ; and in the evening he drank kava, and forbade them to
blow the fire. But when he lay down to sleep the two
women blew up the fire into a blaze, and looked at him, and
he turned into a bird, and flew away. And the two women
cried after him, and he threw down money to them.

9. The Winged Wife. Aurora.

This is about the women that they say belonged to heaven,
and had wings like birds ; and they came down to earth to
bathe in the sea, and when they bathed they took off their
wings. And as Qatu was going about, he chanced to see
them ; and he took up one pair of wings and went back into
the village and buried them at the foot of the main pillar of his
house. Then he went back again and watched them. And
when they had finished bathing they went and took up their
wings and flew up to heaven ; but one could not fly because
Qat had stolen her wings, and she was crying. So Qat goes
up to her, and speaks deceitfully to her and asks her, What
are you crying for ? And she says, They have taken away my
wings. Then he takes her to his house and marries her.
And Qat's mother takes her and they go to work ; and when

the leaf of a yam touches her there are yams as if someone had already dug them up, and if a leaf of a banana again had touched her, just a single one, all the bananas were ripe at once. But when Qat's mother saw that things were so she scolded her; but not Qat; he was gone shooting birds. And when Qat's mother scolded her she went back into the village; and she sits beside the post of the house and cries. And as she cried her tears flowed down upon the ground and made a deep hole; and the tears drop down and strike upon her wings, and she scratches away the earth and finds them, and flies back again to heaven. And when Qat was come home from shooting he sees that she is not there, and scolds his mother. Then he kills every one of his pigs, and fastens points to very many arrows, and climbs up on the top of his house, and shoots up to the sky. And when he sees that the arrow does not fall back he shoots again and hits the first arrow. And he shoots many times, and always hits, and the arrows reach down to the earth. And, behold, there is a banyan root following the arrows, and Qat takes a basket of pig's flesh in his hand and climbs up to heaven to seek his wife. And he finds a person hoeing; and he finds his wife and takes her back; and he says to the person who is hoeing, When you see a banyan root don't disturb it. But as the two went down by the banyan root and had not yet reached the ground, that person chopped the root off, and Qat fell down and was killed, and the woman flew back to heaven. That is the end of it.

10. THE STORY OF TASO. AURORA.

This is a story about Taso a man-eater. This Taso was a man who ate men, and there was a woman, the sister of Qatu, who was pregnant and near her time. Taso found her in the garden ground, in a thicket, and killed her; but he did not eat her, because she was pregnant and her time was nearly come. She lay and rotted in the thicket, never having been brought in for burial. And while this corpse of a woman killed with a club, Qatu's sister, was lying and rotting, her two infants were alive, and as the mother rotted, it left them free. So they lay, and they rolled along on the smooth ground, and by and bye they grew strong. Then they found dry leaves in which rain water had collected and they sipped and drank; and they came on to a root of *qena* (a gingiberaceous plant) and sucked it, for this *qena* has a swollen lump at its root and water accumulates in a small hollow in it. So they clung to the *qena* root till they were strong and could move about, and then they began to wander, and made their way out of the thicket. And as they so wandered along they came to a place where there was a sow with young; and they sat and looked at her. Now this sow was the property of their maternal uncle Qatu; and they sat looking out for the cocoa-nuts with which the sow was fed. After a while their uncle Qatu came and sat down and called his sow, and the sow came with her litter of pigs, and Qatu cut up their food for them; and when he had cut it up he did not sit there till it was all eaten and then go; he went away before that, he turned his back and went. Then these two came forth and drove away the sow, and took from her the cocoa-nuts that had been cut up to eat them themselves, and sat down and ate. But the sow went up into the village and cried to her owner Qatu. Next morning when he came down to feed the sow they did the same thing; the sow went off to her owner, and they gathered up the cut cocoa-nut in their arms and took it off to eat it themselves. And Qatu saw that his sow was always coming back to him, and was thin without any fat about her, and he asked himself, Why is it I wonder that my sow comes back to me, as if I had not fed her, and is not at all fat? Let me sit and observe what it is that makes her come back to me up into the village. So after feeding her he pretended to go back, but went round and returned that he might see what it was that happened to his sow. And he stood and watched them coming out, light in complexion, wonderfully fair, as they came and stood and drove away the sow to take her food. And Qatu jumped out, and called to

them, What, is it you who are always driving away my sow?
I have seen her coming back to me. These two twins let the
food slip from their arms and stood ashamed, biting their
fingers. And Qatu asked them, Where do you come from?
And they told him how they lay and rolled and found their
way out of the thicket, and saw the water and drank it, and
came to the root of *qena* and sucked it; and how when they
did so they grew strong, and saw the sow and filled their
bellies with the food the sow was eating. And Qatu understood without mistake that these were the children of his
sister whom Taso had killed long ago.

Qatu called them and went up to the village and hid them
at the further end of his house; and he bade Ro Motari his
wife to go into the garden and dig some yams, and bring
hibiscus leaves, tender such as locusts eat, and come back to
make a yam-mash for the two twins. And Ro Motari did
so; she went and gathered the leaves and dug the yams and
came back and made the *loko*. And when the oven was closed
in Qatu bade Ro Motari to go and cut down cocoa-nut fronds
for mats, and plait and spread them, and to make up a
pillow. Then Qatu bids Ro Motari go to the further end of
the house; and she goes and sees the two little twins sitting
at the further end of the house in the pig fence; and she runs
back and cries to Qatu, *Lili! Lili!* What are those little ones
to me? my children, or my brothers, or my grandchildren? [1]
Qatu says to her, O-o-o! your grandchildren. So she took
them gladly into the house, she and Qatu, and gave them
food, and they stayed with him and Ro Motari. After a
while they grew big, and Qatu shaped bows for them made of
the rachis of the sago fronds; and when they could shoot
lizards he broke the bows and took them from them, and made
different ones for them. And when they could shoot geckos
he took the bows away from them and broke them and shaped

[1] In another version of the story, 'When Motari saw the two handsome
boys with their white hair, she liked them and asked Qatu, Are these my children or my husbands? And Qatu said, Yes indeed, your husbands, for they
are my sister's children.'

different ones for them, and put points to their arrows. And
when they could both shoot the small birds *tatagoras* he took
the bows away and broke them, and made them bows much
larger than before, and put points to their arrows, and then
they could shoot doves. So they came to be able to shoot all
kinds of birds ; and then he cut clubs for them, and they killed
rats with them, and he took them away and broke them ; and
presently when they were full-grown youths he made clubs
for them again, for one a *oi utu* (Barringtonia fruit) with four
corners to it, for the other a simple *tarara* with a ring and
spike.

Qatu brought them up till they were quite big, and then
one day he told them about Taso, saying that they were not
to go carelessly about or go where Taso was without due
cause, because he had killed their mother and was a man-eater.
When they had considered this they set a taboo upon a banana
belonging to them, and said to their uncle Qatu, If you go into
the garden and see our bunch of bananas beginning to ripen at
the top and ripening downwards to the end, Taso has killed us ;
but if you see that it has begun to ripen at the end and is
ripening upwards we shall have killed him. So their uncle
turned his back and went his way, and the twins started off to
take Taso by surprise. They came to Taso's place, but did
not find him there, because he had gone down to the beach to
sharpen his teeth[1] ; so the twins asked Taso's mother, Where
is this Taso gone? We have come here to see him. And
Taso's mother called to them to come up and sit by the *gamal*
to wait for him, and they came up to the *gamal* and sat there
waiting for Taso. Now short round yams had been dug, and
a fire lighted in the *gamal*, and they heated the yams, and
pulled out the stones that lined the ovens, and put them on
the fire to pelt Taso with. There were two fire-places in the
gamal, at the one end and at the other. And Taso's mother
came down from the house ; and the old woman lay down on
the ground and sang a song, crying down to Taso on the beach.
This is the song : *Taso ! sarosaro ganga tamate, a ganga i tuara,*

[1] A tooth of Taso is still to be seen at Maewo.

gaku i tuara. Taso! (Taso! look out for your dead man to eat, one for you, one for me. Taso!) Taso was sitting on the beach, and heard his mother crying to him, and he got up and came back along the path ; and as he came he turned his head from side to side and struck the trees, and they came down with a crash. But the twins had made ready for their attack on Taso, red-hot stones and cooked yams, and they stood with their feet firmly planted and waited for him inside the *gamal*, one at the one end of it, and the other at the other. Then they heard Taso come up and ask his mother, What is it, mother? And she said, What is it but dead men for us to eat, sitting there in the *gamal*? So Taso went on and up to the *gamal*, and as he got in over the rail at the door, one of the twins took up a red-hot stone and threw it at him and hit him, and when he ran down to the other end of the *gamal*, the other twin threw at him and hit him Taso cried out, It is in vain that you throw at me, I will eat you both to-day. As he runs to one end of the *gamal* one of the twins throws at him, as he runs to the other the other throws ; so they go on at him till his bones shake within him, and he lies down and only groans. Then the twins leap upon him and beat him to death with their clubs. Then they go down to the house and drag out the old woman, Taso's mother, and club her ; they clubbed them both to death. Then they set fire to the houses over them, and went back homewards. But Qatu and Motari were standing in the garden listening to the popping of the bamboo rafters as they burnt, and wondering what was going on over there : 'Those two probably have come across Taso and he is killing them.' Qatu starts and goes off, and as he goes he meets them, and they tell him that they have killed Taso. And he said to them, I forbade you to go there, you have disobeyed me and gone, and very nearly he has eaten you. So it was finished ; they killed Taso and revenged their mother whom Taso had murdered.

11. About Betawerai a Snake. Aurora.

The beginning was in this way; a woman and her child
went to strip pandanus leaves for weaving mats, and the boy
saw a young snake on the stalk of a leaf and begged his
mother to let him have it for he wanted it ; his mother forbade
him to take it. But he said that he wished for it, and so he'
laid hold on the little red snake, and took it and put it in the
hollow trunk of a tree ; and the name of that tree is the
uqava ; he put it into the hollow of that, and he used to feed it
with rats or birds or black lizards, or pig's flesh, and that
snake became extremely large. And one day when he killed
a pig he went to give it some ; but that snake snatched the
pig from him, and ate him up also, and crawled out of the
hollow tree, and came into the village and ate up all the
people in the place. But there was one pregnant woman who
survived ; and she dug a pit, and took a thin flat stone and
laid it over the pit, and she stayed within it.   And she
brought forth her children, twins, and they three remained in
that pit in the ground. And the snake ate up all the people,
and then went and took up its abode on a banyan-tree, and
brought forth exceedingly many young ones, and two the
chief among them. The name of one of these was Betawerai,
and this one was not able to go about, but stayed always on
a branch of the banyan. But we call the branch of a big
tree like a banyan *tawerai*, like the flat of the hand, and this
was named after that, Betawerai, At the branch. And the
other one used to go very far away seeking diligently men or
pigs to eat, and his name was Walolo. But one day those
two, the children of the woman who had lived in the ground,
begged of their mother to make them bows and arrows ; and
after that they said they would go into the village and seek
that snake to shoot it and kill it. But when they had gone
and had seen from a distance that banyan where Betawerai
and Walolo lived, they saw upon the branches, and on the
little twigs, and on the leaves, nothing but snakes on that

banyan. But Walolo was not on the tree, because he had gone across the sea and was still seeking for men to devour. And these two boys went up to the banyan-tree and began to pelt it with sticks thrown end over end ; and while they were pelting so the snakes fell down in very great numbers. And Betawerai began to sing a song to make Walolo come quickly back and kill and eat them. And this was the song, *Risurisu vano, Betawerai, a lang togalau, ti uvi goro nanagoku. Walolo! Walolo! go vano mai! Walolo! Walolo! go vano mai!* Turn and come to Betawerai, the wind is North-west, it blows against my face. Walolo, Walolo, come hither! Walolo, Walolo, come hither! And they say that Walolo heard him singing, and thought that something had happened. And he came end over end like a stick, and as he came near he heard plainly that it was Betawerai's voice, and he thought that indeed there was surely a man there. Therefore he came end over end in haste, and came near to those two ; and one of them shot him, and then the other shot, and both hit him ; and he tried to rush upon them, and one shot, and the other shot, and both hit. And they went on shooting like this, till they shot him to death. And they went after Betawerai, and pulled him down to the ground and killed him. And when they had killed the snakes in this way they heaped them up at the roots of the banyan-tree, and brought plenty of wood and burned them up, a great heap of snakes, as a sign that the devouring snake was destroyed. And they three (the boys and their mother) returned to their village and dwelt there.

12. THE STORY OF BASI AND DOVAOWARI. AURORA.

She was a girl of Dama, and her mother, a snake, lived in a cave there. And there was a young man living at Tanoriki ; and one day Basi and another girl, her sister I suppose, went down to the beach to dip salt-water ; and Dovaowari was the name of the youth, and he also went down to bathe in the sea, but on another part of the beach. You know our ways, that

we always like to dress our hair to make it white, and that the
hair too may be curly, in ringlets, such as you always see
with the Opa people. So these two girls stand looking over
to the other part of the beach, and see the fellow bathing, and
washing his hair till it was exceedingly white, and they say,
Let us two go and see who that is bathing. And they went
and saw that it was Dovaowari; and he asked them what
they were looking for, and they said that they had been
standing far off and had seen him, and were come to look at
him. And Basi said to the other girl, You go home to our
mother, and tell her that I am going after Dovaowari. But
Dovaowari forbade her in vain to follow him, saying that he
was poor, and not one that had money, that he had no
property and no garden ; and she disputed with him, saying
that she would certainly go with him. So he said, Well, we
will go together ; then that other girl went back to the mother
of them both, the Snake, and Basi followed Dovaowari to be
his wife, and so they married. But Basi kept going to her
mother at Dama a long way off, and Dovao was vexed at it,
and he told Basi to go and say to her mother that she was to
move to that place so that all might live together. But
Basi said, Mother cannot come here to this place ; yet she
went and entreated her, and she agreed that it would be
possible to make the move. But the chief thing she thought
of was how she should manage, because she was a snake very
long and large, and if a small house were built for her it
would not be enough. She considered, therefore, and said to
Basi, Go and tell my son-in-law to build me a house, and let
there be ten chambers in it. But Dovao did not yet know the
truth, and when he heard about the house with ten chambers
he was astonished at it, and thought to himself, What is
this ? When the house was finished, Basi carried the news
saying, Your house is finished ; but she had said beforehand,
I shall go in the night, and if my son-in-law should hear
anything don't let him take notice of it. So in the middle of
the night they heard an earthquake, and thunder, and a very
great rumbling as if all the world would come to an end ;

and when she reached that place, her tail entered first and coiled itself in the first chamber, and then in the second, until all those chambers were filled with the big snake; and her head, a woman's, lay opposite the door, though the whole house was full of the snake. In the morning the people came to see this person, and saw that it was a snake with a human head. And whenever Dovao and Basi went anywhere and returned, she would go to her mother, that snake, and rub her nose upon her, and lie close upon her; but her husband did not like that sort of thing. On that account (and because the snake devoured the pigs and fowls that came near the door), when there was a feast at another village at a distance, he told some of the people that he and his wife were going to the dance, and while they were away they were to set fire to the house and burn it so as to burn up the snake with it. But the snake knew this, and called Basi and told her that they were going to set fire upon her and burn her that night, and, When you are standing at the feast, she said, if you see sparks run quickly back to me. So it was done; while she was dancing she saw sparks flying and ran quickly back and leapt herself into the fire, and both were burnt to death. And after a long while the liver that was burnt was found, and still remains, the liver of Basi and of her mother; and I have seen a bone in possession of some wealthy people; there is *mana*, magic power, in it, they say, for pigs, and for wicked intercourse with women when they blacken their faces under the eyes with it [1].

13. The Story of Deitari. Aurora.

They say that Tari went into his garden to work, and as he was working something cut him, and he put the blood into a bamboo vessel, and went into the village, and set it by his

---

[1] The power of the liver to attract women was discovered by a boy playing with his bow and arrow as his mother worked in the garden near where the snake had been burnt. His arrow fell into the ashes of the liver, and seeing it blackened he smeared his face with the black stuff.

fire-place, and there it stayed. And after many days when he was going to work he told his wife to cook some food for him, and she went to get it. But when she came back into the house she found food already cooked, and she did not know who had prepared the food for her. Thus it happened very often, and the woman told her husband. And he when he heard it bade her sit and watch who it was that did it. So she sat by the side wall of the house, and saw Deitari (Tari's blood) creep out of the bamboo vessel which Tari had put aside ; and she saw that he was exceedingly fair, and she hid him. Then when Tari came in from work he asked his wife, Haven't you seen him ? And she said, What was that you put by the fire-place ? I did not put anything there, said he. But his wife said, Not so, you put something small there in a bamboo. Then he remembered about his blood, and he said to his wife, My blood was in that bamboo ; and his wife said, I saw him come out of that bamboo that you had put there. So she brought him forth, and Tari rejoiced very much to see him. And one day as they were living together the boys of the village, and Deitari with them, went to bathe in the stream, and sang songs. And there was a man called Taepupuliti, and they say that he changed himself into a fish, and went and devoured the boy who had come out of the bamboo, and went off with him into a different country. And Tari sent every kind of fish and bird to seek for Deitari ; and he found a little fish, extremely thin, and this fish and Deitari's father found him hidden at the back end of Taepupuliti's house. And they two, Tari and Taepupuliti, sat down to drink *kava* ; and the father of the one whom the other had devoured let the liquor fall from his mouth as he drank, so that the *kava* did not strike (affect) him ; but as for the one who had eaten his child it struck him very much, and his father carried him off again.

14. Tarkeke. Aurora.

They say that he used to devour men in all the islands, and that he made the image of a fish with woven vines, and got into it and turned into a fish. And when he wanted to eat a man he entered into that fish and went to Opa or Raga. One day he went into his garden, and his son was in the village, and his father had forbidden the boy to go to the inner part of the house; but his father had gone away and he and his mother were in the village, and he was playing about alone, and he thought he would go and see what it was that his father had forbidden him to see. So he went into the further end of the house, and saw the image of the fish lying, and got into it. And a kingfisher flies down as a sign if any one gets into the figure of the fish; and the old woman lying in the house when she hears the kingfisher breaks a stick, and the image then goes into the sea. And when the boy got into the figure of the fish, and the king-fisher flew down to the roof of the house, and the old woman heard it, she broke a piece of fire-wood, and the image of the fish with the boy inside it went down into the sea, and crossed to Opa. And the father was in his garden and he heard a noise, and he ran as fast as he could, but found that the fish was already gone. So he weaves together the stuff that is on a cocoa-nut, in no particular shape, and puts it on his breast, and goes into the sea to seek the boy. And he finds him at Opa; and the Opa people, they say, had very nearly shot him. And his father brought him home. And as they were coming back they saw a man in a bread-fruit-tree, and the father said to his son, Go and eat him; and the son said to his father, How shall I go, father, because he is on dry land? And his father hit him hard, and said, Go, for you want to eat a man. Then he went, and as he went up towards the shore the sea went up too upon the shore, and he was carried up into the bread-fruit-tree after that man and swallowed him. And they came back to the back part of the house, and put him there, for he was not yet dead. And when they put him there at the further end of the house, and he moved himself about, he saw the sea, and the shark, and the fishes with their mouths open to devour him. And so he stayed there and died.

15. THE WOMAN AND THE GHOST. AURORA.

This is about a woman who lost her husband, and went in search of him, and she had a child with her. And a ghost met the woman carrying the child on her hip, and the woman thought it was her husband. And the three went down to the beach to burn for fish. Then the ghost said to the woman, You go and burn for fish, and I will look after our child. And when the woman went with the torch the ghost ate one finger of the child. And its mother asked him what hurt the child, and the ghost said, Nothing, a mosquito bit it. After he had spoken the child ceased to cry, and the woman discovered that it was a ghost because it had eaten the child entirely up. Then she knew for certain that it was a ghost, because she had set up cocoa-nut branches along the shore, and the ghost when it had eaten the child went to eat the mother, and as he ran along to eat her he ate the branches she had set up, thinking that the branches were the woman. And the woman ran away fast and climbed into a pandanus-tree, and when the ghost would have climbed up to eat her the woman pelted him down with the fruits. And so she did till dawn ; and when it was light she saw that he turned into a hermit crab.

16. A STORY ABOUT TAGARO THE LITTLE.
LEPERS' ISLAND.

They say that he went to a part of the island called Vagimbangga to pay for a pig there, and that on his return the sun set while he was still in the forest. And he was hungry, for he had nothing whatever to eat. Now beside that path they say there was a single gaviga-tree, with many branches, and also ripe fruit on it ; and he climbed up to eat, and to sleep awhile on that tree ; and in his hand was his conch-shell trumpet to blow as he went along the path. And in the middle of the night, when he had finished eating, he climbed further up to the top of that gaviga-tree to sleep and rest there ; and as he begins to fall asleep he hears the voices

of a number of people coming along underneath the gaviga-
tree. And he woke up thinking that it was probably his
brothers looking for him; but it was not so, these were
different persons; these were Mera-mbuto and his brothers
coming along, and they climbed up the gaviga-tree themselves. And Tagaro-mbiti sits perfectly still lest they should
see him, and he hears one of them say '*Ineu ranganggu ngaha,*'
This is my branch, and another cries '*Ineu ranganggu ngaha,*'
and so say all of them. Then says Mera-mbuto '*Ineu ranganggu
ngaha lo vuhungegi,*' This is my branch at the top; and this
he said with a loud voice. And Mera-mbuto climbed straight
up to the top of that gaviga-tree, and there he found Tagaro-
mbiti. Then says Mera-mbuto, Who are you? And says he,
I am Tagaro-mbiti. Now they say that this Mera-mbuto and
his brothers had a cave for their dwelling. And he asked
Tagaro again, What is that in your hand? And he says, The
voice of you and me to be sure. And he begged of him to
speak in that conch that he might hear it; but he said also,
Wait a bit till I go back to my dwelling-place, and when I
get there you will hear me whistle; then you shall speak with
the voice of us two that I may hear it for myself. And he
made haste down from the tree, and his brothers said, Are we
to come too? No, says he, I am only going to get rid of a
mess and then I shall come back. Thus he deceived them;
and when he reached his dwelling, the cave, he whistled
for Tagaro to hear, that he might blow the conch. And
Tagaro heard Mera-mbuto whistle, and he put forth all his
strength to blow the conch hard, and he blew, and Mera-
mbuto's brothers fell every one of them from the tree; and he
himself was delighted and jumped high again and again in
his cave, and his head struck against the rock, and the rock
stuck fast into his head, and there he died. And his brothers
who had fallen down died every one; and on that account
they say that bushes grew up in that place where Mera-
mbuto's brothers fell. And when it was light Tagaro-mbiti
returned to his home.

17. About Mera-mbuto and Tagaro. Lepers' Island.

Mera-mbuto prepared food for himself, and then he invited
Tagaro to come that they might eat together. So Tagaro
came to him in his house ; and the food of Mera-mbuto was
exceedingly bad, and as they ate Tagaro did not eat at all, but
he wrapped the food up to deceive Mera-mbuto, and went and
threw it away, and then went back to his house. Afterwards
Tagaro sent after him saying, Mera-mbuto, come here to my
house. Mera-mbuto came and they two ate. And the food
was good ; Mera-mbuto liked Tagaro's food very much ; he had
made his own not at all good. So Mera-mbuto considered
silently, What sort of thing is this we two are eating ? So he
asked Tagaro, and Tagaro said to him, I have grated up my
barrow pig. So Mera-mbuto went and grated up his barrow
pig, and in due course they two ate it. After this Tagaro
invited Mera-mbuto to eat with him in return in his house.
So he asked him again, What food is this we two are eating ?
And Tagaro was tired of being asked, and deceived Mera-mbuto,
saying to him, My mother ; I cooked her in the oven. So
Mera-mbuto went home and cooked his mother in the oven.
After this Tagaro said to him, Light a fire over me. So
Mera-mbuto came, and tied up the door of Tagaro's house,
bound it very tight, and set fire to Tagaro's house. Then
Tagaro wept ; Mera-mbuto said to him, Don't cry, you deceived
me formerly, now you are soon to die for it. He thought that
Tagaro was dead ; but not at all, he had dug a hole, and
stayed in it. In the morning thinking that he was dead he
came, and Tagaro had been long sitting ready for him. So
Mera-mbuto asked him, Are you sitting like this ? Tagaro
said, Yes. So Mera-mbuto said to him, My turn now, to-night
you set fire to my house. So Tagaro set fire to his house, and
the fire burnt him up.

INDEX.

—⊷—

THE END.